Sheila
9911
Apt 35
Edmonton AB

MW01536785

LIGHT & TRUTH

Volume Four

The Mormon Battalion

A Historical Novel
Based on a True Story

Visit us at HYPERLINK "http://www.harrispublishing.com"
www.harrispublishing.com; or the author, HYPERLINK
"mailto:dcharris@harrispublishing.com" dcharris@harrispublishing.com.

Copyright 2006 by Darryl W. Harris.

All rights reserved. No part of this book may be reproduced in any form or
by any means whatsoever without express permission in writing from the
publisher, Harris Publishing, Inc. 360 B Street, Idaho Falls, Idaho 83402.

Visit us at www.harrispublishing.com.

Library of Congress Control Number: 2001012345
ISBN: 0-9747376-3-1

First Printing June 2006
Printed at Falls Printing (a subsidiary of Harris Publishing, Inc.), Idaho
Falls, Idaho, USA.

Dedicated to the Mormon Battalion organization
and to all the descendents of the men and women who served
in the Battalion.

"Brethren, you will be blessed, if you will live for those blessings which you have been taught to live for. The Mormon Battalion will be held in honorable remembrance to the latest generation; and I will prophesy that the children of those who have been in the army, in defense of their country, will grow up and bless their fathers for what they did at that time. And men and nations will rise up and bless the men who went in that Battalion. These are my feelings in brief respecting the company of men known as the Mormon Battalion. When you consider the blessings that are laid upon you, will you not live for them? As the Lord lives, if you will but live up to your privileges, you will never be forgotten, without end, but you will be had in honorable remembrance, for ever and ever."

President Brigham Young, 1846

Foreword

As stated from the beginning, *Light & Truth* is a historical novel based on a true story. The two main male characters of this book, Robert Harris and Daniel Browett, served in the Mormon Battalion. Their wives remained behind in Winter Quarters.

Volume one, *The Field Is White*, told of the conversion of Robert, Daniel, and their wives—Hannah and Elizabeth—by the Apostle, Wilford Woodruff. Volume two chronicled their ocean voyage across the Atlantic and their steamboat trip up the Mississippi to reach Nauvoo; it was entitled *The Gathering*. Volume three, *The Nauvoo Years*, detailed their lives in Nauvoo from a British convert point-of-view.

This volume, *The Mormon Battalion*, begins with the enlistment process in the summer of 1846 and ends as the battalion enters California six months later. A fifth volume, to be entitled *The Journey Home*, will conclude the *Light & Truth* series. It will contain the story of the battalion's release in July of 1847 and the struggle for Robert and Daniel to be reunited with their wives and families. My original intent was to end the series with volume four, but as I developed the story it became too long and I had to divide it into two volumes.

This is not only a story about the battalion, but about the Mexican-American War of 1846-47. Events of the war—some not involving the battalion—are interwoven to give the reader an appreciation of the battles and casualties that Mormon soldiers avoided because of the promises given by Brigham Young and other Church leaders. Even though members of the Mormon Battalion did not have to engage the enemy in an actual battle, there were plenty of other dangers, trials, and tribulations that they faced. The author hopes that the reader can vicariously experience what it was like to serve in the battalion.

Every known source on the Mormon Battalion has been used to write this novel (see the bibliography at the end). The author also studied books and sources about the Mexican-American War, history of Fort Leavenworth, the Santa Fe Trail, Santa Fe, the Mexican states of New Mexico and Alta California, San Diego, Los Angeles, Sutter's Fort, the discovery of gold, the California Trail, Winter Quarters, and the early history of the Salt Lake Valley. The author also studied the lives of military personalities such as Captain James Allen, Colonel Philip St. George Cooke, Colonel Alexander Doniphan, Colonel Sterling Price, General Stephen W. Kearny, and Captain John C. Fremont. Notable California characters were also studied, such as John Sutter and Samuel Brannan.

The viewpoint in this novel is obviously Latter-day Saint. The reader needs to keep this in mind because there are also other viewpoints about the events that swirled around the Mexican-American War. A few others would be: American, Missourian, Texan, New Mexican, Californian, and Mexican. For example, the Mormon soldiers had a negative image of Dr. George Sanderson. Sanderson, although a Missourian, was trying to do his job as an army doctor. Calomel was administered for just about every ailment. But Brigham Young counseled the Mormon soldiers not to take calomel, thus bringing to the forefront a heated controversy.

The author would like to thank members of the official Mormon Battalion organization for their assistance, specifically Richard Bullock, Val John Halford, Cap Cresap, and Sherman Fleek.

Principal Characters

All characters are real except those indicated with an asterisk. Bold face indicates main characters. Ages are as Volume Four opens in July 1846.

THE ROBERT HARRIS FAMILY
Robert, 35
Hannah, 32
Joseph, 10
Lizzy, 8
William, 7
Thomas, 5
Enoch, 3
Sarrah Ann, 2

THE BROWETT FAMILY
Daniel, 36
Elizabeth, 33
Moroni,
Martha, 61, Daniel's mother.
Rebecca, 27, Daniel's sister.

THOMAS BLOXHAM FAMILY
Thomas, 34
Dianah, 35
Lucy, 13
Tommy, 12
Johnny, 9
Isaac, 4

HENRY EAGLES FAMILY
*Henry, 37
*Katherine, 32
*Annie, 5

OTHERS
John Benbow, 46
Jane Benbow, 54
John Cox, 37
John Hyrum Green, 47
Susannah Green, 43
Joseph Hill, 42
Orson Hyde, 44
Thomas Kington, 53
Edward Phillips, 33
Levi Roberts, 33
Richard Slater, 32
Robert Pixton, 32
Ezra Allen, 31
Henderson Cox, 17
Wilford Woodruff, 39
Brigham Young, 45

NOTE: A full roster of the Mormon Batalion is located at the back of this book.

PART ONE

The
Enlistment

1

Garden Grove, Iowa

May 1846

SINCE LEAVING NAUVOO, Hannah seldom slept solidly. But when she did, she dreamed. Every dream was a nightmare, and every nightmare frightened her. Now three weeks into the American frontier, she was a product of those nightmares.

"I can't get it out of my mind," she said the day the twelve wagons of her company rolled into Garden Grove, a temporary settlement in Iowa established by early Mormon wagon companies. "This would be a terrible place to be without a husband."

"I'm not leaving you alone out here, so stop fretting about it," her husband, Robert, quickly answered as he led his team of oxen along a dusty trail.

"It just keeps popping up in my dreams," Hannah snapped back through lips ulcerated by sunburn. "And every time I look at poor Katherine and little Annie, my dreams bounce back into my mind."

Robert forced a little laugh. "Well, maybe Henry will show up here in Garden Grove."

From under her sunbonnet, Hannah glared at her husband. "You've been dreaming too if you think that's going to happen. Even if he did, I'd probably throw rocks at him, I'm so mad."

Robert rolled his eyes. "You're impossible. First, you want Henry to come and take care of his family. Then if he did show up, you'd throw rocks at him? You've swallowed too much Iowa dust."

"Well, he ought to grow up and take over his responsibilities as a father and a husband," Hannah said as she pulled up her green short-wash dress and walked around a string of ox manure. "It would help if you'd show a little liking for him instead of always trying to throw him over the fence or something."

"Let's get this straight," Robert shot back. "I don't like Henry. I've never liked him, and there is no way that anyone, including you, will ever get me to like him. So don't pretend that I'll ever change in that regard."

Robert and Hannah Harris, along with eleven other English converts and their families, had left Nauvoo in mid-May as members of the Daniel Browett wagon company. Not only did Hannah dream about being left alone in the American wilderness with her six children, but she dreamed about drowning in one of the swollen rivers they continually had to cross, being eaten alive by wolves, scalped by Indians, or just plain starving to death. She had no idea where Brigham Young aimed to lead displaced members of the Church of Jesus Christ of Latter-day Saints, other than some strange-sounding place called the Great Basin. She missed her new white framed home east of Nauvoo and she missed her feather bed. She never had bad dreams in the feather bed.

"I guess it's not important that you like Henry," Hannah said with a note of conclusion. "It's just important that he get back here and take care of his family."

"Henry ain't normal, so stop expecting him to be normal," Robert said with a shake of his head.

Robert's attempt to humor Hannah didn't work. She harbored a stinging bitterness over her brother's mysterious disappearance, and it worsened her fears. Where was Henry? Why couldn't he grow up and take responsibility for his wife and daughter? The notion that he might be playing faro or keno in the saloons of St. Louis while his wife and daughter were walking alone across Iowa irked Hannah. It was painful to think of her brother that way. Sometimes she wished that the shoulder bullet wound Henry Eagles had received at the hands of his anti-Mormon friends was still festering, bleeding under his shirt, giving him a painful reminder of the sinful life he had led.

It was too bad she and Robert had to leave their home and farm in Nauvoo. Life there hadn't been easy, but it was bound to have more than the wilderness had to offer in creature comforts. At least in Nauvoo she not only had a feather bed, but also a cook stove, a roof over her head, and a root cellar full of vegetables. On the way to Garden Grove they had passed very few settlements, and civilization seemed to be escaping behind them at a rapid clip.

It was true, a fact that Hannah had to admit: her brother was not normal. He had never been normal. He had been an abnormal child growing up on the family dairy farm in England. He had spent an abnormal time at the pubs, and picked an abnormal number of fights. Henry and Robert fought the first time they met, fought over the notion that Robert was going to marry Henry's sister, and fought on the ship that brought them to America. Henry's marriage to Katherine was not even normal; he purposely married a homely Mormon girl in order to be eligible for a cheap ticket on a Mormon immigrant ship. His life in Illinois had not been normal; instead of living in Nauvoo with the Mormons he chose to live in Carthage with the non-Mormons. He had non-Mormons for friends, yet non-Mormons shot him and Mormon-haters killed his brother, Elias, too.

Hannah let her large brown eyes take in Katherine and Annie again. The sight of them walking alongside an old Carthage dairy wagon with a mismatched team of a horse and a mule wasn't normal, either. Henry ought to be with them. They ought to have a team of hearty oxen. They ought to have a regular covered wagon. Annie ought not to have to cry for her father every day and every night. She was too young to realize what an abnormal rotten scoundrel he had been.

On the other hand, it was Hannah's aim to be normal and remain normal. She had married a good, hardworking, and decent man. Robert was big, strong, and husky. It was normal to want to keep him. She aimed never to lose him to sickness, to an early death, to sorrow, or to separation for any reason. She had six normal children, four of them walking beside her, two of them riding in the wagon because they were only two and three years old. She reckoned it was normal to have aching legs, but she reckoned it was normal to complain, for thinking about Henry put her in a complaining mood. A puff of dust rose with every step she took, filling her nostrils. Chains rattled against the hickory yokes of the wagon. Deep coughs shook the worn-out bodies of the four oxen as they strained, heads down.

"Well, if Henry does miraculously appear, right after I throw the rocks, you hogtie him and keep him here," Hannah said, knowing that it was unrealistic to expect anything of the kind.

Running away wasn't normal either, but that's what Henry had done in early April when he fled Nauvoo. He left a note, and now that she thought about it, the note was abnormal, too. Henry said that he would find Katherine and Annie in a year or two, when the Mormons had settled somewhere out West.

America was turning out to be a much larger place than Hannah had ever imagined, maybe a hundred times larger than England where she had lived for the first twenty-five years of her life. America seemed big when she saw the first landmasses as a passenger on the ship *Echo*, the Mormon immigrant vessel that carried her from Liverpool. She saw Florida, the gulf coast, and then a ghastly place called New Orleans. She thought she'd never find Nauvoo, for the steamboat wound endlessly up the huge Mississippi River—a river wider than her hometown, Apperley, was long. It had taken nearly two months to cross the Atlantic, during which her fourth child was born. Now here she was, two children later, on her way across endless Iowa after being forced out of Nauvoo by mobs who had murdered the Prophet Joseph Smith, burned the homes of friends, shot and wounded abnormal Henry, and killed her other brother, Elias.

As she thought about it, all that wasn't normal, either. Prophets shouldn't be martyred. God-fearing, religious people shouldn't be forced out of their homes. Governments with a constitution guaranteeing freedom of religion shouldn't stand by and do nothing.

But here she was, smack dab in the middle of the big, frightening American wilderness. Homeless. Almost penniless. And with a missing brother who seemingly didn't care for his own wife and child.

Elizabeth Browett, Daniel's wife, took a different view about Henry's absence. In most ways, she was glad Henry was gone. He was a bad actor. He beat his wife and sided with the enemies of the Church. Katherine and Annie were better off without Henry. But she could never be better off without Daniel.

"You're handling this *better* than I would," she told Katherine as they made their camp in Garden Grove. A dozen wagons had formed a circle. Lazy smoke from campfires swirled into the sky.

"It'd be nice to have Henry here to help," Katherine said in a forlorn voice. "And Annie needs her father. But she's too young to understand how he abused me."

Elizabeth felt lucky in that respect. It would never be in Daniel's nature to harm her, their nine-month-old son, Moroni, Daniel's plural wife, Harriet, or anyone else for that matter. Daniel was the opposite of Henry. Daniel was kind and had a strong testimony. Henry was mean and poked fun at Mormons. Elizabeth bit her lip; she was about to accuse Henry of being downright evil, but Annie was close enough to hear.

Just like all women, Elizabeth harbored her fears and her greatest one was losing Daniel. She couldn't imagine life without Daniel. During her eleven years of marriage she had never been separated from him for more than one night, or maybe two. There was no chance that Daniel would run away like Henry had done, but there were plenty of other dangers. Husbands were known to get injured or killed in accidents, or killed by mobbers or even Indians.

The first day after they left Nauvoo, for example, nervous oxen broke the tongue out of their wagon and almost tipped the wagon over, right on top of Daniel. Daniel had to fabricate a new tongue, a ten-hour delay. Two days later John Cox drove his wagon into a mud hole and was stuck for several hours. It took a yoke of eight oxen to pull the wagon out and the process broke four chains. One of the chains almost took Daniel's head off, so close was the whipping action when it broke. Another time Thomas Bloxham woke everyone in the middle of the night because he needed help to find his oxen. Daniel took off to help and was gone until dawn. Elizabeth worried all night that savage Indians had found Daniel and had sent arrows into him.

It was dangerous for the women, too. Just after leaving Richardson's Point an accident almost killed Harriet. Harriet had been walking alongside the wagon, delighting in the wind that cooled her as she trudged along, when an unexpected gust of wind whipped her skirts into the wagon wheel. Before she knew it, her skirts were being wrapped around and around the hub. By the time her screams stopped the wagon, she had been drawn so tightly that she could only grasp the spokes with her hand, place her feet between two others, and make complete revolutions with the wheel as it rolled.

As she had done in Nauvoo, Elizabeth kept busy tending to the needs of others in her role as midwife and herbalist. By her count there were more than two dozen children in the company, many of them sick, including Hannah's. It seemed to Elizabeth that during the trip every affliction invented by the devil had at one time or another stricken the camp: diarrhea, dysentery, headaches, piles, mumps, bowel complaint, scurvy, cuts, broken bones, scalding, animal bites, and snake bites.

Henry's absence was the least of Daniel's worries. In fact he was glad Henry was nowhere around. If he were, Henry was apt to make Daniel's job as company leader more difficult. Henry would've been in a few fights by now—especially with Robert—and he would have everyone worked up with his opinions on Mormonism.

While the women fixed the evening meal, Daniel began inspecting the wagons one at a time. It had been no easy job for each man to build these wagons. The wheels had to be high, for clearance, which meant that maneuverability was low. A wagon could not make sharp turns unless both front wheels were small enough to swivel underneath the wagon box. Wagon tongues often snapped in two when the draft animals pulled too far right or left. The wheels themselves had to be made well enough so that they did not fall apart. The Saints were warned that the dry air of the plains and deserts shrank the wooden spokes and rims of the wheels until the iron tires wobbled off.

"Your wheels are staying on fine," he said to Robert from a kneeling, inspection position.

"We ain't hit the dry country yet," Robert replied. When they did, in the arid West, the wheels were expected to shrink. Iowa was wet and humid, like Illinois.

The women had made wagon covers of heavy canvas waterproofed with linseed oil. Being inventive, most women in Daniel's company had sewn pockets and slings to the inner surface of the fabric for extra storage. Supported by hickory bows, the cover provided about five feet of headroom. Pucker ropes at either end were used to tighten the canvas, screening the interior of the wagon from the weather.

Hannah came to the wagon to get a few cups of flour. "Let me know if you see Bishop Miller around here," she said. "I still aim to give him a piece of my mind."

Controversy was one thing Daniel wanted to avoid. "Haven't seen him and I hope we don't," he said.

Hannah scowled, got her flour, and marched back to the campfire.

Bishop Miller, with the approval of Wilford Woodruff and Orson Hyde, had taken the first wagons built by Daniel and Robert. Miller had used them to haul feed for his animals. When Brigham Young had announced that the first companies would have to leave Nauvoo in early February because of political and mob pressures, the original plans for the exodus had been tossed out the window. The Browett and Harris wagons were *loaned* to Bishop Miller with the understanding they would be returned in time for their own exodus in May. It never happened. Everyone knew why: Because of the wet weather and mud, it had taken until late April for those early companies to reach Garden Grove, and Garden Grove was only a third of the way across Iowa. The Daniel Browett Company, with the Browett and Harris families using another set of wagons that Daniel and Robert had built, wasn't that far behind the lead companies. It had taken the Browett company only three weeks to reach Garden Grove, whereas it had taken Brigham Young ten weeks.

It wasn't long—just before supper was served—that Daniel learned Bishop Miller and Brigham Young were no longer at Garden Grove. In fact, most people here were of the opinion that by now they were likely to reach the western edge of Iowa any day. There, they were expected to set up another temporary settlement like the one here, and the one named Mount Pisgah, just beyond Garden Grove. Here at Garden Grove the

Saints here had already broken more than seven hundred acres of prairie sod. Several cabins had been erected, too.

The exodus had begun in February. Now, in May, wagons carrying Mormons were strung out from Nauvoo to the Missouri River, a distance of several hundred miles. Daniel hoped to get his company to the Missouri without any accidents, injuries, or deaths. He had already crossed several treacherous rivers, swollen with spring runoff. Even without Henry, Daniel never knew what terrible thing might happen next. Shortly after supper, a bad thing did happen.

"Rattlesnakes!" someone yelled.

Daniel whirled to see Robert Pixton running madly toward his brown horse. The horse had been struck by a rattlesnake. Pixton and the other men in the company had barely turned their horses and oxen out to graze.

Elizabeth dropped what she was doing and ran to the wagon. In no time at all she was bathing the horse's nose in turpentine and was forcing snakes master root and milk down it. Pixton had dispatched the snake with the butt of his rifle.

"Get the children in!" Daniel screamed. "There are rattlesnakes all over!"

"If Annie gets bitten, it's Henry's fault," screeched Hannah.

The horse was soon so sick it could barely stand. By morning it was dead.

2

On the Missouri River

May 1846

HENRY EAGLES HADN'T THOUGHT ABOUT being a soldier in the United States Army until he talked with a Missourian by the name of Bernard Bogart. Henry had secured a job as a stevedore on a steamboat—the *Radnor*—bound for Independence from St. Louis when Bogart and his black horse came aboard in Jefferson City.

"I'm headed fer Fort Leavenworth," Bogart announced to everyone, sticking out his chest. "I'm volunteerin' ta fight the Mexicans. It'll be quite the shindig. Us Missouri boys'll be the best soldiers yet, for we're hearty and used ta the hardships of frontier life." The more he sipped on his corn whiskey bottle, the greater the volume from his voice box. And the more richly curved became his homespun Missouri accent.

Drawing inspiration from their own bottles of whiskey, a group of Caw Indians was singing in the background; a fat Negro danced while the Indians sang.

Henry felt an urge to get to know Bogart. Bogart sounded like his kind of man.

The main topic of conversation on the *Radnor*, ever since it left St. Louis, had been about the recently declared war with Mexico. Bogart's presence seemed to heat it up. In the cabin were Santa Fe traders, gamblers, speculators, and adventurers of every description. Steerage was crowded with Oregon emigrants, mountain men, Negroes, the Caw Indians, and a party of Kansas Indians who had been on a visit to St. Louis. When the proud Missourian quit strutting around the boat, Henry asked Bogart why he would want to fight Mexicans.

Bogart was a half a head shorter than Henry and several pounds lighter. He was a lot younger, too, in his late teens or early twenties. But he made up for it with his feistiness. His voice boiled like lava. "Say, Englishman. Them Mexicans have been stirrin' fer a fight. Haven't ya ever heard of Texas?"

Henry felt offended, as though Bogart was talking down to him either because he had a British accent or because he whistled when he talked. He had lost his two front teeth pub fighting in England before he came to America. "Of course I've heard of Texas. I didn't just fall off a wagon somewhere," Henry said indignantly.

Bogart was so worked up that he hardly took a breath. "President Polk was elected on the promise of addin' Texas and Oregon ta the Union. Now he's declared war against them Mexicans. Where've ya been all your life, Englishman?"

"In Illinois, fightin' the Mormons," Henry shot back. He hoped his answer would win him a new friend. Henry had long ago concluded that every Missourian in the world hated the Mormons worse than he did.

The remark took Bogart by surprise. His blue eyes lit up. "Fightin' Mormons? You? A Brit?"

A prideful feeling came over Henry and it was his turn to stick out his chest. "I was part of the mob that killed Joe Smith and his brother." The statement just slipped out of Henry's mouth even though he really didn't mean to say it. It wasn't entirely true, but he said it anyway.

Bogart extended his right hand. "Well, I'll be. I've always wanted ta meet one of the men that got rid of that imposter. Tell me all about it."

Henry let a wide smile come upon his dark bearded face. He related the story about the time in the summer of two years ago when he and his brother, Elias, had been serving in the Carthage militia. Both he and Elias had been called into active duty because of trouble with Joe Smith and the Mormons in June of 1844. He told how he and Elias delivered the message from Colonel Geddes to the Warsaw militia, ordering the disbandment of the Warsaw units. He explained how some of the men from Warsaw had jumped up on wagons and organized a mob to return to Carthage where Joseph and Hyrum Smith were imprisoned.

"I was right there when we stormed the jail," Henry said, knowing he was stretching the truth a little. Actually, he and Elias had watched the whole thing from the sidelines, but both had been right next to the mob in the trees when they painted their faces. Henry described how the mob overwhelmed Joseph Smith and his brother, the gunshots, and how the Mormon prophet toppled out of the Carthage Jail window. He didn't bother to mention that the mobbers also shot his brother, Elias, and that the body was never found. Henry assumed the mobbers had taken the body back to Warsaw and dumped it into the Mississippi River.

After more questions and more details of the assassination, Bogart seemed genuinely impressed and soon several other passengers became interested in the story. Unexpectedly, Henry found himself transformed into some kind of a hero. This greatly pleased Henry and he stuck out his chest again and began embellishing the story even more, exaggerating his role in the murders. Bogart shared his bottle of whiskey and so did some of the other passengers, especially those who were from Missouri and knew of the Mormons.

"A man like you ought to come and fight the Mexicans with me," Bogart said when both men were about half stewed. Huge steamboat paddles were making a swishing sound and a shrill whistle pierced the air as the steamer rounded a sweeping bend in the river. The *Radnor* was loaded so heavily that water broke alternately over her guards. Her upper deck was covered with large wagons and her hold was crammed with goods.

"Do Mexicans shoot back?" Henry asked, barely knowing what a Mexican was.

"Oh, I 'spect they will, but not to fear," Bogart said. "Word is them greasers use old flintlock muskets made in Great Britain, and sold as surplus ta Mexico. The greasers use too much powder, so's it hurts their shoulders when they fire. So's they shoot from the hip. Most the shots are gonna fly right over our heads."

Henry paled a little; shot were shots, even if they went over a man's head. He did his best to mimic a Missourian's way of speech. "But ain't there lots of Mexicans? They're apt to hit you if there's enough of 'em shootin' at you."

Bogart grunted in disgust. "There's about seven million of them greasers all together, but only two or three thousand in the country beyond Santa Fe and what we call New Mexico and Alta California. I'm gonna be a dragoon and chase them greasers clear back to Mexico City."

Henry understood the word "dragoon." It meant a horse soldier. He took in Bogart's horse, the black one with one white foot, who was half asleep in the warm late May sun. There were several horses on board, and cows, pigs, and chickens, too.

"But I don't have a horse," Henry sheepishly admitted. Until he came to Missouri he had never heard the term "greaser." The Mormons had never used the word to describe Mexicans.

"Well, you can't be a dragoon without a horse, but you can be a foot soldier, or a teamster," Bogart explained. "The army's put out the word that there's been a grain shortage in New Mexico so the army's gonna have ta haul its own grain and other provisions, too, like pork belly." He went on to say that quartermaster agents had been buying up just about every available wagon in places like St. Louis and Pittsburgh and shipping them by steamboat to Fort Leavenworth. The agents were also buying up oxen and mules.

"I can drive mules," Henry said, his vision now swimming with thoughts of being an American soldier.

Bogart continued to gloat. "They say there's gonna be a thousand wagons or more going down that old Santa Fe Trail to supply our army. The army's hiring as many teamsters as they can, but they'll have ta use a few soldiers, too."

"A thousand wagons?" Henry asked innocently.

"Yep," Bogart answered. "If ya ain't got a horse, be a foot soldier or a teamster. All ya need is an overcoat, so sez the Army."

"I can go to war with just an overcoat?" Henry asked, figuring he could afford that out of his steamboat wages.

Bogart turned visionary, spreading his arms in the direction of the steamboat's bow. "That country out West belongs to these United States of America, and we're gonna drive the greasers out. The prospect of duty-free trade with New Mexico appeals with all us Missourians. Somethin' else, too. Ever heard of 'Manifest Destiny,' Englishman?"

Henry had heard the term, but had no idea what it actually meant. "I suppose I have."

Bogart cursed the Mexicans again. "When this is over, the United States is gonna be bigger by a million square miles. Texas is gonna be a slave state and so is New Mexico. If the greasers don't like it, we'll make slaves of them, too—the ones that stay. They were nothin' more than slaves under the rule of Spain, and Mexico's been independent for only twenty or so years. Them greasers would be better off if we took over all of Mexico, right down to Panama. I don't fear them greasers. They're not ready for war."

"But you think the Americans are ready?" Henry asked. He liked the way Missourians talked. Henry didn't mind the fact that Missouri was a slave state. Joseph Smith had been anti-slavery, so Henry was pro-slavery.

Bogart took on a prideful look. "Why, I'd say we are. We Missourians are. When the secretary of war back in Washington D. C. asked Missouri to help, our governor John Edwards stepped right up. Edwards issued a proclamation callin' for twelve hundred volunteers. I'm one of 'em, and you could be one, too."

"I guess I could if I wanted to, but I'd have to want to, first," Henry said.

"If we asked around, I'd expect we'd find other passengers that are volunteers, just like me," Bogart said as he let his eyes scan the steamboat. "Volunteers are comin' in from St. Louis and towns along the Missouri River, too. Ever heard of Alexander Doniphan or Sterling Price?"

For some reason the name Doniphan struck a familiar chord with Henry but he couldn't remember why. He took off his cap and scratched his broad head through his black hair. "Can't say as I do."

"They've been officers in the Missouri militia," Bogart said. "They're already volunteers and are asking the same of other militia members in Missouri."

Henry was now full of questions. "Are these greasers far away? Are they trying to invade Fort Leavenworth? Where do you go to find them?"

"I reckon we'll have ta go all the way ta Santa Fe to find some."

"Where's Santa Fe?"

Bogart scratched his head. "Where've you been in these United States?"

"Just Illinois, St. Louis, and New Orleans."

"I reckon it's as far from Fort Leavenworth ta Santa Fe as it is from here ta New Orleans," Bogart replied. "It's way out there, that direction." He pointed west.

The distance comparison made sense to Henry, except he had ridden a steamboat from New Orleans to St. Louis, and from there to Nauvoo. He said, "That's a long ways to walk or even drive a team of mules."

"But think of the benefits," Bogart said as he sipped on his bottle. "The army'll pay ya and give ya a gun. It's just fer a year if ya volunteer. Congress has authorized the president to call up fifty-thousand volunteers and you just as well be one of 'em. Ya might end up in Californay, which is not far from Oregon territory. After yer year is up, that'll put ya a lot closer ta where these poor settlers are tryin' to be, with a lot less effort and expense. The army'll feed ya, so if ya save yer money ya kin get a good start out west some where."

"Do you want to stay out west?" Henry asked as he thought of his wife,

Katherine, and his five-year-old daughter, Annie.

"No, sir," Bogart said. "Sometimes they offer land grants to returning soldiers. I'm hopin' fer free land when I get back, right here in Missouri."

Army life for one year didn't sound like a bad idea to Henry. He looked at his worn-out boots. "Will they give me a new pair of boots if mine wear out?"

Bogart nodded. "I'd expect. This here steamboat's full of supplies bound for Fort Leavenworth. There're probably boxes and barrels full of boots, muskets, and ammunition hidden behind all those dismantled wagons and hogsheads full of flour and pork. We've got to capture Santa Fe, which is almost nine hundred miles away. Hundreds of wagons'll be needed to carry provisions. Each dragoon gets single-shot percussion rifle. But I want to end up with a Colt too. You've probably never heard of the Colt revolver. Brand new fancy pistols, five or six-shot. I hope ta get me one. Shoot a few bean-eaters with it."

For the first time since he'd left Nauvoo, Henry suddenly found a place to plant his feet. He could be a soldier. He could shoot greasers or bean-eaters, too, and drive mules, and get paid for it. "I'd like one of them pistols, too," he said.

When the steamer arrived in Independence, Henry found the Missouri city swelled not only with settlers bound for Oregon Territory, but also with more Missourians who had volunteered for the war against Mexico. They were on their way to Fort Leavenworth, located in Indian Territory of the Kansas and Kaw Tribes. To Henry, most of them seemed just as wild-eyed and keyed to spill blood as Bernard Bogart. The Missourians had probably been that way since they drove out the Mormons, or even before, he reasoned.

"I sort of like Independence," Henry said to his new friend. He wiped his brow. However, the humidity here was just as bad as it had been in Illinois during the summer. To the south, storm clouds were gathering.

The town seemed spread out to Henry, a collection of log huts, clapboard houses, a few hotels, a few stores including a large one that held dry goods, a bank, a printing office, a couple of barn-looking churches, four clanging blacksmith shops, harness shops, and three liquor stores. Mexican cowboys from the Santa Fe Trail, along with teamsters and muleskinners, were drinking in the saloons and grog shops, and gambling in the muddy streets. Teamsters were greasing wheels, smoothing the ox-bows, fitting and repairing harnesses, and overhauling their own kits. Long trains of oxen, sometimes as many as ten or twelve yokes, were strung together pulling huge tented wagons, gearing up for the trip to Santa Fe. They were moving along the streets under the whips of teamsters, cracking their whips, making a great noise. With optimism and good cheer a white wagon train disappeared over the rolling green prairie.

"Well, you ought to," Bogart replied. "Independence is about the most important place in the world right now."

"I thought it would be sort of tiny," Henry admitted.

"Tiny? Why, there're five thousand people here," Bogart explained. "I reckon a lot of them are of the transient nature, journeying to and from various parts of the West. But I reckon, too, that twice as many people are likely to strike out on the California-Oregon trail this year than last."

"If I wanted to take a trip to the West, how much are oxen here?" Henry asked.

"Twenty dollars a yoke," Bogart answered.

Henry let out an airy whistle, the best he could with his missing teeth. He couldn't afford that at all.

"See all them mules around here?" Bogart asked. There were mules pulling wagons, mules being groomed, mules being pastured, and mules in pens. There were mules with big bellies, ready to be bought. There were mules with gaunt bellies, ready to be fattened. There were brown mules, bay mules, gray mules, black mules, and even albino mules.

"Never seen so many mules," Henry said.

"Missouri's the mule capital of the world now," Bogart claimed. "Teamsters trade goods in Santa Fe for Spanish gold and mules, bring 'em here, and sell 'em to settlers."

Mexicans with jingling heavy spurs—bearing gaffs more than an inch in length—were mounted on mules. Some of the Spanish saddles had leather skirts so wide that they almost hid the diminutive animals that bore them.

"I'd like a set of them spurs," Henry said.

"When you get to New Mexico kill a greaser and take their spurs as a reward for your killing," Bogart suggested. "That's what I aim to do."

3

HENRY SAW A BUSY TOWN in Independence, with merchants and mechanics in an extremely advantageous position to capitalize on the steady traffic. By necessity, Santa Fe traders, fur trappers, emigrants, military expeditions, and other travelers had to pass through Independence, and towns like Westport, all located at the Indian Country line.

Henry had never seen such wagon-making magic. New wagons were painted red, green, or blue. Signs above the shops read *Andrew J. Royal Wagons, Joseph Murphy Wagonmaker*, or *Robert Stone Manufacturing*, for example. Some of the wagons Henry saw were gigantic, with wheels seven feet high, and the height of the bed so that a man standing inside would barely bump his head. The tongues on those wagons were fifty feet long. Customers lined the streets waiting for blacksmith shops to take care of their needs.

Henry concluded that even loading the wagons was a rite almost religious in its care and precision. Packers were seen expertly arranging the goods so that after the journey of eight hundred miles they would still be in perfect condition.

"A normal wagon costs a hundred and fifty dollars here, and you can sell it for seven hundred dollars in Santa Fe," a trader told Henry when he was caught gawking at the huge wagon. "A tidy sum, all right. But one like this is twice as much. Now's the time for trade caravans—the grass is growin' on the prairies."

A caravan of wagons had just returned from Santa Fe, bearing bales of buffalo robes and beaver pelts. Henry wished he were a trader. He wished he had a hundred dollars to buy a wagon, but he didn't. He felt broke, and he almost was; he was down to his last few dollars.

Overall, Henry was impressed with Independence. He said, "Maybe I ought to get me a job and just stay here."

"I reckon you could be part of the outfitting trade," Bogart said in a disappointed tone. "The settlers sure enough need clothes, firearms, ammunition, saddles, horses, mules, wagons, and foodstuffs."

"Well, maybe that's just what I'll do," Henry said. Building wagons might be safer than having bean-eaters shoot at him.

"But you'd miss all the fun," Bogart said. "I thought you were a man of adventure."

"Well, I am," Henry said. "Maybe I'll join the army, and maybe I won't. I'll decide."

Bogart retreated into silence for a spell, and Henry did too. The two men walked for a few minutes, taking in the cottonwoods, oaks, maples, and hickory trees that seemed to spread their arms above the houses, wagons, and tents. They walked past the courthouse square with a collection of two-story whitewashed buildings around it and a toy-like storybook courthouse. Indians gathered there, selling their crafts.

While Henry took in these sights it began to rain, for it was still the wet season. Dashing rain drenched him and the whole town. Vivid lightning and tremendous thunderclaps struck terror into him for a while. Henry began to wish he had enough money to stay in the Noland Hotel, or the Locust Grove Hotel, but he didn't. Besides, they were already filled up. Visitors who flooded the town were complaining about the lack of accommodations.

"I reckon we'd better run for it," Bogart said.

"Where to?" Henry asked.

"That saloon over there," Bogart said, running as he answered.

Despite his run of bad luck at saloons in St. Louis, Henry followed the Missourian and soon found himself at a faro table again. Henry had pocketed three dollars wages for his labor on the steamer and was crossing his fingers, hoping he could double it on the faro table and buy himself a horse. With a horse, he could be a dragoon. With a horse, he would be able to look like someone important, important enough to get a good job just in case he didn't want to join the army and be a dragoon, or even a teamster.

Henry decided he felt comfortable. The gamblers here didn't look as professional as they did in St. Louis.

As the cards were being dealt, Bogart elbowed Henry and whispered in his ear. "Do you know who that is a sittin' across from us?"

Henry didn't know a single soul at the table other than Bogart and had no clue. His eyes rested on an older man with graying hair and stubby facial hair. He looked to be around fifty. Cigar smoke swirled around him and hung in the air all throughout the saloon. Whiskey glasses, some full, some empty, littered the table. For a second, Henry forgot about Bogart's question and began longing for a winning hand. With a winning hand he could afford a cigar and a glass of whiskey, and a horse, too.

"That there's Lilburn Boggs," Bogart said. "He used ta be governor of this here state. I hear he's fixin' ta go west with one of the companies. I guess he wants to be a settler."

Henry's mind swirled in remembrance. He didn't know Mormon history very well, but he'd heard of Governor Boggs. He said, "I thought he was dead, killed by Porter Rockwell."

Bogart laughed. "Not hardly. He recovered from his wounds. Hard to believe the judge sentenced Rockwell to only *five minutes* in jail."

Henry pulled a face, wondering about Missouri justice.

Boggs had served as governor from 1836 to 1840, during the time the Mormons had tried to make Missouri their headquarters. He had issued the now-famous "Extermination Order" in response to the ongoing conflict between Missourians and new Mormons settlers. He loosed a throng of six thousand militia on the Mormons and soon the mob violence flared to an uncontrollable level. Three days later the Haun's Mill Massacre occurred, resulting in the murder of seventeen Mormon men and boys. On a rainy evening in early May 1842, someone shot Boggs in his home by firing at him through a window as he read a newspaper in his study. Boggs was hit by buckshot in four places. Everyone thought Boggs was dead and at least one newspaper ran his obituary. But here he was, sitting across from Henry Eagles, betting money like it was going out of style, smoking a big cigar, and drinking corn whiskey.

Henry withdrew his betting money. He figured he could not outsmart or out-bet a former governor.

"Are you really Governor Boggs?" Henry blurted out as he pocketed his money.

Boggs narrowed his eyes and returned a glare, making Henry feel small and insignificant. "That's right, and who are you?"

"Why, I'm one of the men who killed Joe Smith," Henry replied, expanding his lie a little. "Henry Eagles from Carthage, Illinois. I hear you hate Mormons. Me too. I hate their guts and livers."

The dark eyes of the former Missouri governor suddenly brightened. "I'll shake to that," Boggs replied as he offered Henry his hand. "I hate their guts and livers, too. But do you mean to say you knew men like Thomas Sharp, Mark Aldrich, and Levi Williams?"

"Oh, you mean the editor of the newspaper in Warsaw, the land developer, and Colonel Williams of the Warsaw militia? Why, of course I do," Henry gloated.

The jaw of Governor Boggs dropped about a mile.

Henry noticed the jaw drop and ranted onward. "Course they're all from Warsaw and as defendants they had to sit through that ugly trial. I was right there in the courtroom, stomping the floor with my musket. But my closest friends were in Carthage—the men of the Carthage Grays who were guarding the jail that day."

Henry named some names, but he left out the names of the three men who shot him just before he left Nauvoo. All of this genuinely impressed Boggs because Henry threw around names like a preacher who knew every person in his congregation.

Suddenly Missourians who wanted to meet Henry Eagles surrounded the faro table. Lilburn Boggs jumped up and shook Henry's hand, practically treating him as a celebrity. All this disrupted the faro game and the dealer took on a look of disgust. Boggs bought Henry a drink and soon, under the influence and the help of a little alcohol, Henry told one story after another about living with the Mormons in Hancock County, the details about killing Joe and Hy Smith, and even the trial.

"Why, it would be an honor if you were to join us for the trip to California," Boggs said, explaining that he was leaving within a couple of days. He talked about the restlessness or "itchy-footedness" as he called it, of the American people. He even mentioned the fear many immigrants had of having collisions with the Mormons, how they feared such encounters, and that many had turned back in consequence of their apprehensions.

Henry felt important. He'd always wanted to talk to a governor. He'd never had a chance to talk to Governor Ford, although he'd seen him close up at Carthage.

"Seems a lot of people are headed west these days," Henry said to the ex-governor.

Boggs turned eloquent, as though he were addressing the legislature, giving Henry reasons why there were so many immigrants. There was the national financial panic of 1837, which led to a depression, he said. As a result, land prices plummeted; farmers couldn't sell their produce, which caused them to go bankrupt. People were looking for a better life out west. Only now were economic conditions returning to normal, but men of the Midwest did not intend to wait for the next downturn in the boom-and-bust economic cycle. Overlanders, Boggs stated, were coming from the "middling sort," previously prosperous farmers, traders, artisans, and craftsmen, who had fallen on hard times but who still had sufficient savings to get to the West before being sucked into terminal financial quicksand of the Mississippi valley or points north. Besides, Boggs said, many settlers wanted to avoid the fever-infested swamps of the Missouri and Mississippi Rivers where the ague caused men to sweat and shiver through the summer months. He said he heard that there was but one man in California that ever had a chill there, and it was a matter of so much wonderment to the people that they traveled several miles just to see him shake.

Henry laughed at the story.

Boggs further claimed that when he got there he was going to push for U.S. annexation of California because that would cause property values to go up dramatically and quickly, and he aimed to acquire as much land as he could.

"Lots of people in California?" Henry asked.

"Only around three thousand Mexicans, not counting Injuns," Boggs said. "But two thirds are women and children. Soon we whites'll outnumber the Mexicans there."

"How many Injuns?" Henry asked.

"A hundred thousand, maybe two," Boggs answered nonchalantly.

Henry gasped at the number.

Boggs introduced Henry to another man at the table, Edwin Bryant, who he said was cousin of the famous William Cullen Bryant. Edwin, it was explained, was a newspaperman who planned to write a book about his experiences along the way. Boggs said, "Just bring your wagon and team to our camp and we'll find you a place. You can entertain us at nights with stories about Joe Smith and the Mormons."

The color went out of Henry's face just a little. He didn't want to admit that he had no wagon, no yoke of oxen, and no family with him. He didn't even have a horse, or even worse, an overcoat.

While Henry paused, Boggs began to swell up again as he extolled the importance of his state. "For years I've watched trappers, voyageurs, and settlers come through St. Louis and Independence, on their way to a more adventuresome life. And now I'm one of them."

"I reckon you are," Henry admitted.

Boggs turned on his oratory skills. "There are three highways that diverge from my great state of Missouri into the wilderness of the great American desert. Of course there's the Missouri River itself, winding two thousand miles yonder to the Continental Divide. It's been well traveled."

Boggs made a broad sweep of his arms to a northwestern direction.

"The second great road runs overland up the Platte River, over South Pass, and on to the farm lands beyond the ranges. I'm talking here of the Oregon Trail, and that's the route I'm takin'. As we speak an untold number of covered wagons are crawlin' their way westward, carrying household goods and greenhorn pioneer families seeking new homes. It's like water runnin' across a field. Immigrants are seekin' the easiest passage and the most favored spots. You better get there while the gettin's good."

Henry wondered if that was the road Katherine and Annie were on with the Mormons.

"The third, of course, is the trail to Santa Fe," Boggs said. "It begins right out the door. I couldn't begin to guess the dollar value of the precious wares of Yankee commerce that's creaked and swayed along that trail, and the number of corded bales of buffalo robes and beaver pelts that have come this way from Santa Fe, and the rich metals from Mexican mines."

Henry's understanding of America's overland trail was becoming complete. The trail, he reasoned, frayed like a rope at its eastern end and was bound in a unit along the Missouri. From places like Independence the chasing of the rainbow's end began. America was an amazing place to him, with little rivulets of humanity trickling westward into an almost endless horizon. England, where he was from, was a landlocked isle, with mighty torrents of humanity flowing to the United States on a consistent basis. America could hold all fifteen million Brits and still have room to spare.

Bryant tapped Boggs on the shoulder. "I have that figure, sir. It's right here in the *Commerce on the Prairies*; I happen to have a copy."

Henry's interest piqued and he locked his eyes on the newspaperman.

"In 1843, for example," Bryant began, "the United States transported nearly a half million dollars worth of merchandise to New Mexico, hauled by two hundred thirty wagons. Just a few days ago a caravan of forty-five wagons left from here, just behind Colonel Kearny and his forces. There was even a lady with them, a Mrs. Magoffin. Her husband is one of the major Santa Fe traders. If she makes it, she'll be the first American woman to make the trip from here to Santa Fe. So you see the war hasn't stopped the trade, and likely won't."

Henry was impressed with Bryant's numbers.

"So what do you say, boy? Going with us?" Boggs asked.

"Well, I guess I might," Henry answered, still feeling important that he was talking to an ex-governor. "But I might go to Fort Leavenworth and fight them greasers."

Boggs squealed with delight. He pumped Henry's hand. "Son, that's the downright patriotic thing to do if I ever heard one. How appropriate it is for one of the killers of Joe Smith to volunteer for the war against Mexico."

Boggs was still shaking Henry's arm. Henry didn't dare break the grip, for Boggs was a governor. But his mind was made up. He had to be a soldier now, because a governor expected it.

Boggs finally let go. "Well, boy, you kill a few of them greasers for me."

4

Council Bluffs, Iowa
July 15, 1846

HANNAH WAS READY TO EXPLODE. She and her six children had made the grueling two-month trek across Iowa only because of the courage and strength of her husband. She had barely arrived in this wilderness setting called Council Bluffs. Now she was learning that her husband was expected to enlist in the United States Army to fight in a war against Mexico. How could she possibly get her family to the Great Basin, Upper California, Oregon territory, Salt Lake, the Bear River Valley—or wherever Brigham Young was leading the Church—without Robert?

Her worst nightmare was coming true.

"But this isn't our war," Hannah complained to Brigham as she threw bits of squirrel meat into an iron pot over a campfire. Her brown eyes flared with anger at Brigham and the three men that were with him, Wilford Woodruff, Orson Hyde, and Jesse C. Little. She was not impressed with their gift of wild strawberries and blackberries, either. Her rapid-fire talk was nonstop. "We're English and we don't even live in the United States anymore. Let the American army go somewhere else to raise volunteers. Like Missouri. The Missourians are close by and they've always seemed to like a fight. I don't want my husband aiming a musket at any human being, not even a Mexican."

The meat sizzled under a bright afternoon sky and the aroma began to drift through the camp, attracting Robert's black and white dog. It had rained earlier; a rainbow now formed a perfect and brilliant arch over the camps. Lazy gray, summer clouds floated overhead, offering moments of shade to an otherwise hot, humid day.

Hannah's impertinence didn't seem to bother Brigham. He turned to Wilford Woodruff and shrugged his shoulders. "These are your converts, Elder Woodruff. Besides, it's your turn to do the talking." Brigham's tone implied that he was worn out in the effort to fill five companies of Mormon soldiers for the United States Army. Other wives had resisted, too. And other wives had given in.

Wilford wore an apologetic expression on his weathered face. He had left England in January, returned to Nauvoo, and then departed Nauvoo as part of the exodus on May nineteenth. After spending several days in Mount Pisgah, he arrived in Council Bluffs on July ninth. At Mount Pisgah he had heard of the government's request for five companies from a soldier, Captain James Allen. Wilford had sent an express letter to Brigham Young in Council Bluffs, informing him of the proposal. Captain Allen had arrived on June thirtieth. When Captain Allen first appeared at Mount Pisgah, it caused a great deal of confusion and excitement. Many Church members feared the army had come upon them.

The short barrel-chested Apostle put on his best smile for Hannah. "I just thought it would be a good gesture for a few of the English converts to show their loyalty," Wilford said. "You folks who came from the United Brethren congregation have been stalwarts in the Church during these past five or six years. With all the trials and tribulations we've had in Nauvoo, you've come out the strongest and the most faithful."

The compliment did little to salve Hannah's feelings. "I refuse to give up my husband out here in this wilderness. How would I take care of six children all alone? And just where are we, anyway? All I've seen since I've been in this place is painted up Indians, starving people surrounding covered wagon camps, and a glimpse of some old trading post when we crossed the Missouri River. I didn't go inside because I didn't have any money to buy anything."

Hannah and Robert and the rest of the Daniel Browett Company—down to nine wagons now—were settled into a Missouri Valley catch basin called the Grand Encampment. The encampment stretched an incredible nine miles. Covered wagons with bright white canvas were drawn up in squares in marshy bottomlands, where the Browett Company was located, and on the hills, too. Tents were pitched between the wagons. Some of the wagon and tent squares were enclosed with split-rail fences. Some roads, too, were fenced, making for some semblance of order in the movement of livestock, riders on horseback, and the running of children and puppy dogs around the communal squares. Smoke from a thousand campfires steamed into the air. Herd boys were dozing on the slopes; sheep, horses, mules, cows, and oxen were feeding around them. Other herds—numbering into the thousands—fed on the luxuriant meadow grasses near the swollen river.

When the Browett company arrived at the Missouri, Hannah had reached the organized territorial limits of the United States. Now she found herself in Miller's Hollow, a part of Council Bluffs. Council Bluffs was the name of a landing on the Missouri River, a few miles north of the Pottawattomie Agency, or Trader's Point. The landing was on the east side of the river, overlooked by the hills of the high prairie.

Husbands and wives of the Browett Company had quickly gathered when the four authorities from the Church of Jesus Christ of Latter-day Saints had approached their camp on horseback.

Hannah did not care if she sounded stern, foolish, or narrow-minded in this matter. She was not in the mood to be rational. She was still angry over giving up her first wagon to George Miller and the trip from Garden Grove to here hadn't been any better than the trip from Nauvoo to Garden Grove. A week ago Robert had tried to get their wagon across the Nodaway River. Because of recent rains the river had risen six feet, partially washing away a bridge that another Mormon company had constructed. Everyone had to unload their wagon boxes, use them as a boat, and take a few things over at a time. The horses, mules, oxen, and cattle had to swim across. And so did Hannah and her children.

Hannah also had to share the burden of helping other families. Her sister-in-law, Dianah Bloxham, had suffered from a variety of ailments the entire trip—fever, stomach cramps, and canker being the most noticeable. Hannah felt she was responsible for not only her own six children, but the five Bloxham children as well. Then there were the wives of her two brothers, one of whom had met an untimely death and another who abandoned his wife just prior to her departure from Nauvoo. Elias had left a widow, Mary, and Henry the runaway had left Katherine and Annie.

Other than the brilliant flowers of every hue she saw along the way, the only thing that had brought a chuckle to Hannah during the entire trip was the realization that the award for the chief complainer did not belong to her. That award went to Daniel's mother, Martha, now sixty-one. By the time the company arrived in Council Bluffs, Martha had filled a twenty-page notebook with her detailed complaints.

Hannah was relieved when the other women of the camp began to side with her about the Battalion. They had just been talking about Brother and Sister Edward Martin, the people who had purchased a portion of Robert and Hannah's Nauvoo lot three years ago. On this very day here in Council Bluffs the Martins had buried one of their children between two small oak trees on a high bluff, south of the camp on Mosquito Creek. All the mothers in the Browett Company had cringed at the news, fearing for their own children.

This was no place for a woman to be alone.

"I'm with Hannah, Elder Woodruff," said John Cox's wife, Eliza, with an icy voice. "I've got four children. I couldn't bear the thoughts of staying here without my husband."

"Me either," said Richard Slater's wife, Ann, who also had four children. "Let those without children volunteer."

"Not only do I have four children, but they've been sick," added Levi Robert's wife, Harriet Ann. "And I'm coming down with something. What if it's serious? My husband can't possibly leave now."

Hannah glared at Brigham Young and Wilford Woodruff. Surely she was winning now.

"They wouldn't want my husband, would they?" asked John Hyrum Green's wife, Susannah. "He's forty-six, too old for army service. Besides that, he can hardly walk from the wagon running over him. Besides, I can't understand the necessity of fighting for America; after all, we're fleeing America— aren't we?"

Mary Bundy turned to Margaret Kington. "That would leave our husbands off the hook, wouldn't it?" George Bundy was fifty-eight; Thomas Kington, forty-eight. Mary's nephew, Job Smith, was too young to enlist.

Hannah agreed that Bundy and Kington were far too old for the army. Both of them had long gray eyebrows, hair growing from their earlobes, and long nose hairs.

"My husband's not even a member," Thomas Bloxham's wife, Dianah, said with a sigh of relief, holding a hand to her chest. "And I've been so sick I don't know what I'd do without him right now."

Hannah knew that if it were not for her curiosity in the Battalion enrollment, Dianah would be lying in bed right now. This was the first time in six years that Dianah had not complained that her husband had not been baptized. Thomas' stubborn refusal to listen to the gospel had been a constant source of irritation to her. Dianah, Robert's older sister, had been one of the first persons baptized in 1840 during Elder Woodruff's mission among the United Brethren. She had been baptized nine months pregnant. When the baby was born dead a few days later, Thomas blamed the baby's death on the baptism. Thomas was also bitter over the death of his eight-year-old son, Charles, who had been lost and presumed drowned during the steamboat trip up the Mississippi in 1841.

Dianah's younger sister, Elizabeth Browett, agreed. "Thomas can't possibly enlist," she said. "If he even *thinks* about it I'll whack him with a frying pan." She had just administered a dose of quinine to Dianah to help suppress her fever.

Dianah sat on a log looking grateful for the support of her sister.

Elizabeth spoke next, and forcibly. "You *can't* have Daniel. He has two wives to protect out here, plus a baby." She bounced her pride and joy on her hip, nine-month-old Moroni. After all these years without a child, I *finally* have a baby, Elder Woodruff. Don't take my husband away now."

Wilford seemed to squirm a little, much to Hannah's delight.

"I suppose Sister Phillips is the lucky one right now," Hannah said to Elizabeth. Elizabeth nodded. Annie Phillips' husband, Edward, had dropped out of the company three days ago because of an injured ox. Edward and Annie would probably arrive in Council Bluffs a few days after the Mormon Battalion left for Fort Leavenworth. The Mormon emigration was still scattered three hundred miles from Nauvoo to the Missouri River.

Wilford took a deep breath. "I appreciate your concerns, sisters. I've been here only a week, but what I've learned about our boys who have volunteered to serve in the Mormon Battalion makes me proud. We've had most of the enlistments take place in a large bowery up there on the bluff on Mosquito Creek, between my camp and John Taylor's. Up that way you'll find our Liberty Pole. We've hung a white sheet with an American flag underneath."

If Wilford's remarks were meant to make Hannah feel ashamed, it was working. She hung her head and longed for the day when the Savior's true religion triumphed everywhere, making a call to arms unnecessary. Muskets and swords could be buried in the ground. In her view right now, the world was full of egotistic, willful, evil people poised to go to war at the drop of a hat.

Wilford continued. "Ezra Allen enlisted in Company C; his wife and *all* his children are sick. Henderson Cox enlisted, and he's only seventeen. Brother Phillip Garner enlisted; he and his wife, Mary, have eight children, and she is expecting again. Brother Richard Sessions of Company A is leaving *seven* children behind, and his two oldest sons have enlisted, too. Brother Sessions is *forty-four* years old, by the way. Allen Compton is now a member of Company D. Brother Compton lost *everything* in Nauvoo; a mob of eighteen malicious men burned their home and all their possessions. They left Nauvoo with only the clothing on their backs. He's leaving five children behind. Hyrum Judd has enlisted. His only little daughter is buried somewhere between here and Sugar Creek. James Brown enlisted; he did it on the same day that he married Sister Mary Black."

Tears sprang to Hannah's eyes. Slowly stirring her squirrel meat and without looking up she said, "Elder Woodruff, we just got here. I don't think any of us understand this war with Mexico. Maybe if you could just explain it …"

CHAPTER NOTES

According to the Job Smith Autobiography (LDS Church files), Robert Harris arrived in Council Bluffs on July 15. It appears that several families traveled together, leaving Nauvoo in mid-May: Robert Harris, George Bundy (including Job Smith), Daniel Browett, John Cox, Levi Roberts, Richard Slater, Robert Pixton, and Thomas Bloxham. Studies reveal that Thomas Kington left about the same time and so did Edward Phillips. All these people were from the same area in England and, with the exception of Thomas Bloxham, were United Brethren converts. Thomas's wife, Dianah, was also a convert, even though Thomas had not joined the Church. Dianah was a sister to Robert Harris, as was Elizabeth Browett, Daniel's wife. For the purposes of this novel, the author placed all these families into the Daniel Browett company for the trek across Iowa.

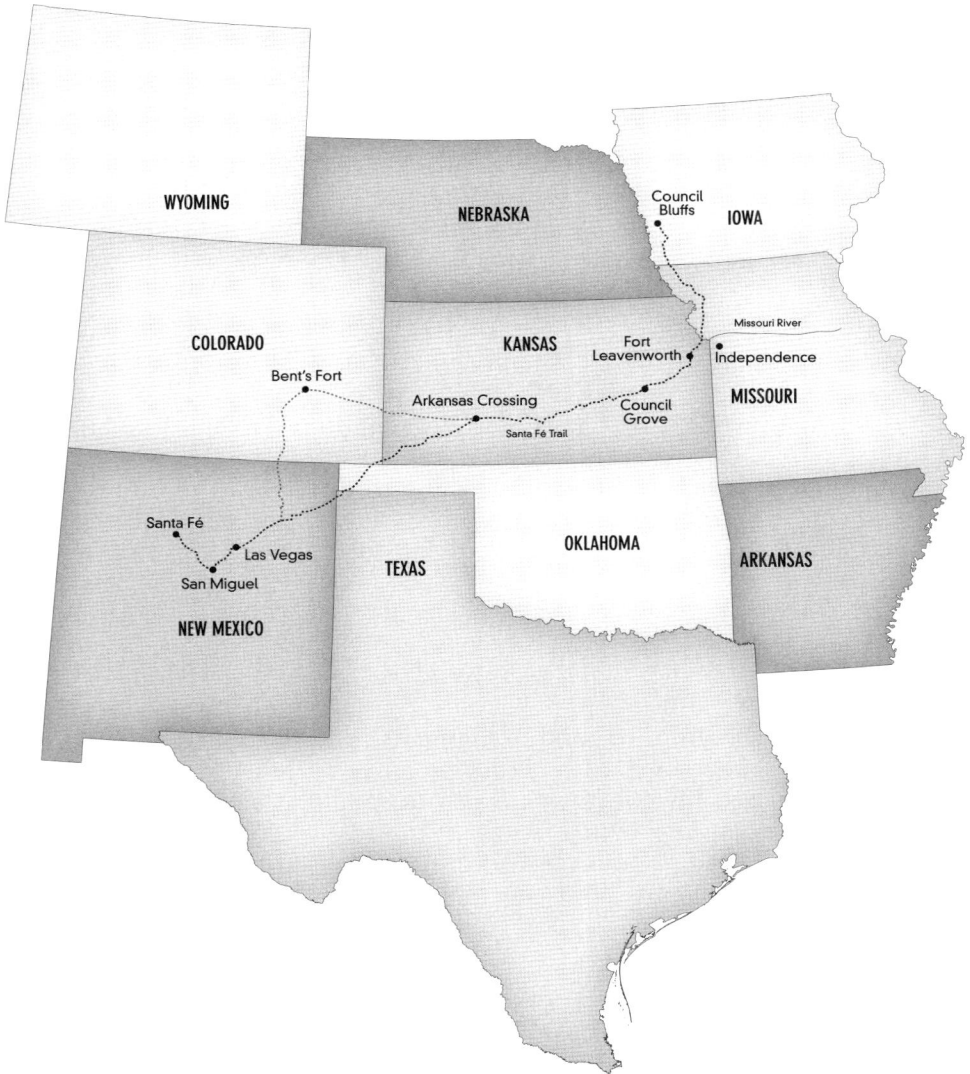

5

ROBERT WAS TORN BETWEEN TWO emotions. He felt duty-bound to enlist, not because it was the patriotic thing to do, but out of loyalty to the Church. But Hannah appeared dead set against it and he didn't want to disappoint her. She was right; wives needed husbands out here in this wilderness setting. If he left for a year or more, who would watch over her? His anxiety deepened as Wilford began to respond to Hannah's concerns.

Wilford flexed his fingers and began to speak. "Members of the Twelve have been visiting camps on both sides of the river in this recruitment effort," he said. "A year ago we could have raised two thousand men in twenty-four hours. But times have changed. Captain James Allen wants the Battalion to leave Monday, but we need almost a hundred more men."

To Robert's eyes, Wilford Woodruff looked as confident today as he when he first laid eyes on him—the time Wilford was preaching in Robert's home in Apperley, England, at Hannah's request, and Robert had tried to throw him out. Since then, however, flecks of gray had appeared in Wilford's brown hair. Hard to believe, but that was twelve years ago. At thirty-nine, Wilford's physical sturdiness matched his spiritual endurance. Despite his short stature, Wilford looked like he could fell a tree with one swing of the axe.

"Monday?" Hannah shrieked, her face now ashen. "You want my husband to leave Monday? That's only five days away!"

Wilford turned to face Hannah. "And because you just got here there are some things you don't understand."

Hannah pulled a face. Her voice was tinged with sarcasm. "The only thing I understand is that you're trying to take away my husband."

"What things don't we understand?" Levi Roberts asked.

"It's too late in the year for us to try for the Great Basin," Wilford explained, his craggy face now set in concern. "Brother Brigham and the Twelve have made the decision that we are going to winter somewhere here in the Council Bluffs area. Besides that, everyone's money is short, and so are supplies. Soon, we'll all be down to squirrel meat."

"But to ask our husbands to leave…" Hannah complained as she tossed wild onions and leeks into her stew.

Wilford's resolve stiffened. "Each soldier who enlists not only will get paid a monthly wage but he'll receive a clothing allowance as well. The army will let each soldier take the clothing allowance in cash instead of an actual uniform. Remember the covenant that all Church members made before we left Nauvoo, that we would assist one another, and bear one another's burdens."

Brigham Young cleared his throat and took off his hat, revealing locks of thick, reddish-brown hair. His blue eyes were intense. "We'll collect the money from the volunteers and bring it back to the camps here, and use it to help survive the winter," he said.

In Robert's view, no Church official had earned more respect than Brigham since he took over leadership of the Church following the murders of Joseph and Hyrum Smith. He had an air of confidence backed up by performance, although today his face was stiff with strain. There was an urgency to fill up the Battalion as quickly as possible.

Robert clearly understood, too, the tenuous situation of his Church. The economy was fragile, and the Church's very survival was in question. With winter coming on, the Mormons at the Missouri and scattered across Iowa faced a raft of formidable economic problems. Few if any crops had been planted; provisions were meager; property sales in Nauvoo were at a standstill; Indian theft of cattle was increasing; and the prospect of trading with Missouri wholesalers, farmers, and merchants was uncertain. The Mormons either had to band together and support one another or reap the inevitable consequences of mass suffering and starvation.

Elizabeth stopped swaying Moroni on her hip and her green eyes brightened. "How *much* cash allowance?"

"For clothing money, forty-two dollars," Brigham explained. "Monthly pay for privates is seven dollars a month. It goes up from there. Some of the Mormon men will be elected officers. Mormon captains will be paid fifty dollars a month. A first sergeant, for example, will get sixteen dollars. The volunteers get to elect their own officers."

Robert let out an airy whistle. He did a quick calculation in his mind for a private's pay. Seven dollars times twelve months equaled a total of eighty-four dollars for a year's enlistment, plus the forty-two dollars for clothing. He had less than three dollars in his pocket. Yesterday, Hannah had sold her teapot for seventy-five cents.

Hannah was doing her own calculations. "If the Church is so hard up for money, why don't you sell the Nauvoo Temple?"

Brigham hung his head. "I've clung to that hope all across Iowa. We've felt much anxiety about that subject. We even lowered our price to twenty-five thousand dollars, but nothing has materialized. We're still trying, but it looks hopeless. We're even trying to sell the Kirtland Temple."

Robert pulled at his chin, putting all this together. The hasty winter departure from Nauvoo, the fact that hundreds more of the Saints were being driven out by mobs, the relative poverty of the Saints, and the inability to sell the temple and even farms and homes, drew Robert into an unwanted conclusion. The Church and its members were in dire straits. "You mean to say that none of our people are going west this summer?" He asked. He knew that Brigham's trek across Iowa had taken sixteen weeks in the mud and rain, three times as long as anyone had expected. Those sixteen weeks had cost individuals and the Church not only a lot of provisions, but time and energy too. Nonstop rainfall, sudden melting snows, and swollen creeks had all combined against them.

Brigham stood on squat powerful legs, his authority emanating from deep blue eyes. His mobile face went a little weary. "We have no choice, Brother Harris. It's getting too late. And we haven't the money to buy proper supplies. The first companies will leave in the spring."

"Not until next April or May?" Hannah whined.

"Sorry," Brigham said, "but it's a well known fact among mountain men and settlers out west that the latest safe date for leaving the Missouri River in time to cross the Rockies before the mountain snows is early to mid-June. And only then with adequate provisions."

"So if the Church as a whole doesn't move out until next spring, where will the Mormon soldiers be by then?" Robert asked, trying hard not to show the emotion in his face. Even though he felt duty-bound to enlist, he could not envision being separated from Hannah for one day, let alone for more than a year.

"Somewhere in California," came the answer. "That's what Captain Allen says."

Robert blinked in exasperation. To him, California meant anywhere from the Missouri River to the Pacific Ocean. He had never studied Fremont's maps personally. He had only heard about them. But he now suspected California meant somewhere along the Pacific Coast. "And when will the Battalion be released?" he asked.

"One year from now," Brigham said.

Robert pulled Hannah to his side, his chest starting to heave with concern. "And where will my wife be one year from now? And my children?" He pointed to his six children playing in the tall grass near a small creek. They ranged in age from ten to two.

Brigham paused to think. "We'll use the Battalion money to get them to the Great Basin. Migration costs for the whole of the Church are going to amount to a staggering sum."

Robert was not satisfied. The thoughts of Hannah and his six children trudging without him across vast plains marked as "Indian Territory" on a map didn't sit well with him. "Just where is this Great Basin?" he asked. "And what is it, exactly?"

Brigham quickly explained that the Great Basin was a vast bowl-like area wedged between two great mountain ranges—the Sierra Nevada on the west and the Wasatch branch of the Rocky Mountains on the east. The basin contained more than two hundred thousand square miles, and it was more than nine hundred miles long and seven hundred miles wide—more than enough to provide a safe harbor for the Church. None of its rivers flowed to the sea; rather they either emptied into the Great Salt Lake or simply sank or disappeared into the earth. Rainfall was admittedly sparse and its scenery depressing.

The parched-desert description of the Great Basin sounded mournful to

Robert. "Are we ending up there, or California, New Mexico, or Oregon?"

Brigham shuffled his feet. "That might depend on the war. So before I answer that question, I want you to hear from Elder Jesse Little," Brigham explained. "He's just come from Washington, D. C., with Captain Allen. He's prepared to tell you about the war that has developed against Mexico, and why the army is here recruiting volunteers to fight for the United States. I sent Elder Little to petition President Polk for help. It is my belief that the Lord is going to help the Mormon people through this war with Mexico. Elder Little will explain."

6

ROBERT HAD HALF EXPECTED Brigham to go off on President Polk and his administration at any time. In the past, Brigham had been critical not only of Polk but other government officials such as Missouri's Thomas H. Benton, a senator. Benton was John C. Fremont's father-in-law. But now it seemed that Brigham looked upon Polk's offer to let the Mormons enlist in the army as a gift from heaven. And it seemed the Church was asking the Mormon men to serve in the Battalion more as a Church calling than as an act of patriotism. In fact, Brigham had instructed all Church members not to be critical of the government anymore.

All eyes riveted on Elder Little, the man who had served as president over the Eastern and Central States Mission for the past year. He had lived in New Hampshire where his business had been carriage and sleigh manufacturing. Robert had never met him, but he looked like a man he could trust.

Hannah, however, gave the man a doubtful stare.

Jesse Little reached into his vest and pulled out a crumpled piece of newsprint. He slowly unfolded it. "This is the best rendition of a map that I've found. It was printed by a newspaper in Washington, a compilation of the Mitchell and Tanner maps, and probably Fremont's, too.

The men and women of the company squeezed together to view Jesse's map. Robert squinted in the afternoon sun and saw that the map had thick lines that bordered all of the states from the Atlantic Coast to the Mississippi River. Robert made out Illinois, Missouri, and Iowa territory.

Jesse used his index finger to outline Texas. "All this area is Texas, which is part of the problem," he began, waxing philosophical. "You probably know by now that Texas has formally been part of the United States just since January. Texas, it should be remembered, declared itself a republic way back in 1836. Since then, Texans have vigorously defended their independence. But there's been a problem. Mexico never did recognize the sovereignty of Texas. Mexico warned us time and again that annexation would mean war. Because of pressure from Americans there, we annexed Texas. It should not surprise any of us that we are now at war with Mexico."

"But what has that got to do with the rest of the map?" Hannah asked, shifting her gaze back and forth on Jesse's map.

"You're familiar with Texas," Jesse said, letting his finger point to that area on the map. "If we win the war, I'd expect Texas to become part of the United States."

"So why is the United States asking for Mormon soldiers to march to California?" Hannah asked.

Jesse let his finger trace a large area of the map west of Texas all the way to the Pacific Ocean. "All of this is Mexican territory. To the Mexicans, it is divided into three provinces—New Mexico, Sonora, and Upper California."

Hannah let out an audible gasp, so large was the territory.

"Up here," Jesse explained as his finger outlined an area along the northern Pacific coast, and then back again toward Iowa, "is the area we call Oregon Territory. It has been jointly settled and occupied by the United States and Great Britain. But very sparsely, I might add."

"Is the United States trying to conquer all that land, and add it to its borders?" Hannah asked.

Jesse smiled. "Who knows what will come to pass as a result of the war? I would say Texas, yes, but what might happen to California and Oregon Territory—that's another matter and open to speculation."

Robert stared at the map, letting this all sink in. Little said that the influx of Americans into Oregon over the past few years had ignited a dispute between his home country, Great Britain, and his former country, the United States. The wrangle originated in the fact that the boundaries of Oregon had never been clearly fixed. The name vaguely embraced the territory west of the Rockies between the northern boundary of Mexican-held California and the southern edge of Russian-held Alaska, which extended south to parallel fifty-four degrees forty minutes. Earlier in the century America proposed a boundary at the forty-ninth parallel, but the British suggested a line farther south. Two years earlier, the 1844 Democratic campaign slogan had been "fifty-four-forty or fight." Temporarily, the issue had been settled by joint occupancy. But now the issue could no longer be avoided. Texas and Oregon fever had become potent political forces.

Jesse paused for a few seconds. "I understand that most everyone in this company is from England."

Wilford stuck out his chest and flashed a satisfied smile. "That's right, Elder Little. They're from the Malvern Hills area." He pointed to Thomas Kington. "This man had organized six hundred people into what he called the United Brethren congregation. They were a prepared people, Brother Little. They were seeking the further light and truth of the restored gospel. They recognized the truthfulness of the gospel immediately. All six hundred were baptized in just a few months."

Jesse smiled grimly. "As former Englishmen, you understand Great Britain's position. The British have been reluctant to give up any more territory in North America."

Hannah's jaw dropped open, her eyes full of fear and apprehension. "Is the United States going to war against Great Britain, too?"

Jesse began to chuckle, sensing her concern. "I don't think so. But President Polk was elected on a platform of fifty-four-forty or fight."

"And that means war with England?" Hannah asked, her expression still clouded.

"President Polk asserts that everything up to this line should be part of the United States," Jesse said, now letting his finger wander up the Pacific Coast toward Alaska. "When I left the city of Washington, Polk was confident that things could be worked out with the British. Now I've heard that Polk reached a compromise, accepting everything below the forty-ninth parallel. At this point our only war is with the Mexicans."

"But how can an army of five hundred Mormon men win a war against the entire nation of Mexico?" Ann Slater asked with a puzzled look. Like Hannah, Ann was the mother of six children. She had recently announced that another baby would be born to her and Richard in a few months.

Jesse rolled his eyes and chuckled again. "President Polk has been authorized by Congress to accept fifty thousand volunteers into the American army, not just five hundred. Pardon me for laughing, but there are some things you need to understand. Mexico is having a lot of internal problems right now. There's unrest and political instability going back to regional loyalties when Mexico was ruled by Spain. An internal war in Mexico broke out just this past January. The president of Mexico has been deposed by a general in what we call a coup. This general—Mariano Parades y Arrillago—has formed a junta, but the junta is hanging on by its fingernails."

"But what about Santa Anna?" George Bundy asked. He was older, and more caught up on current affairs.

"He's in exile in Cuba and he's retired for the third or fourth time, some of it voluntary, some of it not," Jesse explained with a world-wise shrug. "He's not a factor right now, and even if he came back, his country is in too much turmoil for him to turn it around anytime soon. Besides that, Mexico owes Great Britain a lot of money. The Mexicans don't appear to be able to fund much of a war these days."

"So the United States is fighting a weak opponent?" Hannah asked.

"Mexico would be a strong opponent if all the forces there worked together, but it's quite the opposite," Little explained. "In early May, a United States general by the name of Zachary Taylor won the first battle in northern Mexico, along the border of the Rio Grande. The Mexicans lost more than three hundred men killed and seven hundred wounded."

There was an audible gasp from the men and women of the company. Hannah's fears were confirmed. Men get killed in war, and therefore her husband would be in harm's way if he enlisted.

Jesse went on. "But Taylor's army lost only nine killed and less than fifty wounded. The victory has given President Polk great confidence that future battles will go well. Not only that, but Mexico's power in New Mexico and California is on the decline. Powerful independence movements in both places are challenging the authority of Mexico. People who are orchestrating the movements seem to be getting away with it because of the remoteness of the Mexican central government. Indians are another factor. Bands of Navajo, Apache, Pima, and other Indians actually control most of the country between the Rio Grande and California, not the Mexicans. The Mexican government is doing little to protect its citizens in the area from the incessant attacks of

Indians. There're a lot of Indians between the Mississippi River and the West Coast, probably three million of them."

Robert saw Daniel tremble just a little. Daniel had always feared Indians for some reason. There were no Indians in England, where Robert and Daniel had been raised. They were unique to America. Here, Indians were regarded by the government of the United States as a foreign nation. The existence of warlike races of Indians on the margins of settlement naturally called for the occupation of the borderland by troops. But Robert had seen no troops, not even at the trading post.

"But I've heard there are six or seven million Mexicans," Harriet Ann Roberts stammered. "Won't this rile them up?" Like many of the people in the temporary Mormon settlements, Harriet was sick. Curiosity had given her the strength to rise from her bed.

Jesse shook his head no, but he was amazed that Sister Roberts knew the population of Mexico. Not many so-called knowledgeable people in Washington knew the figure. "Only among a few war hawks," he said, "but they've got their hands full trying to hang onto power in Mexico City. And there are very few loyal Mexicans scattered throughout the provinces of New Mexico and California. Just a few hundred. We think there're more Americans living in those areas than Mexicans."

Harriet Ann tugged at her chin. "So if our husbands go on this march, will they be in danger of losing their lives? And what about the Missourians? Fort Leavenworth is just up the river from Independence, Missouri. Won't there be a lot of Missouri volunteers in the army, too?"

Brigham Young took over again. "Good questions, sister. We've had several public meetings explaining all this, but since you just arrived, we'll go over it again. We need to make a distinction between the actions of our oppressors in Missouri and Illinois and the actions of the central government. The central government did not drive us out of those two states; but some very wicked people did. Now let us suppose that in the future the Mormon people are admitted into the Union as a state and the government did not call on us to assist them in a war such as this. We would feel neglected."

"Not me," Hannah said, her flowered dress feeling heavy and sticky in the heat. Oily strands of brown hair hung down her forehead. "I wouldn't feel neglected."

Brigham scoffed and then cleared his throat. "If we want the privilege of going where we can worship God according to the dictates of our own conscience, then we *must* raise this Battalion. I say let the Mormons be among the first to set their feet on the soil of California. We have offered the government five hundred soldiers. I have promised Captain Allen that I would do my best to see that we fill five companies of a hundred men each."

Hannah shook her head sideways. "But I've heard you and other members of the Twelve lament the fact that we have received no help from the government. Why now? Why this?"

"The United States wants our friendship," Brigham said. "The president wants to do us good and secure our confidence. The pay that five hundred men receive will provide the miracle we need to get the Church to the Great Basin. I feel confident that our Mormon men will encounter little or no fighting."

Hannah pulled a face of disbelief. "But isn't that the purpose of an army—to fight?"

Jesse Little held up a hand. "Another army officer—this one named Kearny—has been stationed at Fort Leavenworth. He's the commanding officer of the First Dragoons there, and he's the colonel who signed Captain Allen's letter of introduction. Kearny has been ordered to march into New Mexico, Sonora, and California. Yes, his army of fewer than three thousand men consists mostly of volunteers from Missouri, plus a few regulars. But they will be marching ahead of our Mormon Battalion boys. The brethren and I have discussed this at length. If there are battles to fight, we think that Colonel Kearny will fight them. Our Mormon boys will be used mostly as a show of strength and for the occupation."

"I suppose this Colonel Kearny is qualified?"

"He's earned his stripes," Little said. "Seven years ago he marched against the Cherokees with ten companies of dragoons, the largest U.S. mounted force ever assembled."

Hannah still was not convinced. She stared thoughtfully at Jesse's map. "But what about here, along the Pacific coast? Seems to me there would be a lot of Mexicans there."

"President Polk and the generals think that there are more people loyal to the United States that live there, than to Mexico," Jesse said. "Again, we're talking only of a few hundred people, not thousands, and we call them Californios."

"And an American explorer is there with a small force, too," Wilford said.

Hannah's eyebrows lifted. "Who?"

"John C. Fremont. Jesse tells us that Fremont left St. Louis a year ago on his third expedition to the West. He's on a scientific exploration of the area, but he has two or three-dozen hardened, seasoned mountain men with him. I think these men will be a factor. Not only that, but the United States has a naval presence on the Pacific coast, too."

"And what about central Mexico?" Robert asked.

"What I am about to say is my opinion," Jesse said. "If war does break out, I am confident that President Polk will send other units into Mexico to capture Vera Cruz and Mexico City. It might take a year, but it would be a natural course of events if war formally breaks out. Remember again, Mexico has a highly unstable government. They've gone from a federal constitution in 1824 to a centralized dictatorship in 1835. Since then, there have been various clashing parties of Centralists trying to gain control. All this has caused them to lose control of what we call colonial New Spain. They've already lost Texas, and now I predict they will lose their California and New Mexico provinces as well."

"If Jesse is right, we'll be settling in the United States, not Mexico," Brigham said with a broad, confident smile.

Robert's mood brightened a bit, and so did Hannah's.

Brigham continued. "People back east, where Jesse came from, say that this is the natural destiny of the United States, to stretch our borders all the way to the Pacific. Americans have been migrating westward for the past forty years, most often into lands not belonging to the United States. At times, Mexico actually encouraged people to settle in New Mexico and California. At other times, Mexico was against Americans entering any area—but they didn't have the means to stop it. The Mexican government wanted all settlers to take an oath of allegiance to Mexico and convert to Catholicism, the state religion. Now, however, those settlers want to be included in the United States, and there's a lot of political support back east for that to happen."

"So this so-called 'natural destiny' purely political?" Daniel asked.

Jesse snorted in derision. "No, sir. Back in Washington if you asked what it meant you'd get a variety of answers. I see it as a peculiar mixture of assertiveness and fear. We want to assert our borders to the Pacific Ocean because we fear if we don't we'll regret it later. And we don't want to have Mexico or England border our western frontier."

Daniel nodded, quickly seeing the logic.

Jesse continued, explaining things he'd learned back east. "There are those in our country who believe that God wants the freedoms guaranteed by the Constitution to be extended to as many people as possible, across the greatest expanse possible. Those people believe Providence has obviously chosen the United States as its vessel."

At this point Brigham Young interrupted Jesse. "The Church needs a safe sanctuary, a place where the gospel can grow. The constitution was divinely inspired. Ultimately I believe we'll find the place where God intends us to be."

The adult members of the Daniel Browett company shook their heads in a gesture of understanding.

Robert agreed that the Church needed a safe sanctuary. Missouri had not turned out to be a safe sanctuary, and neither had Illinois. It seemed to him that the American West so far—Illinois and Missouri—was just about void of God-fearing people except for the Mormons. Robert and his wife had come to America to gather to Zion. Americans, on the other hand, often went west because of personal difficulties. Some incident in their life had caused them to flee the more staid east. Having exiled themselves from respectable society by some illicit love affair, a duel, or a more serious crime, these crude Americans could hardly be expected to lead pious lives in the wilds. Too many of them were outlaws. To Robert, that described the Missourians and the people in Illinois who had mobbed together to murder the Prophet. For those kinds of people, it seemed there was no Sunday west of the Mississippi and no God on the American frontier. The attitude of the Western people was antagonistic toward restraint of any kind. It was a case of everybody for himself and the devil take the hindermost. The shrewdest, most fortunate, the strongest, and the most unscrupulous were out to seize America's vast resources without regard to waste, uneconomic practices, or religious freedoms. They had driven the Mormons from Missouri and Illinois. Where out west—on this great map that Jesse Little held before him—could the Mormons really find a "safe sanctuary?"

"Take a look at the map again," Jesse said as he placed his outstretched hand on it. "All of this area constitutes the organized area of the United States." He moved his hand a little. "All of this constituted the Louisiana Purchase, which I am sure you have heard of." Again, he moved his hand. "Now take a look at all this area. What happens to the size of the United States as we annex Oregon, and win California and New Mexico in the war against Mexico?"

There was a combined gasp. It looked to Robert that the United States would gain at least a million square miles of land. New Mexico included Hispanic Arizona. He could see that if the United States did not move quickly to annex territories north of the Rio Grande held in Mexico's grasp, some other nation, probably Britain, would acquire them. No wonder men like Fremont had been sent to survey and make maps of the West.

"I want a better answer to my question now," Robert said to Brigham Young. "If I enlist in the Battalion, just exactly where will the Church be located on this map one year from now? Where will I find my wife and children?"

Brigham Young took Jesse's map. "All this area is called the Great American Desert. It has other names, too, as we've explained: Oregon, New Mexico, and California. Here, between Iowa and Oregon and California, is land we call Indian country. That land belongs to the Indians, not to the United States, not to Mexico, and not to Great Britain. We're going to be out there somewhere, wherever the Lord leads us."

Hannah reacted with disgust. "That's not a very good answer," she said.

"That's the best I can do for now," Brigham countered. "There are too many unsettled issues, like this war. But there's one thing for certain. There are fewer than twenty thousand whites out there. When *we* settle in the West, the number will be doubled."

Daniel Browett nudged closer. "And where do you think the Mormon Battalion will be one year from now?" he asked.

"Captain Allen thinks somewhere here," Jesse said, pointing to his map again. "Perhaps in Monterey, San Diego, or Los Angeles—somewhere on the Pacific coast is my guess."

Hannah turned to Robert. Tears streamed down her face. Counting a few months extra for travel time, there was a possibility that her husband could be gone for nearly two years, not just one. "No, Robert. No."

Robert took Hannah into his arms. Then he turned his eyes to Jesse and to the three Church authorities. "We need some time alone."

As Brigham turned to go, Orson Hyde motioned to Daniel, Robert's brother-in-law. "Can I have a word with you, in private?"

Daniel followed Orson several yards away from the group. Nearly five years ago Orson had dedicated and consecrated the land of Israel for the gathering together of Judah's scattered remnants so that Jerusalem could be built up again.

"I'm camped nearby, in a large hollow," Orson began as he walked to the horses the four men had left tied to trees. The bright red hair of the forty-four-year-old apostle gleamed in the late afternoon sun, with several strands of gray apparent.

"When did you arrive?" Daniel asked.

"A month ago, on June seventeenth," came the answer. "Elder Woodruff got here just a few days ago."

"I know," Daniel said. "We were traveling right behind him most of the time. We camped together twice. He told me about England and some of the problems there."

"That's what I need to tell you," Orson said. "Brother Brigham wants me to go to England again and preside over the mission there. John Taylor and Parley P. Pratt are going with me."

Daniel stared at Orson in disbelief. "Because of the problem with Brother Hedlock?" he asked. When Elder Woodruff left England, he had placed Hedlock in charge of the British Mission. Now there were rumors he had been mismanaging Church funds, especially those connected with the Joint Stock Company. Hedlock probably faced a Church court that would likely result in him being disfellowshiped or excommunicated.

"Yes," Orson answered. "We just decided this during a council meeting this morning."

"Does Rebecca know?"

"No, and she'll absolutely throw a fit when she finds out," Orson said.

Daniel let his air out, wondering when his sister would outgrow her jealousy. Rebecca was Orson's second plural wife. And there was a third, the former Mary Ann Price.

"I want you to come to camp with me and be with me when I tell her. Maybe it will help. Bring your mother, too. And Elizabeth."

"Now?"

"Tonight. I've got to visit other camps with Brother Brigham first. How do you feel about enlisting?"

The men and women of Daniel's company were breaking up now, husbands talking to wives about the enlistment. Daniel turned to spot Elizabeth and Harriet, and his little boy, Moroni. "Elder Hyde, I've never known until now what it was like to be a father. I love my son. He's the light of my life. I can't imagine not watching him learn to walk and learn to talk. The thought of leaving him and my wives for a year or more tears my heart out. But I can see the need. Let me talk to Elizabeth and Harriet, and pray about it."

"The enlistment camp will be open again in the morning," Orson said. "We're counting on you. And you ought to give Sister Bloxham a blessing. She sure doesn't look good."

"We've given her two or three, on the way across Iowa."

"Better give her another."

CHAPTER NOTES:

In 1846, Mexico's three states within territory now held by the United States comprised the present states of California, Nevada, Utah, Arizona, New Mexico, and parts of Wyoming and Colorado. At that time no American mapmaker could have approximated the theoretical boundary between the United States and Mexico. Oregon territory consisted of not only Oregon, but also Washington, Idaho, and parts of Montana, Wyoming, and northward into Canada. The Mitchell and Tanner maps of 1846, and Fremont's map of 1842, were the current public maps of the time.

It is doubtful that people like Brigham Young, Wilford Woodruff, and Jesse Little knew as much about the pending war with Mexico as portrayed here. They were not highly educated people. In this chapter the author is putting words into their mouths merely in an attempt to educate the reader about the circumstances that led to the enlistment of the Mormon Battalion. This process continues throughout following chapters, involving the opinions of people like Captain Allen and Thomas Kane. President Polk actually authorized the Army to enlist the Battalion after the Saints arrived in the West—whether that be the Rockies, California, or some other area—and this is the agreement that Little understood when he left Washington on June 4. But the orders to Kearny were not clear on this point. Thus Kearny ordered Captain Allen to the Mormon camps in Iowa to begin recruiting. When Little arrived from Nauvoo, Captain Allen and Brigham Young were already recruiting Mormon men. And it may be that Jesse Little, Brigham Young, and even President Polk did not know what would come to pass as the result of the war with Mexico, such as the addition of New Mexico, Sonora, and California to the borders of the United States.

7

DANIEL REELED WITH HORROR WHEN he turned to face the campfire again. More than a dozen hawk-faced Indians with braided hair had suddenly surrounded Elizabeth, Harriet, Moroni, Hannah, Robert, and the others. The Indians were gesturing and doing it rather wildly in Daniel's opinion. He felt a rush of protective instinct.

"You didn't tell me about the Indians," Daniel said to Orson as he began a brisk walk back to the camp.

Orson appeared not to be concerned. "They're friendly. They've noticed that you're new here. They're going to try their hand at trading with you."

Orson explained to Daniel that the Omaha and Oto-Missouri tribes lived on the west side of the Missouri and that the Church was negotiating an agreement to use some of their lands for the winter. The Pottawattomie-Ottowa-Chippewa Federated Tribe of Indians lived on the Iowa side of the river, he said. All told, there were more than two thousand five hundred Indians living near the river by the Grand Encampment of the Mormons, and more than two thousand additional Indians lived in at least five other widely scattered villages. The Mormons themselves were now stretched in camps that measured nine miles from one end to the other.

"But I don't like Indians," Daniel said. He had been inwardly disturbed when he saw that there was a vast area labeled "Indian Territory" on Jesse Little's map and he couldn't get the image out of his mind. Men with copper skin stretched over high cheekbones, their expressions penetrating and fearless, had always given Daniel uncomfortable feelings. "I have bad dreams about them. Sometimes I see a tomahawk coming at my nose. Elizabeth doesn't like them either."

Orson laughed. "Patronize them best you can, especially the Omahas and the Otos. We don't want the agreement to be jeopardized."

Elizabeth ran toward them, clutching Moroni to her breast. "Brother Hyde, make those Indians go away. They *bother* me."

The Apostle laughed again. "That might take an hour or more. Just don't trade with them. According to U.S. law, we have no right to trade with the Indians. They're supposed to use official traders at Trader's Point, but the Indians like to break the rules. That's fine for them, but not for you. And watch your livestock. Brigham is waiting for me. See you tonight, Brother Browett. Bring Elizabeth and Harriet if you'd like."

Elizabeth pursed her lips, deep in thought. She had passed through

Trader's Point on the way to Council Bluffs. It was a town composed of twelve to fifteen blocks and none of the houses had windows. Only Indians, French, and half-breeds lived there.

"But Elder Hyde," Elizabeth said as Orson mounted his horse, "will the Battalion encounter *Indians* in New Mexico and California?" She had a habit of over-emphasizing certain words, especially when she was excited.

"I'm certain they will," Orson said from the saddle.

"I don't mind if Daniel is gone for a year marching to Mexico and California, but I *don't* want him killed by Indians, or by Mexicans either."

"You worry too much, Sister Browett," Orson exclaimed. He kicked his horse and followed his three traveling companions to the next camp.

"Come on," Daniel said to his wife. "Let's go help protect everyone's larder."

Elizabeth nodded. What was left of her flour, bacon, sugar, tea, canned goods, salt, dried meats, vinegar, cheese, pickles, oatmeal, molasses, and bran she didn't want to have carted off. There was a danger of starving half to death during the coming winter even with all of her larder, let alone losing some or most of it to Indians.

There were upward of more than a dozen Indians surrounding the campfire now, and more coming. The bucks were dressed in calico shirts with buckskin pantaloons, gaiters, and moccasins. All of them were rouged with vermilion paint. On some, only their eyelids and lips were painted; on others, the paint had been dabbed onto cheeks, foreheads, and noses. There seemed to be a variety of tastes and styles to the application of the paint, with no particular fashion prevailing. The ears on most of the men were bored with large holes, large enough for a man's finger to poke through. A profusion of bone, tin, and brass trinkets hung from their ears. Some had shorn heads except for a small tuft at the crown. Others had long, matted, tangled, black hair. Most were scrawny men, but one man, tall and athletic, carried a broadsword in a bright metal scabbard that glittered in the late afternoon sun. The others carried a collection of bows and arrows and tomahawks. To Daniel's eyes, the squaws looked worse than the men. Several nude Indian children accompanied them. Three of the squaws had babies strapped to their backs with blankets.

Robert's dog, Duke, seemed to like the Indians. Duke offered friendly licks at the Indians' fingers.

"What do they want?" Daniel asked Hannah, who seemed to be in distress. She was guarding her squirrel stew, hoping the Indians would not eat it before her own children were fed.

"Anything and everything," Hannah complained, her eyes flaring back and forth at the unwanted company.

"One of them speaks a little English," Robert said. "He's said words like *whiskey, rifles, meat, tobacco, bacon,* and *bread.*"

Do they have anything to trade?" Daniel asked.

"Moccasins, snake skins, skunk skins, and small bits of silver," came the answer.

Elizabeth shook her head until Daniel thought it would fall off. Then she shivered. "Just get rid of them," she said.

Daniel held up his hand and waved it. "No trade."

The Indians began to trickle to the next campfire, asking to trade with the Cox, Roberts, Pixton, Slater, Bloxham, Green, Kington, and Bundy families. Daniel quickly spread the word that trading was against the law. When most of the Indians had disappeared, Hannah began feeding her children and the Bloxham children.

"I suppose we need a campfire council to talk about the Battalion," Daniel said to Robert.

"The sooner the better," Robert responded.

"I'll invite the others," Daniel said. "But it looks like I'll have to shoo the Indians away again. I'll be back soon."

Hannah slowly and methodically began to ladle the stew into tin bowls. She locked her mournful brown eyes onto Robert. "There's something I haven't told you," she said.

Robert began placing the bowls on a makeshift table attached to the wagon box. "I'm listening."

"I'm in a family way again. Number seven will come in February, eight months from now."

Robert closed his eyes. "No wonder you were so cranky today."

"I've been having dreams, bad dreams."

"What about?"

"It's about death and the unborn baby. Either I die or the baby dies."

"You've never had those kinds of dreams before."

Hannah began to cry and the tears stained her dusty cheeks. "Maybe it's nothing. I'm sorry for the way I behaved."

"Sometimes our dreams come true, or they serve as a warning. I'm worried. I'll not enlist with the Battalion if that's what you want."

Hannah tried to dash away her tears. "That's what I want, but I know it's not fair. When Elder Woodruff told us about the others who have enlisted, and what their family situations were, it made me feel guilty. I guess I can do it if the others can. I suppose Brother and Sister Bundy and the others can help me with Dianah and her children until she gets back on her feet."

Robert pulled Hannah to his chest and wrapped his powerful arms around her. "Let's participate in the council tonight and then say our prayers before we go to bed. We'll get our answer."

Daniel had just convened the council when two men approached riding a brown mule. In faltering daylight, a voice from atop the mule said, "How's my old missionary companion?"

Daniel was sitting in front of a campfire on his haunches. The sun's orange glow was now blotted out by gray clouds in the western sky. As he recognized the voice, he jumped to his feet. "Jacob Kemp Butterfield—how long have you been here?"

"More than two weeks," Jacob said as he slid off the mule and embraced Daniel. "I happened to see Elder Woodruff a while ago. He told me where you were camped."

"Who's the young man still on the mule?" Daniel asked.

"Henderson Cox," Jacob answered. "I'm giving him a ride back to his parent's camp."

Jacob and Henderson shook hands with the other members of Daniel's company.

"Have you enlisted in the Battalion?" Daniel asked.

Jacob flashed a winning smile. "Did so yesterday. I was one of the first to volunteer, so I'm in Company A. How about that? So far, I'm the tallest man in the Battalion." Jacob, who was six-two, scanned the other men and laughed. "Don't see anyone here any taller, neither."

"I volunteered also," the young man on the mule said. "I'm in Company A with Brother Butterfield."

"You look mighty young to be in the army," Daniel replied.

"I'm seventeen, so I reckon I'm old enough," said Henderson. "It's with Ma and Pa's blessing. I'll only be gone for a year. I'm gonna send them my pay."

"That's noble of you," said Daniel. Daniel admired the young man and hoped Moroni would grow up to be just like him.

Hannah had a question for Jacob. "How did your wife take to your enlistment?"

Jacob's countenance changed. His chin slumped to his chest. "She's no longer with me."

Daniel cringed, fearing the worst. "Don't tell me she died."

Jacob shook his head in sad remembrance. "No, not that. My wife's parents got discouraged over all the persecutions in Nauvoo. To make matters worse, two of our children died last winter, both of canker fever. Little Persis Amanda would have been four. And Sarah Lucinda lived to be only three months."

Daniel choked up for a minute. "So where's your wife, Brother Butterfield?" he queried.

"Her father made her leave me," Jacob said as a tear rolled down his reddened cheek. "Right now, I don't know where Louisa is, or if I'll ever see her again. I did the only thing I could do—I hired out to Brother Loren Farr and drove a team to Council Bluffs for him. This is one of his mules."

Daniel embraced his old missionary companion compassionately. They had served together in Illinois during the summer of 1843, mostly in the Springfield area, following the attempted kidnapping of Joseph Smith by the Missouri sheriff. "I'm truly sorry, Brother Butterfield. I'm so sorry."

Jacob shrugged his shoulders and tried to act brave. "Life goes on."

There was a long pause before anyone spoke again. Everyone in the council that Daniel had convened contemplated Jacob's morbid situation.

"I can see why you enlisted," Elizabeth said. "You didn't have a wife to hold you back."

Jacob wiped at his blue eyes with his shirtsleeves. "Oh, you should have heard the talk when Captain Allen and his four dragoons first arrived in Mount Pisgah. I was there. Women almost fainted in fright at the sight of the uniforms. They thought the soldiers were government spies trying to find out how many Mormons were in the Iowa wilderness and what their plans were. The women rounded up their children and hid them while the men reached for their rifles."

"Did anyone believe Captain Allen's story at first?" Thomas Kington asked.

"Not really," Jacob said. "It sounded pretty far-fetched, that Captain Allen had a request from the president of the United States to enlist an army of five hundred men for the war against Mexico. At first, all of us thought it was a plan to destroy us, that it was some kind of plot."

"I can see how that might be," Hannah said.

Butterfield continued. "There was a lot of talk about how the request was unfair, that the Saints had given enough and owed the government nothing. No one wanted to enlist. Hardliners like Hosea Stout argued that the recruitment was a ploy: that either the Americans planned to leave our families here in Iowa defenseless so they could massacre them at will, or they intended to lure five hundred of our men away into the wilderness and do away with them somehow. Or both."

"But things must have changed rapidly," Levi Roberts said. "This afternoon Elder Woodruff told us that more than four hundred men have already enlisted."

Butterfield laughed. "Already enlisted is a poor term. Brigham Young and our other leaders have pushed hard to get that many men—the process has taken many days. But as soon as Brigham Young confirmed that he wanted all the men to sign up who could, the enlistments started happening quite rapidly. He used some pretty strong language. He told us that if we refused to enlist he would shame us by forming a Battalion of old men and women."

Daniel gasped.

"Then to sugar the pill, Brigham promised us that none of us would be killed in battle," Butterfield said. "I believe Brother Brigham. The salvation of the Church is at stake. This will save us. Did they tell you how much money a private will make each month? And how the money can be sent back to the Church here in Council Bluffs?"

"Where is this Captain Allen?" Hannah asked as she placed her hands on her hips. "Since there's a possibility our husbands will be marching away with him, I want to meet him first."

Butterfield pointed to the northeast. "He's camped within walking distance in a grove of trees over there with a man named Thomas Kane. Captain Allen would like nothing better than to meet with more potential recruits. He's anxious to fill the last company and get on his way. I'll drop Henderson off and then take you over there."

Daniel turned to members of his wagon company. "This seems important. We'll reconvene the council after I get back."

8

ON THE WAY, Butterfield explained to Hannah that Captain James Allen, Company J, First Dragoons, had graduated from the U.S. Military Academy in 1829, and had already served an incredible seventeen years on the American frontier. Since 1843 he had established and commanded Fort Des Moines, protecting the Sac and Fox Indians from aggressive intrusions by the Sioux, traders, and settlers.

"What's he like?" Hannah asked as she held her dress above the muddy trail that led to the camp. Robert, Daniel, and a few of the other men followed. The other adult members of the Browett company stayed behind to watch the children.

"On the plus side, he's very likeable for a military man," Jacob said. "And he seems to genuinely like the Mormons. That's probably because of the influence of Thomas Kane. On the negative side, he drinks a lot. He's always got a bottle in his hand. And he has a conflict of interest of sorts. A peacetime army holds few prospects for promotion. Rumor has it that Captain Allen will receive an immediate promotion to lieutenant colonel as soon as he raises the Battalion. So he's very anxious. The strung-out nature of our arrivals in Council Bluffs has required the captain to spend a few more days here than he had planned. He's been known to be grumpy about that, but most of the time he's pleasant to deal with."

This explanation did not sit well with Hannah. She was prepared to detest the army captain.

As they arrived at the camp, two shadowy shapes emerged, visible by the dim reflection of a low setting sun. One was the forty-year-old Ohio army captain of Irish ancestry; he had a narrow, gaunt face, foggy but penetrating brown eyes, a full beard, and thick, wavy brown hair. His rank was denoted on the contra-epaulette of his uniform: two embroidered bars. He wore an officer's dress cap, made of black beaver with a lacquered tip. Captain Allen was not quite the legendary American solider she had built up in her mind, but he immediately disarmed Hannah with his charm. When Jacob introduced Hannah to Captain Allen, he kissed her on the hand, performed a deep bow, and began to heap an incessant flow of praise for the Mormon people on her. Not only that, Allen complimented Hannah on her beautiful brown eyes, her olive complexion, her lovely British drawl, and the fact that she was an attractive woman despite the fact she was the mother of six children. He was a clever, cordial man, different than most non-members she had ever met. He made bright jokes, including bold pleasantries about the Mormon people's perseverance. He expressed deep regard for the men who had already enlisted. He had a copy of the *St. Louis Republican* under his arm, which displayed headlines about the first overt acts of hostilities between the United States and Mexico. For now, at least, he was content to let his brown bottle of whiskey sit on the ground rather than sip on it.

Young Thomas Kane was equally charming, in Hannah's view. Only twenty-four, Kane was the son of an influential Democratic judge and he seemed wise beyond his years. He was a small, dainty man, lean and stringy, but cunningly alert. Kane seemed to have a burning desire to be someday known as an expert on the American West. He impressed Hannah with talk about how the Mormons were going to eventually help settle the Great Basin and be a major factor in the process to tame the West. He complimented Brigham Young on having the wisdom not to proceed to California this season, commenting that it surely would be in vain with winter not that far away.

Captain Allen turned his attention to Robert, Daniel, and the other men. "Because all of you Mormon men served in the Nauvoo Legion, you're already experienced soldiers. I'd love to have you in the Battalion we're forming. I'm already impressed with those who have enlisted. The quality of the United States Army would be greatly enhanced if all our soldiers had the attributes of those men. I'd trust any of them with my life."

Hannah blinked hard. She had expected the non-Mormon to be critical of the Nauvoo Legion, as most other outsiders had been. Before Governor

Thomas Ford disbanded it, the Nauvoo Legion had been a semi-private military force that swelled to four thousand men, armed and uniformed, nearly
half the size of the entire United States Army.

Robert inwardly scoffed at Captain Allen's comments, judging them to be
mere praises to win him over to the enlistment process. In truth, regular army
officers normally had complete disdain for the militia tagged as the Nauvoo
Legion. The Legion was never properly trained. Their leader, the Prophet
Joseph Smith, was not a professional soldier and knew very little of tactics and
training. The Nauvoo Legion paraded often, and that was about it. But the
Legion did strike fear into the hearts of the enemies of Mormonism, mostly
because of its strength in numbers.

Hannah didn't give Robert a chance to respond to Captain Allen. "Surely
you've got to think of us wives in this enlistment process. How do you expect
us to survive out here in this open wilderness without our husbands?"

Captain Allen chuckled, still leaving his bottle on the ground. "I've never
met men like your Mormon leaders. Brigham Young will find a way to take
care of you and your children. And I've agreed to allow the Battalion's pay to
be collected by the Church and brought back to the Mormon camp."

Hannah didn't argue, although she suspected that the money might be
used for the good of all the people instead of just the wives and families of the
men who enlisted. She said, "I don't understand why the government even
wants Mormon soldiers, after all that's happened."

Thomas Kane's florid face had an unusually bright smile. He had just recovered from a bout with intermittent fever. "That's probably because Jesse Little was at the right place at the right time. Have you met Elder Little?"

Hannah nodded stiffly. "He just left our camp."

"Elder Little came to Washington in early May to solicit government help for the Mormon exodus," Kane explained.

Little's trip to Washington was not the first time the Mormons had looked to the national government for help, and Hannah, Robert, and Daniel understood this as well as anyone, thanks to their connection to Orson Hyde, who had made many trips there himself. Shortly before his death, Joseph Smith had proposed federal legislation that would authorize the Mormons to build a string of military posts along the Oregon Trail, and to raise a force of 100,000 volunteers, independent of the U.S. Army, to defend American interests on the frontier. Orson Hyde had proposed this to a senate committee, but the request had been turned down.

"And this is your view of how the government can help the Church after all we've suffered through—is to take our men off on a forced military march?" Hannah asked.

Kane's smile was indulgent. "Every other plea from your Mormon representatives over the years had been turned down flat."

Hannah gave a resigned shrug. Kane was correct.

"After spending ten fruitless days in Washington, D. C., Elder Little and I came up with a plan," Kane continued. "I advised him to play on President Polk's fears of a British plot to take over California."

Hannah cocked her ear to make certain she was hearing correctly.

"Your Church has a strong presence in England, despite the fact that many of you have immigrated to the United States," Kane explained. "Elder Woodruff, in fact, has told me that he had actively courted British support while he was in England this last time. Church officials over there presented a petition to the British government, requesting permission for your members to settle on Vancouver Island, which is in British territory. That's simply because our own government was hindering, rather than helping, the Mormons while you were in Nauvoo."

Hannah nodded her understanding, but this information caused her anger to brim again.

Kane continued. "So Elder Little and I sat down and composed a letter to President Polk suggesting a possible shift of Mormon allegiance to Great Britain."

Hannah's jaw dropped. "You did?"

"Yes, ma'am," he said with a tart smile. "On the day that Polk received Elder Little's letter, Polk agreed to meet with him. It so happened that the president was meeting with members of his cabinet that very day. They were trying to decide what military forces it would take to occupy New Mexico and then move on to invade California before winter. Polk decided to allow a few hundred Mormons to serve in the California occupation forces. He didn't want the Mormons, once they got out west, to turn against the United Sates and upset the delicate international balance of power in western North

America. In fact, he didn't want the Mormons to actually be enrolled into the army until after they reached the west coast. But the war department didn't quite understand that. The authorization came, and here we are taking Mormon enlistments."

Hannah pulled a skeptical face. All of this political talk was almost impossible to follow. All she knew is that she still faced the prospect of losing her husband for a year or more. She countered, "I can't believe that the United States has a shortage of men to fight in this war."

"Oh, that's not the case at all," Captain Allen responded. "Thousands are volunteering as we speak—men from the New England states, the South—all over, really. There seems to be an outpouring of young Americans who want to enlist. It's simply the fact that President Polk is *allowing* the Mormons to enlist."

"I find that hard to swallow," Hannah said, not comprehending.

Captain Allen smiled, flashing his limpid blue eyes. "Well, that's about all I can tell you."

Kane interrupted. "Let me speculate a little. This is not official, so don't take it as that. I'm merely offering my opinion to help calm your fears. Maybe President Polk is holding back the other volunteers for now. Maybe they'll eventually be sent toward Mexico City, not toward California. Perhaps Polk doesn't want to alert the Mexicans that an American army has been ordered to invade California before winter. And perhaps he doesn't want to alarm Americans on the west coast that the first U.S. troops to arrive there will be

Mormons. You have to remember that politics is part of the equation. President Polk wants the Mormons in his camp, not in the camp of Great Britain. Jesse Little opened the president's eyes to the fact that there are more than forty thousand Mormons in Great Britian."

Captain Allen held up a hand, as though Kane were disclosing sensitive military matters. "None of that is really important. Speed is of the utmost importance here. I need the final company to enlist and then we'll be on our way."

"What about the Missourians that are marching with Colonel Kearny?" Hannah asked. "Will my husband be in any danger from them?"

"Not all Missourians hate the Mormons," Captain Allen said. "On June sixth, I swore in a group of a hundred volunteers from Clay County. A man by the name of Alexander William Doniphan was among them."

"Who?"

Jacob raised a hand. He spoke directly to Hannah. "Back in the days of Missouri persecution, Doniphan was a general in the Missouri militia. When Joseph Smith was held prisoner in Far West, the major general of the militia gave orders to Doniphan to take the Mormon prisoners to the public square an execute them. General Doniphan refused, contending it was cold-blooded murder."

Hannah bit on her lip, recalling the story. "Is he still friendly?" she asked.

"He was pleased when he found out that I was leaving Fort Leavenworth to enlist a Battalion of Mormons," Captain Allen answered. "If you don't know yet, all volunteers are sworn in as privates, and so was he, despite the fact that he had been a general in the militia. But he remains a popular figure. The other volunteers elected him to the office of a colonel."

"Is he still at the fort?" Robert asked.

"No, Doniphan is part of Colonel Kearny's Army of the West, just as the Mormons will be," the captain explained. "Kearny and Doniphan are on their way to Santa Fe."

Hannah appeared startled. "Army of the West? That sounds like a hundred thousand men. If so, you don't need our Mormon men."

Captain Allen laughed. "Though Kearny's army is gloriously labeled, the truth is that Kearny will have less than three thousand men, counting the Mormons we've enlisted. Some of the army has already left the fort in groups, so they'll be far ahead of us. Colonel Kearny has been ordered to invade New Mexico, Hispanic Arizona, and Upper California. Thus far he has a large force, about sixteen hundred men, including five dragoon companies."

"What's a dragoon company?" Hannah asked.

"That's a company of mounted soldiers, or cavalry, armed with rifles. They get their name from the fact that some of the early muskets had a hammer shaped like a dragon." He went on to explain that the idea for a mounted ranger Battalion came from a lieutenant named Philip St. George Cooke, who in 1828 was escorting a Santa Fe trade caravan. There had been a constant siege of the caravan by mounted Comanches. With a command of foot soldiers, Cooke was helpless to pursue the Indians or protect individual excursions for hunting. It became obvious, Allen said, that it was impossible for infantry to deal with mounted war parties of the Plains Indians. Four years later Congress authorized the United States Mounted Ranger Battalion for the defense of the Santa Fe trade route. The men of the unit were to be one-year volunteers who would provide their own arms and horses, for which they would receive one dollar a day in compensation.

"Are you providing my husband with a horse?" Hannah asked innocently.

Allen laughed again. "No ma'am, he'd be part of the infantry—a foot soldier. There're plenty of young men who are eager to go to war mounted on a horse, but there's been an aversion in that part of Missouri to serve on foot. That's why I'm here—to recruit five companies of foot soldiers."

"So Kearny is gone, but are there any more Missouri soldiers at Fort Leavenworth?" Hannah asked, being even more perceptive.

"Yes," Captain Allen admitted. "Four more companies of dragoons under command of another colonel, Sterling Price. The Mormon Battalion will try to catch up with Kearny and help secure and occupy California."

"Will there be any trouble between the Missourians that are still in Fort Leavenworth and the Mormons who are coming?" she asked. "I've heard that sometimes volunteers who serve in the army are not much better than common criminals."

"We're gearing up to fight Mexicans, not each other," Allen said. "Don't worry about such things. I'll keep the two groups apart."

Hannah's curiosity was still raging. "And you get a promotion if my husband signs up?"

Captain Allen gulped, regretting the fact that he had earlier disclosed the contents of his letter from Colonel Kearny to a select few. Kearny promised Allen a jump of two full grades—once the Mormon Battalion enlistment was complete—from a company captain to lieutenant colonel. It was a shining opportunity for him, in Hannah's view.

Captain Allen's smile was disarming. He executed another military bow. "Colonel Allen at your service, ma'am."

Hannah's weary tension dissolved a little. She tugged at Robert. "We haven't decided one way or another yet. Don't get your hopes up."

The smile didn't disappear from the captain's face. He had heard all these concerns before.

"One more question," Hannah said, pausing now. "What gives the United States the right to invade New Mexico and California, if that land belongs to the Mexicans?"

"Good question," Allen said. "The Spanish have been in Texas and New Mexico intermittently since the days of Juan Coronado and the conquistadors in the sixteenth century. But what gave them the right, or the Spaniards, to push their borders beyond the Rio Grande River in the first place? Or to go beyond San Diego in California? Expansionism isn't something the United States invented, or Mexico, or Spain, or England. It's been going on since the beginning of time, I suppose. As the European countries have lost control of the New World, the people who live here have gained it. We have just as much right to expand our borders west to the Pacific as Mexico has to expand hers north. If Mexico's expansion isn't stopped, where will it end? Canada? Alaska? Russia? There's a conflict, and it's going to be solved by this war."

Hannah rolled her eyes, deep in thought. And then she trudged back to her camp as darkness settled in.

9

HANNAH WAS PUZZLED WHEN JOHN AND Eliza Cox stood to greet them upon their return. John sat his dessert of wild strawberries and thick, sugared cream aside. For a moment Hannah was distracted by the howls and sharp snarling barks of the wolves in the trees, the mournful hooting of owls, and the rush of the wind through the treetops. Flames from the fire illuminated John's face and his expression was devoid of enthusiasm. He spoke not to Hannah but directly to Daniel, the company leader. "Eliza and I have talked it over. I'm enlisting in the morning. I feel it's my duty."

Hannah choked and turned brick red. She dropped moodily onto a log, not sure if she heard right. "I didn't think anyone would make a decision until morning," she said in exasperation. In her opinion, both Eliza and John were strangely out of character.

"While you were gone, we went into the woods and prayed about it, and got our answer," Eliza explained.

"I suppose it's the right thing to do," Daniel said, letting a smile of acceptance about the whole idea spread across his face.

Hannah gave a negative dip of her head, now fearing what would happen if she presented the same question to the Lord in prayer with her husband. She was surprised that prayers about serving in the U.S. Army could be answered so swiftly.

Levi Roberts, tall and angular, shuffled his feet. "I guess I will, too. Harriet Ann says I should. And that's what the Spirit is telling me to do."

Hannah stiffened, looked away, and then let her eyes come back to Robert's sister, Dianah, and her husband, Thomas Bloxham. Their faces were stern with resistance. This pleased Hannah.

"Not me," said Thomas, feigning a hurt expression. "I'm not a Mormon, and don't plan to be one. Besides, my wife's pretty sick right now. I'm not leaving." His attitude was nothing new. The barrier he had long ago put up against joining the Church seemed to be permanent.

Despite the warm sultry weather, Dianah stood huddled under a blanket. She retained her sense of humor, however. "We could have the men dam up the stream over there and put your under," she said with a painful cough.

Thomas held up a hand. "Don't start that."

A tear came to Dianah's eye. Hannah knew that she longed for the day when her husband would accept the gospel, receive his endowments, and be sealed with her and their children in a Holy Temple.

Thomas Kington spoke next. "My mind hasn't changed. I'm too old to be in the army, way past the age recommended."

George Bundy gave the same response.

Robert Pixton and Richard Slater rose to their feet. "We've both decided to enlist," Richard said.

"Elizabeth, Harriet, and I haven't had much time to visit about this," Daniel said almost sheepishly. "But…"

Elizabeth took Daniel by the hand, and so did Harriet. "Go," Elizabeth said. "You should set the example. You *always* have, so don't fail the Lord now."

Hannah felt the stares of the entire company. She bit her lip in anguish and let tears fill her eyes. Her vivid imagination was working overtime, conjuring up lonely nights in the Iowa wilderness without the companionship of her husband, begging others for something to feed her children, and giving birth to a new baby in less-than-sanitary conditions. She put her right hand to her chest as though it would calm her rapidly beating heart. Her insecurity was showing but she didn't care. She had gone through her married life totally dependent upon Robert; without him, life would be meaningless. Her stubbornness was her only strength in this moment of trial, and she aimed to cling to it.

Robert took her off the hook. "We're going to pray about it tonight. If the Lord wants me to go, he'll tell me."

Hannah turned her head. It was time to give her husband and the others the silent treatment.

While Hannah was sulking, the other members of the company began retiring to their own wagon boxes to prepare their bedrolls for the coming night. With his four-year-old son, Isaac, sleeping on his shoulder, Thomas Bloxham approached Robert and Hannah.

"It's a bad idea to join the American army," he said. "A responsible father wouldn't think of it."

Robert gave Thomas a helpless shrug, feeling the pressure from both sides of the issue. "I know, but the money that would be sent back here might mean the difference in surviving the winter."

Thomas had a quick comeback. "You Mormons have never worshiped money. Why start now?" Most of the time Thomas looked puffed up with anger, like he resented living among Mormons. In the night air he appeared more frustrated than usual as though he resented the thought he might have to help take care of Robert's six children as well as his own five. Thomas was shorter than Robert, but just as bull-necked.

Robert thought for a moment. "It's not that we're worshiping it, it's just a matter of being realistic and practical. Your larder is just as small as mine. Neither of us have enough flour to get through the winter."

"If we have to stay here all winter, we can't live out of a wagon box," Thomas argued. "We need to get our axes and saws out and build some kind of temporary log house. Dianah's already sick, and so are some of your kids and some of mine. Who knows when we'll all be sick in this godforsaken wilderness? How do you know that after you leave Hannah or the children won't come down with the ague? Don't you worry about cholera, black canker, or things like that?"

"Of course I do," Robert countered.

Thomas looked at Robert as though he were daft. "You can't do anything about it on a march to Mexico if one of your kids comes down with black canker," Thomas scoffed. "Try to picture your two-year-old, little Sarah Ann. From New Mexico Territory you won't be able to see the lesions that'll pop out on her skin, her uncontrolled drooling, her painful barking cough, how her neck will swell from pussed-up tonsils, the terrible fever she'll have, how her little heart will almost quit beating from the strain of it all, and how her muscles stop working. I've seen black canker come on kids, and it ain't good."

"See, Robert?" Hannah nagged, sounding as though she appreciated her brother-in-law's mournful description of a disease that might affect her own children.

Thomas was not finished. "And what if Hannah suddenly comes down with the ague? Like Dianah?" Dianah had already made her bed under the wagon box and was lying there sweating underneath a pile of blankets.

"I've had the ague plenty," Robert said, remembering his trip to Galena a year ago to track down William and Wilson Law, two of the apostates responsible for the death of the Prophet Joseph Smith. All during the trip he had suffered from successive undulations of hot and cold streaks, cold chills, hot shakes, a burning fever, harsh sweats, a dull headache, dizziness, an irritating cough that secreted a bloody mucus, and blood in his urine.

"Then it's settled," Hannah concluded. "You'll not enlist."

"We promised Elder Woodruff that we'd pray about it," Robert said. "If that's what the Lord wants me to do, I'll stay here and not be part of the Battalion."

Robert had transformed himself into a religious man over the years since his conversion, but it had been a slow process, not an event. It began that night in England, when he came home from the pub and discovered Wilford Woodruff in his home, teaching the gospel to his wife and some of her friends. Daniel and Elizabeth were there, already baptized members of the Church. The sight of the thing angered him, and he tried to throw the American missionary out on his ear. When an unseen power protected the Apostle not once, but twice, it awakened the spiritual side of Robert. But he entered the gospel as a babe, and he had a hard time shedding worldly feelings. As he walked to the trees with Hannah he recollected the times when he purposefully withheld asking God's opinion about things, fearing the answer. He liked to cling to his stubbornness, his pride, his ability to rationalize, his insensitivity, his way of manipulating others, and his dislike of being told what to do. He did a sharp right turn last autumn after his terrifying dream, the dream where he held a mock trial for the murderers of Joseph and Hyrum Smith. Until then, he had not deviated much from his one-man vigilante hunt of the men who had anything to do with Joseph and Hyrum's deaths. He had never asked God about whether it was right or wrong to hunt down the Law brothers, the Higbees, or the Fosters—all Mormon apostates, or anti-Mormons like Thomas Sharp and Mark Aldrich. He had never gotten over his propensity to use his fists when riled up, and probably never would. But this matter about serving in the army somehow appealed to him, despite the concerns of Hannah, Thomas, and others. He had no fear about presenting his dilemma to the Lord. He already knew the answer: he should enlist. It was merely a matter of having the Spirit whisper to his wife that it was the correct thing to do.

When Hannah went to the wagon she made her and Robert a bed in their tent. She lay awake for a long time, apprehensive, while the men sat by the fire talking about the Battalion. Across the prairie she began to see lightning darting down the sky through the tent door, and within a few minutes big drops of rain hit the tent. In a minute the grass was wet. Robert came to bed without talking because she pretended she was asleep as were the children. Soon lightning was crashing all around and the thunder came in big, flat cracks, as if a tree had fallen down. It frightened her so that she hugged her knees and trembled. When the lightning struck, the whole Missouri basin would be bathed for a second in white light.

The rainstorm soon passed, but she lay awake for a long time thinking about Robert and the Mormon Battalion. It grew very dark. She still didn't know what to do.

Hannah's confirmation didn't come until morning. As she stepped upon the wagon tongue to get her flour she thought she heard a voice. The voice asked her if she desired the greatest glory in the heavens. She answered, "Yes, of course," in her natural voice.

"Then how can you get it without making sacrifices?" the voice seemed to say.

"How do I lack?" she answered back.

"Let your husband serve in the Battalion."

"But there are others. The Battalion will fill up."

"It's your decision. But remember the promises you made in the temple during your endowment. I am bound when you obey."

Hannah felt properly chastised; she hung her head and sobbed. And then she found Robert and gave him her decision. Her husband should enlist; he should support Brigham Young and the Church leadership.

10

BY THE TIME HE REACHED PAWNEE ROCK, a thirty-foot sandstone monolith on the Santa Fe Trail some three hundred miles from Fort Leavenworth, Private Bernard Bogart wished he hadn't enlisted. Desertion wasn't an option, however. It would break his mother's heart. She, along with hundreds of other mothers, and wives, had spent more than a week camped near Fort Leavenworth. The women had flown homemade flags with mottos such as: *Death before Dishonor*, or *Love of Country Is the Love of God*. His mother had admonished Bogart by alluding to the ancient Greeks, saying she felt like a Spartan mother who presented a shield to her boy as he was going to battle and said, "Return with it or return upon it."

Leaving Fort Leavenworth had been a delight for Bogart and for every soldier. Hundreds of girlfriends and wives and come to see them off, causing a celebration that rivaled the Fourth of July. Wives and families had arrived by steamboat, keelboat, buggy, carriage, and horseback. There were patriotic addresses, presentations of flags and banners, and lots of excitement. A few visitors complained that the troops assembled at the fort were the "dirtiest, rowdiest crew" they had ever seen, but the remarks didn't bother Bogart. When the men actually left it had been amidst the fluttering of banners, the sounding of bugles, the rattling of artillery, and the clattering of sabers and cooking utensils. All that frightened many of the horses, mules, and cattle and they had taken off to running pell-mell across the prairie in all directions. But the march between Fort Leavenworth and Fort Bent proved to be a hard one. After the lush prairies, the army passed over un-wooded areas where cooking was mostly impossible, where water was brackish, the mosquitoes and gnats pesky, fresh fruits and vegetables scarce, and scurvy prevalent.

"Dern, I ain't never been this saddle sore," Bogart complained to another dragoon, Sergeant Waldo Peck of Liberty, Missouri. "Or this hungry, or this thirsty."

"Me neither," Peck agreed. "They didn't tell us we'd be on our horses sixteen hours a day." Peck was young, too, in his early twenties. All the Missouri volunteers, with the exception of the officers, were either in their late teens or early twenties.

Bogart had been in a fine mood for the first few days, burning for the battlefield, panting for the rewards of an honorable victory, and confident the war would be won quickly—in time to be home in Missouri by Christmas. Those were the days when the boundless plains, lying in the ridges of wavy green not unlike the ocean, seemed to unite with the heavens in the distant horizon. This newness, this beauty, had long worn off.

"Are you gonna write about all this suffering?" Bogart asked. He hadn't complained about all the training he'd undergone at Fort Leavenworth, the hoofbeats of hundreds of horses as they trampled the grass on the fort's parade ground, churning up clouds of powdery dust that settled over him, over the sweating volunteers, and over the horses. Most of the volunteers had balked at all the training, but not Bogart. He had not even minded their training officer, the stern Lieutenant Andrew Jackson Smith of the First Dragoons. Smith never cracked a smile, no matter what high jinks the volunteers perpetrated.

Peck had enlisted as a volunteer in order to send battlefield reports back to the Liberty *Weekly Tribune*. "Why, I suppose I ought tell the truth, even though it is rough out here."

"That ain't the half of it," Bogart said, shaking his head. Pawnee Fork was flooded so bad that the dragoons had to swim their horses across, an expanse of more than fifty yards. Two soldiers had already drowned in the process. The good news was that General Kearny and Colonel Doniphan had decided to wait a few days to get the rest of the army across. The whole bend of the river was strung with tents, horses, oxen, mules, wagons, soldiers, and even trade caravans that were traveling with the army. "The goin's gonna get worse from here," Bogart continued. "If I have ta drink any more water fouled with buffalo chips I'll puke my guts out." At one place Bogart stirred up swarms of angry mosquitoes when he stooped to drink out of a stagnant pond.

In Bogart's view, moving an army from Fort Leavenworth all the way to Santa Fe and then to California was proving to be an almost impossible task. Kearny had ordered his army out at staggered departure times. Even finding the Santa Fe Trail for some had bordered on the near impossible. Some detachments strayed off course right from the beginning. There were creeks to cross in order to find the trail, some with high and rugged banks. Soldiers had to dig the banks down before the wagons could cross, causing delays. Even once they found the trail, in some spots the road was so soft the heavy wagons sank up to their hubs. At other times boggy quicksand caused wagons to sink almost out of sight. And it was worse for the heavy artillery. More than once Bogart had to get off his horse and put his shoulder to a wagon. Dragging heavily loaded wagons, several of the oxen and mules grew so tired they refused to walk. Some dropped dead in their tracks.

"It wouldn't be so bad if the army'd feed us decent," Peck added.

Bogart put a hand over his forehead to shield his eyes from the blinding summer sun. The prairie seemed endless. "We're gonna kill every deer, turkey, rabbit, and lizard out there to feed us, and still it ain't gonna be enough."

Feeding sixteen hundred men was proving to be an insurmountable task, even with all the supply wagons and the cattle that accompanied Kearny's army. The general was adamant about not using up the beef too soon, and many of the provision wagons containing flour were lagging behind or just plain lost. Measles, cholera, fevers, and dysentery were beginning to show up among the soldiers.

"What if the Injuns set fire to the prairie?" Bogart thought out loud. "That'd drive the game off. Then we'd die of starvation sure enough. Or what if the greasers scare away our draft animals, or burn the supply wagons in hit-and-run raids? Dern it all. I wish they'd just march toward us and let us shoot 'em.'"

His traveling companion had something else on his mind. "Think I'll take off my clothes and bathe in the river," Peck said as he tore off his shirt. Both he and Bogart were from well-watered Missouri; they were not used to the dry desert.

"Ye otta go upstream or downstream," Bogart advised. "Dead buffalo are here." It was true. The river and the prairie were littered with bones, skulls, and carcasses of animals in every state of decay. "Help yourself to some more whiskey." He handed Bogart his canteen.

Bogart smiled and took a few swigs. He had voted for Peck for the rank of sergeant in Fort Leavenworth. Peck had given a lively speech. "I ain't afraid of greasers," he had said. "I want to be your sergeant. I'll lead you against the yellow-bellied Mexicans. I have treated you to twenty dollars worth of whiskey, I have, and when elected sergeant I'll spend twenty more, I will!"

To Bogart's delight, the hardships of the journey had been mitigated a little by the inexhaustible supply of whiskey the sutlers carried in their provision wagons. Also, he was constantly entertained at how the soldiers seemed to vie with each other about who could commit the greatest excesses in drunkenness and debauchery in the few hours the army wasn't marching toward Santa Fe.

Fights among soldiers broke out every evening. During daylight hours, cursing Kearny and Doniphan was a major daily entertainment. After all, they were responsible for the sixteen-hour days spent in the saddle.

Robert was only going as far as Sarpy's, a French trading post on the Missouri River, but Hannah still felt gloomy. Within another day or two Robert would be leaving for good. As she took stock of the situation, gloomy was the only way to feel despite her confirmation by the Spirit that his enlistment was the right thing to do. She dreaded parading her children in front of her husband and saying her final goodbyes.

"I'll be back tonight," Robert had said when he joined his company for the short trip. Sarpy's was eight miles downriver where each man would be issued a few supplies and then return to Council Bluffs.

"I can hardly stand your being gone one day," Hannah moaned. "What's it going to be like for a whole year? Maybe a year and a half by the time we're together again?"

Henry had already been gone for three months, but that was different.

George Bundy and Thomas Kington had promised to do their best to take care of her and the other wives in the Daniel Browett Company, but they were old. Robert was young and strong. Robert, with Daniel's help, could erect a new log cabin in just a few days. Without him, she would be left to live out of a wagon box for who knows how long.

Hannah had felt patriotic for a little while during the morning enrollment ceremony, but the feeling didn't last long. It had taken place at the camp square under an American flag brought out of the storehouse from Nauvoo. The flag had been hoisted on a tree mast liberty pole, sixty feet high. Brigham Young, Wilford Woodruff, Orson Hyde, and Heber C. Kimball had been there representing the Twelve. Elder Jesse Little had been there too, along with Thomas E. Kane and Colonel Allen. Two embroidered oak leaves had replaced the two bars on Allen's contra-epaulette, denoting his new rank of lieutenant colonel. Robert, Daniel, Levi Roberts, John Cox, Robert Pixton, and Richard Slater had all been placed in Company E, the fifth company.

"Daniel wonders how Sarpy's will be able to accommodate so many men," Elizabeth said to Hannah as they watched the men march away. They had been formed into a square by their captains at a place called Redemption Hill, where members of the Twelve had addressed them.

"I know," Hannah replied with a sad shake of her head. "Robert wonders about that, too."

The men were disappearing over a knoll. Elizabeth shielded her eyes from the bright and scorching midday sun with her right hand and wiped the perspiration off her brow with the other.

"How did the meeting go with Rebecca?" Hannah asked, her hopes of Robert staying with her now dashed. He was in the Battalion and there was no turning back. The situation wouldn't allow for it.

"Not well," Elizabeth said. "She thinks the British Saints ought to do a *better* job of governing themselves. She *doesn't* want Orson to go, but she's being naïve again, and *very* immature. She refuses to stay in the Hyde camp after Orson leaves, so she'll come and stay with her mother."

"Oh, no," Hannah exclaimed. "One more woman for Brother Bundy and Brother Kington to take care of." Her memories of Rebecca's immaturity were recent and she deemed it a terrible task for Bundy and Kington to have to put up with her.

"Rebecca doesn't get along too well with Marinda and Mary Ann, so I suppose we're stuck with her," Elizabeth concluded. "If only Dianah would get better, it wouldn't be so bad."

11

DANIEL WAS FEELING GOOD ABOUT HIS enlistment as he marched off to Sarpy's. His thinking had slowed down to a crawl because it was so hot and humid, but he thought he had done the right thing. The talk among the men seemed to dwell as much on the excitement of being a soldier and marching off to war as it was about the concern over wives and children. Inwardly he put more of his trust in Elizabeth to take care of things in his absence than he did in the likes of Thomas Kington and George Bundy. Elizabeth was a strong-minded, independent sort of woman who could almost fend for herself in spite of being planted smack dab in the middle of a wilderness. It might be a trial for her and Harriet to get along in his absence, but he was confident he could spend a year in the Battalion and contribute to the good of all the Saints.

Daniel had decided he liked Peter Sarpy two days earlier when he used Sarpy's ferry to get his company's wagons across the Missouri River to

Bellevue. Actually, the ferry was now known as the Mormon ferry and that was another reason Daniel had taken a liking to Peter Sarpy. When, in mid-June, Brigham Young proposed that the Mormons almost take over the ferry, Sarpy was a picture of cooperation. More than a hundred Mormons of varying skills, on a voluntary basis, built a new ferry in less than three weeks. The ferry that carried Daniel's company across the river was capable of carrying three loaded wagons with oxen harnessed. It was a far cry from Sarpy's old dingy type ferry.

Sarpy struck Daniel as a fair-minded man who was not taking advantage of the Mormons. Sarpy had already given a ball for the Mormons, which was a delightful affair. It had been the first time the emigrants had any use for the better clothes packed away in their chests since they left Nauvoo.

The trading post was located on the Iowa side of the river, so the five hundred men of the Mormon Battalion were ferried across again. As Daniel stepped off the ferry, he recalled that two days ago the trading post didn't seem to be that well stocked. Unless Sarpy had restocked the post with goods unloaded from a steamboat arriving from Independence, Missouri, Daniel wondered what Lt. Colonel Allen was going to do to supply the Battalion men until they reached Fort Leavenworth. The last thing Daniel wanted to do is take food away from Elizabeth, Moroni, and Harriet.

Sarpy established his trading post in 1840 across the river from the tiny settlement called Bellevue. Sarpy had been in Nebraska Territory since 1823, working for a fur company's trading post. Most of his customers at the trading post were Indians. But during this past summer, Sarpy's business had flourished because of the influx of Mormons wanting to cross the river, and Mormons and other settlers wanting to buy supplies from him. Sarpy also held the title of superintendent of Indian Affairs.

When Daniel's turn to enter the trading post came, his suspicions were quickly confirmed. The forty-five-year-old Sarpy was running around like a chicken with his head cut off, and so was his Omaha Indian wife, *Ni-co-mi.* Sarpy's black hair was flared out in frustration, sensing that he could be selling far more than he was going to, if he had the goods. He was a funny-looking man, well knit but thin as a wire, and with an Adam's apple that looked as big as a turkey egg, even through his dark beard.

"If you can give me more time," he was saying to Colonel Allen, "I'm sure a steamboat from Independence will be here soon with more food stuffs."

Colonel Allen exhaled his breath in a long silent sigh, and shook his head rapidly. "There's a war going on and I'm on a strict timetable. I've got to get these men to Fort Leavenworth as soon as I can. We're leaving Monday. If there's a steamboat coming, hold it. I'll put my five hundred men on it and commandeer it to Fort Leavenworth. If not, I'll have to march these men the entire distance."

Daniel went pale because he understood Fort Leavenworth to be near Independence, or two hundred miles south of Council Bluffs.

Sarpy bore a sad look. "But I have only a handful of tents."

"How many blankets?" Allen asked.

"Dozens and dozens. Indians are good customers for blankets."

"We can probably use all of them."

"Sold."

Colonel Allen drew another deep breath. "I'll take all the food you have. And my men will need kettles and utensils."

"I have more than enough coffee and sugar to last until you get to Fort Leavenworth. Aside from a little flour and pork, that's all I have right now." Sarpy paused to smile, thinking of his profits. "The Mormons have cleaned me out. Only four kettles are left."

"I'll take that flour and pork—all of it. Will it be enough to feed my men until we get to Fort Leavenworth?"

Sarpy laughed out loud as he began packaging the army's order. "Not unless you shorten their ration to one bite each. What's this war all about?"

"I'll give you the short version," Allen answered. "We're defending the rights of a free people to determine their own destiny, namely the people of Texas. They have a right to join the American union of states if they want to. The government of Mexico wants to deny them that right, so we're at war."

"Well, I support it," Sarpy intoned. "I just wish I had more food to sell you, and more tents."

Daniel cringed. He could see himself sleeping out in the open without so much as a tent or a blanket and he dreaded taking even a morsel of food from his or anyone else's larder back at camp. If a steamboat was not going to be available, he now knew he would have to walk to Fort Leavenworth. And he knew he would be a hungry man during the entire trip. At least he was going to have a blanket, even though the army would deduct its cost from his first month's pay.

Two days later, in a light rain, Hannah broke out in tears. She was now feeling guilty that she hadn't given Brigham and the other Church leaders the blind loyalty they deserved. She had been doubting and obstinate, and the realization of that now haunted her. In her morning prayers, however, she promised God that she would be forever grateful that Company E had been given an extra day in Council Bluffs. The other four companies had left Monday on schedule. But last-minute enlistments to fill Company E were still taking place as late as Monday night so Colonel Allen pulled out, leaving instructions for the last company to catch up.

"Do you think there'll actually be a steamboat at Sarpy's?" Hannah asked Robert, tears already showing. The quick glimpse of Company E mustering to leave Council Bluffs left her in such a perplexity of spirit that she could hardly focus her thoughts.

"I hope so," Robert replied. "It's a long ways to Fort Leavenworth and Colonel Allen is anxious." Robert's dog, Duke, looked up at him as though he were going, too.

"What'll you eat if you have to walk?" she asked, suddenly showing a motherly concern. "Brother Brigham already cautioned you not to take things from farmers, even though that's the way of the army." She hoped Colonel Allen would keep her husband on the Iowa side of the river, away from bloodthirsty Missourians on the other side, the people who had driven Mormons out of that state in 1838.

"I don't know, but somehow the Lord will provide for us," Robert said, showing a little blind faith of his own.

Bright lightning cracked down from the gray sky, forking behind the camp in jagged streams. It was raining hard to the north, but where the E Company had mustered it had quit to a drizzle.

One-by-one, Hannah watched Robert hug their six children and give them last-minute counsel. Robert's backpack was light—only his scriptures, a change of clothes, and the blanket purchased from Sarpy's. He had left behind his gun, telling Hannah to sell it if she had to.

"Here, take this," Hannah said as she thrust Robert's fiddle at him.

"I don't want to pack that to California," he answered.

"Think of the lonely nights on the trail," she replied. "I insist, for the good of the other men. When you play it, you'll think of the children and me. You can store it in one of the wagons."

Robert took the fiddle, but he refused Hannah's offer of food from her larder. He said that the army had the responsibility to feed him, even though there had not been much at Sarpy's to buy. He had been issued some flour and some pork, enough to last for only a couple of days.

"And what about your butcher knife?" Hannah asked. She felt a little perked up that Robert was taking his fiddle, but she knew he hated what the knife stood for.

"I have it. I just hope they don't make me the official butcher," Robert answered. "I had enough of that back in England."

Hannah scoffed. She had always prided herself that her husband knew how to not only kill a steer but to cut it up just right. "Your talents might turn out to be a blessing to the men."

Robert turned his attention to his children. "Joseph, you're the oldest," he said as he ran a hand through his son's tousled hair. "You take good care of Mother and help with the other children."

In Hannah's view, none of the children really comprehended that they would not see their father for a more than a year. Nor did they understand the war with Mexico, the so-called Manifest Destiny of the United States, the fact that Missourians would be in Kearny's army, how far away California really was, and whether or not Indians and Californios posed a threat to their father's life. She did not understand these things herself but she felt pleased with herself that she was handling her emotions better than expected. Now that Robert was an official member of the Battalion, she was slowly resigning herself to fully support him and the war effort.

"Yes, Father," the boy said. As he looked up, raindrops wet his face and there were tears showing, too. "I trust Brother Brigham. If he says it's okay to serve in the army, then I think you'll be fine. I'll say my prayers for you every day."

Hannah bit her lip. Perhaps Joseph understood more than she gave him credit for.

Lizzy had a tender heart, a little like her mother, but with more emotion. Sick with symptoms of ague, she sobbed openly. Robert drew the eight-year-old girl to his side, and then stooped to kiss her on the cheek and mouth while the other children clung to their mother's dress.

"Papa will be fine," Robert said. "Aside from baby Julia Ann, you're the only other girl in our family. Papa is counting on you to help your Mama."

Lizzy nodded her feverish head, still sobbing. Finally she said, "Don't you be late coming home. One year is all you get, Papa. I won't forgive the army if they keep you any longer."

"One year is all they get, sweetie," Robert replied as he gave her another kiss. "I promise."

Robert stooped again and gathered his three youngest boys, William, Thomas, and Enoch, ages seven, five, and three. "You've got to take care of your Mother, too. I'm counting on you."

Next, he picked up his year-old daughter, Sarah Ann. "Papa's gonna miss you." He kissed her on one cheek and then the other.

Daniel C. Davis, the Mormon who had been elected captain over Company E, called for the men to move out.

Hannah fought back tears. The fact that Robert was actually leaving for more than a year was now striking her hard. "Well," she blubbered, "at least you're among friends. You've got John Cox, Levi Roberts, Robert Pixton, and Richard Slater all with you in your company, as well as Daniel." Daniel had been selected as fourth sergeant of the company.

"We'll try to represent not only the United States, but the English converts as well," Robert promised. "Goodbye, darling. I'll write you from Fort Leavenworth."

Hannah closed her eyes, tilted her head back, and prepared to accept Robert's kiss. For a long moment she kissed her husband, gripping him tightly around the neck. How long they clung together, neither could remember.

"Goodbye," she whispered, her emotions in a swirl. She caressed his face with her hands.

"So long," Robert responded, kissing her again. He could taste Hannah's salty tears as they ran down her cheeks. As they parted, Robert patted Hannah's tummy. "Goodbye, number seven. See you when you're a few months old."

"If it's a boy, I'm giving him your name," Hannah whispered.

Under gloomy skies, Robert walked toward the Bloxham wagon so that he could say goodbye to his sick sister, her husband, Thomas, and their children. Robert's black and white dog followed. "Go back, Duke," Robert said. He took a few more steps, but the dog followed again.

"Take him with you," Hannah said as she wiped away tears. "He'll be good company. He might be as valuable as your compass. He can catch rabbits along the way. Besides, they're threatening to shoot dogs here if they're caught worrying the sheep."

Robert called the dog to his side.

"Better say goodbye to your sister," Hannah said.

12

❧

"YOU'LL BE STORING UP manna in heaven volunteering like this," Dianah Bloxham told Robert. Beads of sweat dotted her forehead.

Robert suddenly regretted not tending to his older sister's needs more over the years, and especially during the trip across Iowa. For an instant it gave him a tremendous case of the sulks. Somehow he suddenly understood the burden she had carried for the past years: being a member of the Church with a husband uncommitted to baptismal covenants. Now here she was, sick with the ague, looking like she might even die here on the prairie, and he was going away for a year.

"You're the one storing up manna in heaven," he told her as he drew her hands into his. Momentarily they separated and she stood huddled under a tent fashioned with a piece of canvas that had been purchased out of the supply Orson Hyde had shipped to Nauvoo from back east. The tent was held up with poles that Thomas had cut out of spindly trees.

Dianah had married Thomas Bloxham when Robert was twenty-one. Back then Robert wondered if Dianah and Elizabeth were really sisters; they were so unlike each other. Dianah was quiet and subdued; Elizabeth was noisy and bubbly. Dianah had a nice female figure, but she was squarely built—more like her father, and had medium brown hair. Elizabeth was dainty and thin, like her mother, and had blond hair. Dianah was fruitful; she began having children less than a year after her marriage and had one almost every year or two thereafter. Were it not for the fact that she lost one baby right after her baptism, and another boy to drowning off the steamboat, she would have seven. It had taken Elizabeth ten years to conceive her first child. And Dianah seemed more susceptible to disease. The cold, wet weather in England never seemed to suit her but it never bothered Elizabeth much. And the hot, humid summers in Nauvoo had always affected Dianah, too. More than once she had suffered from the effects of the ague, and now it was getting her down again. Elizabeth got by with mild symptoms of the ague, and less frequently.

Dianah seldom complained. Even with five children to worry about, she took the rigors and hardships of traveling across Iowa in stride, as though she had done it all her life. Whenever the Daniel Browett Company encountered other families who were running out of food, Dianah was the first to share her larder. One morning she milked her cow and gave nearly all the milk to a family who had lost their cow, run off by wolves. The family had been living on elm bark for two days. Another time she found a young girl in a family destitute of clothing. Dianah rummaged through her daughter Lucy's things and found a dress and bonnet to fit.

Elizabeth had been with Dianah earlier, although now she was saying her goodbyes to Daniel. She had administered a dose of medicine.

"The quinine must be helping a little," Robert said as he gazed into his sister's blue eyes. Because quinine had to be imported from South America—made from the bark of the Cinchona tree—one ounce was as expensive as a new cow, fourteen dollars.

"I shouldn't have taken any," Dianah complained, appearing self conscious and ill at ease. She had wrapped both arms around herself now, obviously going through a chill. Robert suspected that any minute a hot streak would undulate through her body. "There're people in other camps who need it more than me."

Robert pointed a bony finger at his sister. "You do as Elizabeth says. If she gives you a double dose that makes your ears ring, just be a good girl and be obedient." Everyone was well aware there had been deaths attributed to the ague all along the Iowa frontier, mostly the last two or three weeks since the weather had turned hot.

"You're the one to preach," Dianah said. "You about died of it yourself last year. How do you know you're not going to come down with it again, on your way to Fort Leavenworth?"

Robert noticed Dianah's spunk, something she had rain or shine. "I didn't come to argue," he countered. "I've come to say goodbye." He reached out and pulled his sister to his chest and gave her a brotherly squeeze. Then he kissed her on the cheek, after which he turned to Thomas. "You take good care of my sister. I want to see the color back in her skin when I return."

Thomas's chin muscles twitched. "I'm going to miss you, Robert. I still think you're making a mistake, but good luck anyway."

"I expect you to be baptized by the time I see you again," Robert said.

The fog in Thomas's brain over joining the Church seemed permanent. "If a bolt of lightning strikes me and I see a sign written in the sky, I guess I might. But I don't expect that to happen. I'll be the same old holdout when you see me." But Thomas embraced Robert and then shook his hand.

Robert felt a surge of boldness. He was surprised how fast life could suck a person along and keep him from noticing the things that were the most important. "Thomas, the gospel is true. I testify to you in the name of Jesus Christ that this is his Church, that he appeared to Joseph Smith, and that the Book of Mormon is the word of God, just as the Bible is."

Thomas took a step backwards. "My, aren't you the intrepid missionary? I've never known you to be this direct before."

"What if one of us dies before I get back, Thomas? I don't know how the crowds will be handled in the world to come. But when that day comes, I don't want you to look me in the eye and say, 'Robert, you knew. Why didn't you tell me?' Know what I mean?"

Thomas looked at the ground. "You've told me," he said, a bit testy. "Have a good trip."

Robert walked a few steps away and turned, suddenly feeling terribly alone. "I hope the year passes by quickly. Goodbye. I love you both."

"Goodbye, Robert," Dianah said. "I love you, too."

"Let's go to Kansas, Duke," Robert said to the dog.

The rain had started again, with a whistle of wind, a rumble of thunder, and a whoosh of raindrops from a light gray sky. The deteriorating weather made Daniel feel even bluer, and he was in a tizzy. He felt a responsibility for all the families left behind, but there was nothing he could do except leave conversations of encouragement to George Bundy, Thomas Kington, and John Hyrum Green. Between the three of them, they had five extra families to care for: his own, Robert's, John Cox's, Levi Roberts', and Richard Slater's. He was especially concerned about how they would endure the winter months.

Brigham Young had already announced that because there wasn't enough grass, wood, and water in the Grand Encampment area to support ten to fifteen thousand people—and thirty thousand cattle, flocks of sheep, and herds of horses and mules—members of the Church were going to have to fan out on both sides of the river for the summer and fall. Where Elizabeth, Harriet, and the other wives would spend the winter, Daniel did not know. This put him in a quandary of worry because that was his nature. He always saw himself as a lighted beacon of goodness and truth and he took his responsibilities seriously.

Minutes earlier he had said goodbye to Wilford Woodruff and Orson

Hyde, who had been busy giving last-minute instructions and blessings to Battalion members. Daniel had also been able to bid a goodbye to John Benbow—the man who funded the United Brethren organization in England. Benbow had just barely arrived in Council Bluffs, traveling with Joseph Fielding. Before he left Nauvoo, Benbow had finally sold his hundred and sixty-acre farm to his nephew. He now had two wives, the second a sister to Apostle John Taylor.

Daniel kissed and embraced Elizabeth, Moroni, and Harriet and then turned to go. As he did, Elizabeth caught Daniel's hand. "Here, take this," she said. She pressed a small bottle into his hands.

"But this is your supply of quinine," he gasped.

"I know," she replied, quick on her feet in her thinking as always. "You and the others will probably need it. The ague fever just *sits* in your blood. It erupts every season when the weather is hot."

Elizabeth had been vocal about the volunteers not receiving any kind of physical examination before they enlisted.

"But you'll need it too, and especially the children will need it," Daniel argued as he heard the final call to leave.

"If you have to *walk* to Fort Leavenworth in this summer heat, you'll practically die," Elizabeth countered. "We can shade up when we have to. You won't be able to."

Daniel opened the bottle and peeked into it. "There's not much left, is there?"

Elizabeth kissed Daniel again. "No, there isn't."

"Find another bottle," Daniel said sternly. "I'll take a third of it with me, but no more." Daniel strongly suspected that the small quantity of quinine would be the only quinine in the entire Battalion.

From her wagon box, Elizabeth found another bottle. After splitting the quinine she said, "I need another kiss and another hug."

Daniel began to breathe in short spurts. He already felt his loneliness growing. "I'm going to miss you terribly."

Elizabeth pulled back and took Daniel's face in her hands, fighting back tugs of emotion. "And me, you."

"I have this feeling that I shouldn't go," he said, gazing into her large, radiant eyes.

There was a bugle call. It came from Levi Hancock, the fifer for Company E. Daniel knew him well. He was one of the seven presidents of the Seventy, the only Church general authority that had enlisted. Heber C. Kimball had given Hancock the assignment to be the Battalion chaplain.

"I think it's too *late* to change your mind," Elizabeth said as she wiped away her tears. "Read your Book of Mormon and the Bible every day. And be sure to keep a journal or a pocket diary, like Brother Brigham *asked* you to."

"I will. Do you believe Brother Brigham's promise that if we are faithful in our duties not one of us will fall in battles with the enemy?" Daniel asked. "That our only battles will be with wild beasts?"

Elizabeth, in an old brown wool dress that she normally wore on chilly days, looked decidedly odd in this setting. But Daniel found the contrast as exciting as everything else about her. He loved her more than ever. He remembered that first time in England when he laid his eyes on her, when he hopelessly craved to seize her in his arms and kiss her. They had never been apart in their married life. He wondered how he could get along without her.

"Yes, I believe him," she said. "But what about *after* you are released? Does that protection apply to you *then*, too? And all the way back to me?"

"I hope so," Daniel said as he took one step away, still touching fingertips with Elizabeth. He stood there admiring her green eyes, her sharp features, and her blond hair. A hundred daydreams about Elizabeth came swirling by, intense and delicious. "Hold still for a moment and let me look at you. I want to burn your image in my mind, like a daguerreotype."

"I'm doing the same to you," she replied.

"I love you." He backed away for a second and faced her, his eyes blazing. Then he embraced her again. He was dazed with the happiness of having a family and flooded with gratitude for being alive. He did not want to leave.

"I love you, too."

"How old will Moroni be when I get home?"

"He's nine months old—add *twelve*. Then add *another* two or three months for you to find us in the Great Basin. He'll be two years old."

"Don't let him grow up without me. I want to be around when he says his first words."

"I'll freeze him in time."

13

DANIEL'S SPIRITS FELL TO ROCK BOTTOM when a soldier named Samuel Boley died on the way to Fort Leavenworth. Boley's death didn't have a single thing to do with the lack of flour and food, or even with the suffocating heat that hung like a pall over the Missouri River basin. Boley had been sick from the start and never should have enlisted. But Daniel had gone into the army thinking God would absolutely protect each Mormon Battalion soldier to the fullest extent, especially from death. Boley proved him wrong on that count. Now Daniel wondered where else his thinking might be flawed. Would God protect him from sickness? Wild animals? Enemy bullets? Indians?

Daniel's company had caught up with the other four companies in a day. Now all five companies were together and Daniel felt like Colonel Allen was trying to kill all five hundred Mormon soldiers all at once with his long, forced marches, and without much food. There were no bowls to mix flour in, so the men had opened up their bags of flour and poured a little water into a hollowed-out place in the flour.

"It ain't Colonel Allen at all," Robert said one evening. "It's Dykes. He's the one who insists on these long marches."

Daniel gasped and felt betrayed. Dykes, a first lieutenant in Company D, was one of their own—a Mormon volunteer. But Dykes had the luxury of a horse and wanted to impress Allen with his enthusiasm for army life. Allen had actually favored traveling moderate distances only; Daniel was surprised to find that Dykes had recommended the long marches.

Colonel Allen's goal was to get the Battalion to Fort Leavenworth right away. There, the Mormon soldiers were to get a few days hard training and receive their clothing allowance, muskets, and accoutrements. Provisions would be gathered—flour, bacon sides, pork belly—along with wagons, mules, oxen, and a herd of beef cattle to help sustain them until they got to California. Daniel supposed that five hundred men could devour three or four of the animals in just one day. It would take more than just a few buffalo and wild game to help feed them as they left Santa Fe and traveled along the Santa Fe Trail.

"What can we do about it?" Daniel asked as the men laid out their blankets on the tall, damp grass.

"I can jerk him off the horse and break his jaw," Robert said.

"You can't act that way in the army, Robert," Daniel warned. "Dykes is not an apostate like Wilson Law and he's not a Mexican soldier. Think of something better."

"You think of something—you or one of the other officers," Robert said. "You've got to do something; it's wearing us down too fast."

"If we all had the money we could buy horses from the Missourians," Daniel said. "That way we could keep up with Dykes and ride into Fort Leavenworth in style." Daniel said it knowing nothing of the kind was a possibility. He didn't have any money to spend on a horse and neither did Robert. And neither did ninety percent of the men. William Hyde and William Coray had each purchased an Indian pony, but they were the exception.

Daniel noted that despite the long marches there were few complaints. More important, there were no desertions.

He prayed for something to eat.

Robert had never gone two full days without even a morsel to eat. He'd fasted for two meals every month, just as he was supposed to do as a member of the Church. He'd been taught that it was good for his health and that the money saved was a proper way to give to the poor of the Church. Although Hannah tried to get him to fast for a full twenty-four hours, like the Apostles taught, he usually cheated and made it only nineteen or twenty hours.

Two days without food, marching in the hot sun, was a different matter. His energy was zapped and he felt himself getting edgy, to the point that he decided he hated army life. He was so hungry he could imagine himself shriveling away to nothing. If he made it back to Hannah, he would be skin and bones.

"It would be more terrible to die from starvation than from an enemy bullet or an Indian arrow," he said to Daniel as they marched through grass up to their shoulders along the Missouri River. "A bullet would kill you almost instantly. An arrow or two would take only a few hours. But I've heard starving to death takes a few weeks. I'm not up to that."

"Don't talk about such nonsense," Daniel said. "We'll find some food somewhere."

Robert was not only half starved to death, but he suspected the ague might hit him at any minute. The hot season had definitely arrived. The boiling sun was high in a hazy blue sky, stalled like a mule. Rain had soaked him and his blanket the night before. He had tried to keep the rain out by building a little shelter out of brush, but it hadn't worked.

He felt that the combination of no food and hot weather had taken at least ten years off his life.

The Battalion was now on the Missouri side of the river. A few of the men had seen John Eagle, a member of the mob that had murdered Joseph Smith, standing in the door of a stable in one of the settlements. Robert was amused by the fact that many Missourians were fearful at the approach of the Battalion. Many locked up their houses and temporarily deserted their homes. The Missourians were openly astonished that the Mormons had raised the Battalion. If all the soldiers were like Robert, they were not prone to make rash moves right now. They not only lacked the disposition for it, but they were too weak to fight.

The way Colonel Allen marched the Battalion through Missouri brought a smile to Robert's lips, and it inspired confidence in his new leader. It was as though the colonel was trying to show off his Mormon boys to the Missourians. Allen had the Battalion's drummers and musicians playing as loudly as possible, and the men marching in time whenever they approached a village.

The area around the farm impressed Robert. Missouri was a beautiful land of green, rolling hills, magnificent timber, and a good supply of water. There were thousands of acres of barren prairie land, too, kept that way because the Indians burned the land every year to keep the spread of timber down. But in many places the grass was up to their shoulders as they marched, but that seemed to add to the heat and sultriness.

Robert kept stepping to the marching music but he let his eyes wander. One by one, little farms passed by. Each had its share of livestock and tidy little garden spots. It seemed that every Missouri settler had a black slave; some had three or four.

"I sure wish that farmer over there would give us one of his pigs or a few of his chickens," Robert said with a wistful look.

Up until now, Missouri farmers had been driving Mormon soldiers off their farms as they marched by, swinging hoes and whatever they could find at them. One soldier, who must have been even hungrier than Robert, had driven a cow off a farm and milked her. Another had raided some beehives.

The Missouri farmer was less than a hundred yards away, fanning himself in the shade. He also looked like he was ready to defend what few head of cattle he had, and his sheep, horses, hogs, plus a few chickens, ducks, and geese.

"Do you think he knows we're Mormons?" Daniel asked Robert as he wiped the perspiration from his brow.

"I suspect he does," Robert said, his keen eye also on the Missourian's little garden. He couldn't see a black slave. "Word about the Battalion has traveled through the settlements around here a lot faster than our march."

Earlier, Robert and Daniel had talked about the fact that their march would take them close to Independence, Missouri, in Jackson County. Joseph Smith had taught that the garden known as Eden had been located there. Someday, Joseph taught, the City Zion or the New Jerusalem would be built there. Levi Hancock told them that Independence was exactly halfway between the Atlantic and Pacific coasts. So hot and humid the weather, Robert found it difficult to envision the area's glorious past, when Adam and Eve and been here.

Hancock came walking up to Robert and Daniel. The Garden of Eden was not on his mind. "Boys, remember what Brigham Young told us before we left about not stealing from farmers."

Robert's eyes remained locked on the little Missouri farm. He made a brave effort to smile. "Brother Hancock, I'm so hungry I can't remember who said what. I've always fed my dog better than the army's feeding us." Robert began to rationalize in his mind. The Missourians had killed Mormons. It wouldn't hurt for Mormons to steal fresh vegetables from Missourians' gardens, or to grab a chicken or two.

Two days ago the men had been given several ears of old corn from a farmer. They decided it was only good for cornmeal, but they had no mill. To compensate, they had boiled the corn slightly, then rubbed it in a homemade grater—made by punching holes in a piece of tin, bending it, and nailing it to a board. It was a slow method of grinding, but they did make a little cornmeal. A few soldiers ahead of them had secured food from farmers, some with pay, and some without.

Robert was certain Levi Hancock was just as hungry as he was, maybe more so. But Levi threw his shoulders back and began to recite Brigham Young's words from memory, which made Robert a little peeved.

Levi said, "Brother Brigham said we would be traveling in a foreign land, even in our enemy's country—Missouri. But he promised us that if we live our religion, obey our officers, attend to our prayers, and not disturb orchards, gardens, livestock, or chicken coops, or beehives, and never take anything that does not belong to us, we would be blessed."

"I've a better memory than you, Brother Hancock," Robert said dismissively.

The church authority looked a little out of sorts.

"Brother Brigham said never to take anything that didn't belong to us unless it's a matter of starvation, and that's a fact. It's also a fact that I'm starved."

Levi Hancock fell silent and a tight look came to his face. His stomach was growling too.

"And Colonel Allen said that if we ran out of food, we've got to help ourselves—isn't that right?" Robert said.

Hancock began walking toward the farmer. "Let's at least ask the man if he'll share before we take it from him."

As they approached, Robert began to think about the stories Levi Hancock had been telling them the past three or four nights about the Missouri years. Levi had been baptized way back in 1830 by Parley P. Pratt and had suffered through the persecutions heaped upon the Mormons in Missouri. Robert couldn't help but wonder if there was a little thought of revenge swirling around Hancock's brain as he trudged through the grass toward the farmer, despite the fact that Hancock was one of the seven presidents of the Seventy.

"I s'pect you boys're Mormons," the farmer said as Robert and his dog reached the rustic log cabin with Hancock. Daniel, Levi Roberts, John Cox, Robert Pixton, and Richard Slater trailed behind. A dozen or more other Battalion members were watching the proceedings from shade trees by the creek where the soldiers had nooned.

"Hungry Mormons at that," Hancock said to the farmer. "Got anything you can share?"

The Missourian seemed to rake over his visitors with dark eyes, obviously trying to fathom what was in their minds. He was dressed in buckskin and his footwear was of homemade tanned leather. "Might have," he said as he stuck out his paw. "Appleman's the name. You got one?"

Robert almost fell over, not from the weakness of his forced two-day fast, but because the farmer exhibited a warm smile and seemed rather friendly—strange for a Missourian.

Hancock introduced himself and the others. "We're on our way to Fort Leavenworth, Mr. Appleman. There're five hundred of us who have volunteered as soldiers. The army's gonna march us to Mexico and California. There's been war declared against Mexico."

Appleman fanned himself as his wife appeared from inside the log house. They were victims of the heat and humidity too. "I see. I know about the war. I commend you. Before we talk about food, I've got something to say to you Mormons."

Robert pulled himself one step back, fearing the worst. An eerie silence fell over his fellow soldiers.

"You Mormons have been gone for a few years," Appleman said as his features softened. "But we'd like ta have ya back. I'm not the only one who feels this way around here. We were misled. You'd be a lot better neighbors that most folks I've ever seen. When yer army thing is done, you'd be welcome. Folks around here caint understand how persecuted Mormons could volunteer for service to a country which made no effort to protect you in your times of distress."

Levi Hancock took off his brown felt hat in respect. "You're very kind. Thank you."

Robert didn't know what to think. He hadn't expected such crazy talk from a Missourian.

Appleman chose his words carefully. "You say there's five hundred of you? I can't possibly feed ya all. But I'd be glad ta donate what I kin afford. I'll give ya a dozen bottles of canned fruit, ten pounds of taters out of my garden, and three chickens."

Hancock's face was lit with happiness. He motioned to Robert. "If you'll get the canned fruit, we'll catch the chickens and dig the potatoes."

The other men were standing around like statues, not knowing what to do, so complete was their shock.

Robert nodded. But he began to wonder how many bites of food each of the nearly one hundred men in his company would get. Three? Four?

Now that the shock was over, the other men had sprung into action. Some were chasing chickens; others followed Robert inside the log home.

Inside, Robert couldn't help compare Appleman's home to the typical log cabin in Nauvoo. Wooden pegs driven into the walls served as a hanging place for the couple's wardrobe. All the clothing appeared to be made with linsey-woolsey, a mixture of flax and wool. The walls were not whitewashed. A rough bench made with the aid of an axe alone was the only furniture he saw, aside from a rough-hewn table and a bed anchored to the wall. Two wide-eyed children stared back at him, their hands in their mouths.

Robert thanked the lady for the canned goods and turned to go. She said, "When ya get ta St. Joseph, there'll be plenty of goods you kin buy. Joseph Robidoux always keeps his trading post well stocked. But watch him—he's a sly one."

Robert gave her a blank look.

"One day, so the story goes, runners arrived, announcin' that a Pawnee camp was draggin' in ta trade their furs. Joe had only one competitor in town, old foxy Manuel Lisa. Both Manuel and Joe put out all their goods. Manuel went over ta see what his competitor was displayin,' and ta his surprise Joe invited him in ta split a bottle of champagne—ta drink ta their mutual success. Manuel was thrown off guard and agreed. Joe complained that his gout made it painful for him ta stoop, and asked Manuel ta go down into the cellar and fetch a bottle. When he did, Joe let the trapdoor fall, rolled a heavy cask over it, and called down to his prisoner that he could come out after the Pawnees had gone. Old Joe had the trade all ta himself that day."

Robert laughed. Stories about Missourians never ceased to amaze him. "Thanks for the information, ma'am. But we left all our money with our wives at our Mormon encampment about a week's travel up the river. We have no money and we have no food. But when we get to Fort Leavenworth we'll be paid."

"It's a four-day walk from here," the woman said. "Good luck."

14

ROBERT FELT HANNAH WOULD BE proud of him. He had survived his first crisis. He had faced death by starvation and had been saved by a Missourian. He felt he would live, but by no means did he have a full stomach. It still growled for more food.

"I'd sure like to line my flue with some bacon or a pork chop," he said to Daniel from the E Company nooning camp. The Missouri farmer had been generous, but Robert suspected he could have eaten everything the couple had in their cupboards all by himself. Now he had his eye on the hogs that were asleep on the farmer's porch.

"We were lucky to get what we got," Daniel replied.

"Too bad the kind farmer didn't see fit to give us one of his fat hogs," Robert said as he picked his teeth clean of the one bite of chicken he'd been able to salvage. He licked his fingers, savoring that little bite. "Or one of his beef cows. One or the other, it would have soothed our hunger pangs just a little more."

"You volunteering to be our butcher?" Daniel said with a chuckle. "I thought you hated the trade."

"Oh, I loved being a butcher when I was in England," Robert shot back. "It's just that I hated the killing, the blood, the skinning, and the cutting up of meat."

In truth Robert also had his eye on a yoke of oxen that the men in Company B had purchased to pull a wagon. The oxen were grazing on lush grass, not far away. He envisioned clubbing one of the oxen right between the eyes, slitting its throat right in front of the other men, and carving out some beefsteaks.

"Wagon coming!" John Cox yelled out.

Robert jerked his head up, shielded his eyes with a hand, and saw a wagon lumbering toward camp. It was pulled by a team of two mules; a teamster and an army officer sat in the wagon. Four mounted dragoons guarded the wagon, making it somewhat an impressive sight. Puffs of dust rose from under the feet of the mules and the horses.

"What do you suppose this means?" Daniel asked.

Robert intensified his gaze. The oak leaves on the officer's shoulder told Robert he was a colonel. His trousers were dark blue with a buff stripe down each leg. When the wagon drew closer, Robert almost fainted in surprise. The barrel-chested man driving the team of mules had deep-set dark eyes, a square jaw, and thick, stringy black hair hanging out of his army cap. Robert came to a stupefying conclusion.

"Why, that there's Henry Eagles, my brother-in-law," Robert announced to the soldiers in E Company.

"Well, it is at that," Daniel said as he let his jaw drop to the ground.

Duke, Robert's dog, suddenly became uneasy. He growled at the wagon and the men in it.

"Henry! What are you doing here?" Robert asked.

Henry looked as though he had just seen a ghost. "Hoping I wouldn't see you," he said as he pulled the mules to a halt. "Me and the colonel here have waded through heaps of Mormons looking for your quartermaster. Imagine my surprise when I heard the army had recruited five Battalions of Mormons."

Duke growled again.

"Keep your dog away from me."

Robert calmed the dog down. Henry had killed one of Robert's dogs back in England. That dog had also been named Duke.

"Katherine and Hannah will be pleased when I write to them," Robert said. "We had no idea where you went."

Henry was about to let out an uncomfortable snort when the colonel held up a hand. "You two can talk later. I have a load of flour from Fort Leavenworth." The colonel had an oval face heightened by long muttonchops, dark brown eyes and hair, and deeply creased worry lines between his eyebrows. "Someone get me your quartermaster, on the double."

Before Robert or any of the other men could answer, Quartermaster Sebert C. Sheldon came running up to the wagon with Levi Hancock. "I'm the quartermaster," he said. "I'll have the men start unloading the flour. We're starving around here, so thanks."

The colonel's icy stare chilled Robert. The man looked to be about his same age, in his mid-thirties. Henry sat silent, obviously in fear of the colonel. The mules were restless, slinging their heads.

"Are you one of the Mormons?" the colonel asked Sheldon.

"Why, yes, sir. We're all Mormons," came the answer.

"I'm not turning this load of flour over to any scoops," the colonel said in a steely voice. His reddened face was contorted in rage and hate and he began to swear, bitterly and vilely.

It struck Robert that the officer was a Mormon-hater. He recognized the colonel's terminology. Missourians sometimes referred to Mormons as "scoops," a derogatory reference meaning that their brains had all been scooped out. Robert turned his gaze to the wagon. It was loaded with more than three-dozen sacks of flour. His mouth watered thinking of the bread that could be baked with that flour. There were also several jugs of liquor. Robert wondered whether the colonel's irritable garrulity was due to whiskey or to fact that he just plain hated Mormons. Too many years of army life showed in his lack of manners. This half-crazed biased colonel wouldn't take this wagonload of flour back to Fort Leavenworth with him, would he? Or wouldn't he? A deep gloom settled over Robert.

"Get Colonel Allen, on the double!" Sheldon commanded John Cox. Cox ran toward the interior of the camp, to a grove of thick trees.

Levi Hancock motioned Robert and the others away from the flour wagon. "Do you know who that colonel is?" he whispered.

Robert shook his head *no*. "Never seen the man before. The teamster is my brother-in-law." Briefly, Robert told Hancock about Henry's strange disappearance.

Hancock was more interested in the colonel. "Well, I've seen the colonel before."

"You have?"

"Do you remember the story when Joseph Smith was held in the Richmond Jail, back in 1838, when the Prophet rebuked the guards? You've probably told the story to your children."

This time Robert shook his head *yes*. The incident happened more than two years before Robert arrived in Nauvoo. Joseph Smith had been transferred from Independence to Richmond for a preliminary hearing on charges against him. Joseph had been fastened by chains to six other prisoners—including Sidney Rigdon—in a miserable, noisy, cold room and compelled to sleep on the floor. Joseph and the others had been placed under guards who were the most foul-mouthed, vulgar, disgraceful rabble that ever defiled the earth. One night, after Joseph and the others had lain there and endured hour upon hour of obscene jests, horrid oaths, dreadful blasphemies, and filthy language, with the guards recounting their deeds of rape, murder, and robbery they had committed among the Mormons—even boasting of defiling by force wives, daughters, and virgins, and of shooting or dashing out the brains of men, women, and children—Joseph rose to his feet stating that he had enough. Witnesses declared that the Prophet spoke in a voice of thunder, or as a roaring lion. He said, "Silence, ye fiends of the infernal pit. In the name of Jesus Christ I rebuke you, and command you to be still; I will not live another minute and hear such language. Cease such talk, or you or I die this instant."

Robert felt a deepened anxiety as he scratched his head. "Does this colonel in the flour wagon have anything to do with the incident in the Richmond Jail?"

Levi Hancock nodded his head up and down, emphatically and slowly. "Colonel Sterling Price was the head guard in the Richmond Jail. It was he who was silenced by Joseph Smith. Back then Price was serving as a colonel in the Missouri militia. The man in the flour wagon is probably one of the most passionate Mormon-haters on planet earth." He went on to explain that Price moved to Missouri from Virginia in 1831 and at the time of the jail incident was serving as a member of the Missouri General Assembly, and that he was probably one of Colonel Kearny's most important officers.

Robert let out a low whistle as he turned his head and shot Colonel Price an unfriendly stare. Without realizing it, he balled both fists. How he would love to jump the Mormon-hating army officer and pulverize him. Joseph Smith would return from the dead and pin a medal on his chest. Robert wondered if Henry would help him beat on Price, or oppose him.

As Robert continued his stare, Colonel Allen came strutting up to the flour wagon like a red rooster. He fixed the other officer with the gaze of a hound staring at a cornered fox. "What's the problem, Colonel Price?"

The officer in the wagon narrowed his smug eyes. "I have flour, but I'm not turning it over to a Mormon."

By now, nearly two hundred Battalion members had crowded around the wagon.

"Oh, yes you will, colonel," Allen barked, drawing courage from the whiskey bottle he had been nurturing in the woods. He had been in the army seventeen years and had little use for this kind of ridiculous prejudice. "You'll give this flour to my quartermaster. His name is Sheldon. And he's a Mormon all right, through and through. You may be a higher rank than me, but this is ridiculous. I'll fight you right to the top if you want to make an issue over this wagon load of flour."

Colonel Price sat motionless, giving Allen a most unfriendly look. To Robert, Price appeared he as though he were not going to back down; he folded his arms in an act of defiance. Henry looked away as though he wanted no part of the controversy. Colonel Allen appeared quite peaked and a little inebriated, but he had a determined look. The four dragoons looked puzzled but had their hands on their swords, ready to back their colonel.

"Colonel Price," Allen growled, "you will release this load of flour to Quartermaster Sebert or I'll give orders to these Mormon soldiers and place you under arrest."

At the suggestion, Robert took several menacing steps toward the supply wagon. Others followed. Price's dragoons backed away.

The men around the wagon let out a chorus of cheers. "Hurrah for Colonel Allen!"

Colonel Allen leaned forward, a growing look of triumph and satisfaction in his eyes. "I mean it, Colonel Price."

Reluctantly, the Mormon-hating officer slowly melted. He jumped out of the wagon, grabbed a sack of flour, and tossed it on the ground at Colonel Allen's feet. "Be my guest. The flour's yours. At least *you're* not a Mormon."

There was a scowl on Colonel Price's face that seemed etched in stone, one that Robert knew he would not forget. He had the sense that this confrontation would somehow come back to haunt members of the Mormon Battalion. Nevertheless, Robert reached into the wagon, grabbed another sack of flour, placed it on Daniel Browett's shoulder, and told Daniel to run toward the Company E campsite. "Build up the fire, boys. Daniel's coming with flour. I can taste the bread now! We have enough flour to last until we get to Fort Leavenworth!"

While the Mormons unloaded the wagon and Colonel Price sought the shade of a tree, Robert turned his attention back to Henry, who still had a stunned look on his face. "You've got a lot to explain."

Henry shrugged his shoulders and gave Robert the quick version of what had happened to him since he left Nauvoo, interspersing it with questions about Katherine and Annie. "I never thought I'd end up in the United States

Army," he said. "And I never thought you Mormons would enlist, either."

Robert, in turn, told Henry about their trek across Iowa and that Church members were going to spend the winter on the Missouri River, north of Sarpy's Trading Post. Henry had heard of Sarpy's and also of places like Bent's Fort on the Santa Fe Trail, Fort Laramie and Fort Hall on the Oregon Trail, and Sutter's Fort in California. He repeated his promise to find Katherine and Annie after his enlistment was up, in one year.

Those words pleased Robert and, for the sake of Hannah and Katherine, he began renewing his awkward friendship with Henry. "What's the army like for you?" Robert asked.

"Oh, it has its good points and its bad," Henry answered. "We're gonna overwhelm the Mexicans. You wouldn't believe the supply trains Kearny sent out in advance of his army. Probably twenty-five to thirty wagons in each of them, and still the general worries about running out of food. He says an army's no better than the soldier's empty or full stomach. He's got a big army. Sixteen hundred men have already marched toward Santa Fe."

"Sounds like he hardly needs us," Robert said.

Henry laughed. "Oh, you wouldn't believe the bungling that goes on. I'm just a private and I see it from the teamster point of view, but it's a comedy. Most of the wagons the army bought out of Missouri were old and in poor condition. They're breaking down all over the prairie out there. And there're not enough teamsters. I've only had experience back in Carthage driving my dairy wagon around, but I know far more about mules and wagons than most of the teamsters. Then there's the quartermaster. His men load the wagons wrong. They get poorly balanced and break down. Some are overloaded, and the wagons fall apart. Wagons get stuck in bogs and wheels and axles get busted."

Army life suddenly sounded far worse to Robert than he ever supposed it to be. He had a notion to make a run for it and return to Council Bluffs. But that would be desertion, and desertion wasn't a good option. "So are provisions getting to Kearny's men?" he asked

"Only some of them. We hear reports that some provision trains get too far ahead, and some lag too far behind. There's a colonel by the name of Doniphan who had to borrow provisions from another colonel named Ruff because his men were starving. And Ruff didn't have much to spare. There're shortages everywhere. Colonel Price hates you Mormons for good reason, but he doubly hates you when you need provisions that are also needed elsewhere."

Robert scoffed at that last remark and then asked, "We're not going to starve to death between Fort Leavenworth and California, are we?"

"I think the colonel hopes you do."

"Henry, I have to ask you this. Don't you miss your wife and daughter?"

Henry looked at the ground and shifted his weight. "I've never loved Katherine. I guess that's no secret."

"What about Annie? I saw her before I left. I rubbed my thumb across her cheek. Her eyes were sad. She misses her Papa. I thought I was going to cry."

Henry let out his breath in short spurts. "I guess I have to admit I lie awake at night thinking about little Annie."

"It can't be hard to figure out what you ought to do."

"I've enlisted in the army for a year. I'm more comfortable with the Missourians I'm with than with Mormons."

"Would you like me to tell you exactly what's wrong with you?"

Henry kicked at the ground. Before he could answer Colonel Price stormed back to the wagon. The scowl on Price's face had deepened.

"I don't have time for you two to visit," Price said, his anger still brimming. "I didn't take you for a Mormon, Private Eagles."

Henry pulled a long face and looked like he was thinking of ways he could appease the colonel. He dropped his concerns that he had expressed to Robert. "Oh, I'm not, I assure you. I was married to a Mormon, but I left her. I came to Missouri to enlist in the army and fight greasers."

The colonel gave Henry a suspicious look. "You'd better be telling me the truth or you'll end up in the stockade. I won't have any Mormons in my outfit. Now get us back to Fort Leavenworth on the double, away from these scoops."

"See you around, Henry," Robert said. "We can finish our conversation later."

CHAPTER NOTES

The stories of the encounter with Missouri farmers and the delivery of flour to the camp by Colonel Sterling Price in late July 1846 are true, both contained in the book, *The Mormon Battalion, U.S. Army of the West,* by Norma Baldwin Ricketts (Utah State University Press, 1996). Price was a congressman from Missouri when he resigned his seat to accept appointment as colonel of the Second Regiment of Missouri Volunteers. During the war he led the garrison forces in New Mexico and put down the rebellion against the American government. After the war with Mexico, Price served as governor of Missouri from 1853 until 1857. After Missouri seceded from the Union at the outbreak of the Civil War, Price was made a Confederate Army brigadier general. Later, Price went to Mexico to live and was leader of a Confederate exile colony in Vera Cruz. When the colony proved a failure, he returned to Missouri where he died in 1867 at the age of 58.

The reader will remember that Henry Eagles is a fictional character while people like Robert Harris, Daniel Browett, and Colonel Price are not. While Robert and Daniel may not have personally met Colonel Price on the day mentioned in this chapter, they certainly knew of him.

George P. Dykes was the chief assistant to Colonel Allen, acting as intermediary between him and the soldiers. Many of the Battalion members developed bitter feelings toward Dykes because of his actions during the march. In later years, Dykes joined the RLDS Church and was one of its missionaries.

PART TWO

Fort Leavenworth
To
Santa Fe

15

EVEN BEFORE THEY STARTED FOR Fort Leavenworth again, Henry knew he was going to have trouble with Colonel Price. Henry had volunteered to be a teamster immediately after his arrival at the fort, although he regretted he did not own a horse and could not be a dragoon. Bernard Bogart made it into the dragoons and in fact was in Colonel Stephen W. Kearny's crack regiment. Kearny's "Army of the West" left for Santa Fe a little more than a month earlier, and it was a big one. Henry had been amazed at the number of wagons, mules, and cattle that it took to support an army of sixteen hundred men.

Kearny had a simple strategy. He had divided his troops into three separate bodies. He was leading the first command in person to Santa Fe, where he planned on a swift victory and then proceed from there to the Pacific Coast. After securing Santa Fe, another force of a thousand volunteers, under the leadership of Colonel Alexander W. Doniphan, was to march into the State of

Chihuahua. And after the capture of Santa Fe, Colonel Price was to hold it. The Mormon Battalion was to meet up with Kearny in Santa Fe and would proceed to California as quickly as possible and be the occupation force there.

The conversation between Henry and Colonel Price began awkwardly. "You don't need to take me for no Mormon," Henry stammered. "I lived in Carthage, not Nauvoo. I married an old dish-nosed Mormon, but I left her. All my friends hated the Mormons, and I did, too. I was in the mob that killed old Joe Smith."

Henry's explanation was met with an icy stare. "I doubt your story, private," the colonel said. "If you have a brother-in-law that's a Mormon, and he's from Nauvoo, that makes the possibility that you're a liar. If you're lying about your part in the mob, I'll cut out your tongue."

Henry felt that the colonel meant it. He began to shake, almost dropping the lines to the mule team. He couldn't remember when he'd ever been in such a tight spot. His voice quivered as he began to explain. "Oh, I was there, sir. And I can prove it if you'll just give me a chance."

Most of the infantrymen who left Fort Leavenworth with Kearny had been dressed in their own clothing, and were a ragtag group, but one thing Henry had noticed about Kearny and Colonel Price was their immaculate dress. Today Price had worn a buff general staff uniform, neatly pressed, with his insignia showing prominently—all of which highly intimidated Henry.

"Tell me your story straight out, private," Price said. "I have my ways. I'll find out if you're lying."

Henry cleared his throat and told his story, which highly entertained the colonel for more than an hour. Price asked detailed questions and Henry gave detailed answers. Henry had convinced ex-Governor Boggs, Bernard Bogart, and all the rest of the Missourians, and Price acted as though he believed the story too. After all, Henry knew the names of just about every member of the Carthage Grays and the Warsaw militia by heart, he had actually been in the woods with the mob, had watched them storm the jail, and his own wife had been in the courtroom during the trial of Thomas C. Sharp, Mark Aldrich, Levi Williams, William N. Grover, and Jacob C. Davis. Henry described their looks and their mannerisms. He explained that although his wife was a Mormon, he had left her because he refused to travel with the Mormons, let alone even be one. Again, he said nothing about being shot by anti-Mormons. When Missourians at the fort had seen his shoulder scar, Henry explained that the Mormons had shot him. He was prepared to give the same explanation to Colonel Price if he had to.

"Very well, Private Eagles," the colonel said as he reached for his corn juice jug. "You sound mighty convincing. I still have my ways of checking you out. But if your story is bona fide, I might decide I like you. Might even give you a promotion."

Henry breathed a sigh of relief. The hundred-degree sun suddenly felt twenty degrees cooler. "Thank you, colonel. I think we're two-of-a-kind. I hate scoops and greasers, just like you. I'm more Missourian than English now that I'm with you."

"Have a swig of whiskey, my boy," Colonel Price said as he handed Henry the jug.

Colonel Allen was a hero in Daniel's eyes, and in the eyes of every member of the Battalion. He had stood up to Colonel Price in fine fashion, sending him away with his tail between his legs. With full bellies, the soldiers clamored around Allen to thank him. The colonel felt the appreciation and took the opportunity to talk to his Mormon soldiers after the evening meal, and brief them about the war. They circled him around the low embers of a campfire. Lazy smoke curled through the men, making Daniel think of the campfires he had lit during his trip across Iowa. It also made him think of Elizabeth, Harriet, and Moroni.

For the first time in several days, Daniel felt sluggish, so good was it not to be hungry. He wanted to take a nap, but his commanding officer wanted to talk. He'd always been taught to respect authority, so he slapped himself to a bright stage of alertness and then sat on a log.

Allen didn't hide his drinking. He took a sip of his whiskey, held it in his right hand, wiped his mouth, and began his oratory.

"There's been a lot of talk that the Mexicans might not put up much of a fight," Colonel Allen began. "Let me put the war in perspective for you. If you faced losing half your country to the United States—would you fight?" He nursed his bottle again. It bothered Daniel a little, but he figured the colonel deserved it after his successful putdown of Colonel Price.

Daniel gasped. He had never thought of it from the Mexican point of view. But then the Mormons had left Nauvoo without much of a fight, but that was because Church leaders had instructed them to do precisely that. Now that he was in the army, fighting was the thing to do.

Allen continued. "Once we begin our march out of Fort Leavenworth, within a few days we'll be in an area that was once part of Spain's New World Empire. The Spaniards were in New Mexico by 1600, Texas by 1716, and California by 1769. Now I ask you, what were they doing in this desolate land known as the Great American Desert?"

At this point Colonel Allen paused. Daniel expected one of the captains of the five companies to make a venture at the answer, but instead it was seventeen-year-old Henderson Cox who hazarded a guess.

"Herding sheep?" Henderson asked.

All the men laughed, but the laughter didn't seem to bother Henderson. So he ventured another guess.

"Killing the Indians?"

The men didn't laugh this time. The Spanish had killed their share of Indians in South America, and in North America, too. It was in all the history books. The thought of traveling through country where Indians hated the Spaniards, and all white men for that matter, depressed Daniel. A shiver of dread crept along his spine. He hoped the colonel wouldn't dwell on it.

"Well, I suppose that's part of it," Allen said. "But they were looking for gold and silver. They thought there'd be really wealthy kingdoms up here, something like the Aztec and Inca nations they'd found in South America. To secure those areas while they looked, they planted permanent missions, military posts, and ranchos."

The colonel paused, allowing all this to sink in. So it was the missions, military posts, and ranchos that he emphasized. He told them that the Spaniards had established settlements from Florida to California and had tried to pacify native Indians by converting them to Christianity as they searched for their gold, silver, and other riches to cart off to Spain. Santa Fe, he said, was central to that search in North America. Conquests had been made in the name of God, country, and gold—but not necessarily in that order.

What a way to do missionary work, Daniel thought to himself. Conquer by the sword, not by the Spirit. No wonder the Mexicans—half Indian and half Spanish—were all Catholic. The Spanish had conquered by breeding, too, taking Indian wives.

"The prospect of finding riches only whetted the appetites of Spanish explorers and conquistadors, most of whom came from proud but very poor families," Colonel Allen explained. "So they instinctively sought wealth and power. When the Spanish first arrived, the natives thought Cortez to be the Aztec god-king Quetzalcoatl. So the Indians gave him a gold necklace set and other jewels. Another Spanish explorer, Pizarro, was given a whole room full of gold and silver in exchange for releasing an Aztec chief. All this set off a frenzy of gold explorations, and a rape of natural resources—all sent to Spain. Having found such riches in Central and South America, the Spaniards expected North America to yield similar wealth."

Daniel could only vaguely recall these historical items. In England, he had been taught little of these things.

Allen took another sip and continued. "So you can see how the history of this area is connected to the Spaniards. Mexico now has her independence, but the Mexicans lay claim to this Spanish territory. People who are loyal to Mexico—call them New Mexicans, Californios, *pobladores* or settlers, or whatever—are apt to be edgy if not angry. We Americans are not their only threat. They are also threatened by Russia and England on the north."

Levi Hancock raised his hand. "All this may be true, but I believe in the words of our Prophet, Brigham Young. If he says we will not fight battles against the Mexicans, I believe him."

If there was one thing that gave Daniel at least a little peace about being a soldier, it was Brigham's promise that none of the men would fall into enemy hands, and that they would pass *over* battlefields. Brigham also promised them that there would be battles in front of them and battles in the rear, but none of the Mormon soldiers would be harmed; rather, the enemies in the war against Mexico would flee before them. At one point Daniel had felt so strongly about this promise that he almost dared ride right in the face of gunfire. But now that Samuel Boley had died, he had backed off that daring.

Colonel Allen smiled to answer Hancock. "You know what? I believe him, too. Not just because he is your Prophet and your leader, but also because common sense tells me the same thing. Here's why."

Daniel cupped his ear; he didn't want to miss this part.

"First, there *will* be battles fought," the colonel emphasized. "New Mexico is a prize worth having, and so is California. The war south of the border will be ferocious. Our president is sending the army to invade Mexico, all the way to Mexico City if necessary. Colonel Kearny may face some opposition as he enters New Mexico and California. But as you've already learned, there's not much of a population there, and not much of an army either."

Daniel wondered what life was like for President Polk right now. With a perplexity of spirit Polk and members of his cabinet were probably meeting every day, perhaps around the clock. Daniel suspected the President was still worried about the Mormons, too, how they could upset the balance of power.

"And you don't think the Mexican army will fight?" Hancock asked.

"Oh, yes, they may fight," Allen stated. "But the bigger question is will the common people join that army, or will they be complacent observers? Or will they actually support the army of the United States? I've had the opportunity to study this with Colonel Kearny before I left Fort Leavenworth to find you Mormons. I'll give you our conclusions first, and then explain the details. This will surprise you, and calm your fears."

Daniel sensed that the colonel was about to say something profound.

Despite the whiskey, there was a raw, uncompromising strength about Colonel Allen. He said, "Here's why we are going to win the war, and why I doubt that we'll see any serious action. First, the Mexican government has failed miserably in keeping its citizens happy in New Mexico and California.

Most of the *pobladores* want to break away from Mexico anyway, almost to the point of rebellion. And why not? They are far more dependent upon the United States for markets and merchandise than they are on their own country. Political independence from Spain did not bring economic independence to Mexico. Their economy is in shambles. If you were a Californio, would you have a better chance at a quality life as an American or as a Mexican? Mexicans who live across the river from Texas in poverty and ignorance can't remain unaware of the fortune enjoyed by citizens of the United States who live on the other side of the bank."

"So it is a question of economics?" Hancock asked.

"That's only part of it," Allen answered. "There no longer is any real strength in the Mexican frontier. Their missions have collapsed. The influence of the Catholic Church has suffered as a result. Their presidios or forts have withered away, too, and along with it the military control Spain and Mexico used to have. They can't control the economy, and smuggling is a big problem."

Daniel considered all this to be good news for him and for all the Mormon soldiers.

"To govern is to populate," the colonel went on. "There may be upwards of forty thousand Mexicans in New Mexico, counting women and children, but most of them are considered to be friendly to the United States. And we think there are more citizens of the United States in California than Mexicans. We're playing the Texas game again. Texas is part of the United States because the people there wanted to belong to us, not to Mexico."

James Pace, the first lieutenant in Company E, asked, "You mean to say there is no patriotism among the New Mexicans and the Californios?"

"There is to a point," Allen responded. "But it's like one New Mexican, a trader, said to me when he visited Fort Leavenworth a few weeks ago. He admitted that their central government is like a very mean stepmother to them. Its way of administering governing is corrupt and archaic. There are grotesque social inequalities. But he was having a tough time deciding whether or not to give up his birthright. His government is bankrupt, and it is not populous, powerful, or stable enough to people its frontier, neutralize Indian raiders, and control the commercial and political links between places like Santa Fe and Mexico City."

The men of the Mormon Battalion were intrigued. Several had questions. Jacob Kemp Butterfield, a private in Company A, asked, "Why did their missions and military posts collapse?"

"With the missions, it was a process called secularization," Allen explained.

Private Butterfield pulled a face. "Secularization?"

"I'll use California as the example here," the colonel said. "You have to remember that California is a sleepy, backwater country. Its main feature has been a string of about twenty Franciscan missions established from San Diego in the south to Sonoma in the north. Secularization is a big word, new to all of you. Simply stated, though, secularization was the replacement of state-supported missionaries with parish-supported priests. In theory it meant that the government wanted the Indians to cease being wards of the mission—a liability—and become real parishioners and taxpayers. It also meant that Indian communal property, held in trust by missionaries, would be returned to the Indians. It was fine in theory, but in reality it failed miserably. The padres found that the Indians placed little actual value in private property, thrift, or hard work. Instead of becoming settlers, the Indians rapidly returned to their former unrestricted habits. The missions rapidly fell into disrepair, and the Indians became raiders again."

Raiders again. The words didn't sit too well with Daniel, or with the other men.

"When Santa Anna came to power he wanted the Jesuits to return, re-establish the missions, and by force and conquest get control of the Indians again. It never happened. Yesterday the missions produced grain, livestock, hides, and other goods. Today, they produce nothing. The California ranches, run by foreigners, produce just about everything. Of course this has jeopardized the Catholic Church there, too. The church found itself weakened throughout Mexico and unable to move effectively onto the frontier."

"And the Mexican military in the presidios?" Andrew Lytle, another lieutenant in Company E asked.

"Under Spanish reign, the tried and true bastion of frontier defense had always been a line of presidios, manned by small units of light cavalry. Along with the collapse of the missions, Mexican independence, and a bankrupt economy, it only stands to reason that the presidios failed, too. Mostly from a lack of funding. That left the responsibility for defense to the frontiersmen themselves. The presidios, in New Mexico and California, weren't too effective in controlling the Indians, anyway. Too much distance between those locations and Mexico City, and the garrisons were undermanned."

"How much undermanned?" a corporal in Company B, Thomas Dunn, asked as Allen nursed his bottle again.

"On paper, there're supposed to be three presidio companies of ninety men each in New Mexico, one in Santa Fe, Taos, and San Miguel del Bado. We know that five years ago Taos had only twenty-seven men. We expect that's the case in about all the presidios in the settlements. The presidios are run down, too. They're just tiny squares of adobe huts without any defense of ditches, stockades, walls, batteries, or even an adequate food, water, and wood supply. In the past few years the government hasn't paid their soldiers. Morale has dropped. Desertion rates have climbed. Officers have had to conscript vagabonds, criminals, and Indian peasants. Often they have to keep them in chains to keep them from running away. Indians steal the cavalry's horses and the cavalry has no artillery."

Most of the men in the Battalion laughed.

"You'll get a chuckle out of this, too," the colonel said. "Ten years ago, in San Diego, the townspeople went off on a campaign against the Indians. Mexican soldiers, who could not go along because they lacked guns and ammunition, stayed behind and robbed their homes."

The Mormon soldiers laughed again.

Daniel had another question, this one serious. "Does the Mexican central government know we're coming? Will they send an army from Mexico City to intercept us?"

"Possible," Allen said, "but not likely. They fear an American invasion, which will certainly happen. It's highly unlikely that the New Mexicans could raise battle-worthy local militias to supplement the small regular garrison in Santa Fe. And it's even less likely that the Mexicans could dispatch significant reinforcements from Mexico City, or from Chihuahua, and send them northward in time to protect New Mexico from Kearny's advancing army, or from us."

Daniel let his air out and smiled. Perhaps Brigham Young was right. The Mormon soldiers had more to fear from wild animals than from Mexican soldiers. He felt like penning a letter to Elizabeth to tell her that she should have no fear of becoming a widow.

"So the trick is just to cross the prairie to Santa Fe, and then on to California?" Daniel asked.

"Not so easy," Colonel Allen replied. "Any competent frontiersman with a horse can do that. The trick is to walk there, as infantrymen. Plus we've got to hitch mules and oxen up to drag a bunch of wagons full of provisions."

Allen turned to address all the men. "Can we do it? Can you Mormons make it to California?"

The men threw their hats in the air. "Yes! We can make it to California!"

16

PRIVATE BERNARD BOGART HAD SPENT the day on his black horse with an advance party of dragoons on the south bank of the Arkansas River, a few miles downstream from Bent's Fort. He was now around six hundred miles west of Fort Leavenworth. Kearny's Army of the West had traveled that far in a month, now on the far brink of civilization, and was scheduled to invade Santa Fe in a few days. For most of the time, the army had been strung out over several miles due to its immense size. The provision wagons were scattered everywhere, some of them missing. In addition to the sixteen hundred men, there were hundreds of horses, nearly four thousand draft mules, and fifteen thousand cattle. The animals had annihilated the grass as they moved across the prairie.

There were signs that the Mexicans might put up a fight, although the common people around the area seemed to favor peace. It was natural to assume, in Bogart's view, that those Mexicans in power and wealth did not favor peace. They were the ones to worry about. Three Mexican spies had just been captured near Kearny's camp and taken to him for questioning. Kearny did a smart thing, in Bogart's opinion. He ordered Bogart and a handful of other soldiers to take the Mexicans around and show them the guns, the men, the wagons, and the animals, and then release them. This was with the intent that they would return to Santa Fe with saucer-sized eyes and tell people, especially Governor Manuel Armijo, what they had seen.

After completing that assignment, Bogart and some of the dragoons headed for Bent's Fort.

Not all New Mexicans were taking the war seriously, or at least the American traders weren't. He had seen an eastbound wagon train operated by the firm of Bent, St. Vrain & Co. traveling to Missouri with furs from Bent's Fort and livestock from New Mexico. They were driving two hundred sheep and forty horses and mules.

"I'm glad to be out of that desert back there," Bogart said to Sergeant Waldo Peck and his other companions as they rode along in the approaching dusk.

"Me, too," Sergeant Peck agreed. "It was a bad desert."

"I don't know what we want with this worthless area," Bogart said, shaking his head. "I've changed my mind. The greasers can have it."

For the first few days the Army of the West had traveled over pleasant Kansas prairies with beautifully undulating hills, reminding Bogart of a painting he had once seen of the ocean with its unending swells. Since then, all he had seen was deserts, shifting sand, whirlwinds of dust, snakes, lizards, prairie dogs, buffalo, wild Indians, and cactus.

Large mountains were now in sight, but Bogart could see no use for them, either. A tinge of disgust came over him and he told Peck and his companions, "I'd never vote to take one red cent from the public treasury to try to place the Pacific coast one inch nearer to Missouri than it is now."

His words hung in the air like a heavy layer of smoke. It caused a reaction from Sergeant Peck.

"I feel sorry for any soldier that'll come this way from Fort Leavenworth after us," Peck said. "Our animals have eaten all the grass and the hotter it gets the less water there'll be."

A mile behind the men buzzards picked at the remains of wild animals the soldiers had killed for food, and the carcasses of cattle that had also been killed.

The high adobe walls of Bent's Fort loomed in the distance on the summer-scorched plain. Its towers overlooked hundreds of miles of uncultivated wastes of nature like an old baronial castle that had withstood the wars and desolations of centuries. As Bogart galloped closer he could see Indian women tripping around its battlements in their glittering moccasins and long deerskin wrappings. Indian children, with high Saxon cheekbones, followed them. A collection of Indian men with long locks of black hair, traders, and clerks sat on the shady side of the fort engaged in serious talks. They passed around a long native pipe, drawing smoke into their lungs by short hysterical sucks, ejecting it through their nostrils, and grunting in Spanish.

Bogart found the giant exterior walls of the fort to be of sun-dried brick almost the height of three horses and one horse thick. There were high towers that stood at the northwest and southeast corners, all rounded, allowing weaponry to sweep all walls in event of an assault. Bogart had heard the towers contained plenty of heavy lances with long sharp blades, along with pistols and flintlock muskets.

"No wonder them greasers ain't brought the war to here," Bogart replied as his eyes surveyed the fort. He trotted his horse to the entrance, which was covered by a huge wooden door, itself almost two horses high and one horse wide, spanned by heavy iron. Overhead there was a belfry and a flagpole that held a huge American flag. Altogether, the fort looked to be about six or seven steamboats long by about five or six wide. The fort had been built in 1833 by William and Charles Bent, the only stop travelers and trappers could use to relieve livestock and get supplies between Independence and Santa Fe. The space between was known as the "great American desert," and Bogart had lived to cross it. Indians had normally harassed travelers but they had kept their distance from the Army of the West. There had not been a single Indian incident.

Outside the fort, Bogart could see a racetrack but it wasn't being used today. He could feature wild races there with frantic onlookers betting and gambling. Horses were never turned loose to graze unguarded, so Bogart and his companions put theirs in the adobe corral behind the main walls of the fort, where there was a collection of wild mustangs, mules, and oxen for sale. Chickens and peacocks strutted around.

Inside, Bogart found himself in a small square surrounded by a collection of large and small rooms—about twenty-five of them by his count, all with dirt floors. Sick soldiers from Kearny's army occupied several rooms. A wooden staircase, almost like a ladder, led to the roof where defenders could shoot if necessary. Every once in a while the people living and working in the rooms sprinkled water on them to keep the dust down. Boarders—mostly traders and soldiers—occupied most of the sleeping rooms. Others rooms served as a kitchen, a barbershop, a blacksmith shop, a dining room, an icehouse, and a fairly large store or trade room.

The trade room put to shame other trade rooms Bogart had seen. Shelves were lined with dried foodstuffs, whiskey, tinware, blankets and cloth, tobacco and pipes, beaver pelts, buffalo rugs, gunpowder, powder horns, tools, bell, and beads. Muskets were held in a neat row by a new wooden gun rack.

Along the Santa Fe Trail Bogart had witnessed freight wagons loaded with goods destined for the fort as well as destined for Santa Fe. Regardless of the large military presence on the trail, the wagon trains had pulled into a circle every evening, the mules unhitched and driven to water, and then picketed to long ropes inside the circle so that they could graze during the night. Men had stood guard, watching for Indians. Dutch ovens heated over dried buffalo chips provided the grub.

For a brief moment Peck and Bogart were able to speak with two of the

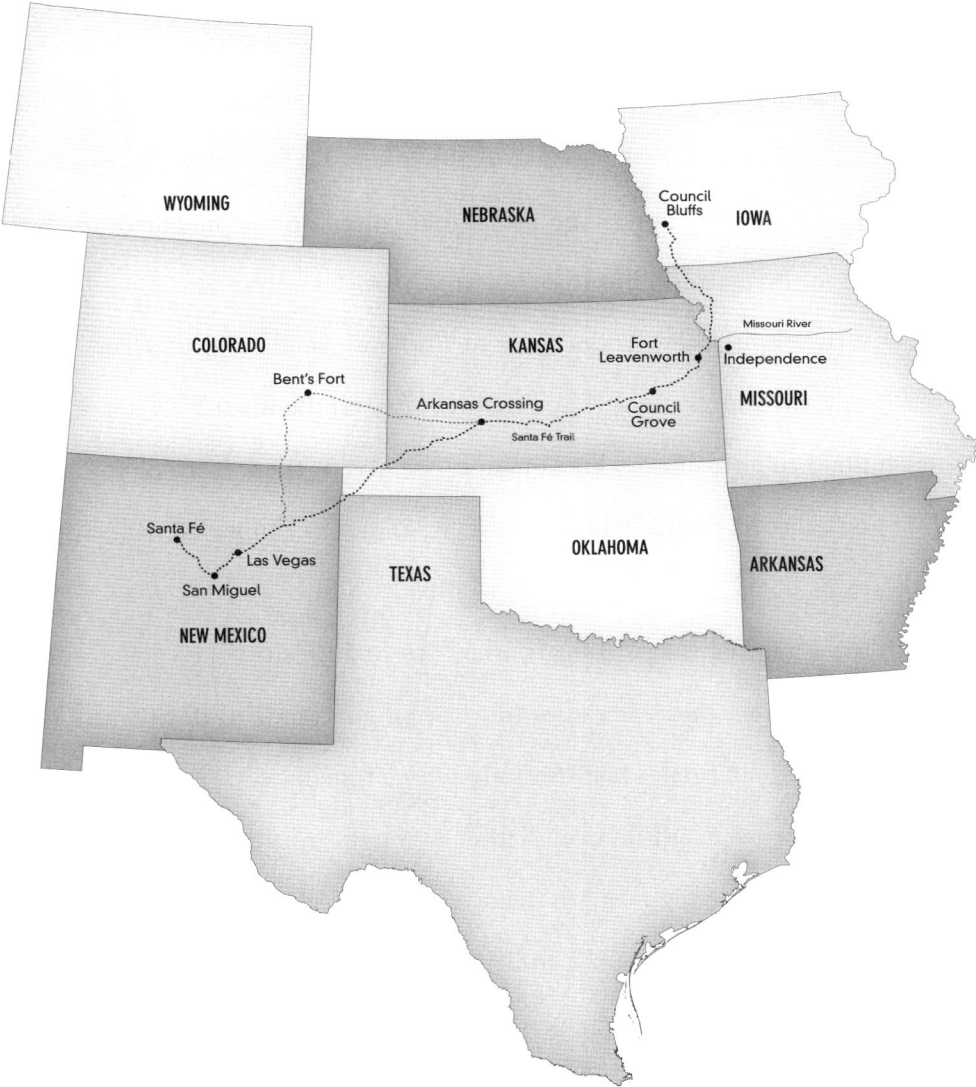

Mormon Battalion route from Council Bluffs to Santa Fe

Bent Brothers, Robert and William. Both were dressed more like Indians than white men. They wore deerskin trousers and shirts with long fringes, and moccasins garnished with beads and porcupine quills. They said that the Indians around the fort were friendly, but they never knew when the Comanches would strike. One time, they said, Indians sprang from hiding places outside the fort to run off fifty horses and mules that grazed on the outside of the fort, and sending three arrows into the heart of their Mexican guard.

"What are the rules around here for Indians, then?" Bogart asked.

"Only the chiefs get inside the fort," Robert Bent said. "They display their buffalo robes and deerskins outside. We accept them in trade for tobacco, beads, calicoes, flannels, knives, spoons, and even things like whistles and jewsharps."

"How about whiskey?" Bogart asked out of curiosity.

"Rarely," Bent said. "It causes too many fights. Indians don't waste time fighting with their fists. They use knives and tomahawks. Whiskey trading usually leads to the death of an Indian or two right outside the fort."

"Sounds like a rough way to make a living," Peck told Bent.

"It is, and it's rough on the Indians, too, I suppose. Life out here in this wilderness, close to the *jornada*, is not easy."

Waldo Peck posed a question to Bogart as they climbed the stairs to a second level. Here, they found a billiard table in one end of the room and a bar generously stocked with liquor on the other. "How would you like it if you were in the next Battalions and regiments and Kearny asked you to skip Bent's

Fort entirely and go through the *jornada* to reach Santa Fe?"

Jornada was a Spanish word for the bleak desert that covered that area. Bogart had discovered that once he began his trip on the plains, misery took on new and diverse forms. Swarms of buffalo gnats rose from the grass. When he reached the Arkansas River, great clouds of mosquitoes had attacked with a ferocity he had never experienced—not even in Missouri. He had been the victim of insect bites, whipped by a ceaseless wind, blinded by driving rains, numbed by a burning sun, choked by great columns of dust, almost bitten by rattlesnakes on a daily basis—and that was before he came to the Cimarron Desert.

"Not possible," Bogart stated emphatically, basing his reaction on what he'd heard. "Even Jedediah Smith couldn't make it. He had his back turned, diggin' for water, when the Injuns got 'im."

"That's what Kearny is asking the Mormon Battalion to do, so that they can catch up," Peck said. "Skip Fort Bent and go directly to Santa Fe."

"Now that's a clever way to kill Mormons," Bogart said with a curt smile. "Make them cross the *jornada* in Indian country."

CHAPTER NOTES

Records of the quartermaster general, United States Army, show that during fiscal year 1846-47, Kearny's Army of the West was provided with not less than 1,556 wagons, 14,904 oxen, 3,658 mules, 459 horses, and 516 packsaddles. Chalfant, William Y., *Dangerous Passage, the Santa Fe Trail and the Mexican War* (University of Oklahoma Press, 1994), page 5.

17

❧

ROBERT FELT HALF DEAD BY THE TIME the Battalion reached Fort Leavenworth. The midday heat was sweltering, almost unbearable. Just as it had done a year ago on his trip to Galena to track down Wilson Law, the ague had set in and had his blood boiling plenty.

"It's hot enough here to melt cheese," he said to Daniel as Company E was barged across the river to the Kansas side. Martial music played by eighteen-year-old Jesse Earl was impressive, but it didn't make Robert feel any better. It had taken five long hours in the hot sun for the first four companies to cross the river and now it was Company E's turn.

"We've got to get you feeling better," Daniel said as they watched Fort Leavenworth come into view. "It's a long tough road between here and Santa Fe, and I hear there's bad country out there—far worse than where we've been."

Fort Leavenworth sat on the bluffs overlooking the river, built there to overcome the unhealthy living conditions in the river bottoms where the Battalion had traveled. Below the bluffs lay the steamboat landing where military provisions were being unloaded. Stacks of barrels and hogsheads littered the wharves. Supplies were being transported from the wharves up a road to the post, which lay just to the southwest.

"Oh, I'm feeling just fine," Robert moaned, wiping beads of perspiration off his brow. "Don't feel sorry for me just because my fingernails are blue and all my muscles are sore."

"I wish you wouldn't joke about such things," Daniel said. "You've got no close rivals when it comes to making jokes, but joking won't make you better."

Robert's fake smile faltered. "Well, it's no joke that my head feels like the inside of a hearth when the coals are burning bright orange. Then every once in a while I get a bad case of cold chills and the shakes."

Daniel grimaced as though the ague could strike him at any time, too—and it could. "I'll give you a dose of quinine when we get to the parade grounds. Maybe that'll make you feel better."

"Maybe the feel of a musket will make me feel better, too," Robert said as his voice trembled a little. "That way I could shoot myself and end my misery."

Obtaining their army muskets had been one of the main topics of conversation among the men as they crossed the river and approached the fort.

The fort was an impressive sight to Robert's dull eyes, but something less than he had built up in his mind. It had been established by the army as a cantonment in 1827 and officially designated a fort in 1832. But no wooden palisades lined the fort's perimeter. Only a couple of sturdy blockhouses guarded each corner of a twenty-acre-square parade ground. On the eastern lateral, two imposing brick barracks, each two stories high with wide porches, gave an air of permanence and decorum to the post. Married officers and their families occupied a row of handsome brick quarters lining the north side of the square.

"Think they'll let me sleep in one of those barracks?" he asked Daniel. Frustration sat heavily upon Robert in his feverish condition; he hadn't slept in a bed since leaving Nauvoo in mid-May.

"No," Daniel replied, "but maybe in that hospital over there, if you're lucky."

The hospital stood at the southwest corner of the fort, a large brick building featuring wide wrap-around porticoes.

"Maybe it's filled up with the Missouri volunteers," Robert said weakly. "We'd tussle, each of us too weak to put up much of a fight."

Commissary and quartermaster buildings lay to the northeast. Scattered brick and wood frame structures dotted the western side of the fort: an arsenal, bachelor officer's quarters, and houses for a few civilians employed at the post. Log stables ran all along the fort's southern edge, with a log guardhouse a short distance away. The men in Robert's company were now talking about the fact that the fort was regarded as the "permanent Indian frontier" for both the Plains Indians and the immigrant eastern tribes that had been relocated nearby. The fort's frontier army had the assignment to protect the Indians from encroaching settlers and to suppress the liquor traffic coming into the Indian villages. "Doesn't remind me at all of any of the castles back in England," Robert said stiffly. A hundred or so white tents could be seen, too—the obvious camps of enlisted men like himself. Even though he was sick, he concluded that he was doomed to sleep on the ground again.

"No, but I guess it's been a busy place the last few years," Daniel said with a shoulder shrug.

He was referring to the fact that Fort Leavenworth had quickly evolved into a primary destination of thousands of soldiers, survey crews, and settlers who were passing through on their way to the West. Soldiers from Fort Leavenworth protected wagon trains hauling supplies over the Santa Fe and Oregon trails to most forts, posts, and military camps in the West—some as far away as the Pacific Ocean. It was named after General Henry Leavenworth, who had the responsibility to protect the increasing trade over the Santa Fe Trail twenty-five years ago, although the trail was several miles to the south.

The fort was called a fort, but it really wasn't. It had no defensive works, except those two blockhouses.

It didn't take too long for Robert to lock his eyes on the Missouri volunteers. To his surprise, they didn't look too serious or even busy. They were running races, wrestling, some of them wandering around aimlessly on the grassy area that surrounded the fort. At first they gave the Mormons wary glances, but soon went back to their normal activities.

A few soldiers could be seen leaving for the government farm, now under cultivation, about a half mile southwest. Several small log and frame houses had been erected on the northern and western suburbs of the fort, occupied by the families of regular soldiers.

Daniel pointed to the middle of the square. There stood a powder magazine, surrounded by a beautiful lawn and shaded by forest trees. It was the heart of the fort, obviously fireproof and bombproof. "Too bad we can't lie in the shade over there."

As the men stood in formation waiting for Colonel Allen to address them, Robert collapsed to his knees and waited in the shadow of Daniel's body. "I wonder where Henry is," he said in a voice barely audible. "He's in Colonel Price's regiment, so he's still here in Fort Leavenworth somewhere. He probably watched us march in from under a shade tree."

Henry Eagles, in fact, had become an unofficial trusted advisor to Colonel Price. At that moment Price was having Private Eagles drive him around the perimeter of the fort to assess the new arrivals. Five other members of the Second Missouri were in the wagon, inhaling rumors and clucking their concerns.

"Keep them Mormons away from us," a captain with narrowed eyelids said to Price.

"It 'pears to me they outnumber our regiment by a hundred," said a sergeant who spit out foul curses as he talked.

"You shouldn't have given 'em that load of flour," said another captain who had gasped in horror at the sight of the Mormons.

Colonel Price tugged at his chin. His stern features hardened. "How much of a threat do the scoops pose to us here, Private Eagles?"

Henry relished the trust placed in him. "They're more interested in the money they'll pull from the government for their clothing allowance and monthly pay."

The first captain was unconvinced. He chaffed with impatience. "Colonel, you ought to get rid of Colonel Allen. Then you'd have control over them scoops."

The colonel leaned toward Henry. "Mingle among the Mormons, my boy. You be my eyes and ears. Tell me what they're thinking."

Henry returned a brisk salute. "Yes, sir."

Daniel reached into his backpack and drew out the quinine Elizabeth had given him. He mixed a few grains in a cup of water and gave it to Robert. "It's time to take some of this," he said. "No sense in saving it any longer."

Robert drank it down. "I'll be up and running laps around the parade ground in no time. I need to get back into fighting shape. There are Missourians all over this place."

For just a moment Daniel thought about Elizabeth. He could still taste her lips. He could see her sparkling green eyes and her sharp, delicate features. He longed to embrace her again and hear her laughing so uproariously that he could barely manage to kiss her. He thought about Harriet, too. And Moroni, his son. By now, Moroni might be taking his first unassisted, awkward steps. Daniel wished he could be there to see that. Reluctantly, he shook himself back to reality, the reality of army life.

"Maybe you'd better give some to Brother Phelps," Robert said as another hot undulation passed through him. "He looks worse off than me."

Alva Phelps was also a private in Daniel and Robert's company. He stood shaking in the hot sun. Daniel mixed a little quinine and gave it to Phelps.

"Thank you, Brother Browett," Phelps said, almost too weak to stand.

"Got any of that left?" a voice from behind asked.

Daniel whirled to find Ezra Allen, a musician from Company C. "Ezra, you sick, too?"

Daniel remembered the time Ezra had come to his house in Nauvoo, asking for Elizabeth to come and tend to his sick wife and child.

Ezra, like Robert, had maintained his sense of humor. "I'm not sick at all unless you count fever and the shakes so bad I can't control them."

"I guess I've got enough of this quinine for at least one or two more doses," Daniel said as he began measuring out some of the powder.

"Thanks brother," Ezra said. "You're a life saver."

"I can't imagine a worse pickle than being in the army in Fort Leavenworth on a miserable hot day, can you?" Daniel asked Ezra.

"Not unless we were surrounded by wild Indians," Ezra shot back as he downed his medicine.

"If we were I'd tell you who I'd want to have with me to fight the Indians off," Daniel said almost without thinking.

"Who'd that be?" Ezra asked.

"Henderson Cox of Company A," Daniel answered. "He's a young one, only seventeen, but he's strong and wily."

Colonel Allen's speech was short. He welcomed the men to Fort Leavenworth and told them that Colonel Kearny's army had left the fort on June twenty-seventh, more than a month earlier.

Robert had that date burned in his mind. Two years ago Joseph and Hyrum Smith had been murdered in the Carthage Jail on that date. And two years ago right now Robert was trying to hunt down the men who had done the foul deed.

Allen said that as soon as the Battalion rested, received their muskets, arms, accoutrements, and other supplies, they were under orders to meet Kearny and his "Army of the West" in Santa Fe. More cattle, mules, and oxen were being brought up to the fort after being purchased in Missouri. It would take a few days to outfit the Battalion with provisions, train a number of balky mules and oxen, and move as far out as Council Grove, Kansas, where they would assess any need for wagon repairs.

"By the time we arrive in Santa Fe, Colonel Kearny will have captured it," the colonel said in a happy voice. "From there, we'll march to California and capture it, too. You will be the occupation force of California."

The term "occupation force" sounded just fine to Robert, even in his still feverish condition.

After the men were organized into messes of six men each, Robert and Daniel began walking with the Battalion toward the garrison where each mess would receive its tent and cooking utensils. Robert Pixton had volunteered to be the cook for their mess. John Cox, Richard Slater, and Levi Roberts were the other members.

"Is the quinine working yet?" Daniel asked.

"My head's ringing," Robert answered. "That means you gave me a little too much. Don't waste it—someone else might need it, too."

"Sorry, you're right," Daniel said as he accepted the tent from the post's assistant quartermaster. "There's not much left as it is." The tent had a musty smell from the humid heat that overwhelmed the entire Missouri River basin.

The six men trudged to the Battalion's assigned staging area, the public square west of the fort. With Levi Hancock assisting, Daniel gave Robert a blessing. Except for Robert and a few other men who were sick, there was a merry atmosphere. There was singing somewhere, so Daniel and the others broke out in a song, which made even Robert feel better—or at least he said he did. Adjutant George P. Dykes came along and ordered them to place shady branches of trees in front of their tents in order to cool the canvas.

"You don't look so good."

Henry's words startled Robert, who had been lying on his woolen blanket outside his tent. The sun had set and the temperature had moderated a little. Still, he wished he were in a comfortable bed in someplace like the Rookery, the living quarters for regular soldiers.

Activity at the fort had picked up. Missourians had organized dogfights, with vicious-looking dogs representing various units. The officers had a jockey club and a horseracing track had been laid out on the prairie. Large amounts of money were being exchanged as the horses lined up. A few soldiers were amusing themselves, trying to throw a lasso—a skill a few teamsters had learned from Spanish cowboys in Santa Fe. Others were spinning yarns and lies, trying to outdo each other. In spite of warnings about card playing, the cards were out in stables and workshops, the men gambling. There were also games of dominoes, chess, and checkers. A Presbyterian clergyman was strolling through the Missourians, trying to drum up interest in a revival. A few teamsters had gathered around a new grave with a priest. Indians had killed a soldier during an expedition out on the prairie. A salute was fired over the grave.

Robert sat up. "Hello, Henry. You come to join the Mormon Battalion?"

"You keep forgetting—I'm not Mormon."

Robert felt well enough to banter. He rose to his feet. He didn't tower much over his brother-in-law, perhaps only an inch or two. Henry had lost his potbelly, probably owing to the fact that he had not enjoyed Katherine's cooking the last few months.

"We can take you down to the river and wash your sins away," he said.

"Some representatives of the Church will be here soon. We could write Katherine and tell you you've been baptized. She'll be pleased. You could even write your own letter."

All of a sudden Henry looked uncomfortable. He hadn't thought much about the possibility that Robert might write Katherine a letter, telling her that he was in the U.S. Army stationed at Fort Leavenworth. He changed the subject. "How many Mormons you got in this here Battalion?" he asked, trying to sound genuine.

"I thought you knew army terms by now," Robert said as he rubbed his aching neck and legs. "We have five companies so there're more than five hundred of us."

"Are you ready to kill some greasers?"

"Greasers?" Robert hadn't heard of the term.

"You know—Mexicans. They got the name because teamsters used to hire them to grease the hubs. They call us gringos, so it's fair play."

By now a little crowd had gathered around Henry and Robert, including Alva Phelps, who looked just a bit better, and Levi Hancock. The term riled Hancock. "Brother Eagles, our leader, Brigham Young, promised us we wouldn't have to fight. Wild animals maybe, but not Mexicans. The Lord is not going to require us to shed the blood of any man, not even in war. The Mexicans are our brothers, too. They're not greasers, they're sons of God, just like you, and just like me."

Robert could tell that Henry resented being referred to as "brother." To emphasize that he was not, he took out a plug of tobacco and inserted a pinch into his mouth. He said, "The army's gonna issue you Mormons one musket each. You'll be expected to use them."

"If we have to, we will," Hancock answered. "We'll follow orders. But I don't think we'll have to use them against the Mexicans."

Henry spat a spittle of tobacco juice at Hancock's feet and pointed to the West. "There're lots of greasers out there. You might be surprised."

Daniel was more interested in the army's strategy. "Colonel Kearny is so far out in front of us that they'll do the major fighting, won't they?"

The question apparently pleased Henry. He puffed up like he was an army officer himself and knew all the answers. "Kearny has the greasers scattering. But you're supposed to catch Kearny in Santa Fe. There'll be more greasers in California to fight. By then there might be boatloads of 'em shipped in from Mexico City."

Robert scratched his head thinking of the hardships that lay ahead. "We're supposed to catch Colonel Kearny in this heat? I hope there's lots of water along the Santa Fe Trail."

Henry already knew some details about the Santa Fe Trail and he was glad to share them, mostly because the news was bad. "There's plenty of water for the first few days, but the country soon turns to desert. You should have seen all the mules and cattle Kearny had with him. They've probably eaten all the grass and sucked the desert dry. There won't be much left for you Mormons, or for us."

"Us?" Robert queried.

"Colonel Price's Second Regiment will be leaving Fort Leavenworth in three or four groups about the same time as you scoops, all four hundred of us. More coming every day."

Robert Pixton was lancing a blister on one foot with his knife. "I saw the recruitment posters in the garrison. I suspect they've been posted all over Missouri, and places like New York and Boston, too."

Henry still played the part of the expert soldier. "President Polk received authorization from Congress to accept thousands of volunteers. We'll need every man. The greasers think we're gonna wipe out the Catholic religion and make slaves out of 'em. They're gonna fight, believe you me."

"But the soldiers I've talked with spoke of how Mexico's generals fought with each other for the presidency," Levi Roberts said. He looked weary, the effects of the march from Council Bluffs apparent. His shirt was black with sweat.

John Cox said, "But they say that Mexico's army is bulging with untrained officers who are commanding underfed, under-equipped Indian conscripts."

Henry's jaw dropped as though he didn't believe any of the soldiers would talk to the Mormons. After all, most of the other soldiers were from Missouri. "That may be true, but Colonel Price says that Mexico's army is larger than our country's army, and they're more experienced in formal warfare. The United States and Mexico have been at each other's throats a long time over the Texas question. This armed conflict is a good thing. It's the only way to set-tle the dispute. We'll kill all the greasers we see and send the others running back to Mexico."

Robert tapped Henry on the shoulder. "You really ought to quit calling the Mexicans greasers and the Mormons scoops. It's not nice."

Henry spat again and laughed. "You Mormons call the Missourians 'pukes,' don't you? Tit for tat. See you around."

With that, Henry walked back to his camp. He had the clear impression that members of the Mormon Battalion didn't want to shoot any Mexicans.

Daniel searched in his backpack for a piece of paper. "I suggest we get busy writing letters to our wives and families. Someone from the Church will be here in a day or two to collect the money. I hope they have room to take back our letters."

Daniel's eyes glassed over as he thought of Elizabeth, Harriet, and Moroni again.

Later, Levi Hancock came to Robert and Daniel's tent, saying that one or two of the weaker Mormon men had already succumbed to the temptations of the fort, sampling strong drinks. He warned their messmates to steer clear of such vices. He also reported that Colonel Allen had appointed a man from Platte County, Missouri, to be surgeon for the Mormon Battalion—bad news as far as he was concerned. The doctor's name was George B. Sanderson, but Daniel didn't know anything about him.

18

FOUR DAYS LATER, ON A WEDNESDAY evening when the sky had pinked up nicely over the western horizon, Daniel was rewriting his letters to Elizabeth and Harriet. A rumble stormed through the Battalion's camp of nearly a hundred tents. Earlier, men had been singing and humming, just as they had done on Sunday evening, bringing a nice conclusion to another day at Fort Leavenworth.

Ezra Allen came running by, spreading the news, and out of breath. "Elder Hyde has just arrived."

Daniel found his heart marching double-time. There would be letters from Elizabeth and Harriet, and his mother and sister, too. "Who's with him?" he asked Ezra.

"John Taylor, Parley P. Pratt, and Jesse Little," Ezra said.

In the center of the camp there was an outburst of greetings, men shaking hands with the Apostle and saying their how-de-do's. Daniel found Orson and the other church officials surrounded by Battalion men. In the bright sun Orson's red hair was easy to spot.

"I don't suppose you had to walk all the way here like we did," Daniel said jokingly after he greeted his apostle brother-in-law.

"No, not even by horseback," Orson said. "We came on a flat-bottomed boat and slept nights on the shore."

Orson quickly accepted Daniel's invitation to share a camping spot with him and his messmates, which was near Levi Hancock's tent. Hancock was the only Church authority who had joined the Battalion.

"I'm on my way to England again," Orson said as he spread out his bedroll. "We have problems there." He told Daniel about Rueben Hedlock and the mess the British Mission seemed to be in. Orson hoped to be in Liverpool by early October.

Over a supper of biscuits and stewed beef, Orson told Daniel and the others the situation at Council Bluffs hadn't changed much. Elizabeth, Harriet, and all the other wives that had traveled to Council Bluffs in the Daniel Browett Company had been moved to Cutler's Park, one of the many temporary settlements. Other than a huge windstorm that had ripped through their camp a few days after the Battalion had left, the women were content and well taken care of by George Bundy, Thomas Kington, and the other men. They were waiting for Brigham Young and the Twelve to decide where a permanent camp would be set up for the winter. Rebecca was staying in the same group with her mother, and was her same old feisty self. The most startling news was that Wilford Woodruff had finally entered into plural marriage, sealed to a widow by the name of Mary Ann Jackson.

"You're timing's good," Daniel told Orson. "We've just received our clothing allowance money."

"That's excellent," Orson replied. "Without the Battalion money, the Church would be in terrible shape for the coming winter. Even with it things will be tough."

Daniel told Orson how the army officers here at Fort Leavenworth had been surprised that every Mormon Battalion member had been able to actually sign his name. In contrast, most of the Missouri volunteers had merely signed their "X."

"I trust the men have been faithful in attending their Sunday worship services," Orson said.

Levi Hancock reported yes. Dykes preached the sermon last Sunday.

"And they gave you your muskets and accoutrements?" Orson asked.

Daniel reached into his tent and pulled out his musket. It was a smoothbore Harpers Ferry 1816 model manufactured in 1827, able to shoot a ball a mile. Daniel showed it to Orson; it looked similar to the muskets the Nauvoo Legion used to carry. Daniel also displayed his white leather strap, two and one-quarter inches wide, which carried his cartridge box when strapped over the left shoulder. An identical strap, designed for the right shoulder, carried a one-pound bayonet and a scabbard. Daniel strapped them on. A belt with a circular brass baldric—with an eagle on it—two inches in diameter, went around his waist to hold everything tight to his body. A knapsack for his daily ration also hung over his shoulder, and yet another strap held his canteen—also over the shoulder. All this was topped off with a leather backpack that contained his change of clothes and personal items. His rolled-up blanket was attached to the top of the backpack.

"It's gonna be quite a burden to carry this all day long," Daniel said, not looking forward to the march from Fort Leavenworth to Santa Fe. "Do I look like a soldier?"

Daniel felt overloaded from his neck to his waist. He drew the musket to his shoulder and looked down its long forty-two-inch barrel, positioned over a walnut stock. The colonel had instructed him to clean it every day.

Orson was honest. "Military-wise you don't look as much a soldier as the other men here at the fort. But you look just fine to me."

Orson was referring to the regular army soldiers at Fort Leavenworth, not necessarily the Missouri volunteers. Privates wore simple but smart gray or blue fatigues with army forage caps. Officer's combat jackets were gray trimmed in gold. A few officers were decked out in dress uniforms adorned with plumes, fringe, and scarlet silk. In full dress, the diameter of the fringe on an officer's shoulders indicated his rank while a brass numeral identified his regiment. Several of the volunteers had arrived at Fort Leavenworth in the uniform of their hometown militia. Each of them proudly flaunted their own distinctive style, a reflection of the provincials' disdain for the federal government and its standing army. An Indiana soldier, for example, had arrived in a uniform decked out in dark blue and silver lace. He had told Daniel, "I'll be derned if they make a regular out of me." Daniel in turn had thought how woefully inappropriate the uniform was going to be on an actual campaign. The dark blue uniform was wool, too hot for the weather.

In contrast to the regular uniform which the army usually gave soldiers, Daniel had two pair of linsey-woolsey trousers, both already badly worn from the trip across Iowa. He also had two cotton shirts and only two pair of under garments, the special kind Church members wore once they had been endowed in the Nauvoo Temple. He wondered if they would last another twelve to fourteen months until he would reunite with the Church and have some more made.

Daniel also showed Orson his small cotton haversack that held barely enough rations for two days, a canteen that held three pints of water, and a heavy, wide, one-and-a-half-inch white leather waist belt. Daniel also displayed the camp kettle, frying pan, and coffee pot issued to his mess. The Quartermaster Sergeant made certain that proper receipts were issued for everything, including the blankets issued from Sarpy's back in Iowa. Daniel C. Davis, captain over Company E, showed Orson his receipt. It showed that Company E had been issued eighty-seven muskets and infantry cartridge boxes, the same number of belts, scabbards, slings, brushes, flint caps, pikes, musket screw drivers and wipers, ten musket ball drivers, ten musket spring vices. There was even a receipt for rations. Daniel told Orson that the

Battalion was fortunate to receive all these things because a steamboat bound for Fort Leavenworth carrying ammunition and supplies for the army had sunk.

Daniel told Orson that Colonel Allen had allowed each company to purchase a baggage wagon and a four-mule team to haul knapsacks, clothing, and bedding.

"Where'd that money come from?" Orson asked.

Daniel sensed Orson's distress. "From the clothing allowance, sorry to say. It's been hard for us to decide what's necessary to buy for our trip, and how much to send back with you."

The army required each volunteer to have one dress cap, one forage cap of glazed silk, two flannel shirts, one coat, one cotton jacket, one linen fatigue frock, one pair of cotton overalls, three pair of woolen overalls, four pairs of boots and socks, and one blanket. Most of these requirements had been waived in the case of the Mormon Battalion so that the money normally required to purchase these items could be sent back to families.

Lieutenant Samuel Gulley displayed the receipt for the wagon, mules, oxen, lariats, bridles, chains, and saddles issued to Company E.

"You had to buy all that out of your pay?" Orson gasped.

Daniel laughed. "No. That receipt was for the wagon, mules, and oxen for our military equipment—regular army issue. We had to pool our money for one extra wagon and four mules."

Orson's blue eyes seemed to narrow a little in disappointment. Daniel felt

Orson personally understood the need for the men to buy such things for their trip to California, but it might well be a different case when it came to Brigham Young. Brigham had already counted on nearly the full forty-two dollars per man. Elder Pratt would be disappointed too. He had been selected to return to Council Bluffs with the money.

"I hope you men don't waste money on knickknacks," Orson said.

"I suppose that's already happened some," Daniel said. "I don't know how we could avoid it unless we take every soldier down and hogtie him."

"Maybe we'd better do that," Orson said.

Daniel gained the impression that he'd better change the subject, but the subject he came up with was bad news, too. He told Orson that Colonel Allen was sick, so sick that he ought to be in the hospital.

What's wrong with him?" Orson asked.

"Part of his problem is the ague that afflicts a lot of the men," Daniel said. "But he's got a problem our men don't have."

Orson was not clueless. "His drinking?"

"Yes," Daniel sadly added. "Constant drinking. I'm afraid for him."

Even though he had not been feeling well, the colonel had drilled the Battalion two days ago, teaching them how to form ranks and use their muskets. It gave Daniel a good laugh when he thought about what Colonel Allen had said as the Battalion boys had crowded around the arsenal before it opened, anxious to get their muskets.

"Stand back, boys," he had said. "Don't be in such a hurry for your muskets. You'll want to throw them away before you get to California."

The colonel had been right. With its bayonet, each musket weighed nearly fifteen pounds.

"I take it you've gotten along splendidly with Colonel Allen," Orson said.

"Despite his drinking, we have a tremendous amount of respect for him," Daniel said. "He stands up to the Missouri officers, who otherwise would be tormenting us daily. He's a good man, strict, but I guess we need strict. He read the military law to us. He even warned us that desertion means the death sentence, Mormon or not. He even complimented us on our obedience, saying that we learn how to do something the first time he tells us."

"You must be getting along with the Missourians then," Orson said.

"We stay away from them," Daniel said. "They can't even get along with each other. They've been fighting and quarreling with each other ever since we've been here. This morning, one of them wounded another Missourian with a hatchet. He's in the hospital, not expected to live."

"How about Church members?" Orson asked. "Everyone getting along?"

Daniel nodded yes.

"Just keep it that way," Orson said to Daniel and Levi Hancock.

CHAPTER NOTES

The author is grateful to the official Mormon Battalion organization for assistance in describing the Battalion's accoutrements—specifically Richard Bullock, Val Halford, Cap Cresup, and Sherman Fleek.

19

HENRY LIKED BEING COLONEL PRICE'S favorite teamster. Lately, Price had even let Henry serve as a sort of private valet, taking him even to some of the less-important high-level strategy meetings. Whenever the meeting turned boring, Price asked Henry to tell another Mormon story. "Old Pap" Price especially liked hearing the one about how Joe Smith was captured and killed.

Today's meeting was being held in the upstairs room of the headquarters building. All the windows were open, letting a gentle breeze fan the room. The humid weather had brought a musty smell to every building at Fort Leavenworth.

Price peered out of a window. "Them Mormons look a little restless."

"I guess they're anxious to get going," Henry said as he leaned back on a chair with his hat pulled over his eyes. "Colonel Allen's sick and he can't lead the Mormons out until he's better."

"I hate Mormons," Price said as he sipped on his precious corn juice.

"You've told us that," one of Price's captains said. "But what can you do about it? If you cause them too much mischief, Kearny will find out. We're all in the same army, you know."

One of the Missouri Second Regiment quartermasters spoke up. "Some of the teamsters are greenhorns, or worse. I could send the Mormon Battalion's provision wagons with the worst of the lot. The road between here and the main Santa Fe Trail is poorly marked. They'd probably get lost out there."

"I don't see how," Price said. "Think of Kearny's army—they went that way. Thousands of horses, mules, cattle, and wagons."

"Give me a few bottles of corn whiskey," the quartermaster said. "For a bottle of corn whiskey, some of them Missouri teamsters will do anything, especially if it's against the Mormons."

Price laughed at the idea and thought it a good one. "Just don't get me in trouble with Wharton." Lt. Colonel Clifton Wharton was the fort's commanding officer.

"He'll never know."

"What about Colonel Allen?" Price asked.

"He's too sick to know or care."

"Colonel Allen disgusts me," Price said. "He acts like he's in love with every Mormon boy out there."

Another captain tilted his cap and yawned behind his hand. "He's sicker than you know. It's doubtful the colonel will recover with the heat and all. His drinkin' has taken a toll."

Still another officer said, "Besides that, there's a Missouri sawbones volunteer that's tending to him. Colonel Allen had no choice but to assign him to the Mormon Battalion, because that's all that was offered. Worst doctor I've seen. His name is Sanderson. Behind his back the soldiers are already calling him 'Calomel Sanderson, 'cause that's his favorite remedy. With Dr. George Sanderson treating him, and if my suspicions are right, Colonel Allen doesn't have a chance of recovering."

The officer didn't mention the fact that calomel was the normal remedy for just about all ailments, especially gastrinomical, and that a doctor's normal medical training included how to prescribe and use calomel.

"Allen has told the scoops to go to Council Grove and wait for him there, but what if he doesn't make it? Who will lead the scoops?" another officer asked.

Price's eyes lit up with the possibilities. "Why, I could make them part of my command once we're on the trail, out of the reach of Wharton."

"The Mormons would revolt," Henry predicted.

"What about Lieutenant Andrew Jackson Smith?" the officer asked.

"What about him?" Price countered. He knew Smith, a young officer, only thirty, from Pennsylvania, and a graduate of the U.S. Military Academy. He had served as Kearny's training officer and was known to be hard-nosed man who never cracked a smile.

"If Colonel Allen can't continue to lead the Mormons, send Smith out to take over. You can control Smith, but you can't control Allen. Smith is a hothead, and is just what them scoops need."

With Colonel Allen in the hospital there was no one to drill the soldiers of the Mormon Battalion. One morning Robert found himself fascinated with the teamsters in the field beyond the fort, such as Jacob Kemp Butterfield. From his sickbed Colonel Allen had sent word that the teamsters needed to make certain all the mules were trained and ready to pull supply wagons along the Santa Fe Trail. Robert, Daniel, and Jacob were watching John Murdock of Company B hitch his mules to a wagon when Henry strutted by. This was going on while the three visiting Church authorities were meeting the captains of the five companies.

"It's about time we saw you again, Henry," Robert said. "Where've you been? Seems to be we have some unfinished conversation."

"No more talk about Annie. She's off limits."

Robert flushed, his disappointment apparent. "What else is there to talk about?"

Henry looked toward the barracks. "What'd ya have ta eat this mornin'?" he asked Robert, trying his best to sound like a Missourian rather than an Englishman.

"Food," Robert curtly replied. It was obvious Henry wanted to revert to his past ways and banter a little.

"I was up a day's dawn with the dragoons," Henry said. "I watched 'em drill fer two hours on horseback, amidst great clouds of dust. All the while I was a workin' my mule team in the cool of the mornin'. Then, after feeding and curryin' down our horses and mules, we heard the call fer breakfast. We et it in the comfort of the dinin' room over there. Pickled pork, lean beef, strong coffee, and sour loaf bread."

"Great snort!" Robert said. "You mean you actually ate the bread?"

Henry took on a puzzled look. "Why, it's good bread."

Robert laughed the best he could. "I've heard the dough is mixed barefoot by an old Dutchman, and the man's not particular about washing his feet."

For a few seconds Henry appeared to take on a green look; he had no idea how Robert knew that one of the cooks in the mess hall was a Dutchman. He quickly changed the subject again.

"Your man's gonna have problems with them mules," Henry said, referring to Murdock. Henry suddenly lost some of his Missouri accent. "I've seen it a hundred times since I've been here."

Henry was dressed like a typical teamster. His pants were tucked into thick boots that reached to his knees. Around his waist was a thick leather belt that supported a large sheathed knife. He wore a red and black-checkered shirt and a brown felt hat already stained by dust and rain.

"I'm thinking the same thing," Jacob said, tugging on his chin with a worried look.

"New mules?" Henry asked.

"The army brought them up from Independence just this morning," Jacob said. "Brother Murdock has no idea about their experience."

The six mules were a mixed lot; two were hinnies—the progeny of a male horse and a female donkey—and the other four were regular mules—from a female horse and male donkey. The mules, one a grulla, had heavy donkey-like heads with long ears, and horse-like tails that appeared wispy and sparse. The bay hinnies were smaller than the mules, their heads more horse-like, with shorter ears and fuller tails.

One of the very tame mules, a thin one that looked overused, lifted a foot. A soldier inspected it, finding it clean as a whistle.

"That old mule's a smart one and just wants attention," Henry said. "Mules are like that."

"You seem to know a lot about mules lately," Robert said.

"Perfect animal for the desert out west of here," Henry replied, displaying the benefit of being around Missouri teamsters for more than a month. "Mules have a built-in mechanism, similar to a camel or an ass. They can drink a whole gut full of water after a hot, dry day and not flounder like a horse. More surefooted, too."

Robert felt that Henry was just trying to show off in front of the Mormons.

Show off or not, Henry went on to say that Missourians had long since learned that the small Spanish mules had incredible strength and endurance, faring better than horses on the Santa Fe Trail where forage was poor and water scarce. Their flinty hooves withstood the shock and abrasion of rocky terrain better than horses. Mules, he said, possessed a native canniness that made them wary of precarious trails and impossible tasks—probably a combination of instinct, stubborn caution, and intelligence. Henry credited Mexicans to be the best at handling mules and horses. After all, their Spanish ancestors had introduced horses to the plains and Mexico had bequeathed mules to Missouri.

"Too bad you don't use your time to learn about the gospel, Henry," Robert said in a huff. "You could get baptized, go back to Katherine and Annie, and make us all happy."

Henry ignored his brother-in-law. "Them hinnies hadn't ought to be hitched in the lead," Henry observed. "Your man ought to get a mare for the lead during training, at least. Hinnies like to follow 'em 'cause they were raised by a mare."

Murdock was attaching a harness to the sixth mule and threading the leather lines through the harness rings and back to the wagon box. He was getting plenty of help from Company B soldiers. Four of the six mules were fidgety, acting as though they had never been harnessed. One seemed terrified, ready to buck. The fidgety mules looked fat, their stomachs bulging from grazing on the lush summer grasses that surrounded Independence and Fort Leavenworth.

Murdock appeared terrified himself.

"What them mules need is some rough muleskinner treatment," Henry said. "If you don't know how to swear like a muleskinner, you ain't gonna control them mules. They don't understand normal language. They only understand words that make Mormons and women weep."

"Kindness ain't a bad way to go," said Butterfield.

"Greasers know how to treat mules," Henry retorted. "They lasso scrub mules and hitch 'em to a wagon wheel with scarce two inches of spare rope to relax the right noose around their necks. Then they starve 'em for twenty-four hours to subdue their fiery tempers."

Robert gasped. "Twenty-four hours?"

"Yep," Henry continued. "Then they harness 'em to a real heavy wagon, and lash at 'em if they don't pull. After an hour or two of plungin' and kickin' them mules start to settle down real good."

"Kill or cure?" Butterfield said to himself.

"Kill or cure," admitted Henry. "I've learned the process myself."

Only a few yards away, Murdock grimaced at Henry's remark and tried to ignore it. Then he asked the soldiers of Company B to turn the mules loose. From the wagon box Murdock shouted a command for the mules to start— and that they did. But the first step turned out to be unfortunate. The skittish mule in the shaft position reared and plunged, and then burst its straps, which frightened the others. Soon Murdock had a runaway team of six mules and the sight was a comic one, in Robert's view. The soldiers of Company B were running after them but losing the race. The mules were in a panic, not knowing which way to go. Robert cringed when he saw Murdock pitched out of the wagon. The wheels of the empty wagon ran over him but quickly he was tended to by several of the soldiers. The mules were still going and the wagon was still bouncing, headed for the fort's farm ground.

Murdock was conscious, but he had to be placed in another wagon. The wagon made a beeline for the fort hospital.

"Looks like Colonel Allen is going to have some company in the hospital," Robert said, shaking his head.

"I just came from there a while ago," Daniel said. "Some of the officers were allowed in to see him."

Henry's ears perked up as though Colonel Allen were a blood brother.

"How's the colonel doing?" Butterfield asked Daniel.

"There's a doctor by the name of Sanderson who's treating him. He was trying to talk the colonel into taking an increased dosage of calomel."

Henry brought a hand to his face to hide his smile.

20

❧

BY MID-DAY THE SUN was beating down on the parched ground of Fort Leavenworth like a blacksmith's hammer against red-hot iron. Daniel paced back and forth as though he were the captain of Company B rather than its fourth sergeant.

"It must be a hundred and twenty degrees in the shade," Robert said from the inside of his tent. "I hope my blood stays calm. I don't want another round with the ague."

"I think I'm already having another round," a less cheerful Alva Phelps said from a nearby tent.

Some of the Battalion members were returning from a shopping trip in Weston, Missouri, just across the river and a few miles north. They had an assortment of blue and red flannel shirts, calico and hickory shirts, vests, cotton and woolen socks, waterproof ponchos, buckskin pants, and broad-brimmed, low-crowned hats of soft felt. The fastidious bought extra razors, towels, bar soap, combs, brushes, and toothbrushes. Even whetstones for sharpening their belt knives were purchased, as were clothing repair kits consisting of strong needles and stout thread, complete with a bit of beeswax, extra buttons, a paper of pins, and a thimble.

It wasn't but a couple of hours later that Daniel made a remark about the shopping. "Good thing we didn't go, Robert. Maybe we would've spent our money on some of the same things—it's a temptation. It's going to reduce the amount of money that'll be sent back to Council Bluffs for our families and for the Church."

Robert didn't answer. He apparently had his eyes on a young soldier from Company E who was wobbling and had a faraway look in his bloodshot eyes. Daniel had seen this look on a man's face before, especially Henry's. The man was obviously drunk and it wasn't the first time.

Daniel heard a ruckus. He whirled to see Robert confronting another private in Company E, a young soldier by the name of Walter Davis. Robert knew him as a Canadian, born there about 1821, making him eleven years younger than himself.

"I'm tired of you coming back to camp half drunk," Robert was saying, acting as though the heat had set him on edge. "You're spending money on liquor, and that money really doesn't belong to you. It belongs to the Church."

Robert felt justified in getting after Davis. Technically, liquor was forbidden for use by American soldiers, and Robert knew it. Prohibition had been part of the soldier code of ethics since 1832. Some generals tried to punish drinking soldiers by ordering them to dig their own graves and threatening to throw them in it. Twenty percent of all military deaths had been attributed to alcohol. But prohibition orders failed to stop intoxication. Bootlegging thrived at Fort Leavenworth, and so did whiskey peddlers.

Walter Davis swayed on his feet, his hands clutching a bottle. His eyes seemed hard and cold, and Daniel detected no fear in his eyes. Not smart, thought Daniel. The young, drunk Mormon obviously didn't know about Robert's past—he'd been a contender for the British heavyweight championship.

Davis crudely pushed Robert out of the way. "None of your business," he slurred. Davis was short, barrel-chested, and had legs as thick as oak trees. His pompous grin showed sparse, foul teeth.

Robert calmly placed his stout frame in front of Davis again. "Yes, it is my business. It's the business of everyone in the Battalion. You'd be wise to give me all the money you have left. You'll only drink it up. I'll give it to Elder Hyde."

Those words did not sit well with young Davis. Without warning he doubled his fists and rammed one of them toward Robert's head, barely grazing it. Reacting with cat-like speed and instinct, Robert stepped away from the punch and launched one of his own. It caught Davis squarely behind the ear and a shout of pain went up as he collapsed to the ground. Dazed but not broken, he staggered to his feet again as Daniel stepped between the two men.

Levi Roberts and John Cox grabbed Davis by the arms and held him back.

"If I were you, Brother Davis, I'd do as Brother Harris says," Daniel pleaded. "He used to be a professional fighter and you're lucky your ribs and your jaw aren't broken."

Davis cast Daniel and Robert a contemptuous look. "Let go of me. I'm not afraid. It's his jaw I'll break."

Other men came running to see the spectacle, among them Orson Hyde, Levi Hancock, and Daniel C. Davis, captain of Company E.

Captain Davis narrowed his eyes at Private Davis, who was not related. "You, again. We've warned you about drinking. This time you're going to the guardhouse."

"But this man hit me," the private complained as he rubbed a knot forming behind his ear. He pointed to Robert.

"Take him away," Captain Davis ordered Levi and John. Robert followed them, his blue eyes still seething.

Orson Hyde winked at Daniel. "I thought you said all the Battalion soldiers were getting along."

As Private Davis was led away, Daniel joked with Orson about Robert's past, his career as a pugilist in England, his altercations with Henry Eagles, and his attempts to hunt down apostates like Wilson Law.

"You'd better put a bit in his mouth and a harness around his chest," Orson warned. "If he strikes out with his fists at every abhorrent thing he finds wrong with the Battalion and army life, he'll wind up in the guardhouse himself."

"It would take a dozen men to get him there, but you're right," Daniel acknowledged.

"But on the other hand, we can't tolerate bad behavior like getting drunk, swearing, and wasting money," Orson said with a shake of his head. "As members of the Church, we need to remember the covenant we made with God at our baptism, and in the temple. We're not at liberty to participate in the sins of the world." He began to chuckle. "Maybe a bop on the head once in a while isn't a bad idea. Keep Brother Harris handy, just in case."

Levi Hancock's face turned serious. "I think we ought to go tent-to-tent and warn the men about drinking and cussing."

Orson scanned the tents and the soldiers. "Take Brother David Pettigrew with you. You two are among the oldest and most respected."

For a brief moment, Hancock regarded Orson as part of the military. "Yes, sir," he snapped as he saluted.

Orson turned to face Daniel as John Taylor, Parley P. Pratt, and Jesse C. Little approached. "We've come to say goodbye."

"Good luck in England," Daniel said, feeling a little lonely again. It seemed to him that in the current year all he'd done was say goodbye. He'd said goodbye to his home and farm in Nauvoo, goodbye his two wives and child in Winter Quarters, and goodbye to his brother-in-law in Fort Leavenworth.

"Thank you. I'll see you in a year or two. When do you think the Battalion will strike out?"

"It depends on Colonel Allen's health," Daniel said. "There's talk of delaying our departure, which won't make Colonel Kearny happy when he learns about it. There's even talk about leaving without him, and letting him catch up on horseback when he feels better."

Daniel's curiosity was raging. He and Robert had turned most of their clothing allowance into the Church fund that Elder Pratt was taking back to Council Bluffs. But he had heard that some men had only parted with half of their money, some less, and some none at all, like Private Davis. This, he reasoned, was why Robert erupted so quickly.

"How much of our clothing allowance total will end up in Council Bluffs?" he asked Orson.

Orson smiled briefly. "We just counted it. There's $5,860. We were hoping for more, but this will help the Church tremendously. I've also received some contributions to help with my travel expenses to England."

Elder Pratt patted the fat purse. "I've got a ledger in here, too, detailing what everyone contributed." Pratt, along with Brigham Young and the others of the Twelve, had been dissatisfied from day one with the information on the appropriation rolls filled out by the officers in the Battalion. They had not filled out how much money each man would send back to the Church. Colonel Allen had ordered the Battalion to march before the rolls could be returned. This had created a spirit of uneasiness in the minds of the Twelve and the Battalion officers.

Daniel began doing the math. If every man had forwarded the entire forty-two-dollar clothing allowance, Elder Pratt would be going back with nearly $20,000. But it was unreasonable to expect that to happen. Each Battalion member needed to spend a little of the money on essentials such as an extra pair of trousers or a shirt. But Daniel reasoned that Elder Pratt ought to have at least $10,000 and he began to share the disappointment. He had seen some of the men buying luxuries like ice cream. There was no ice cream in Council Bluffs. And he had seen a few of the men spending money on vices of the world at the fort's grog shop and card tables. He handed Elder Pratt the letters he had composed to Elizabeth and Harriet. "I don't want to burden you any more, but would you deliver these?"

Pratt added the letters to his mail sack. "No problem."

As Daniel shook hands with the four men, he was tempted to tell Elder Pratt that he wanted every penny of his money to be given to his family. But something told him that the request was a little on the selfish side. The Battalion money was not only to aid the families of Battalion members, but the Church as a whole. So he bit his tongue.

Before Orson turned to go, he had one more comment for Daniel. "Do us proud. You're a soldier in Colonel Kearny's army now."

Daniel let his mind wander. By his reckoning, Kearny should be approaching Santa Fe where it was rumored that he anticipated relatively little trouble. Santa Fe was so far from the Mexican capital that for years not much effective Mexican control had been felt there. Its people had little commerce with Mexico but had long engaged in a highly profitable trade with merchants in St. Louis.

California was another matter.

With young Private Davis in the guardhouse, Robert strolled alone to the road that led south to the Santa Fe Trail. His mind had to begun to dwell on the West for long stretches. Particularly at night when he had nothing to do but walk around the fort or lay on his blanket, listening to the small noises the bedded mules and cattle made, or the singing of the men, he thought of the West, trying to imagine what it would be like. Sometimes he would lie on his blanket for hours before he went to sleep, looking up into the starlit sky, talking to Daniel and the other messmates in low tones, with campfires casting a radiant glow across the camp. Duke would always sleep next to Robert, barking if he heard a strange noise, and making strange moaning sounds when he was asleep—as though he were dreaming about being home in Nauvoo as well.

He had grown up in England with a wet climate, with oak and elm trees, and a patchwork of green farms. He had never seen a desert, and he could not imagine anything so bleak as the stories he heard. The Cimarron Desert was not a true desert, but a sixty-mile stretch of arid land with scant vegetation, alkaline dust, and precious little water. The country between Council Bluffs and Fort Leavenworth had been green and wet, like England. He felt dazed at the prospect of being stuck in a place where there was nothing but dry grass, sand, cactus, and no trees.

In a few days, he would strike out west on the Santa Fe Trail. The first few miles, he understood, would be easy going with rivers, creeks, and springs available. However, caravans that hit the desert in the early spring were far more apt to find a few waterholes than those who crossed it in the summer. Now it was August, the driest part of the year. Robert had never been without water one day in his life and he began to wonder how it would feel not to have any water at all for one full day, or even two full days. The stories he had heard about mirages shocked him too, and he wondered if mirages were really dreams or the imaginations of a warped mind. He couldn't imagine seeing crazy images dancing in the sky, and he couldn't imagine his tongue turning black for lack of water, either.

But in a strange way, unexplained almost, the prospect of seeing adventurous places like Santa Fe and California was so exciting that for hours at a stretch he was taken away from himself, into imaginings. He could imagine himself chasing and killing a buffalo, although he had never seen one. He had seen drawings of the mangy beast, and buffalo hides. They were much larger than steers he had seen, and they apparently smelled bad, too. He could scare himself to the point where his breath came short visualizing himself standing his ground, firing his musket at the monstrous hump-backed critter, and then jumping on it with a knife to cut its throat. He also wondered at the prospect of wild black bulls in the country beyond Santa Fe, and grizzly bears in California. He hoped he'd never come face-to-face with one of those angry black bulls, or a grizzly.

The days had dragged along slowly here at Fort Leavenworth, partly because the army had not kept him busy, which was attributed mostly to Colonel Allen's absence. Perhaps that's just the way army life was going to be. He hoped the days wouldn't drag on the trip west, and during the Battalion's occupation of California. If they did, the burden of being separated from Hannah and his children would be unbearable, and it almost seemed that already. He tried to picture what Hannah was doing right now, where her camp was, who was watching out for her, and how the children were. He had suffered from the ague and he suspected that some of his children were, too. Lizzy, especially, was sick when he left. He hoped he would dream again about Hannah tonight, as he had done nearly every night since his departure. He missed her sparkling brown eyes, her soft moist skin, the smell of her auburn brown hair, and especially her companionship.

Just below him he could see a wagon train out of Independence bound for Oregon and it reminded him of his own wagon train, when he trudged across Iowa with Hannah and his children. The optimism of these American emigrants amazed Robert; they were not dampened one bit by the extremely unsettled political situation in New Mexico, California, and Oregon. His eyes fixed on one settler in particular, because it reminded him of his own family. The settler had a bright red wagon overloaded with furniture, heavy farm implements, food, clothing, a chicken coop strapped on back, and heavy iron kettles dangling underneath. There was a sturdy wife and six children, too. One barelegged girl in a bonnet, astride an old mare, kept the milk cows moving. The young girl reminded him of Lizzy.

With a tear in his eye, Robert trudged back to his tent, now dwelling about the trails west that had carried trappers and other adventurers into the Rocky Mountains and beyond. Those trails were nothing more than parallel wheel ruts traced by wagons across the sod of the prairies, the rock and the rubble of mountain passes, and the sands of the western deserts. They were intermittent ruts at that; when they arrived at the bank of a river they stopped and then resumed on the other side, leaving the traveler to devise his own connection. He and the Battalion would follow those trails and ruts, and so would Hannah next spring, on her way to the Great Basin.

It was exciting to Robert to think that right here, in this very place along the Missouri River, was the westernmost edge of the formally constituted United States. Like Jesse Little had pointed out, California appeared on the map as a northern province of Mexico. Oregon country was a large tract of wilderness that extended north from California all the way up the Pacific Coast to Alaska, and from the Pacific Ocean in the west to an eastern boundary running from the Continental Divide in the Rocky Mountains. The families he'd just seen were emigrants, going out from their own country into what was really a foreign land, and an uncivilized one at that. They differed from the Mormons in that they weren't seeking religious freedom. But the emigrants and the Mormons were similar: both groups were to commence their farming and homemaking somewhere out west. Out west, where there was elbowroom, blacker soil, bluer skies, and a rosier future. It was said that Oregon couldn't be outdone in wheat, oats, rye, barley, buckwheat, peas, beans, turnips, cabbages, carrots, or even fat and healthy babies. He hoped that would be the case, too, where Brigham Young was taking the Church.

CHAPTER NOTES

The incident about young Private Davis is related in the book, *Saints in the Wilderness*, Volume 2, David R. Crockett (LDS Gems Press, Tucson, Arizona, 1997), pages 85-86. "With the idle time, Walter L. Davis had been drinking and got into a dispute with a member of his company and struck him in the face. One of the officers tried to break it up, but this enraged Davis. While in this rage, the company commander came up and ordered Davis to be taken to the guardhouse. He calmed down and went as ordered. David Pettigrew went to each tent to counsel against swearing and drinking."

It is, of course, fiction to believe that the soldier who struck Davis in the face was the character of this book, Robert Harris. But then—who knows?

21

Santa Fe, New Mexico

August 12, 1846

THE FIRST THING SERGEANT WALDO Peck and Private Bernard Bogart noticed about Santa Fe was that the central plaza was crowded with what was supposed to be the Mexican resistance army. A few of them were beating drums, accentuating the eerie atmosphere. Others stood rigidly displaying a collection of bows, arrows, lances, and antiquated muskets. By Peck's estimation, there were likely more than four thousand men. A hot late afternoon sun bore down upon them; there were only a few scraggly trees in the plaza and they offered no shade at all.

There were some fighters in the crowd, that was certain, and the sight of them put Peck and Bogart on edge.

Captain Philip St. George Cooke had commanded the last company to leave Fort Leavenworth on July sixth. He, however, with an escort of twelve dragoons, was the first of Kearny's army to enter Santa Fe, on assignment from Colonel Kearny. An American trader, James Magoffin, had come from Santa Fe to lead Cooke into the village. So had Senor Jose Gonzales of Chihuahua, an obese and shadowy figure. Gonzales favored capitulation and was prepared to say that to the governor.

Magoffin had warned Cooke and his dragoons that the governor of New Mexico, Manuel Armijo, had declared the entire territory under martial law and that he had rounded up an army.

The army was a large one, Peck concluded, but not a formidable one. Most of the Mexicans standing at attention in the square looked mean and ready to fight, but some looked like they'd run if someone accidentally discharged a musket or even a firecracker.

Magoffin had a reputation for drinking wine, making friends quickly, speaking fluent Spanish, and being on friendly terms with not only the governor but also all the leading men in New Mexico.

"Dern, I hope them greasers don't start shootin' now," said Bernard Bogart, one of the dragoons chosen to be part of the escort. His black horse hung its head, dead tired from the trip from Bent's Fort.

Peck and Bogart had left the Anglo world and were now entering the Hispanic world.

"Me, too," said Sergeant Peck. "I can't write stories about the war from six feet under the ground." Peck's stomach did a tumble, tied up with nerves as he surveyed the large crowd. He highly respected Cooke, a Virginian and a West Point graduate of 1827. Cooke had been patrolling the western frontier since 1829.

"But they ain't all greasers, looks like to me," Peck said. "There's Injuns, too." Half the men in the plaza were Pueblo Indians. The other half was a rag-tag militia made up of New Mexican farmers and merchants. There were also two or three hundred armed Mexican dragoons.

One-story adobe buildings surrounded the plaza, all practically hidden by the crowd of New Mexican men. On the east side were government offices, private homes, and a squalid, ruined house where the town council met. More adobe homes were strung out on the south side, too, along San Francisco Street. There were also stores rented by American traders, along with the military chapel of La Castrense, no doubt the handsomest building in town. There was another church on the west side of the plaza, the chapel of the Holy Trinity, and more adobe homes.

"Do ya suppose we'll have to kill Injuns, too?" Bogart asked.

"If they fight on the side of the greasers, we will," Peck promised.

The governor of New Mexico, Manuel Armijo, had placed the country under martial law when he heard of Kearny's approach, calling for its people to take up arms against the invaders. Armijo was successful in assembling an army consisting of a couple thousand Pueblo Indians, a thousand or so New Mexicans, and around three hundred Mexican dragoons. Armijo had a lot to fight for—one sixth interest in land grants that totaled nearly a million acres.

"Where's Governor Armijo?" Bogart asked, scanning the village.

Captain Cooke and Magoffin had already briefed his dragoons about Armijo. He was the best known of the Mexican governors in New Mexico, but he was no Spanish knight. Born into a rich Albuquerque family in 1793—a *mestizo* of Spanish, Mexican Indian, and Plains Indian stock—he grew up to be handsome and portly, arrogant and charming, quick-tempered and tough. Although he served three separate terms and proved to be a fine administrator and clever politician, he was not popular, especially with Americans.

In Cooke's view, Armijo was a tyrant, a monster of lust and greed, an enemy to Americans, and a coward. He had recently increased the duty to six hundred and twenty-five dollars per wagon from five hundred dollars, pocketing much of the money himself. His mistress was the most famous woman in town, Gertrudes Barcelo—known as *La Tules*—who ran a bar and gambling casino that stretched the length of Burro Alley. He, along with the Catholic priests, had already spread the rumor that American soldiers would rape women and brand men on the cheek like cattle. Many families had already abandoned their homes and fled to the mountains. One time, Magoffin had told Cooke and his dragoons, Armijo was determined to stop illegal fur trapping by Americans in Mexican territory. So one day American trappers impudently cleaned their contraband beaver pelts in the plaza in front of the governor's plaza, in full view of all Santa Fe. Armijo ordered his guard to seize the furs and arrest the trappers, but when the trappers began loading their guns,

Armijo became uneasy and ordered the guard to retreat. The trappers thus escaped with their furs and jeered Armijo as a coward.

"Probably in the governor's palace," Peck answered as he pointed. "That's where governors hang out." Peck suspected Armijo was trembling inside from the news that Armijo's three spies had brought to him, that Kearny's army was large and formidable.

Armijo had been in and out of office in Santa Fe almost as many times as Santa Anna had been in Mexico City.

"That's a governor's palace?" Bogart asked, eyeing a long single-story adobe apartment on the south side of the presidio near the plaza. It was longer than fifteen yoke of oxen plus two freight wagons. The presidio looked worse than the palace and he couldn't feature any soldiers actually staying in the ruins of the presidio. Stray chickens, cows, horses, burros, and donkeys wandered around aimlessly. Cooke had said he believed that there were probably no more than two hundred and fifty operable muskets in Santa Fe, and usually fewer than a hundred trained presidial soldiers.

Captain Cooke had dismounted and before Peck could answer, Cooke summoned him to his side. "Get your pencil and paper out, Sergeant Peck. I want you to accompany Mr. Magoffin and myself as we visit the governor."

Armijo served not only as governor, but as general as well.

Cooke had been sick the previous day, the victim of bad turtle soup prepared by Magoffin's steward. Torpid with medicinal opium, Cooke had spent that day in Magoffin's carriage, unable to arouse more than a flicker of interest in the town of Pecos when they had passed through. He revived sufficiently to let his eyes scout Apache Pass, the gateway to Santa Fe, but the effort was too much. He spent much of last evening under a bush where he suffered until midnight, when he was coaxed into accepting some claret from Magoffin. Today he was nearly his old soldier self.

Peck let a happy look cross his face. "Yes, sir!" He had studied the situation enough to know that Governor Armijo had been placed in a difficult position at the outbreak of the war. New Mexico's only financial support—its only business—was the trade with the Americans. Yet, as a general in the Mexican army, Armijo was obliged to fight Kearny's army if ordered to do so. He had known for more than a month that an American army was camped at Bent's Fort.

As Peck turned to enter the so-called governor's mansion, he reeled in horror. Between the more than two-dozen wooden pillars of the building was a string of Indian ears, weathered by the sun. Armijo must be a hard character, Peck thought to himself. Especially if he killed all them Indians himself.

The interior of the palace was not much better than the exterior, in Peck's opinion. The doorway led the three men into the governor's office: a small, plain room about sixteen feet square with two calico-covered sofas against the walls. Most of the earthen floor was covered with a cheap homespun carpet; elsewhere the dirt floor produced an unusual sheen—the dirt had been mixed with animal blood to pack it tight. Governor Armijo was seated at his desk with eight military and civil officials standing behind him. On the wall was a bill of lading from an American steamship company and dinner plates of various American manufacturers, indicating to Peck that the governor had a passionate interest in trade with the United States.

Armijo was large for a Mexican, and not bad-looking either although a little portly. He had a wide, high forehead, penetrating dark eyes, and appeared to be around fifty years of age. He wore a blue frock coat with a rolling collar, general's shoulder straps, blue striped trousers with gold lace, and a red sash. As he let his dark eyes survey the American intruders, Armijo remained stone silent.

Captain Cooke did not flinch. He pulled a letter from his leather satchel and spread it on the table. "By virtue of the annexation of Texas, I have come on behalf of General Kearny to take possession of New Mexico."

Magoffin translated the text, making certain there was no room for ambiguity.

Peck knew Cooke's words were well chosen and designed to deflate the governor. In 1841, three hundred fifty well-armed Texans had arrived on New Mexico's eastern border to capture Santa Fe in the name of the Republic of Texas, then at war with Mexico. Armijo met them on the eastern frontier, professed friendship, and persuaded them to lay down their arms. Without their guns the Texans were helpless. Armijo tied them together and sent them on foot to Mexico for the disposition of the president. Even though that incident happened several years earlier, Armijo had to view Kearny's approaching army as an act of revenge, Peck thought.

Although disappointment was etched deeply in Armijo's face, he remained polite. In subdued tones he declined to relinquish control of Santa Fe and New Mexico, but in the same breath he offered to negotiate. "Our negotiations shall be in private."

"Mr. Magoffin must be with me," Cooke said coldly.

"Agreed," Armijo replied coolly.

"You're well aware of the strength of General Kearny's army?" Cooke asked.

The governor's voice turned dejected. "I'm told more than fifteen hundred soldiers."

"And more on the way from Fort Leavenworth," Cook said with a note of pride. He went on to describe the five hundred foot soldiers of the Mormon Battalion and Colonel Price's four hundred mounted cavalrymen, and the fact that the president of the United States was prepared to send more if necessary.

Peck watched Armijo melt.

"Nevertheless, we shall negotiate," the governor said.

Negotiate what? Peck wondered. If Magoffin's assessment was correct, and he was sure it was, the vast majority of New Mexicans waiting in the plaza would much rather be citizens of the U.S. than citizens of Mexico. Despite the influx of goods from the Santa Fe Trail, the wealth had not trickled down to them, and the central government in Mexico City had been shaky ever since the revolution that brought Mexico's independence from Spain.

Two hours later, Peck paced back and forth around the plaza waiting for developments. Nothing of consequence happened until a New Mexican rider galloped in from the direction of Bent's Fort. The rider turned out to be one of Armijo's messengers. Taking a chance, Peck followed the messenger into the adobe palace. Peck didn't speak Spanish, but he understood perfectly. General Kearny's army was advancing.

The governor ignored Peck's presence and jumped to his feet, fear written on his face. He embraced Magoffin almost in tears. "For God's sake, ride out right now and stop Kearny. If you don't, the Americans will overrun Santa Fe within a week."

"Sorry," Magoffin answered, taking a firm stand on the side of the United States of America. "That is impossible."

Armijo fell into uncontrollable despair. He announced that negotiations were over and sent the messenger out again, asking him to bring his second-in-command, Colonel Diego Archuleta.

For a while Peck strode through the streets of Santa Fe with Cooke, Magoffin, and Gonzales. Cooke had recovered from his food poisoning. He kept casting side-glances at the ordnance in view. As a show, Armijo ordered his ragtag army to deafen the plaza with all the noise trumpets and drums could make. Cooke rode past the governor's mansion again. Armijo stood there, trying to look defiant.

"I'll call again in a week," Cooke yelled out.

As Peck rode with Cooke back toward Kearny's advancing army, he felt a glow.

"What do you think Armijo will do now?" he asked.

"He has only two choices, as we outlined in the meeting," Cooke said. "He can fight or surrender. Kearny's made that plain."

"If you were Armijo, what would you do?" Peck asked. If Armijo surrendered, at that instant the United States would obtain the empire of the Southwest.

"First, I'd plaster proclamations on every adobe wall in Santa Fe and all the surrounding villages, calling upon New Mexicans to make a last ditch effort against the Americans. Then I'd take my army and deploy it at Raton Pass."

Peck pulled at his chin, thinking. The pass was the most difficult part of the Santa Fe Trail between Bent's Fort and Santa Fe, guarding the approach to a New Mexican village known as Las Vegas. The approach to it was steep and difficult, and the elevation at the top was high enough to make both men and animals gasp for breath. Freight wagons had to be hauled up by double or triple team, making only two miles a day. The road over the pass was around twenty miles long, requiring a week's travel for wagons. It was the perfect spot for Indian ambushes. And it would be the perfect spot for Armijo's army to make a stand. It was his only chance for his dwarf army to deal with the giant force commanded by Kearny. It was at the crest of Raton Pass where a Mexican once maintained a small shop where ox-carts and wagons were greased before they made the descent to the New Mexico plateau. Americans began calling Mexicans "greasers" from then on.

"I didn't sign up to get killed in Raton Pass," Bogart said suddenly. "I want to shoot greasers, not the other way around."

Cooke smiled at the private's insecurity. "That may be the place Armijo makes his stand."

"Really?"

"There's one other scenario," Cooke added. "Armijo may make his will out and make preparations for his escape to Old Mexico."

22

❧

Fort Leavenworth, Kansas

August 13, 1846

DANIEL BROWETT LET HIS GAZE RAKE across the Kansas prairie. His company and two others, to the lively music of the Battalion bands, were taking their first steps toward Santa Fe. He wondered what he would find there— a city captured by General Kearny, or a city filled with determined resistance on the part of the New Mexicans.

Daniel felt more than a little hurt that the only people watching him march away were the other two Mormon Battalion companies, a few army regulars, some of the staff, and several jeering Missouri volunteers. The entire garrison had assembled to see Kearny off, with several bands playing, homemade flags waving, and several American flags waving from the crowd. Today the garrison was curious but unmoved, consisting mostly of Colonel Price's Second Regiment of Missouri Mounted Volunteers.

The three companies of the Mormon Battalion were marching south where they would find the Santa Fe Trail, and then turn west toward Council Grove, Pawnee Fork, the Cimarron Cutoff, Bent's Fort, and Santa Fe. Companies C and D were scheduled to leave tomorrow. Their captains needed more time to rig up for the trip.

"Do you wish Hannah and your children were here?" Daniel asked Robert as Company E marched out briskly. Each company carried its own colors. The American flag waved in the background, at the fort's parade grounds.

"Yes and no," Robert answered. "I'd hate for them to be here, subject to more persecution from the Missourians. But I'd like to be able to give them all a big hug."

Daniel felt the same way about Elizabeth, Harriet, and Moroni.

"I'm thinking about the contrast to our Battalion boys and the other soldiers of Kearny's army that left here a few weeks ago," Daniel said.

"I've thought about that, too," Robert said.

First off, every Battalion in Kearny's group had a commander. The commander of the Mormon Battalion was in the hospital, with some question as to whether or not he would actually live.

Kearny had departed with much more than his army of sixteen hundred men. There had been fifteen hundred wagons, three thousand seven hundred draft mules, fifteen thousand cattle, more than four hundred horses, and an assortment of cannons, rifles, pistols, and wagonloads of ammunition. The Mormon Battalion, just about all on foot, had just a few dozen wagons, numbered slightly more than five hundred men, and only the weapons each man carried with him—a musket and a bayonet. Daniel carried his flintlock over his right shoulder and a white-leather cartridge belt draped over his left shoulder. The bayonet and its scabbard were attached to another white belt that fit over his right shoulder. He carried his canteen on a strap that went over his left shoulder and a knapsack of daily rations that went over his right shoulder.

Kearny had only one enemy to worry about: the Mexicans. The Battalion had two: Mexicans and Missourians. Some of Colonel Price's Missouri volunteers had left two days ago. Others were said to be ready to leave in another day or two. And Price and his staff would leave shortly after that. The Mormon Battalion would be virtually surrounded by Missourians, some in front, and some in the rear.

Kearny had wagonload after wagonload of provisions, consisting of flour, salt pork, bacon, dried beef, and oil, calculated to be enough to sustain his army on the seven hundred-mile journey to Santa Fe. The Battalion had barely enough provisions to last but a few days. The command at Fort Leavenworth had promised to send more provisions with C and D Companies, however.

Although there were some in Kearny's army who were dressed in civilian clothes, most wore the uniform of their local Missouri militias. Daniel's old

Nauvoo Legion uniform had been left behind, probably still hanging in his home on the outskirts of Nauvoo unless it had been taken as a souvenir by its new owners, whoever that might be, or cast out or burned. Daniel wore the same blue flannel shirt he had worn the day he left Council Bluffs and a pair of brown woolsey pants. His eyes were shielded from the hot sun by a loose-fitting, dusty brown felt hat. His wooden three-pint canteen was already seeping water. Some of the men had chosen tin canteens and yet others rubber ones, although rubber, it was said, caused the water to taste funny. His haversack contained his daily rations: twenty ounces of beef, eighteen ounces of flour, two ounces of beans, two ounces of sugar, one ounce of green coffee, and a little salt, vinegar, and soap. His knapsack contained a red flannel shirt, another pair of half-worn pants, and personal items such as his toothbrush, soap, razor, and a towel.

Daniel did have a new pair of leather boots, however, with loose toe space for walking. They were high tops, coming halfway up his knee. He suspected they would be worn out long before he got to California. There were a few teamsters who worked for the post sutler following the Battalion, their wagons stuffed with things to sell to both the soldiers and the Indians, but they had room for only a few boots. The sutler teamsters were a mixed lot, a couple of them former buffalo hunters, and one of them a Missourian.

"I guess you look like a soldier," Robert kidded Daniel as they marched out, "but from the looks of things you won't make it to the crossing to find the

Santa Fe Trail."

"I'll make it farther than you," Daniel remarked. "You're the one who's been sick, not me."

"Not if a snake gets you," Robert said.

Yesterday a rattlesnake had bitten a soldier by the name of John Spindle. Levi Hancock had promptly split the wound open with a knife, sucked out the poison, given the man a blessing, and Spindle was in formation today.

Daniel was walking behind a wagon and a dozen other men and didn't answer. He was daydreaming about Elizabeth now.

"A snake is more apt to bite the men up front, not us," said John Cox.

Robert marched to the music of the fifers for a few minutes and then said, "Well, watch for Indians then."

The mention of Indians woke Daniel from his momentary daydream. He hated Indians, partly because for four months, ever since he'd left Nauvoo, the fear of them had kept him from getting a good night's sleep. In his weeks and months on the plains in Iowa he never closed his eyes without expecting to open them and find some huge Indian getting ready to poke him with something sharp. Most of the Indians he had actually seen had been scrawny little men, but it didn't mean the huge one who haunted his sleep wasn't out there waiting in some kind of ambush.

"Talk about snakes again, not Indians," Daniel pleaded. "Or even Missourians."

His plea went on deaf ears.

"What did you think of what the veterans around the fort said about Indians?" John asked Daniel.

"In what regard?" Daniel said.

"That Indians around these parts consider soldiers as men who sold themselves to die, and consequently are afraid of nothing," John said.

"Well, that might be true for a few of Kearny's dragoons, but that description doesn't fit me," Daniel said as he shuddered from head to toe. "Keep me away from Indians."

"Do you think we'll see Arapaho or Comanche first?" Robert Pixton wondered.

"It'll be interesting because the Santa Fe Trail crosses both their hunting grounds," said Richard Slater.

Daniel tried to plug his ears. Up north, the government was making a good effort to constrain the Sioux. But not so here on the southern plains. Daniel was headed straight for the Arapaho and Comanche, and he knew it.

"Do you think its true that the Comanche have killed and tortured more whites than any other Indian in the West?" John Cox asked.

"That's what they say," Robert said. "They're specialists in pain and cruelty."

"And they're specialists in kidnapping women and children, too," Slater said.

"That's enough, boys," Daniel whimpered. "No more talk about Indians. Think of what you're gonna have for supper. Think of your families back at

Winter Quarters. Think about poor Colonel Allen in the hospital."

"Colonel Allen doesn't stand much of a chance of recuperating in this hot weather, does he?" Robert asked after a while when the men had quit talking about Indians. The dust was kicking up from the trail, a thin, tan film settling over man and beast.

"They say he doesn't look good," Daniel replied. The five Mormon Battalion captains had been able to visit with the colonel in the hospital yesterday. "But he's a fighter. And he's a friend of the Mormons now. We need to continue our prayers for him. I want him to lead us all the way to California."

From his hospital bed, Colonel Allen had instructed the Mormon Battalion to proceed to Council Grove—an agreeable point where trade caravans traditionally stopped. It was the last place on the outbound trail where hardwood could be obtained and wagons repaired. There was a blacksmith shop there, and a small settlement. The colonel said he would catch up to the Battalion there, traveling by wagon.

Robert hooded his eyes and looked west. "How far's California?" The afternoon sun was almost blinding.

Daniel had studied a map. "Twice as far as New Orleans was to Nauvoo."

Robert swallowed his astonishment. "That was a snap compared to this trip. We were on a half-reliable steamboat, with plenty of water all around us. I hear the water's gonna get scarce after a few days on this trip."

"The colonel says were gonna take the southern route to Santa Fe,"

Daniel said.

"I didn't know we had a choice," Robert said.

"In about a month and a half we'll reach the Cimarron Cutoff," Daniel said. "That's where the Santa Fe Trail splits. The best route goes north to Bent's Fort, and then south to Santa Fe. The other route takes you through the deadly Cimarron Desert."

"I hear there's no water along the Cimarron route," John Cox said.

"You're right," said Daniel

"And I hear some of the provision wagons have already been sent to Bent's Fort ahead of us," Pixton said. He was the cook for Daniel and Robert's mess.

"What'll we do for provisions in the meantime?" Robert asked. "Seems to me there exists the possibility for a foul-up."

"I don't know," Daniel answered. Army life was new to him, too.

Henry Eagles stood in the shade of the headquarters building, watching the Mormon Battalion disappear over the southern prairie. He hadn't bothered telling Robert goodbye; he knew he would have the misfortune of seeing him on the trail. As a teamster in Colonel Price's regiment, he was scheduled to leave Fort Leavenworth within a week. With Price's soldiers on horseback and everyone else in a wagon, he would overtake Robert within a few days, two weeks at the most. And with Colonel Allen lying in bed sick, administered to by Dr. Sanderson, who knows what might happen?

"Do you miss them scoops?" Colonel Price asked Henry later in the day as the colonel drilled some of his dragoons. The weather had cooled down just a pinch.

"Not in the least," Henry replied. "They have their ways of putting you on a guilt trip. My brother-in-law wanted to dunk me in the river to wash my sins away. I don't have any sins to wash away, I reckon." Henry was almost on a first-name basis with the colonel, and Henry called him "Old Pap Price."

"Neither do I," Price said with an odd chuckle. And then he cursed the Mormons. "How's the quartermaster doing with the supply wagons for the Mormons?"

"Assigning them to the greenest greenhorns," Henry answered. "How's Colonel Allen doing?"

"Worse," Price said, chuckling again. "Much worse."

23

Pueblo de Los Angeles

August 13, 1846

MAJOR JOHN C. FREMONT HAD JUST reached a conclusion so stunning that it made his heart jump. Kearny's army wasn't needed in California. Pueblo de Los Angeles, the Mexican capital of California, had just fallen. So had San Diego three weeks earlier. The American flag not only flew in both places, but in Monterey, Yerba Buena, and Sutter's Fort as well. California was in American hands.

Now that it was over, Fremont swelled in pride and patted himself on the back. He had played a successful part in the drama. He had been the first to hoist up the American flag anywhere in the vast territory. That happened way last February when he and his sixty-two men threw up battlements in the

Gavilan Mountains near Monterey. Even though a Mexican commander by the name of Jose Maria Castro ousted him three days later, the stage had been set for hostilities. But in May and June, Fremont had been instrumental in capturing Sutter's Fort and Sonoma, which led to the Bear Flag revolt and the establishment of the independent California Republic on July fourth. By late July, Commodore Robert Stockton had recognized Fremont's ragtag followers as the California Battalion, a horse cavalry of sorts. By the end of July he and Stockton had captured San Diego. And to top it all off, today he and Stockton had captured the Mexican capital of California, Pueblo de Los Angeles. Not one shot had been fired. Not one drop of blood had been shed.

It all seemed so simple, so easy.

"You just wait," said Kit Carson, one of his mountain-man ragtag soldiers, as Fremont's men set up camp next to the river. "There'll be a big prize for what you've done here. I wouldn't be surprised if Commodore Stockton appoints you to command all the military forces in California. And I wouldn't be surprised if he eventually names you the governor. He likes you. He promoted you from captain to major almost on the spot, only a few days after he met you."

Carson was tolerant of the other men but careful to keep himself a bit apart from them. That was one of the reasons he still had his scalp. He had a taste for fish and looked forward to trying the river.

Fremont nodded and smiled in appreciation. Most men would have felt sorely at a loss, but the idea of being governor strongly appealed to him. He had plenty of pride and not a little vanity. The promotion had come only three weeks ago, aboard the *Savannah* in Monterey Harbor. Commodore Stockton had liked Fremont's aggressive successes in California. Fremont, in turn, liked Stockton. He was an aggressive nationalist, like him, who believed Americans could do anything they deemed necessary. Both of them believed whatever was good for the United States had to be good for the rest of the world. Fremont had the sense right then and there that he and Stockton's relationship would be one filled with energy, self-belief, and a never-say-die attitude. They believed action to be the key to success. Their quick capture of San Diego and Los Angles proved this theory to be correct.

The camp spot was in the open; very few trees stood between Fremont and the walls of the Government House where Stockton and his men were quartered. Fremont had grown to love the California weather. Here it was, the middle of August, and the temperature was only in the low eighties and the humidity was very low. In Missouri, the home state of his father-in-law, Senator Thomas Hart Benton, both the heat and humidity would be stifling today. Same in Washington, D. C.

Fremont's eyes lit up at Carson's suggestion. Governor of California? Senator Benton would be proud of him. So would his wife, Jessie, and his two daughters. The appointment might springboard him to a seat in the United States Senate someday, perhaps even to the White House.

"What if Commodore Stockton wants the governorship for himself?" Fremont asked Carson as his men began digging fire pits. "Or General

Kearny?"

"They've got bigger fish to fry," Carson replied. A reddish mustache drooped over the sides of his lips and auburn hair fell down the back of his neck. "The commodore will have to take his men back to the ship soon and resume his patrol of the coast. I predict Kearny will tire of California when he gets here and want to get back either to Fort Leavenworth or Washington, D. C."

Fremont was amazed at Carson's astuteness. As a guide, he could sniff out trails through western mountain passes and he could sniff out Indians better than a dog. As a friend, he was always paying him compliments. *Governor Fremont.* The ultimate compliment.

The first time Fremont met Carson was in 1842, by accident, just prior to his departure from St. Louis on his first exploring expedition to the West. Fremont had tried to hire a reliable guide, but he could not find the man he wanted. Carson's appearance on the steamboat *Rowena* seemed like divine providence. Fremont was immediately impressed by the fact that Carson seemed to be cut out of different cloth than the usual run of mountain men. Carson was not tall, only five-six, but his shoulders were broad and his deep barrel chest heavily muscled. His gray-blue eyes, quick and piercing, looked honest and he spoke with frank words, albeit in a quiet and unassuming way. Fremont hired him on the spot for a hundred dollars a month.

One of Commodore Stockton's marine officers came marching toward Fremont and Carson. "My commander would like to visit with you at the

Government House."

Fremont's jaw dropped. *So soon? Who will I appoint as my assistants?* He thought of his blue uniform, packed in a truck at Sutter's Fort. He wished he had it now.

Minutes later, Major John C. Fremont sat staring at Commodore Stockton. Swallowing with astonishment, Fremont thought of the events earlier in the day. His men had met Stockton's army on the outskirts of Los Angeles about four o'clock. The two commands combined as they marched to the town square. He and Stockton rode in front, and just behind them came Stockton's brass band and all the others—the carts, the marching men, and the men on horseback. As they entered the town the citizens looked at their conquerors with a mixture of anxiety and curiosity, but there was no fighting. With horses dancing back and forth in the dusty streets, and with uniformed marines and sailors trying to keep some semblance of order in their ranks, the invaders headed for the main plaza. Here, the men came to attention and the band played "Hail Columbia." Then the Stars and Stripes were unfurled and run up the flagpole.

"Good evening, Major Fremont," Stockton said, pointing to a chair. "There're a few things I'd like to discuss with you."

"Yes, sir," Fremont said, his eyes alive in anticipation.

For a brief moment Fremont compared himself with Stockton. Stockton was in full uniform complete with epaulets and an ostrich plume hat. He was in a deerskin hunting shirt, blue cloth pants, and moccasins—all nearly worn out, hardly the dress of a governor. Instead of a hat he wore a light cotton handkerchief bound tightly around his head. Stockton was clean-shaven; he had a full beard. At fifty-one, Stockton was much older; he was only thirty-three. Stockton's army, true, consisted of motley, tender-footed sailors, but it was much more an army than his. Stockton marched three hundred fifty men into Los Angeles. At the head of Stockton's column had come the brass band followed by his marines and sailors, four-oxen carts pulling quarter-deck guns, carts loaded with ammunition and supplies, and carts holding Stockton's officers and medical staffs. Fremont's force of one hundred twenty was an unusual mixture of mountain men, voyageurs, and Delaware and Osos Indians. Fremont rode a Mexican sorrel horse given to him by Don Juan Bandini in San Diego, its mane and tail decorated with green ribbons.

"We need to impress upon the minds of the people here that the Americans are in control now," Stockton said, raising his bushy eyebrows. "As soon as possible I want to issue a proclamation to be read to everyone."

Fremont smiled through his thick, dark beard. This was a sign that the commodore trusted him. Quickly the two men discussed ideas. They expected loyalty from local citizens. Anyone caught with firearms outside his home would be deported to Mexico. Thieves were to serve hard labor on public works. Everyone was to obey a curfew from ten o'clock at night until sunrise with no exceptions to the rule.

"Within a few days," Stockton said, "I'll need to withdraw my naval forces and go back to my ship. Mexican privateers will probably prey upon merchant vessels in the Pacific Ocean, and I'll have to protect them. After that, I plan to sail south, land at Acapulco, and attack Mexico City."

Carson was right about Stockton getting back to his ship.

"How many additional men do you need to hold key positions on land?" Stockton asked.

Fremont again thought of the ease in which they had captured Los Angeles and San Diego. "Three hundred should do."

"I'll give the matter some serious thought," Stockton said. "Before I leave, I'll give you a letter authorizing you to raise some more men for your California Battalion. I'd say we need to leave fifty men here in Los Angeles, fifty each in Monterey and Yerba Buena, and less than that in Santa Barbara and San Diego. That would leave a hundred men under your command to be on call for any place within California."

Fremont began thinking of the type of men he could round up to enlist: Americans who had settled here, Mexicans totally loyal to the California Republic, and a handful of friendly Indians.

"If you keep things under control, you'll earn the governorship."

This time Fremont smiled big, beyond boyish gratification. He felt as though he were sitting on top of the world.

"Report to me on October twenty-fifth in Yerba Buena," Stockton ordered. "By then I'll be able to sweep the coast and you'll have your men garrisoned in all the key places. I'll make the appointment official there. Whom do you recommend as your secretary?"

Fremont had an immediate answer. "Lieutenant Gillespie."

Fremont had never heard of Lt. Archibald H. Gillespie of the United States Marine Corps until early May. Fremont and his expedition made up mostly of mountain men were camped on the southern end of the Upper Klamath Lake in Oregon territory. Two messengers rode in from Sutter's Fort in the middle of the night to let them know that a young military officer by the name of Gillespie, only thirty-three, was about a long day's ride behind them. Gillespie had an important message from the United States government for Fremont's ears only.

Sensing the message was critical, Fremont rode off at dawn, taking Carson, four other mountain men, and four Delaware Indian scouts with him. He didn't want to have Gillespie killed by Indians before he delivered the message. Weeks earlier newly arrived emigrants from the States had asked for his help in protecting them from hostile Indians. Fremont didn't take part, but he allowed Kit Carson and most of his men to become involved in a vicious killing spree against local Indian tribes. Nearly two hundred were killed and the survivors had taken cover in the hills. No doubt in Fremont's mind, Indians would be out there seeking revenge against any white man.

Gillespie had quite a story to tell when Fremont found him that evening camped by the Klamath River. He was not an ordinary officer, in Fremont's view. Gillespie's orders had been cut by four men: His father-in-law, Senator Benton; Secretary of Navy Bancroft; Secretary of State Buchanan; and the President of the United States, James K. Polk.

And what orders they were. Simply stated, he was to dress as a civilian, travel to Mexico City, assess the war situation and the mood, and then travel to California and report his findings to the highest ranking members of the American military he could find.

Fremont remembered how Gillespie's report had alarmed him. Gillespie had traveled by ship across the Gulf of Mexico and by stagecoach across the Sierra Madre Oriental to Mexico City. The turmoil there was staggering. President Jose Herrera's government was toppled right under Gillespie's nose by the revolutionary forces of General Mariano Paredes. Paredes was openly anti-American and the hostility toward all foreigners, especially Americans, was as thick as bread pudding. The new government had been offended by President Polk's offer to buy Mexican territory north of the Rio Grande for forty million dollars. In the Mexican view, Texas had been stolen. Newspapers called for war against the Americans, angry that American troops were not far from the Mexican border. Angry speeches in the capital city were a daily affair. The central theme was always the same: Mexico had to defend her honor against the aggressive Americans.

After a month of seeing all this, Gillespie had been convinced that war was inevitable. As he fled the country, he traveled northwest across the great central plateau and saw the first steps toward war as Mexican troops marched northward toward the Texas border. Gillespie followed steep roads and trails in and out of the barranca country and emerged at Mazatlan, a key Pacific port. Here he observed elements of the British fleet. It was not a token naval force.

It was a power to be reckoned with. Gillespie feared the British were going to help defend Mexico from the Americans. Gillespie's trip aboard a ship took him to the Sandwich Islands and then to California.

After hearing Gillespie's report, Fremont's concern about Indians was confirmed that night in their camp near the Klamath River. As he drifted off to sleep, Kit Carson and another scout awakened him. There were noises from another part of the camp, like an ax striking something. An investigation revealed that one of Fremont's men had been split wide open with a tomahawk. Another of his men was making the last sounds of life as blood spurted out of the many wounds he had received from sharp, iron arrowheads. As he made these discoveries, the whole camp came under attack. Before it was over, one additional man had been killed and others wounded, one-fourth of his number. But they had repulsed the Indians. Gillespie recognized one of the dead Indians to be the same Indian who had given him a salmon at the outlet of the lake two days earlier. Kit Carson flew into a rage, grabbed a hatchet, and knocked the dead Indian's head to pieces. The next day, Fremont and his men found the Indians who attacked them, killed two and wounded many others, before they escaped again into the woods.

Fremont shook himself back to the present. Gillespie had become a good friend during these past three months, even becoming part of his California Battalion. At this moment Gillespie was in San Diego with a force of fifty men, firmly in control, he believed, of the small port. Gillespie's courage and self-pride impressed him. He had proved to be resourceful, brave, and very fluent in Spanish—a great asset. He could make a great secretary; together they could set the wheels in motion to make California stable and apply for statehood. Gillespie may have been right about his assessment of the war with Mexico, but in Fremont's opinion, the battlefront would be along the Texas-Mexico border, and deep within Mexico's interior when the United States invaded, not here in California. San Diego and Los Angles had proved that.

"It seems a waste to have General Kearny bring his entire army to California," Fremont told Stockton.

"I think you're right," Stockton agreed as he devoured a desert of sugar cakes. "He could split his forces and send most of them to the front in Texas where they'll be needed. If he brought just one Battalion of men to California, that's all we'd need. Just enough to put down what's remaining of the rebels."

Fremont gave Stockton a quizzical glance. "Do you think Governor Pico and General Castro are still on the run?"

Pio Pico had been the Mexican governor of California, a man who had preferred British to American rule if it came down to that. Pico had been vocal for years, complaining about "Yankee hordes" pouring into his province. Anticipating a jump in land values, however, Pico had given large grants to friends earlier in the year. Fremont worried about those friends; they might still be loyal to the now former governor.

Jose Maria Castro was a self-appointed military chief who had ruled from Monterey in the north. He had been at sword's point with Pico over control of the treasury and customhouse at Monterey, almost to the point of civil war.

After Fremont's moves in northern California, Castro removed himself to Los Angeles, mended his fences with Pico, and tried to put together an army to resist the Americans. But as Stockton and Fremont approached, he warned Pico that he could muster no more than a hundred poorly armed men and was thinking of quitting the country. On August tenth, both leaders and key supporters fled south, while the rest of their forces dispersed to their homes.

"If they're smart they are," Stockton answered. He could see no way that Governor Pico or General Castro could stir up the Californios against the Americans.

Fremont laughed.

"What do you recommend we do with the governor's brother, General Pico?" Stockton asked. "He's begging for clemency."

General Andres Pico had been captured in Los Angeles without so much as firing a single shot. In Fremont's opinion, General Pico was a coward. He proved that fact two weeks ago during the invasion of San Diego. General Pico ran away with his Mexican lancers, driving a herd of horses ahead of them. This afternoon, as Stockton and Fremont's combined army marched into San Diego, he meekly surrendered.

Fremont laughed. "Give him the clemency he's asking for. Send him back to Mexico. He's such a coward that he won't be a danger in future battles."

General Pico had an army of Mexican lancers that could pose a problem if Pico rallied them.

"I'll spare his life if he'll promise to lay down his arms and not take them up again in California," Stockton concluded, a hostile expression on his face.

Fremont nodded his agreement. "If he paints up for war again we'll annihilate him."

"I need to send word to President Polk about developments here. And a message to General Kearny," Stockton added.

"I'll send Kit Carson," Fremont said. His eyebrows went up with pride and delight. "He knows how to get through desert country with limited supplies and how to avoid hostile Indians."

This idea pleased Stockton. "Give me a day or two to prepare a detailed report for the president and the secretary of the Navy."

Fremont began thinking of whom to send with Carson. He would need a dozen or so men and a string of about fifty mules to carry supplies, baggage, and enough corn to serve as fodder in the long stretches of arid country that would have to be crossed.

Carson would not only report the news of victory and conquest to Kearny, but to the whole nation as well.

CHAPTER NOTES

Yerba Buena, a short time later, was renamed San Francisco. Yerba Buena is Spanish, meaning good herb.

24

Las Vegas, New Mexico

August 15, 1846

PRIVATE BERNARD BOGART NUDGED HIS black horse into formation with hundreds of other dragoons near the village plaza of Las Vegas, a primitive agriculture settlement of about a hundred dwellings. There were plenty of corncribs and pigpens, too, surrounded by irrigated fields and livestock pastures. Flocks of sheep grazed in the dry hills.

"Dern," Bogart said with a shake of his head to Sergeant Peck. "I wish these greasers would've put up a fight. It don't seem right taking this territory without firin' a shot."

The sun shone with a dazzling brightness. Bogart watched as the guidons and colors of each squadron, regiment, and Battalion of Kearny's army were for the first time unfurled. Bogart's black horse seemed to take courage from the bright array. Trumpets blared, echoing against the hills.

"Me, too," Peck said at first with a shake of his curly head. And then the rationality of being a newspaperman took over. "But I suppose a bloodless victory by the terror of arms is better than one provided by the loss of life."

"But dern it, I didn't get to shoot even one greaser," Bogart replied. He was beginning to wonder if the trip was worth it, or even his enlistment.

Peck tipped his hat toward the mountains. "Maybe they'll fight us at Raton Pass." He had described to Bogart the four thousand men he had seen in the town square the day Peck accompanied Captain Cooke into Santa Fe.

Bogart had felt excited at the prospect of battle as the dragoons reached a gorge outside the village where Armijo supposedly was waiting. His black horse had broken into a brisk trot with the other horses, and then into a full gallop, charging at the gorge. But Armijo had evacuated the vicinity several days earlier, deciding at the last moment not to defend Las Vegas.

"Good," Bogart said. "That's why I enlisted."

Peck smiled. "We'll see."

"Look at Kearny," Bogart said. "He's wearing his general's stars."

"It's his reward for taking New Mexico," Peck said. "It was pre-arranged."

Kearny, who stood atop the roof of a yellow adobe building that overlooked the small and dirty plaza, indeed wore his new insignia. He could be seen taking out his notes and preparing to address his audience of awe-struck Mexican farmers and ranchers, dressed in serapes and sombreros. Their wives and children had been concealed among rocks and trees near the village, just in case. For the past twenty years they had lived in peace, finding a ready market among weary wagoners of the Santa Fe Trail for their fresh vegetables, fruit, grain, and meat. Theirs was the first settlement of any note between Missouri and Santa Fe. Yesterday it had been part of Mexico. Today, the Americans were in control.

Las Vegas was typical of New Mexican settlements; it had taken shape around a rectangular plaza, faced on all four sides by one-story, flat-roofed structures with thick walls made of adobe bricks. Bogart could see a small adobe church on the west side of the plaza—Roman Catholic, not Mormon.

Peck pointed to the church. "The Mormons'll probably try to convert these greasers when they get here," Bogart said.

"It's better to convert than to kill," Peck said. "Now that the United States is takin' over New Mexico, the greasers will have freedom of religion. The Catholics can't impose on them any more."

Above them, on the roof, Kearny drew a heavy breath and unfolded his notes. With him were several of his own officers including Colonel Doniphan, two Las Vegas militia leaders, and Juan de Dios Maese, the *alcalde* or mayor. Worry lines on the forehead of the forty-six-year-old mayor were deepening. All his military leaders were wringing their hands, and an odd quietness settled over them.

Kearny began his speech, obviously trying to take a grip on the reality that he was almost in Santa Fe. "Mayor and the people of New Mexico: I have come among you by the orders of my government to take possession of your country, and extend over it the laws of the United States," he said, puffing out his chest to the point he almost popped the buttons off his blue uniform. He was reading words prepared for him by Doniphan, whose profession was an attorney.

To the consternation of the New Mexicans, soldiers of Kearny's Army of the West applauded loudly. They had taken the first step to conquer New Mexico, and they had done it without the Mormon Battalion and without Price's mounted regiment.

"We consider New Mexico to be part of the territory of the United States," Kearny went on. "We come amongst you as friends—not as enemies; as protectors—not as conquerors."

Bogart let his gaze scan the southwest horizon, toward Santa Fe. President Polk had encouraged Kearny to take it without spilling blood. Armijo was on the run and maybe wouldn't even defend Raton Pass. Kearny would get his glory, but he, Bogart, might have to go home without shooting a single Mexican.

Kearny's smile was wide as he spoke to the New Mexicans. "I absolve you from all allegiance to the Mexican government, and from all obedience to General Armijo. He is no longer your governor; I am your governor."

He paused, seemingly to let this sink in. Peck assumed that Kearny was also thinking of the speech he would have to make in another two months, following their conquest of California. Kearny would have to announce himself as governor of that territory also, by written authority from the President of the United States.

Now that he was governor of New Mexico, Kearny began making promises. "Those of you who remain peaceably at home, attending to their crops and herds, shall be protected by me in their property, their persons, and their religion; and not a pepper, nor an onion, shall be disturbed or taken by my troops without pay, or without consent of the owner. But he who is found in arms against me, I will hang."

Kearny held a hand to his ear, waiting for his new citizens to applaud at his first words, and gasp at the second.

"From the Mexican government you have never received protection," he continued. "The Apaches and Navajos come down from the mountains and carry off your sheep, and even your women, whenever they please. My government will correct all this."

There was a round of applause.

Kearny moved to the subject of religion. "I know you are all great Catholics. Some of your priests have told you all sorts of stories—that we should ill-treat your women and brand them on the cheek as you do your mules on the hip. It is all false. My government respects your religion as much as the Protestant religion, and allows each man to worship his Creator as his heart tells him is best.

"Our laws protect the Catholic as well as the Protestant; the weak as well as the strong; the poor as well as the rich. I am not a Catholic myself—I was not brought up in that faith. But at least one third of my army is Catholic. I respect a good Catholic as much as a good Protestant."

There was a murmur through the small crowd of New Mexicans. To Bogart's view, they seemed to accept his words. Kearny descended the ladder and rejoined his troops. Within minutes his army was moving out toward Santa Fe under a bright sun with unfurled guidons and colors, and with the sounds of bugle calls.

Bogart rode not far behind Kearny. He heard Kearny say, "If Armijo's still around, let's find him. I'll give the same speech to the other small villages we come to." He was referring to Tecolote, San Miguel, and Vernal Springs.

"And Santa Fe, too?" Captain Cooke asked.

Kearny scanned the southern horizon. "Yes, Santa Fe, too. We'll be there within four days."

Private Bogart could tell that Kearny had grown bored after duplicating his speech in Tecolote, San Miguel, and Vernal Springs, and so had he. At least the women and children had come down from the hills, not fearing the Americans any longer.

"Smell that?" Sergeant Peck asked Bogart as they rode out of Vernal Springs.

"Smell what?" Bogart asked.

"It's the smell of battle. Armijo's waiting at Raton Pass. We're gonna fight. Our boredom's gonna be over."

Bogart hesitated, feeling a sudden chill. "Dern, I don't want them greasers shooting at me from above my head. Why can't they just meet us out in the open, and fight like men?"

Peck laughed, but not Bogart. Bogart lapsed into silence. Getting killed was no laughing matter. He began to regret what he had said about getting into real action. Kearny had told his men that there were at least two thousand men waiting at Raton Pass where the canyon walls narrowed in places to less than forty feet apart. Not a good place for a showdown.

A few hours later, with his black horse barely moving and his head hanging low, a comical sight took place near the Spanish ruins of Pecos, where a few New Mexicans still lived. A large, overweight Mexican rider approached the lead dragoons on a little mule. He identified himself as the *alcalde* of Pecos. Bogart could hear his yell in broken English:

"Armijo and his troops have gone to hell and the canyon is clear."

Bogart took off his army forage cap and wiped his sweaty brow. He had the feeling both him and his black horse might have died in that canyon.

It wasn't until camp that night that Bogart learned the details of Armijo's flight. The man on the mule had been Nicholas Quintaro, Armijo's secretary of state. The defense of Santa Fe and all New Mexico had collapsed when Armijo's army of dragoons, militia, and Indians failed to hold together. After canvassing his officers and finding them quarreling and unwilling to fight, Armijo ordered them home on the grounds that they had neither the means nor the experience to successfully oppose the Americans. Desertions were running rampant, anyway. And Armijo had become so paranoid about his own men planning a treasonous mutiny that he trained his own cannon on them to prevent such an occurrence. This all was despite the fact that Armijo a day earlier sent Kearny a letter with a detachment of lancers promising to engage the Americans, and despite the fact that they had dug into a narrow portion of Raton Pass called Apache Canyon. As for Armijo himself, he had fled south toward Chihuahua with a bodyguard consisting of all his artillery and a hundred dragoons.

"Dern, that Armijo's a coward, ain't he?" Bogart remarked around the campfire that night in the canyon.

"Either that, or full of common sense," Peck answered as he drank coffee. He had learned to accept Bogart's changing emotions.

"Am I ever gonna kill a greaser?" Bogart asked with a faked tone of impatience.

"Sometime, maybe. Maybe before we get to California."

Bogart entered Santa Fe at three in the afternoon with General Kearny's army in an eerie silence. He felt eerie, too. Except for the wails of frightened women, there was hardly a sound—only the clip-clop of the horses, and the crunching of soil under weight of the wagons carrying the six-pound cannon and twelve-pound howitzers. There were so many soldiers, horses, livestock, and wagons that Bogart figured it would take another three hours for all the units to be in town.

"Dern, there ain't nobody ta fight here no more," Bogart said to Peck in his faked tone.

Bogart's black horse was dead tired, walking as though he were on his last legs. The soldiers hadn't eaten since five in the morning, and the horses had snatched precious little grass on the way from the mountains. The plaza was deserted. There was not one Mexican dragoon, not one New Mexican militia, not one Pueblo Indian as there had been before.

A few Americans began to appear from their rented shops. "Well, don't shoot them Americans, whatever you do," Peck said with a laugh.

New Mexicans came out, too, some with sullen looks and muttered curses, others with winsome smiles.

Finally one American trader dared speak to the mounted dragoons. "Where's General Kearny?"

Peck laughed again. Kearny and his staff were dressed in battle fatigues and looked like any other dragoon. Peck pointed him out. "That's him on the gray horse with the black mane and tail."

Soon a bevy of Americans ran toward Kearny and began following him, their feet keeping pace with the advance of the horses. Kearny responded by reaching over his horse to shake their hands. The next man to appear from the adobe huts was a man who identified himself as Juan Bautista Vigil, the lieutenant governor.

"Welcome to the capital of New Mexico," Vigil was heard telling Kearny. "My compliments on running Armijo out of town. There are many here who have hated that man for a long, long time." Vigil's face was lit with happiness.

Kearny let a smile come over him. "Thank you."

As Kearny dismounted, Vigil had more to say. "I've known you were coming. I've prepared a feast. Please bring your staff to dinner in the governor's office. It's being prepared as we speak. Plenty of wine and brandy, too."

Bogart gasped at the thought that Kearny and his staff were going to get treated to a sumptuous meal. As for him, he had been on one-third rations for the past two weeks, and no coffee or sugar at all. He felt slighted; he hadn't eaten anything all day. His meal yesterday consisted of a meager share of a beef boiled for six hours from a "not-being-able-to-walk-any-longer diseased cow." The trail behind him, in fact, was littered with the decaying carcasses of oxen too thin to get much meat off from. Deliberately set fires and a lack of rain had reduced the amount of forage along the trail. To Bogart's chagrin, Kearny quickly issued an order that his soldiers were not to disturb the local food supply.

It wasn't until after Bogart had eaten his own meager rations in a camp just outside of town, and after a thirteen-gun salute from atop a nearby hill, that he learned that Vigil had indeed entertained Kearny, Doniphan, Cooke, and others of the staff to a real feast, prepared in the manner of a French dinner. One Mexican dish after another had succeeded itself in an almost endless variety. On the hill, an American flag was hoisted for the first time.

"Amazing, isn't it?" Sergeant Peck said as the soldiers bedded down for the night in their tents. "New Mexico is in the possession of the United States, and not a single man has been lost. This makes for quite a story."

"It's amazin' all right," Bogart countered. "Its amazin' that I didn't get to shoot one greaser. Maybe California will be better."

Bogart had planned to party all night, but Captain Cooke—assigned provost duty that night—had taken care of that. When Cooke discovered that all the taverns and saloons of Santa Fe were being overrun by thirsty soldiers and Missouri volunteers, he had driven them out.

At the end of the second day, Bogart was more than amazed at the rapidity in which Kearny had issued orders for the occupation. He gave his occupation speech from atop an adobe building on the plaza early in the morning. Vigil accepted the government of the United States on behalf of the inhabitants of New Mexico, asking Kearny not to find it strange if there were no manifestations of joy for the first few days. Kearny ordered Lieutenant William H. Emory, his chief engineer, to begin immediate construction of a fort to protect Santa Fe, to be called Fort Marcy, named after the Secretary of War, William L. Marcy. Kearny charged Colonel Doniphan with drawing up a constitution for the new territorial government. He asked Captain Cooke to organize a ball within a few days and let the soldiers dance with the women, a victory dance of sorts. "Let the soldiers dance until dawn," Kearny said. He made long-range plans, too. He promised to name territorial officials before he left for California within a month. He instructed Doniphan, as soon as Colonel Price arrived to relieve him, to restore peace in the Navajo country before heading south into Chihuahua. Price, known for his tough ways, was to be in charge of the New Mexico occupation force.

"I'm going to announce to the local authorities that my army has not come as conqueror," Kearny said in a briefing, "but as a peaceful occupier. No one is to be molested at all unless they take up arms against us. Anyone who does will be hanged. Not a pepper, not an onion, shall be disturbed or taken by my troops without pay or by consent of the owner."

Peck nodded his head in agreement. Without these stern warnings, he knew his fellow Missourians would run rampant in the territory.

"There will be those among us, including the wealthy who will see their influence and profits wane, and some of the Catholic priests, who will oppose our occupation," Kearny said. "Begin now to watch for uprisings and revolt. A few will consider themselves patriots to the central government in Mexico. Conspiracies will take place."

Kearny had plans to be a model soldier: attend Mass, carry a candle in a church procession, keep his soldiers under control, promise to end the Indian menace, and tour nearby settlements to let the inhabitants see that his troopers had no horns.

Bogart wrung his hands together in anticipation. "Dern," he said to Peck, referring to the conspiracies. "Maybe I'll get to use my rifle even before we ride off to California." Instead of muskets, each dragoon carried a Hall's carbine.

Kearny spoke of his next goal. "California is like a piece of ripe fruit ready to fall from a tree. I can hardly wait to get there."

Me neither, Bogart said to himself.

CHAPTER NOTES

Kearny's August 15 speech at The Vegas, Mexico, is taken from *Notes of a Military Reconnaissance, from Fort Leavenworth, in Missouri, to San Diego, in California, including part of the Arkansas, Del Norte, and Gila Rivers* (Washington D. C. 30th Congress, 1st Session, 1848); as quoted in the book *Eyewitness to the Old West*, edited by Richard Scott (Roberts Rinehart Publishers, 2004) pp. 66-67.

The adobe building that Kearny used for his speech is now a western bookstore.

25

ROBERT FELT HALF SICK, BUT THIS TIME it was not because of the ague. He had eaten so many plums and green corn out of the Fort Leavenworth farm fields two days ago when Company E marched away, that he had a stomachache. He figured it would be the last time he would have access to fresh fruits and vegetables until he reached Santa Fe, and he didn't want scurvy, the great curse of the plains that he'd heard about. Many green-horns came down with it due to their diet of only flour, salt pork, and a little red meat.

Robert didn't expect many delicacies like beaver tail, rattlesnakes, skunks, or unborn buffalo calves—popular dishes with old-timers on the trail. He did look forward to the dryness of the plains and the improvement to his overall health that would bring.

"I hate this knapsack," Robert said to Daniel. He carried it a little lopsided, unbalanced. It carried his bedding, extra clothing, and a few rounds of ammunition.

"I suppose you hate your haversack, too," Daniel retorted.

"I do," Robert replied. "But I don't hate the food in it." The soldiers were required to carry two days' rations in their haversacks.

Robert had seen his first caravan yesterday, near the place where the Santa Fe Trail accepted the roads leading from the main starting-off points—not only Fort Leavenworth but Independence, Franklin, and Westport.

"I've never seen anything like it," he had said to Daniel when the caravan had come into view. It made him feel lonesome; it reminded him a little of the wagon company he had traveled across Iowa with. Thimbles rattled rhythmically. Tongues whipped from side to side. But the creaking of the wheels of the heavy Conestoga wagons was mostly muted in the deep prairie soil. There were no runaway mules in this train. And just as Henry had said, the muleskinners and the bullwhackers fouled the air with colorful language, aimed at their mules and oxen.

Until he came to Fort Leavenworth, Robert had never seen the kind of whip the bullwhackers and muleskinners used. It was a monster whip or *panache*, a braided rawhide lash twenty feet long. On the end was a replaceable "popper," an eight-inch piece of rawhide that could crack like a pistol shot, and could cut the hide of an ox like a knife. Teamsters bragged they could get to Santa Fe and back without drawing blood. The point was to "pop" it at just the right spot, by the correct animal's left or right ear, to guide or inspire the animal.

Today, in the hot air, the poppers were popping.

In contrast, in the nearby trees Robert could hear the sharp whistles of partridge, the chirp of larks, and the croaking of ravens. And that made him feel lonesome, too. The sounds were about the same as they had been in Nauvoo and across Iowa. The prairie here sparkled with lush green grass, sprinkled profusely with flowers of many hues, and crabapple thickets. The sun was exerting itself; there was not a breath of air stirring. The heat was scorching; within a few days the green grass was certain to turn brown. Whenever he neared the trees and the water in this country the mosquitoes tormented him and tormented the animals, too. He had mosquito bites on his face, arms, and hands—every inch of exposed skin itched. Some of the bites were bleeding because he had scratched them so much.

A salty old teamster dressed in a bright calico shirt and a wide-brimmed felt hat waved. "Are you the Mormon soldiers we've heard about?" The caravan consisted of around three-dozen wagons traveling three abreast for maximum protection against Indians.

"Yes, we are," Daniel answered with a big smile.

In front of Robert and Daniel were hundreds of Mormon soldiers. Every man wore a broad-brimmed hat, trousers of rough material, woolen shirts of a variety of colors, and carried a musket. Swords and bayonets were in the baggage wagons. The Battalion had started out with a long roll on the drums, and now the men were marching to the music of the fifers.

Robert let Daniel do the talking; Robert worked at his mosquito bites, making them bleed even more.

"And you're walking all the way to Californay?" the man asked.

"Yes, sir!" answered Daniel.

"Are you certain salvation's worth it?"

"I'm certain," Daniel yelled back, not knowing if the teamster was a Mormon-hater.

"If you see some Injuns, shoot 'em away if they're unfriendly," the teamster shouted. "Don't let 'em at our goods. My boss has a daughter in a finishing school in St. Louis and his wife wants a new home in Independence. Can't afford any losses."

All through the territory Robert expected to see Indians—the prospect was one of the main things the Mormon soldiers talked about. With all the soldiers on the trail, Robert reasoned that there wouldn't be too many problems with Indians. Even so, they would be in a circle tonight with the guards ordered to shoot at anything that stirred. The guides claimed there were all manner of Indians between Fort Leavenworth and Santa Fe, and they were far from whipped. The claim had visibly upset Daniel, who liked to believe there wouldn't be any Indian encounters.

The wagons were two or three times larger than the wagon Robert had used to cross Iowa. Many wagons in the caravan were painted bright red or blue. Their wheels were larger, too, and even their stay-chains and traces. Most were pulled by teams of eight mules, some by oxen. Use of larger wagons had been mandated by an import tax of five hundred dollars on every wagon entering New Mexico. The harnesses were heavy-duty, too, with the backhands of most of them looking more than a foot wide, the hip-straps that wide, too. Bridles were adorned with loops of red trimming, fringes, and shining buckles. Over every team swung a set of finely toned bells, as large as dinner bells, fixed on wrought-iron bows above the hames.

"There's a fortune in those wagons," said Levi Roberts as the caravan slowly passed.

Robert nodded and agreed, and he felt like the poor Mormon immigrant that he was. Someone—probably quite a few someones—was a wealthy shipper. He had heard how the wagons were stuffed with barrels, hogsheads, and boxes. Popular goods in Santa Fe—to be eventually resold to wealthy farmers and merchants in Mexico—included cotton goods, coarse and fine cambrics, calicoes, domestic shawls, steam-loom handkerchiefs, cotton hose, woolen goods, blankets, super-blues, pelisse cloths and shawls, velvets, silks, and ribbons. Also traps, knives, axes, hatchets, lead, powder, trinkets, writing paper, hats, and looking glasses. There were even pianos and liquor. Lots of liquor. Between the wagon sheets was spread a pair of Mackinaw blankets for protection.

Robert had heard there were often contraband items, too, well concealed from Mexican custom officials.

"We'll be back this way in a few weeks, loaded with beaver pelts, buffalo hides, wool, gold, and specie," the teamster said. "Unless the greasers win the war. But we don't expect that, do we boys?"

"No, we don't," Robert answered as the wagons rolled past. He wondered if he'd ever get used to that derogatory term. "Kearny will have Santa Fe secured by the time you get there." The traders were not afraid of anything, not ever war, he concluded.

During the time spent at Fort Leavenworth, Robert had learned how trade on the Santa Fe Trail began. William Becknell, a hard-working frontier settler who traveled across the Appalachians with Daniel Boone, once borrowed three hundred twenty one dollars and couldn't repay it. In debt and worried, Becknell opted to risk all on a venture that in those days, twenty-five years earlier, could make a man rich or dead. He decided to cross the dangerous, unknown prairies to trade with the Indians. He crossed the Missouri in 1821 and rode west. He wound up in Santa Fe and instead of being jailed as foreign intruders, he and his companions were mobbed with customers eager for their goods. The rest, Robert concluded, is history.

Even today, though the first caravan had long disappeared, another one was about to catch the Battalion, its wagons stuffed with bales and boxes. The Battalion, too, was a conspicuous sight out on the lonesome prairie with its five hundred men, its dozens of wagons, and its cattle, Robert thought. Again, just as yesterday, the sun beat down on his head like an oven. Scrubby but conspicuous sand sagebrush dotted the landscape, along with a smattering of silky prairie clover plants, milkweed, and fiery goosefoot. Pronghorns grazed in the distance. An occasional porcupine sauntered across the trail. Roadrunners darted away. Mountain plovers, chickadees, rock wrens, and scrub jays sang their songs. Robert was now spotting rattlesnakes, horned lizards, and box turtles.

There was still no sign of Colonel Allen. Captain Jefferson Hunt of Company A was in charge of the Battalion until the colonel could recover and join them.

"What do you think, Daniel?" Robert asked as they marched toward Council Grove, his face a mask of bewilderment. "Will Colonel Allen ever get better?" The latest news was not good.

Daniel's voice sounded uneasy. "There might be a chance if he quits drinking and don't let the calomel doctors near him."

"And if he dies? There're no other friendly officers back there in Fort Leavenworth."

Robert recalled Colonel Allen as a man who had been strict but kind, even complimenting members of the Battalion on their willingness to learn and obey commands. He even apologized for the weight of the army-issued muskets. When John Spindle of Company E got bit on the hand by a rattlesnake, the colonel saw to it that Private Spindle received proper medical treatment. Back at Council Bluffs during the enlistment, the colonel had happily agreed to some of the wives signing on as laundresses.

Daniel pursed his lips, deep in thought. "Captain Hunt can lead us to Santa Fe just as well as anyone else."

"We've never been on the Santa Fe Trail, and neither has he," Robert remarked.

Daniel stretched out his hand. "You'd have to be blind to lose your way. See how deep those ruts are?"

Robert pulled a face as a terrible thought came over him. "What if Colonel Price takes over our command?"

"He has his own regiment to worry about," Daniel replied, "but he could send one of his officers."

26

On the Santa Fe Trail

August 26, 1846

DANIEL FELT LOW WHEN HE HEARD THAT Colonel Allen had passed away. Quartermaster Samuel Gulley brought the news; he had just arrived from Fort Leavenworth. The news spread through the Battalion like wildfire.

"Dang, I really liked Colonel Allen," Daniel said to Robert at the Battalion boys' camp at Bluff Creek.

"Me, too," Robert agreed, shaking his head in a gesture of sadness. "He may have drank too much whiskey, shaved with an ax, cut his hair with a bayonet, and stirred his coffee with his thumb, but I liked him."

"Don't joke like that," Daniel shot back. "Death's not a time to be funny."

"I wasn't joking, and I'm not trying to be funny," Robert said. "I said I liked him."

John Cox ignored the little argument and said, "If he had lived, Daniel and Levi Hancock might have converted him to the gospel."

Daniel took on a serious look. "I'd like to think you're right."

"This leaves us in a quandary," Robert said. "Now who'll lead us?"

One of Company C's wagons, carrying sick soldiers and flour, had taken a tumble from the steep banks of the swollen creek, and Daniel stared at the mess absentmindedly. Two laundresses and six of the sick men had nearly drowned as they struggled to free themselves from under the wagon. Half the Battalion was still on the other side, dripping with increased general anxiety about their turn to cross the creek. It was a tragedy, but the tragedy of Colonel Allen's death struck Daniel as worse.

"Don't know," Daniel replied, trying to shake himself loose from these endless tragedies. "The officers have already talked about it. Some don't feel that Captain Jefferson Hunt should assume command simply because he has no formal military experience. But others totally oppose the thoughts of an unknown regular army officer taking over. Jesse Hunter and Adjutant Dykes are examining regulations and are expected to give us a report."

"I guess all we can do for now is just keep going toward Council Grove," Robert concluded.

"You're right," Daniel answered sadly.

Daniel's mind suddenly swirled into not only sadness over the loss of Colonel Allen but also imaginations of what it would be like to die.

Apparently only one relative, a niece of seventeen, had been at Colonel Allen's bedside when he died. Allen had suffered greatly; the army doctor, Sanderson, had not been able to relieve any pain, much less save him. Daniel thought that a man of forty-four ought to have been surrounded by parents, a wife, and children when he died. It was tragic, too, that Allen died of a combination of alcoholism and the ague after all the years he had spent on the frontier fighting Indians.

Samuel Boley had died, and now Colonel Allen. If God were with the Battalion, why did either man have to die? Daniel now felt vulnerable to death and no Mormon soldier was therefore safe. He thought how terrible it would be to die as a Mormon soldier somewhere along the Santa Fe Trail, or in California, so far away from Elizabeth, Harriet, Moroni, and his mother. Being buried on the prairie or in the desert in a shallow grave covered by rocks, with the potential to be ravaged by wolves, would be a terrible conclusion to life on earth.

At least Colonel Allen would be buried at the fort, or taken some place where he had a family to tend to the grave, and the grave would be dug six feet down into the earth.

In Robert's view, the controversy over who would command the Battalion was no worse than the news that several of the Battalion's provision wagons were missing. The teamsters were apparently lost, somehow missing the correct road. He could feel a smoldering rage building within him.

"How could a teamster miss the Santa Fe Trail?" Robert wondered out loud. "Henry must be leading them, and doing it on purpose out of meanness and spite."

"I don't know," answered Daniel, equally puzzled. "No one seems to know, not even Captain Hunt, Quartermaster Gully, or Lieutenant Pace."

The march from Fort Leavenworth to Bluff Creek had been slow but steady in the intense, stifling heat. It didn't matter much, anyway; Colonel Allen had instructed Captain Hunt to move at an easy pace toward Council Grove, Kansas, where Allen had been expected to catch up. The Battalion made only six miles the first day due to trouble with many of the mules and the fact that the wagons sunk a foot deep in the sand and dust. It seemed the mules had forgotten all they ever knew about pulling wagons. The old practice of choking them with a lasso had to be put into practice. They got going again, but shied at the sight of every dead oxen left strewn along the heavily traveled trade trail.

The rolling prairie consisted of bottoms that were perfectly flat, covered with rosinweed that grew as abundant as the grass. The summer's riot of wildflowers had peaked and waned, leaving only the hardier survivors. The timber on the ravines consisted of white oak, black mulberry, black walnut, hickory, red bud, and nettles that extended into the air to the height of a man. Occasionally millions of mosquitoes invaded the Battalion, causing the animals to act half crazy. Prairie dogs were everywhere, as were gray wolves, and rattlesnakes, too.

The first Plains Indians the men saw, the Shawnee, had made their appearance as they neared the Kaw River, but they looked comfortably fixed. They had numbers of fine looking cattle and responded with friendly answers to questions about the terrain. Some were dressed in their buckskins embellished with blue and white pony beads, and beaded moccasins. Most of the men were outfitted only in breechclouts, barely covering their vitals.

Robert found out what it was like to carry a heavy musket and the accoutrements of a foot soldier on a hot, melting day with the dust settling like a blanket over him. He also learned all about lice; they infested man and beast.

The next two days the Battalion averaged fifteen miles and would have done the same after that except for bad luck. They camped at the mouth of the Wakaroosa Creek, more of a river at eighty yards wide. It had clear water but the stream ran sluggish. Everyone bathed in the water. But that night heavy rains drenched the camp, splattering the tents and soaking not only the supplies but bedding and clothing as well. Three or four horses broke free from their ropes, driven almost mad by the horseflies and mosquitoes. Iron wagon tires came off three wagons in the heavy mud. The following day, nearly fifty beef cattle came up missing only to have the Indians bring them in for bounty later in the day, which really frosted the men to think they had to pay for their own cattle.

The next night the heavy rains came again, this time accompanied by winds that could outrun an antelope. It took six men to hold one tent down. Even lofty oaks along the banks of the creek seemed as though they would be uprooted. Two heavy government baggage wagons were overturned. Other wagons were pushed ten or twenty rods away from the camp. Hats, caps, fragments of tents, and wagon covers could be seen flying through the air. Rain and hailstones filled up the boots of nearly every soldier. Powder casks had been wrapped in painted canvas, but even some of them were wet.

The weather improved the next day, bringing out the chatter of bluebirds, doves, flickers, towhee buntings, and crows. The day was spent drying out and gathering up supplies that had been scattered by the storm. As is the practice on the prairie, several men were sent in advance with axes, spades, and mattocks, so that by digging the banks of rivers and erecting temporary bridges over quagmires, the Battalion's wagons could keep moving. Temporary bridges were made in a few minutes by cross-laying the quagmire with brush, or even long grass, and then covering it with dirt.

By nightfall, all the camps had turned mournful and the men cranky over the news of Colonel Allen's death. Caw Indians were turned away; no one was in the mood to trade. Grapes and plums the men had eaten at noon, picked along the small creeks, seemed to give Daniel and everyone else indigestion and gas. The mules and oxen were frantically kicking at the horseflies and using their tails to swish them away. Turkey buzzards settled in the trees, now roosting. Catbirds were screaming in the brush beneath the trees. Daniel's every breath drew a pound of mosquitoes up his nostrils. The distractions resulted in bread scorched to nearly black in the camp kettle.

Daniel felt that Captain Jefferson Hunt was the man to lead the Battalion boys to Santa Fe. This confirmation came after Captain Hunt came by Daniel's mess and spoke to him, Robert, Robert Pixton, Richard Slater, Levi Roberts, and John Cox.

"I had been praying for the colonel's recovery," Captain Hunt said. "I am as shocked as the next man. If the army sends a replacement, I'll salute and follow him. If they want me to lead us to California, I'll do it, despite the fact I feel inadequate."

"You have my support," said Levi Hancock, who had accompanied Hunt on the rounds.

"Mine, too," said Robert. He turned to face Levi, the only general authority in the Battalion. "Are we gonna have a service of some kind for the colonel?" Yesterday Hancock had baptized a nonmember soldier, Leonard Scott.

"Yes," said Hancock. "We need to pay our respects. I'll organize a service in the morning."

Captain Hunt signaled his approval and then turned to go. Suddenly, he wheeled. "Brother Harris, I understand you have experience as a butcher."

Daniel watched his brother-in-law turned a shade of green.

"Who told you that?" Robert asked.

"Lots of people. We need a few men to serve as Battalion butchers." Hunt pointed to the large herd of beef cattle bedded down in the trees. "When our rations run low, we'll have to eat them beeves out there. And we'll be in buffalo country soon. I'm assigning you to be one of the butchers. There are axes, hatchets, and knives in the supply wagon. Make yourself ready, soldier."

There was a brief sound of released breath. "Yes, sir," Robert said as he suppressed a contemptuous look. The sultry air suddenly weighed heavier.

Daniel just looked at his frazzled brother-in-law and gave him a tart grin as Hunt marched away swatting mosquitoes. He could taste a big portion of roast beef. But he could see a new weariness come over Robert.

"I wish I could play a flute instead of a fiddle," Robert said, looking half sick. "Then maybe I could be a musician in the Battalion instead of a butcher. I hate blood and offal. I feel a fever coming on."

"I'm out of quinine," Daniel replied, who had been sharing it with other members of his mess. "And I know Dr. McIntire doesn't have any—he had none from the start." Dr. William J. McIntire, a member of the Church, was a member of the command staff by appointment of Colonel Allen. Brigham Young had told Dr. McIntire and other Mormon officers that they should treat the sick with blessings from priesthood bearers and with herbs and mild food, just as outlined in the Doctrine and Covenants, Section 42, and not to use chemical medicines of any kind. His specific words had been: "If you are sick, live by faith, and let surgeon's medicines alone if you want to live, using only such herbs and mild food as are at your disposal."

That evening Daniel and Levi Hancock anointed Robert with oil and gave him a priesthood blessing. Robert's fever went away.

Alva Phelps was still sick, still suffering from the ague.

27

TWO DAYS LATER THERE WAS NEWS that descended upon Robert with a weight far beyond anything he had felt since the trip began. Three men had come riding into camp from Fort Leavenworth. One was a lieutenant named Andrew Jackson Smith and he claimed he was taking over for Colonel Allen. The other was the infamous calomel army doctor, George Sanderson, and he had a black servant.

"This is a bad development," Robert said to Daniel as he watched Smith and Sanderson converse with Captain Jefferson Hunt and the captains of the other companies, Jesse Hunter, James Brown, Nelson Higgins, and Daniel Davis.

Robert and Daniel had been helping their messmates repack wagons and dry out goods that had been wetted by a passing rainstorm.

John Cox said, "I have a terrible feeling already."

The Battalion had reached its first goal—Council Grove, Kansas, about a hundred and twenty-five miles west of Fort Leavenworth. Under orders of Colonel Allen, the Battalion had been ordered to wait here until the colonel caught up with them. With the news of the colonel's death, the orders had been reconfirmed and the Battalion command had waited, not knowing really what to do next.

A little earlier, Robert had walked to a bluff that overlooked Council Grove. The road from Fort Leavenworth formed the dividing line between the last settlements and Indian country. To the east he could see the last of civilization—fine farms with cornfields, orchards, dwelling houses, and all the comforts of home. To the West he could see the lonesome, far stretching prairie, without house or cultivation—the abode of the savage Indian and the highway of the adventurous white man. Below him the cattle of the Battalion grazed on lush green grass that grew in the cottonwoods.

"I hope the captains have the authority to tell Smith to go home," Daniel said. "Captain Hunt ought to be our new leader."

Hunt was huddled under a cluster of shade trees with Smith, Sanderson, and the captains.

Council Grove had been nothing more than a camping site for travelers along the Santa Fe Trail, with good water, blue stem grass, and abundant wood due to the extensive groves of hardwood trees. The main grove consisted of a continuous strip of timber nearly half a mile wide, extending along the valley of a small running stream known as Council Grove Creek, the principal branch of the Neosho River. Along this stream and other smaller ones were fertile bottoms and beautiful upland prairies. The grove itself consisted of a hundred and sixty acres and contained many fine old trees, mostly ash, oak, elm, maple, and hickory, all festooned with enormous grapevines. Its dense shade gave a delightful resting place to the Battalion after the glare of the sunburned plains.

In 1825, a treaty had been signed here, forged between U.S. commissioners and Osage Indian chiefs, which granted whites safe passage on the trail. In 1827, Kit Carson scratched "Council Grove" on a buffalo hide and attached it to a tree where the council had been held. By now it had become a government post and rendezvous point for caravans moving west and it is here that the Battalion waited for instructions from Fort Leavenworth. The Battalion was camped at a spring called Gravel Creek, near the Neosho River, at a spot where it was said that John C. Fremont had once camped. Fremont had called the place an "oasis in the wilderness," one of the most agreeable stopping places on the trail.

"Do you think we'll even have a choice over who'll take over?" Robert asked Daniel, who was a sergeant.

"Too early to tell," answered Daniel. "I suspect the captains will call a meeting soon."

"Well, I don't like the looks of it," Robert said as he went back to work. To him, Lieutenant Smith looked mighty young and inexperienced, no more than thirty years old. Smith was short and reminded Robert of men he had known in his lifetime who had suffered from the runt syndrome. Smith's head looked too large for his shoulders, and his butt looked too large for his legs.

Other Battalion men were engaged in a variety of tasks. Fires crackled under iron kettles. Robert Pixton was kneading bread using the standard recipe of flour, bacon grease, salt, soda, and water. Then he was going to bake it in the spider, or Dutch oven, using burning buffalo chips both underneath and on top. Laundresses were already washing clothes in the creek. In another area, many of the men were washing themselves, too. Some were making trades with Shawnee, Delaware, and Sac Indians that had found their way to the camp.

"You know what I remember?" Daniel asked his messmates.

"What?" countered John Cox.

"We get to vote on our leader," said Daniel. "In fact, we get to vote on all important matters. It's an army principle that governs volunteers. Colonel Allen went over that with Brigham Young back in Winter Quarters."

"I hope so," Richard Slater said.

"Me, too," Robert said. "Smith could turn out to be another Mormon hater, just like Colonel Sterling Price." At the mention of Price's name, Robert automatically thought of Henry. It wouldn't surprise him if Henry turned up as suddenly as Smith and Dr. Sanderson. After all, Colonel Price and his Second Regiment of Missouri Mounted Volunteers were rumored to be not too far behind the Battalion.

"Well, I hope the captains remember all that," said Levi Roberts.

All through the night and the next morning Robert felt restless and wanted the controversy to be resolved quickly. He retained those feelings during the service for Colonel Allen.

The service was a good one. Drums called the men to order in a square with the officers in the center. Adjutant Dykes gave a stirring talk about the resurrection, which not only melted Robert to tears, but most of the other men as well, including a non-member guide—Philip Thompson. Levi Hancock sang a song and Captain Jefferson Hunt also talked. Afterward, in an effort to stem the restlessness and quarreling among some of the men, twenty-eight members of Company C were rebaptized in the Neosho River.

In the afternoon, all the men were summoned to a meeting.

"What it's boiled down to is that the captains are going to give us a choice between Jefferson Hunt and Lieutenant Smith," Daniel said to his messmates as they walked to a canopy of green trees.

Robert felt the same way as he walked to the meeting, and he knew most of the Battalion boys felt the same way. Hunt by a landslide; send Smith back to the fort. After all, Hunt was not only a member of the Church, an experienced officer in the Nauvoo Legion, but he had been second in command under Colonel Allen.

It was therefore a big surprise to Robert to hear arguments in favor of Lieutenant Smith during the meeting. And it was non other than Adjutant

George P. Dykes, the officer who had persuaded Colonel Allen to force long marches those first days along the Missouri River, who took up the banner for Smith.

"I can't believe Dykes is doing this," Robert murmured to Daniel during the meeting.

"I'm only half surprised," Daniel answered. "Ever since enlistment Dykes considers himself more of a soldier than a member of the Church."

Dykes was in the middle of a speech. He was arguing that Smith was a West Point graduate and knew army rules and regulations better than Captain Hunt. Dykes pointed out that Smith was not from Missouri, like Colonel Price, but hailed from Pennsylvania.

This piece of news seemed to allay the fears of some of the men, but not Robert. He smiled, sensing a victory. The Battalion boys were talking amongst themselves; Hunt seemed to be the clear favorite.

"Lieutenant Smith wants to say something," Dykes said as he got control of the meeting again.

Hunt stepped aside. "Certainly. Let him say his peace."

New fears came over Robert. He sensed Smith was going to say something that neither he nor most of the Battalion boys wanted to hear.

"You men need to understand some things," Smith began. "First of all, I was sent here by Colonel Price, who, as you know, commands the Second Regiment of Missouri Mounted Volunteers."

"Yes, I'm aware of that," Hunt said, "and I'm certain the other boys are aware of it too."

Smith now threw his oversized head in the air. "You boys have a choice, and this is the way it's gonna be. Either you accept *me* as your commander, or Colonel Price will attach the Mormon Battalion to *his* command."

A wave of murmuring swept through the Battalion.

"Did he say what I think he said?" Robert asked Daniel.

Daniel's jaw had fallen into his lap. "I think we heard right. We're being strong-armed."

Smith raised both arms in an attempt to quiet down the Battalion boys. His voice hardened. "Furthermore, unless you yield to my command you cannot draw rations from the provision wagons because none of you, not even Captain Hunt, have an army commission like I do. No one has the authority to make out any kind of requisition, not for rations, not for ammunition, not for anything."

"This is a setup," Robert said to Daniel as another wave of murmurs swept through the crowd.

"We ought to call his bluff," John Cox said with an angry shake of his head.

Captain Hunt looked as though he'd seen a ghost. "If we are forced to yield to this, what about the promises Colonel Allen made to us?" he asked.

"What promises?" Smith asked, looking skeptical.

"There are several wives serving as laundresses, which the colonel approved," Hunt said. He pointed to Melissa Coray, wife of Sergeant William

Coray, and the other women, and a handful of teenage children.

Smith seemed to do a quick calculation, not wishing to lose any momentum. His narrow eyes scanned every member of the Battalion, including the women. At first blush he could see no harm in letting the women and children stay. "I'll let you keep the laundresses. I won't divide you."

"I think it's time the officers voted," said Dykes.

A young soldier by the name of Henderson Cox jumped to his feet. The veins on his forehead seemed ready to burst. "What do you mean, it's time for the officers to vote?"

"That's the way Smith wants it," Dykes said. "All the enlisted men voted for the officers; the officers will represent you fairly."

The answer seemed to satisfy Henderson. He sat down.

Robert held Daniel's arm as Daniel left to join the officers. "I guess I don't have to ask you how you're gonna vote."

"Captain Hunt, all the way," Daniel said with a stern smile. "Not for Andrew Jackson Smith."

The moment Robert had been waiting for had arrived. The officers from all five companies returned to the canopy of trees, ready to announce their vote. There was only one thing wrong with this scene, Robert quickly concluded. Hunt looked like he was drowning in humiliating anger.

Dykes, on the other hand, was flashing a winning smile.

"I can't believe what I'm about to hear and see," Robert said to his messmates.

"The officers couldn't have done this," said John Cox.

Jefferson Hunt was taking it like a man, however. It was him who announced the vote: Smith had won by a narrow margin.

Robert felt a creeping numbness come over him. "Oh, brother," Robert moaned to Daniel when Daniel returned. "What happened?"

"Smith's speech did it for him," Daniel said. "He was successful in intimidating a lot of the officers. They didn't want to take a chance that we'd be put under the command of Sterling Price."

"It was a bluff," Robert flatly speculated. Inwardly he detested the other officers for their cowardice and disloyalty.

"I suppose it was, but it's done now," Daniel said.

Robert made no effort to hide his disappointment as he walked back to camp. "If A. J. doesn't treat us right I'll have to break his legs."

"Don't say that too loud," Daniel whispered. "He's our commander now."

To Robert's dismay, it wasn't long until Lieutenant Smith began exercising his authority. To prove that he knew army rules and regulations better than Captain Hunt he immediately mustered all five Battalions, inspected their guns, and buried officers with stacks of paperwork. Smith also ordered each man to take a turn at guard duty. Robert's watch came at the worst time of the day, from midnight to four in the morning.

"So much for a good night's sleep," Robert moaned to Robert Pixton, the mess cook. Wolves were howling in the background, and the coyotes were yapping, too. "What's for supper?"

"Lieutenant Smith just put us on half rations, so not much," Pixton said with a sad face. "I wish that lost provision wagon would get here. I've picked a few more wild grapes. You're the butcher. You might have to kill an antelope or a buffalo, if we ever see one."

A soft chuckle came from Robert's mouth. "I wonder what butt steaks off A. J. would taste like?"

28

AT DANIEL'S REQUEST, ROBERT suppressed his antagonism toward Lieutenant Smith for two days. But an event happened as the Battalion marched southwest along Cottonwood Creek that changed all that. Several Battalion boys, all sick, had been riding in a wagon owned by Sergeant Thomas S. Williams of Company D. When Lieutenant Smith discovered this, he ordered the sick men out of the wagon and told them they must walk like everyone else.

The Battalion had just entered Comanche territory.

"The man has no compassion at all," Ezra Allen said. He was still suffering from the ague and was barely able to walk without assistance. Robert watched as members of Ezra's company came to assist him.

Sergeant Williams looked as though he were ready to explode. Smith was pulling out the sick men, one by one, renting the air with his foul cursing as he did it.

"Colonel Price may as well be here commanding our outfit as Lieutenant Smith," Robert said to Daniel as they watched the ugly scene. "He couldn't be any worse."

Williams erupted. Hiding no insubordination, he tried to sound as menacing as he could. "This is my wagon and if I want to haul sick men, I'll do it."

Lieutenant Smith was a runt of a man, but he had in his possession both a sword and a whip, both of which he promptly placed in his hands. He rent the air with foul cursing. "I order you men out of the wagon. Step away. If you don't, I'll run you through."

Robert wondered if he heard right. A. J. had just threatened to kill some of the Mormon Battalion boys.

Robert was amazed at the speed in which Williams jumped out of the wagon and took hold of Smith's whip. With deadly finality he said, "This wagon is my personal property and I'll haul all the sick men that want to ride. Those men are my brothers and I won't leave a one of them lying on the ground as long as my team can pull them. Furthermore, we don't believe in taking poisonous medicine like calomel, so leave us alone."

Robert had heard rumors that Dr. Sanderson had tried to administer calomel to some of the men and this confirmed it.

A flush of red stained Smith's cheeks. He ground his teeth together and began to mutter to himself. As he walked by Robert, Smith asked, "What's that soldier's name in the wagon?"

"Never met the man," Robert fibbed.

Smith was still drowning in humiliated anger, but he returned to his own wagon.

Robert promptly walked up to Sergeant Williams and put his arms around him. "If Smith gives you any more trouble, I'll knock him on his backside. I'll lead the mutiny if there is one."

Williams said thanks, returned to his wagon, cracked his whip, and proceeded down the trail.

The altercation with Lieutenant Smith turned around and that evening bit the Battalion boys in the form of Dr. Sanderson. Smith had stopped the Battalion for the evening at Cottonwood Creek, forty-one miles west of Council Grove. Instead of camping by the creek, Smith forced the Battalion to camp out in the open with the grasshoppers and sunflowers.

Captain Davis of Company E announced that Dr. Sanderson had signaled a sick call and wanted every man who was currently sick, or had been sick at any time during their enlistment, to come to his wagon and be treated.

The request hit a raw nerve with Robert. "I'm not going," he announced to Daniel.

Robert had been in a bad mood anyway over the camp location and the vote that had put Smith in charge of the Battalion. He had been digging a trench for Robert Pixton because Pixton had said the only way he could cook anything was to build a fire out of weeds in some kind of protective area. There would be no meat for supper because Smith had put a kibosh on killing beeves.

"You've been sick with the ague on and off and everyone knows it," Daniel answered.

Robert hitched up his trousers on his narrow hips a notch. The hikes between Council Bluffs, the hot weather, and his bouts with the fevers had taken their toll on his weight. His face was a little gaunt, too—at least it was the last time he looked in a mirror, but that had been several days ago when he last shaved.

"Come on, I'll go with you," said John Cox.

Robert retained his stubbornness. "You go, I'll stay."

Pixton was lighting a fire in the trench, using weeds the boys had accumulated. "Get out of here, the both of you, and I'll have something fixed for you when you get back."

Richard Slater pulled on Robert's arm. "I'll go, too. We'd ought to meet this doctor face to face, don't you think?"

Daniel said, "Take Alva Phelps with you, too."

Alva, in fact, was still sick whereas Robert hadn't had a sick day for quite a spell.

The remark broke the tension and broke Robert's resistance, too. He was as curious as the next man about the new doctor even though he felt the experience would end up being a bad one. He was already prepared to detest the doctor. After all, he'd heard Sanderson was a Missourian. Worse than that, Sanderson was an English Missourian, having settled there after his immigration. That made Sanderson equal to a traitor in Robert's book. Sanderson was a slave owner from Platte County, and had even brought one of his slaves as his assistant.

When the boys arrived at Dr. George Sanderson's wagon, Robert felt his skin crawl with rage. Sergeant Thomas Williams' wagon was there, too, and Lieutenant Smith was pulling sick men out of it and forcing them to stand in a long line of men that were waiting to see Sanderson.

Cox was already reading Robert's mind and body actions. He held onto Robert's arm. "Better let it pass," John said. "If you do anything it'll get us all in trouble. Smith could cut our rations to nothing or even hang us on a tree."

Robert's fists were already balled and he struggled to keep from making a mad dash at Smith. His mind swirled into darkness. He refused to accept the preposterous thought that Smith was now commanding the Battalion instead of Colonel Allen. He couldn't feature himself being this angry with Allen, no matter what. He prayed for a miracle—that a resurrected Colonel Allen would suddenly come riding into camp on a white horse.

"Let's just be good boys and get in line," Slater suggested.

"I'd like to knock Smith's sorry butt back to Leavenworth," Robert said.

"I know you would, but think of Hannah and your children," John said. "It'd be a sad thing to tell them you died in the stockade."

Robert found quick cause to hate Dr. Sanderson far worse than Lieutenant Smith. It rivaled the hate he'd had for Wilson Law and the other apostates back in Nauvoo, and for the men who had stormed the Carthage Jail and killed Joseph Smith. Battalion boys had crowded around Sanderson's wagon, some of them forming a line. The were exchanging stories of how Sanderson had all day long been attacking Mormonism with personal venom and no restraint on decency. He had spun long, lachrymose tales of woe about how Mormons had tried to take over Missouri and Illinois.

"How'd we get stuck with a doctor like this?" Robert asked Ezra Allen who was also in line.

"The devil himself sent him," Ezra said with a drained look.

"I wish Sanderson would go back to Fort Leavenworth," said Alva Phelps.

The line moved faster than Robert anticipated. The reason, he discovered, was that Sanderson's way of practicing medicine was to spend almost no time at all in the diagnosis and almost no time at all with his prescription. Every prescription was the same, no matter the complaint: calomel, one pill, two pills, or even three. Sanderson, with the help of his shiny black perspiring slave, was forcing the calomel pills down the throats of the men with a steady stream of offensive, foul oaths.

Robert could feel himself inflate with rage again. He was getting closer and closer to the so-called doctor, with only a few other Battalion boys separating him.

"Ague and fevers?" Dr. Sanderson asked Robert almost without looking when Robert's turn came. Sanderson was tall and wide-shouldered, with a lean, dark face shadowed by the slant of his dusty, flat-crowned hat. There was a raw, uncompromising strength about him. He glared at Robert with wild, unsettled, coffee-brown eyes.

"I'm just fine," Robert said with a firm resolve.

Sanderson's medicine bag was open, revealing bottles of calomel, Epsom salts, jalap, and even a lancet and a turnkey for pulling teeth. There was also a small supply of herbs that Robert suspected were bayberry bark and chamomile flowers, things that Elizabeth had used as strengthening bitters.

Sanderson consulted his chart. Robert was surprised he had one.

"Says here you've suffered from intermittent fevers and chills," Sanderson said without looking up.

"But I'm fine now."

Sanderson glanced up from the chart as though his patience had long ago vanished. His hardened, chiseled features were set in an icy mask. "I have had enough of this Mormon insolence today." Using the Lord's name in vain, he told Robert to open his mouth.

The black slave, his fingers still moist from the saliva of other men, stood ready to thrust calomel pills down Robert's throat.

Robert unclenched his fists and held one hand out. He remembered Brigham Young's counsel not to take chemical medicines. "Just put those pills in my hand."

The doctor fouled the air again with his curses, taking the Lord's name in vain again. "I won't tell you one more time. Open your mouth." Sanderson jerked the calomel pills from the sticky hand of his black slave.

Robert had never lost an eye-to-eye confrontation, but he was losing this one. Sanderson continued his stare, perfectly immobile except for the glint in his ghostly eyes. Robert concluded that his own obstinacy was useless at this point. Cracking his fists against an army officer would be bad for him and bad for all members of the Battalion. Almost vacantly he opened his mouth. Sanderson forced in three calomel pills with such force that Robert felt he might have loosened several of his teeth.

Fuming, but holding his tongue, Robert turned and walked away. He exchanged stunned looks with John Cox, Richard Slater, Ezra Allen, and Alva Phelps.

Sanderson welled up in victory. "Next!" he hissed.

Alva Phelps struggled forward. Sweat dripped from his brow as Sanderson repeated the process of briefly glancing at his chart and announcing the remedy. "Three pills of calomel," he announced to his black assistant. The slave placed the pills into Alva's mouth. Alva loosened like a tall ship that had just run sheets first into a dead calm. He choked a little as he swallowed.

Robert did not swallow the pills; rather he placed them under his tongue and felt them begin to dissolve. When he had walked a few paces away from Sanderson's wagon, Robert spit out the calomel into his hand and stared at it. The grains were a mixture of translucent gray, white, and yellow crystals.

"Better not let Sanderson catch you doing that," John Cox told him.

"My sister claims calomel is nothing more than poison," Robert shot back. For an instant he could hear Elizabeth's voice, repeating her warnings.

"Then why do doctors like Sanderson prescribe it?" Slater asked.

Robert again thought of what Elizabeth had taught him. "Well, it's made up of mercury chloride and acts as a purgative. I guess it kills bacteria. But it's so toxic it'll kill a man. It's so insoluble that it'll just lodge in your gut. That's what happened to Alvin Smith, Joseph's brother."

Elizabeth had learned all this from Dr. Willard Richards, an Apostle, who had also served as Joseph's personal physician. Richards practiced the Thomsonian method of administering natural herbs. Alvin Smith had died from a calomel overdose.

"It'd be better if we could all go see Dr. McIntire instead," John Cox said. Sanderson's assistant was Dr. William McIntire, a Mormon volunteer who administered herbs. Trouble was, Sanderson kept McIntire under wraps almost twenty-four hours a day.

"I wonder how many of the men are actually swallowing their pills?" Ezra Allen asked. He had seen Alva Phelps swallow his.

"I hope none," Robert said as he tossed the calomel onto the ground and mashed it into the soil with his foot. Then he talked to the calomel. "I wouldn't wish you on the meanest Missourian, the apostates back in Nauvoo, or even Governor Ford," he said. Then he rethought. "Well maybe I would at that. And if this happens again, I'll stuff you right back down Sanderson's throat, or A. J.'s."

29

LONG BEFORE THE BATTALION stopped the next day, Robert knew that Battalion soldiers were going to have more trouble with Smith and Sanderson. What Smith didn't know about Mormon-hating, Sanderson was trying to teach him—weaving Satan's tentacles with lusty enthusiasm.

After a twenty-five-mile march, the Battalion was now camped near McPherson, Kansas, a tiny settlement made up of hardened prairie people trying to eke out a living on the dry dirt, living in constant fear of the Indians.

Smith was strutting around again, giving unreasonable orders and causing general mayhem. He had picked out another campsite without water, apparently trying to prove his authority over the Mormons. Not only that, but on purpose he had sent the provision wagons on ahead, keeping them a full day ahead of the Battalion. The other provision wagons still had not caught up with the Battalion, apparently still lost somewhere south of Fort Leavenworth.

Smith not only refused a request from Robert to slaughter beef cattle to eat for supper, he also refused the use of flour.

Robert shook his head incredulously. "What'll we eat, grasshoppers?"

Pixton, the cook, scratched his chin through a beard that was growing longer and thicker every day. "I hear they're not bad when fried in molasses."

"He's trying to starve us into submission," said Levi Roberts.

The sound of a bugle resonated through the camp.

"Oh, oh," John Cox said to Robert. "Sick call again."

Robert had just returned from the creek where he'd filled his canteen and brought Pixton a bucket of water. He had dawdled there some, fearing another confrontation with Sanderson. "Well, I can spit out calomel just as well this time as I did last time," he said with a resigned look. "Maybe Smith and Sanderson will mellow out some today."

"I'll go with you this time," said Daniel.

Just before they reached Sanderson's wagon, Robert saw the unmistakable form of Lieutenant Smith dressing down a private from B Company, a man named Durham. Smith's head looked a size larger than yesterday, and so did his butt.

"Have you taken your medicine?" Smith asked Durham, looking like he was ready to use his whip on the poor man.

"Yes, sir," came the answer.

"Medicine from Dr. Sanderson?"

Dunham was honest. "No, sir. Medicine from Dr. McIntire."

Smith jumped on top of the wagon box. He looked delirious with anger as he cursed and faced the men who had surrounded the sick wagon. "You Mormons need to learn to obey orders. My orders are that you must use Dr. Sanderson, and use his treatments. If any one of you go to Dr. McIntire without my consent, I'll cut that man's throat, and I mean it."

Robert's hopes for a mellower Lieutenant Smith had faded to black. He balled both fists again and took a step toward the wagon. Smith had threatened to kill members of the Mormon Battalion. Suddenly Robert felt a heavy hand on his shoulder.

"Don't do it," Daniel whispered. "He'll have you skinned alive."

Smith's dark eyes were still flaring with anger. He turned his vehemence toward Private Dunham again. "As for you, if I ever catch you taking medicine from McIntire again, I'll tie a rope around your neck and drag you behind a wagon all day long."

Robert, in a low voice, said to Daniel, "Just one punch is all it would take. I'd like to see him belly up."

"Patience, brother. Patience," Daniel pleaded. "You throw a punch and you'll wear a wooden overcoat the rest of the trip."

Robert understood the terminology; in past times soldiers were placed in a barrel as punishment for crimes.

Smith was still cursing, vowing to send any man to hell that disobeyed his orders. "Now all of you Brighamites get into line, all of you, and Dr. Sanderson will treat you. Take your medicine like a man. If you're on Dr.

Sanderson's sick list, get in line."

Robert cringed and old emotions of hate surged into his consciousness. He was still on the list even though he had no current fevers or chills. As the men formed, there was low murmuring.

The young soldier, Henderson Cox, was in line. He turned to Robert and Daniel and said, "Smith and Sanderson are as bad as our worst enemies that surrounded Nauvoo. I wish I hadn't said anything about the blisters on my feet."

Daniel grunted in disgust. "I agree; bad men there stained their hands with the blood of the Saints. Now these two officers are threatening to do the same thing."

The line moved rapidly, with Sanderson administering doses of calomel with alarming regularity. Sanderson asked Henderson Cox if he had any complaint other than blistered feet.

"No," replied John. The complaint had managed to get his name on Sanderson's list.

"Open your mouth," Sanderson said. When Henderson did, Sanderson shoved calomel into it. He had quickly caught onto the fact that most of the soldiers had spit out the calomel as soon as they were out of sight. "Wash it down with water from your canteen. Right now, in my presence."

Henderson complied with the preposterous request and then moved away.

Alva Phelps was next in line.

"You don't look any better," Sanderson said.

Phelps stood in silence, fearing the worst.

"Arsenic for you," Sanderson said. "Open up." The doctor had long ago lost his compass for human decency.

Sanderson's black servant poured arsenic into a rusty spoon, the same rusty spoon that had been used to administer arsenic to all other men who had a history of intermittent fevers and chills. Robert noted that the black servant had not even wiped the spoon, let alone wash it.

"No calomel today?" Alva asked almost helplessly.

"Calomel yesterday, arsenic today," quipped the doctor. "I'm just about out of calomel."

When Alva stepped away gagging, Robert found himself facing Sanderson.

The doctor let his eyes fall to his chart, and then back at Robert.

"Still no fever or chills?" he asked

Robert braced himself. "No fever, no chills."

"Bitters of bayberry bark for you," Sanderson said. He handed him a crumpled piece of paper with bits and pieces of the herb. "That's in addition to the calomel."

Robert's jaw dropped in complete surprise. Elizabeth had used bayberry leaves, obtained from the store—bayberry shrubs grew only in drier regions—to combat minor fevers, colds, and sore throats. He had none of those symptoms, but he accepted the remedy and quickly stepped aside. Perhaps there was a sliver of humanity in Dr. Sanderson after all. But only a sliver.

Under the stare of Sanderson and the black servant, Robert swallowed the bayberry along with the calomel.

"Next!" Sanderson roared as Robert darted away holding his throat.

When Robert returned to his mess he found John Cox thrusting a finger down his throat, inducing the urge to vomit out the calomel he had taken. Robert did the same, invoking strong heaves.

"Ain't army life wonderful?" Robert said as he spit the last of his vomit out of his mouth and reached for his canteen. He swirled some Kansas water around his mouth and spit again; he could taste the calomel.

"I wish I were back in Iowa with my wife," John said.

"So do I," Robert said. "Things are apt to be better there than they are here."

CHAPTER NOTES

Background information about Lieutenant Smith and Dr. Sanderson is footnoted in the book, *Army of Israel*, Mormon Battalion Narratives (Utah State University Press, Logan, Utah, 2000), edited by David L. Bigler and Will Bagley. In another footnote, the book documents that Colonel Allen was "a man of a few unfortunate habits which doubtless was the cause of his death," referring no doubt to an addiction to alcohol, a common harmful habit among frontier army officers.

Although the author alleges that there may have been a conspiracy on the part of Colonel Sterling Price to harass and harm members of the Mormon Battalion, the reader will remember that this is a work of fiction. However, the facts speak for themselves. The facts are: (1) Colonel Price was, indeed, a vicious Mormon hater and in charge of the guards at the Richmond Jail when the guards were rebuked by the Prophet Joseph Smith; (2) Price was, indeed, a high ranking officer, in charge of the Second Regiment of the Missouri Mounted Volunteers. He could have been the highest-ranking officer at Fort Leavenworth at the time, after General Kearny left for Santa Fe; (3) Several sources confirm the fact that supply wagons containing provisions such as flour and bacon were sent south along a wrong road and took a long time to catch up with the Mormon Battalion.

Mormon Battalion journals are unanimous in their opinions of Dr. Sanderson. The men did not like him and did everything they could to avoid his calomel doses. Dr. Sanderson's personal journal has recently come to light. Readers agree that Sanderson was trying to do his job as an army doctor. Calomel was used in those days for nearly every ailment.

30

Iowa Mormon Settlements

September 2, 1846

ELIZABETH'S SUPPLY OF QUININE WAS GONE. There was none to be had at Sarpy's, and even if there were, there was no money to buy some. The ague season had struck hard at the Mormon encampments around Council Bluffs. There were a lot of people under Elizabeth's care who were sick but there wasn't much she could do for them. Dianah and Lizzy's symptoms were about the same; their fingernails had turned a bluish color and they complained of chills with flushes of heat. Dianah could hardly breath because of a severe pain in her liver area. Daniel's mother, Martha, complained of a dull headache and dizziness. She also had an irritating cough that secreted a bloody mucus. Katherine's fever had turned into a harsh sweat. Annie had uncontrollable shakes, intermittent but violent.

The heat along the Missouri River basin had been horrendous since the departure of the Mormon Battalion. Members of the Daniel Browett wagon company were now camped in a wooded area called Cutler's Park, but the trees did little to protect everyone from the drab, humid, hot, suffocating conditions. The temperature hovered at or above a hundred degrees for a high, and had been that way for more than three weeks.

Brigham Young, Wilford Woodruff, and the other members of the Twelve had been meeting with representatives of two Indian tribes to formalize an agreement to make a winter camp on their lands on the west side of the river. The men in Elizabeth's camp—Thomas Bloxham, John Hyrum Green, George Bundy, Job Smith, and Thomas Kington—had been trying to get their cattle, and the livestock of others, across the river where there was fresh grass. Thomas had sold two of his calves at the Indian village for two dollars and forty cents each. Yesterday, the men had swathed wild grass for hay. Brigham Young had firmed up his decision not to send an advance company over the mountains this season. Nearly everyone had made tents out of their wagon covers. It had taken several weeks, but Elizabeth had learned how to keep the tent from collapsing every time a strong wind came through.

Elizabeth was bent over Annie Eagles, who lay in a burning fever on a quilt under an oak tree next to Annie's mother, Katherine. Harriet was at their tent, baking bread in an iron campfire oven. Smoke streamed up from hundreds of surrounding cooking fires. Hannah's son, Joseph, and other herd boys were dozing on the slopes; sheep, horses, cows, and oxen were either feeding or lowing in the shade. Along the creek, women were washing all manner of white muslins, red flannels, and colored calicoes, hanging them on bushes to dry. A few crude log cabins were going up, and others at places like Hyde Park, where Orson's other two wives were camped. Indians paraded by, some of them painted up for an evening war dance to entertain people.

With all this to worry about, Elizabeth's sister-in-law, Rebecca Browett Hyde, received news that set her jealousies on fire again. Mary Ann had given birth to her first child. Rebecca wasn't even pregnant yet and was in a low mood as she visited Elizabeth.

"I think Urania is a bad choice of a name," Rebecca was saying. "Mary Ann should have named her baby after Emma Smith. I don't know where she got the name Urania."

Elizabeth knew she should slip a comforting arm around her sister-in-law and give her a little sympathy. Instead, she shuddered in disgust. She felt there were more pressing things to worry about than argue over the name of a new baby girl. She fired back a reaction. "Maybe Mary Ann chose the name from somewhere in her father or mother's family. It's a *nice* name. I don't mind it; besides, it's none of my business."

Just as Rebecca and herself, Mary Ann had been born in Gloucestershire, England, and joined the Church in 1840, also a convert of Wilford Woodruff. However, Mary Ann's first husband, Thomas Price, did not join and divorced Mary Ann because she did. Mary Ann Price had become Orson's third wife.

Rebecca frowned and helped herself to Elizabeth's bowl of wild grapes. "Well, I don't like it one bit."

"At least the child was born healthy," Elizabeth commented as she wiped little Annie's brow. "There's a *lot* of sickness going around." She wondered if Rebecca would ever get over her jealousies of Orson's other two wives.

"I'm glad you got to midwife, instead of Patty Bartlett Sessions," Rebecca said with a melancholy sigh.

Elizabeth's shoulders sagged for a moment. Patty's name was a menacing reminder that no one was immune from the trials and tribulations of a mortal body. "I worry about Sister Sessions. She's so sick some fear she'll die."

Mormondom's most prominent midwife had been sick since early August with a stomach inflammation, even to the point she had planned her own funeral. For days she had only been able to take a teaspoon of water at a time. A priesthood blessing from Brigham Young and Heber C. Kimball finally pulled her out of death's doorstep.

Elizabeth said to Rebecca, "I'm worried about Dianah, Martha, Mary, and Katherine, too. You're *lucky* that your ague symptoms are mild."

Rebecca's complaints kept coming. "It's so mournful around here without our husbands."

"Well, at least your husband is expected to return from England by next spring," Elizabeth said as she fed some hot soup to Annie. "I don't suppose I'll see *Daniel* again until more than a year from now, sometime in the fall of next year."

"Do you miss him?"

"I dream about him every night."

"Tell me the truth…did you detest sharing him with Harriet?"

"Strangely, no," Elizabeth answered. "I thought I would, and that's why I resisted for so long, an *entire* year. But I'm at peace with the whole thing. I *love* Harriet like a sister."

Rebecca drew a deep breath and withdrew a few steps. Her good side finally came out. "Anything I can do to help?"

Elizabeth pointed to the bowl of withered grapes, the last of the season. "Take some of these to your mother, and to Dianah. Without *quinine*, I suppose the best thing they can do for the ague is to get a *lion's* share of fresh fruits and vegetables. We arrived *too late* to plant a garden. There're no peach or apple trees. The chokecherries and gooseberries are long gone. I hope the grapes are a good substitute. See if your mother has any muskmelons left. And *force* some barley coffee down Dianah; it'll do her good. If she's out, parch some more for her. When the men come back, tell them that Mary and Katherine's tent has about had it. It needs a new ridgepole. That last windstorm about did it in."

The Bloxham wagon and tent were located a stone's throw down the creek. Hannah was there with Dianah, washing clothes in the creek, and all the Harris and Bloxham children were either on their way to help Joseph watch the livestock or playing in the woods. Like Katherine, Dianah was laying on a quilt looking worse by the hour.

Hannah responded to Rebecca's offer to help by having her wring out a pile of pants, shirts, socks, and underwear. She thanked Rebecca for the grapes and soon the two women were kneeling at Dianah's quilt watching the sick lady nibble on them.

Dianah's voice was barely audible. "I wish Elizabeth had some more quinine, or the blessing Brother Bundy gave me would take effect."

"Elizabeth said to eat a lot of these grapes, and force as many liquids into yourself as you can," Rebecca said. "Barley coffee, tea, or even water. She's says it's important because you're losing so many body fluids with your hot and cold sweats."

"I'll try," Dianah whispered.

Hannah peered into her sister-in-law's listless red eyes. "You look worse than ever."

Dianah somehow found the strength to ask a question. "Do you wonder how Robert's doing in this heat? It's got to be bad where he is, too."

Hannah felt a pang in her heart. The only thing that had kept her from slipping into a deep depression over the fact that she and Robert had been separated now for six weeks was her hectic schedule of finding food, feeding children, washing clothes, and caring for the sick. Joseph was old enough to milk the cow and supervise the other children in simple chores like finding firewood and scouring tinware with creek water. The mosquito and bug population was beginning to dwindle, but it was still thick enough to plague her night and day.

"I'm certain the army's taking good care of him," Hannah answered. "The Spirit told me that his enlistment was the right thing to do. Don't worry about Robert, just take care of yourself. Eat another grape."

"Brigham Young is sending two men to Santa Fe to collect the Battalion money," John Hyrum Green told Elizabeth and Hannah. "They're leaving tomorrow. They'll deliver letters to your husbands, so get them ready. You need to take your letters to Cutler's Park by eight in the morning."

Elizabeth glanced up at Brother Green. "Thanks for the message. Did Brother Brigham make a decision on *where* our winter camp will be?" As all the other Mormon women in camp, Elizabeth wore a white apron over her dress. Brigham and the Twelve had stressed the importance of the women maintaining their femininity despite the harsh conditions. Women never wore men's clothing.

The Mormons had used the Cold Spring Camp as their headquarters all during July and up through August sixth. Since then, most everyone had been camped at Cutler's Park, several miles northwest. Brigham Young and members of the Twelve had been exploring a new area for the permanent winter camp, east of Cutler's Park, but on the west bank of the Missouri River. When Daniel and Robert had enlisted, the Mormon pioneers had used an area now known as the Grand Encampment, on the north side of Mosquito Creek.

Elizabeth realized they were in Indian Country. When the first Saints reached the Missouri River in mid-June, they had reached the organized territorial limits of the United States. What lay west of the Missouri River had been designated as "Indian Country" by an act of Congress. Elizabeth found herself smack dab in the middle of more than two thousand Pottawattamie, Ottawa, and Chippewa Indians in southwest Iowa, thirteen hundred Omaha Indians west of Sarpy's in Bellevue, and nearly another thousand Indians who lived in a village southwest of Bellevue. For this reason, Indians were always visible and always on Elizabeth's mind.

The Omaha Indians had already agreed to let the Mormons stay on the west side of the Missouri for at least two years.

John Hyrum Green dismounted and let his horse graze on the sparse grass that spread itself among the elms and aspen trees around Elizabeth's camp. "Word is that Brigham likes the new area. There're plans to lay out streets, build small log homes, and get some mills built as soon as possible. In fact, Brigham has been appointed supervisor. The first mill will be at Turkey Creek."

"Well, I'm *tired* of living out of this wagon box and tent," Elizabeth said. "It would be *nice* if all of us had a log house, even if it were small."

"How's Sister Bloxham?" John Hyrum asked.

"I'm afraid she's worse," Elizabeth admitted. The ague season was just about over, but not Dianah's sickness. She had been growing weaker by the day, it seemed. "I think she has consumption now. I'm *really* worried about her. And I worry about some of the children, too. Especially Robert's."

31

ROBERT GOT HIS FIRST TASTE OF BUFFALO meat from "Toothless" Moses Bayer, the old teamster sutler. Bayer had filled his provision wagon mainly with barrels of rye and corn whiskey and champagne, along with red and blue flannel shirts, trousers, wool and cotton cloth, home remedies, and a small variety of foodstuffs.

Bayer's boss was the man in Fort Leavenworth who kept the store, and he had a monopoly of all buying and selling in the fort's jurisdiction. The boss sent teamsters like Toothless Bayer to follow the Army of the West as a huckster, or traveling store. The boss had sent a purser and a bookkeeper, too, and they kept the pressure on Toothless to sell as much as he could.

Toothless talked in a perfect frontier drawl. "I can't waste my time a followin' you soldiers if ya ain't a-gonna buy whiskey from me," he had said to the Battalion boys a day or two after they left Fort Leavenworth.

It was illegal to sell liquor to soldiers, but Toothless did it anyway—on orders from the boss. At the fort, liquor had been bootlegged into the barracks because the Missourians demanded it. Officers had turned a blind eye to the practice for they were only human and they, too, liked to drink. The enlisted men encouraged the officers to drink because drinks had a tendency to mellow them materially. But occasionally, when enlisted men became unruly, the officers cracked down on liquor consumption.

Toothless had been following the Second Regiment of Missouri Volunteers and Robert hadn't seen him for more than two weeks. Born in Germany but brought to Missouri by his parents at age four, Toothless had been one of the first buffalo hunters on the plains west of Independence. His claim to fame, or so he said the first time Robert met him, was killing a white buffalo near Cimarron Springs in 1837, which brought twenty times the amount of money as a regular buffalo hide.

"You shoulda seen that hide," Tooth had said on that first occasion. "Hair was long and soft, perfectly white, like a sheep's fleece. The Injuns tried to kill me fer it, and when that didn't work, they tried to trade me outta it."

Toothless retired from buffalo hunting not because he was getting old—he was only fifty-one—but because he had broken his back in a fall off a horse and walked bent over and with a limp. He lost all his teeth except seven due to his habit of drinking his coffee thick with brown sugar. He would never sell much sugar or molasses out of his wagon for fear of running out. He had a limited supply of cheese for thirty-five cents a pound, herring three for five cents, peaches one dollar a can, and chewing tobacco for a dollar sixty a pound.

"When I first came to America the frontier was just spilling over the Appalachians into the Ohio River Valley," Toothless said with a noted lisp. "Now it's butted against the muddy Missouri. And thanks to me and my mountain men friends, we're pushing toward the Pacific. Next thing you know, you soldiers will have New Mexico and California as part of these United States of America."

"I suppose," Robert said. He had taken a liking to the old sutler. To him, Toothless was an island of sanity in a world of biased Missourians. Temporarily, it made Robert forget how much he loathed Dr. Sanderson and Lieutenant Smith.

"Yer people are headin' fer the Great Basin I hear," Toothless said in his drawl.

"Not by choice, but I guess that's where I'll find my wife and family in a year," Robert admitted.

"Well, children's geography books say that's all Indian land, but you're welcome to it," Toothless added with a lazy grin. "But why not go to Oregon?"

"Don't know," Robert answered.

Toothless spit a wad of tobacco juice. "Oregon ought ta suit you Mormon farmers more'n the Great Basin. I hear in Oregon the pigs are runnin' under the acorn trees, round and fat, already cooked, with knives and forks stickin' in them so that you kin cut off a slice whenever yer hungry."

Robert laughed. "You tell that to Brigham Young."

"I will if'n I ever see 'im. If'n ya go to the Great Basin you'll have a fork stickin' in you and the Injuns will have *you* fer supper."

Robert recoiled at the remark, and so did Daniel.

The Missourians had killed two buffalo the day previous and Toothless brought a kettle full of roast with him to test the Mormons again on their resistance to his barrels of whiskey larder. Private Davis, the young soldier who had fought with Robert at Fort Leavenworth, looked as though he wanted to try some of the sutler's whiskey, but Robert's icy stare and Duke's growls drove him away.

"Just tell me if this ain't the most tenderest meat you've ever et," he told Robert and the other soldiers who crowded around his wagon. He was hard to understand, given the fact that his lips flapped together due to his loss of teeth. "Yer the Battalion butcher, ain't cha?" he asked Robert.

Toothless's head was cocked and there was tobacco juice trickling down his bearded chin. His face was sharp and thin, and there was a long nose and a chin hob-knobbing each other. He appeared to look neither to the right nor left, but in fact his twinkling eyes were everywhere. Despite the heat, he worn a fringed deerskin-hunting shirt, bedaubed until it had the appearance of polished leather, and it hung in folds over his bony carcass. His legs were clothed in pantaloons of the same material, which scattered fringes down the outside of both legs. These were well shrunk and clung tightly to his short, spare, spindly legs. Robert figured he was living in the past, and it showed in his dress and mannerisms.

"Yep," Robert admitted, "I'm the butcher and I agree that the buffalo meat is tender, and sweet, too."

Robert had seen a few buffalo during the day near Cow Creek, but at a long distance. He had seen wolves also, trailing the buffalo, looking for an easy meal from wounded buffalo or new calves. They sent up hideous howls whenever they smelled food or blood. There were no hardwood groves in this country, and only a few cottonwood, elm, box elder, and willows when they came to creeks and waterholes. Buffalo grass hugged the ground, along with the crumbling bones of buffalo left behind by hunters. Buffalo gnats, small and black, were getting thicker.

"By tomorra the plains'll be black with buffalo," Toothless predicted as he pointed west. Despite his statement, he seemed to have a lack of consciousness of time. "Ya kin count on it. Make yer camp early and I'll show ye boys how ta hunt buffalo." Toothless had a little quirt and was always nervously popping himself on the leg with it. When he took off his hat, spiky gray hair stuck out in all directions.

The Battalion had passed several buffalo carcasses of animals killed by Kearny's Missouri volunteers. Nothing but the tongue had been used, and the rest of the meat lay rotting in the sun. Daniel had reminded Robert of the scripture, *Woe unto those who take life and waste flesh when they have no need.*

The thoughts of all the tender buffalo meat you could eat excited the men, and the talk at dinner was of almost nothing else—except Dr. Sanderson and the way the doctor treated the Mormons. Sanderson had been filling Lieutenant Smith with more stories about killing Mormons in Missouri, delighting in his descriptions of the corpses that lay in the smoldering heaps of the Haun's Mill massacre. Toothless stayed in another section of the camp for a while and entertained the soldiers with his stories, how buffalo sometimes blocked the trail, trampled down tents, upset wagons, stampeded mules and oxen, wallowed in the mud, and marched in long majestic files to drink at the river.

The thoughts of hundreds and even thousands of buffalo roused the heart of every man in the Battalion. Robert began imagining what the hairy beast would look like up close, and what it would be like to skin and butcher one. Toothless said that late summer was the season of fury with the buffalo. The bulls had rejoined the cows and hundreds of battles would be going on, for it was the rutting season.

"The prairie'll look like a plowed field in places," Toothless said, casting his eyes westward. "Them bulls'll wanna hook other bulls, and you, too. We'll let the bulls fight and go after the cows. It's those cows what's good eatin'.

Robert went to his haversack and got his knife, and then he began sharpening it. Robert Pixton was cooking supper over buffalo chips and the smell was strong. Soon Pixton was boiling parsley plants and making bread in an iron oven. He brought out clusters of grapes he had picked along Cow Creek.

"When ya camp tomorrow night, take precautions," Toothless advised. "Camp in the trees and protect yourselves with the wagons, and even fell some trees if you have ta. Them critters can run right over you in the night. I've seen herds thicker'n fleas, thicker'n mosquitoes. Saw a herd one time a hundred miles long and fifty miles wide."

"Easier to shoot that way?" Daniel asked as his eyes grew round.

"Don't waste a ball unless you aim at one critter at a time, and aim at the lungs. You hit 'em in the heart and they'll still run a mile. Them muskets the army give you pack a big enough wallop, but you've got ta get yer aim just right."

Daniel gasped and gave a little nod, as though he understood.

"If we run into large herds, you'll learn to hate 'em," Toothless predicted.

"Why?" Robert asked, looking unconvinced.

"Ever had buffalo tea?"

"Why, I can't say I've ever heard of such a thing."

"If we see big herds, they'll have ruint the water holes with their urine and droppin's. Wherever the critters pass the water is so fouled that not even the mules and oxen will drink it. When ya get closer ta the desert and find ya have ta quench yer thirst on buffalo tea, you'll acquire a hatred for them shaggy beasts alright."

The stories Toothless told about hunting buffalo kept Robert in awe. He told of standing in one spot and, even with the slow system of powder and ball, killing a dozen buffalo. Another time he narrowly escaped death among a large herd when a tornado caused the buffalo to stampede in terror. They would stampede after lightning strikes, too, and prairie fires.

"I've seen whole herds with their hair singed off, others blinded and maimed, and others scorched and roasted. One time the ground was littered with dead and dying critters."

Toothless told of watching Indians hunt buffalo: men camouflaged beneath wolf pelts, on horseback with bows and arrows, and spears, too; driving small herds into a corral where they were quickly slaughtered, and running them over cliffs to kill hundreds at a time.

"They's strange creatures, them buffalo," Toothless said. "In ruttin' season, like now, them ole bulls will hook ya and kill ya. But sometimes, they's docile as an old milk cow. Years ago, up yonder, I came inta a swale where there wuz clear water and high green grass. A great herd of buffalo was a grazin' there. I moved slowly through 'em, comin' so close ta some that I could touch 'em, and I did touch 'em. The long, dusty hair of their hides was crinkled and coarse. Their breathin' was like the sound of a huge, close swarm of bees. I just kept quiet and walked real slow and they paid me no mind."

Robert was intrigued. "Will it be that way tomorrow, when we see the great herds?"

"Why, ya don't wanna get close to them bulls tomorrow, my boy," Toothless said with a shake of the head. "They'll be a fightin' each other. Meats no good anyway in the rut. Go fer the cows."

One thing about Toothless Bayer, he was easily found. By evening, any evening, he would be running his sutler wagon from one company to the other, and pestering one mess and then another, drawing occasionally on his jug. When Robert looked up from his dinner plate, Toothless was there trying to get the Battalion boys to buy some of his wares, promising credit until pay-day at Santa Fe.

"No, I'm not buying anything, but I have questions for you," Robert said to Toothless.

Toothless had an armful of shirts, but he set them down on the grass. "I reckon I'm plumb pooped out from sellin', so what's yer question?"

"I'm wondering about Santa Fe," Robert said. "We're all hoping it'll be a good place to rest for a few days."

"It's no St. Louis, or even Independence," Toothless said. "The Spaniards found a place that even the Indians had abandoned and made them a settlement there."

"It's an old place then?" Robert asked. In his mind, every town and city in America was relatively new. England, where he was raised, was the place for old parishes, dating back to Roman times. In America, the only place Robert had ever lived in was Nauvoo, and Nauvoo only dated back to 1839 or so.

"Old as in 1610," Toothless explained. "Spanish frontiersmen picked out the site near a river. At one time tame Pueblo Injuns lived there."

Robert already knew the difference between tame and savage Indians. Tame Indians farmed. There had been a lot of tame Shawnees and Delewares just beyond Fort Leavenworth; they had fine farms and were quite civilized. Savage Indians hunted and stole anything and everything, and killed at the drop of a hat.

Daniel had a hat over his eyes, but he removed it and looked at Toothless. "Are they still tame?"

Toothless giggled through his flapping lips. "Yep, they are. But at one time they weren't by cracky. Around 1680 the Pueblos got plumb nasty with them Spaniards. They were tired of the Spanish rules and tired of havin' the Catholic religion forced on 'em. The priests wouldn't even let 'em communicate with the old familiar Injun spirits in their kivas. In the old days practically ever' village spoke a different dialect, but now they all speak Spanish. It sort of enabled 'em to talk about their griefs in a common tongue. To make a long story short, the Injuns revolted and kilt not only soldiers but the priests, too."

"Killed the priests?" Daniel asked. "The Pueblos don't sound too friendly."

"Oh, the Spaniards reconquered Santa Fe about a dozen years later," Toothless said. "The Pueblos are back to farming and trading with the whites. It'll be peaceful enough all right."

"Most of the people are Pueblo Indians then?" Robert asked.

"Oh, no," Toothless shot back. "Santa Fe is made up mostly of Spaniards—more than half. Course they's a lot of mixed blood there, too. The Spaniards called these people quebrado, or broken color. It's a tight caste system that exists there. If yer background is not Espanol, Crillo, or other European, the Spaniards look down on ya. They's a lot of different names for the mixed blood—mestizo, castizo, mulatto. The pecking order is determined by the amount of Spanish blood ya got in ya. Or whether yer pure Injun or black. There's ever' possibility in Santa Fe. Spanish blood is mixed with Injuns and Negroes, and then back again."

"All good Catholics?" Daniel asked.

"If yer definition of a good Catholic means ya go to mass in the morning to confess and then gather in the plaza fer more sin—I guess that fits," Toothless said with a laugh. "There's sin of every description in Santa Fe, enough to make even a Missourian blush, let alone you Mormon boys. They say gamblin' is illegal in Mexico, but it's the national sport in Santa Fe."

"I guess I know where I'll find Henry," Robert said with a sigh.

32

❧

SICKNESS WAS ALL AROUND HANNAH and she wished she were back in her frame home east of Nauvoo. She had come to the conclusion that Council Bluffs was a poor place to be in the late summer, or any time for that matter. She had heard that in some camps everyone was sick except for two or three persons. A severe storm had just hit, lasting for more than an hour, and it blew down most of the tents. The clouds had rolled up white and circling in all directions, and then they seemed to be driven crazy by a west storm of wind and rain. It came while George Bundy was milking old Victoria, the cow Robert had named after the Queen of England. Victoria had lost a lot of weight during the trip from Nauvoo, and didn't give much, but a little milk was better than no milk at all. George spilled part of the milk and the storm left leaves and other debris in the bucket, but Hannah strained it out and fed Lizzy a big cupful anyway.

The person who worried her most today was Lizzy. She had been sick since Robert left, getting worse every day. All the bedding was wet and there was no place for Lizzy to lie that was dry. The other children were all wet, too.

"Aunt Elizabeth's coming, Mother," Joseph said, his face lit with excitement. Joseph was ten years old and loved visitors.

"Keep churning, she's coming to check on Lizzy," Hannah said. Her old butter churn had made it across Iowa and Joseph was making a little butter. Her camp was a mess and both George Bundy and his nephew, Job Smith, were helping to straighten it up. Thomas Kington was helping Katherine and Mary, and little Annie.

"Laws alive, I hope Brother Brigham can find us a better spot to camp for the winter," Hannah told Elizabeth when she got there.

Elizabeth gave Lizzy the last few grains of quinine and said there was no money to buy a new supply. Bishop Newel K. Whitney and others had been sent to St. Louis to buy provisions for the camp, but because the hot season was about over, Elizabeth doubted Whitney would buy any quinine. Brigham Young had given him some of the Battalion money to buy food that could be distributed to Church members scattered throughout Council Bluffs, Cutler's Park, and other locations. Brigham, along with Wilford Woodruff and Orson Pratt, had found a new location a few miles north and herds of cattle were being moved there. The favored spot, eighteen miles north of Bellevue and Sarpy's, was located on a bench of land above the river, drained on the north and on the south by two creeks. It was to be called Winter Quarters, and it was bounded on the north and west with high bluffs naturally suited for defensive purposes, Brigham said.

Elizabeth pressed a hand to Lizzy's forehead. The eight-year-old girl looked feverish and pale. "What we need is a roof over our heads," she said. "I don't know if we'll ever dry out."

Cabin building had been postponed, however. Virtually all the Mormon men were cutting and stacking wild grass from the prairie into hay. At last count nearly two thousand tons had been stacked. Fences were being built, too, and wells dug.

Brigham, in fact, had told the Saints that he was thinking that the Church might be better off to stay along the Missouri for a year or two and work on getting better outfitted for the trip west. With nearly fifteen thousand people that would eventually migrate to the Great Basin to establish the Church in the mountains, crops needed to be planted here first, mills built, and an economy started. Brigham and the Twelve were still negotiating with the Oto and Omaha Indians on final terms for using the land.

"Anything more I can do for you?" Elizabeth asked the child as she stood up to leave. There were so many sick people in camp that she hardly had time to take care of Moroni. She was not only out of quinine, but out of her herbs, too.

Lizzy shook her head, yes. "I want another letter from Papa."

Hannah had read Robert's letter to her a dozen times. Tearfully, Hannah said, "He has to reach Santa Fe first, and that'll be awhile. I'll read you the old one again."

Robert's letter had told of his March through Missouri, meeting the one friendly Missourian and getting a little food, the encounter with Colonel Price, what Fort Leavenworth was like, Colonel Allen's sickness, the need for the Battalion to get to Santa Fe and join Kearny's forces, and that the Battalion would be used to occupy California. But the most shocking news to Hannah had been the fact that Henry was in the army, too, serving as a teamster in Colonel Price's regiment.

Katherine, Annie, and Mary had been among those who crowded around Hannah as she opened Robert's letter and read it. She could tell Katherine's emotions were swirling when it came to the part about Henry. For the life of her, Katherine had said several times she couldn't figure Henry out. Katherine said that sometimes she suspected that there were two Henrys, one that loved for and cared for her, and loved Annie, too, but the other side of Henry was mean, ornery, and he loved drinking and gambling more than her. Even after the letter Katherine doubted Henry would come back for them some day. Hannah read into the reaction that Katherine wouldn't mind it if Henry had died from his gunshot wound; then she could become a plural wife of one of the other Mormon men—if anyone would have her. Hannah dashed that thought from her mind for fear that the Church might someday ask Robert to take her. For that reason alone she began praying that Henry would return after his year's enlistment, get Katherine and Annie, join the Church, grow up, and take his family responsibilities seriously.

"Is Papa going to come back?" Annie would say about once or twice a day to Katherine, especially around meal times when Hannah and her children shared meals with them.

"I don't know, Annie," Katherine would answer. "I don't know at all. I hope so. His note said he would, so let's believe in that."

"How will he find us?" Annie asked.

"He's in the army with Uncle Robert now. Uncle Robert will help him find us."

"Does he love us, Mother?"

"Oh, I'm sure he does. He loves you as much as Uncle Robert loves Lizzy."

33

THE BUFFALO WAS A STRANGE IF NOT clever animal in Robert's view. He could tell right away bison did not like the odor of men and cattle. Occasionally he could see bison, on coming to the ruts in the trail, stop, sniff the trail, and then jump over it quickly like sheep jumping over a stick. That was different behavior than animals like Old Victoria, his cow, or the horses he had owned, like Bendigo and Tapper. Cows and horses didn't mind the scent of humans at all, and neither did pigs. The buffalo he saw in the distance always moved with the wind, except when the Missourians hunted them, and then the bulls would turn against the wind to avoid being approached from the leeward.

The Battalion had broken camp early in order to reach water at Walnut Creek before the mid-day heat suffocated man and beast. During the morning march Robert met a man and his family of six who were returning to Missouri, disenchanted with the Rocky Mountains—talking of blizzards even in July. He said he had enough of the "rattlesnake-ridden hot-bed of Indian country."

Toothless Bayer proved to be right; Buffalo were spotted all morning, and soon more than five hundred were seen at a time. Buffalo bones were scattered all over the prairie. Long lines of buffalo lined the creek to drink. Some wallowed in the mud, smearing their shoulders with wet clay as armor against blowflies, gnats, and mosquitoes. Others rolled in the dirt, creating massive buffalo wallows. Most of the cows had new red calves. Bulls, fat and sassy, pawed the ground, shook their heads, tossed tall plumes and banners of dirt and sand into the sky, and challenged each other. Most of them exceeded the height of a tall man at the top of their humps and they charged with a vengeance, rushing together with a terrific impact and the thud of broad foreheads. Then they would thrust at each other, clashing with their tough black horns, moving back and forth until the muscles of their thighs stood out like huge welts. The struggle would continue, with the small, dark eyes of both bulls rolling in their stubborn heads, until one finally gave way, pushed to his knees, and suddenly finding a huge hole ripped into his side. Then the victor, wheeling, would trot off driving the cow—the cause of the dispute. Hunters preferred cows and so the bulls far outnumbered them. Each season, Toothless said, as the disparity in numbers increased, the fury of the bulls mounted.

Camp was no sooner made than Robert saw an old bull that looked like he weighed more than two oxen mingling with the cattle. Duke went a little crazy at the sight of the bull, so Robert had Daniel hold the dog back. When

Robert approached he saw that the younger, lustier bulls had gored it. The old bull looked content, however, and when Robert inched closer the bull just slung a long string of slobbers over its back and went to grazing again.

"Waugh! Don't shoot 'im," Toothless said to Robert and the other soldiers who were with him. "He'll be tougher'na old board. Old bulls like this always hang back of the main herd. Go fer cows. Tonight you'll feast on dark-red meat, sweet fat, hump-ribs, marrow, and tongue."

The thoughts of all that intrigued Robert, especially after living off salt sowbelly for the past few days, which had terribly upset his stomach.

Robert and Daniel mounted mules for the hunt. Robert felt funny, as though he ought to be on a horse, like a real buffalo hunter.

"The trick is ta get near a critter on the walk; don't run the mule if ya don't have ta. It'll just frighten the buffalo," Toothless said, looking as though he wished he could straighten his bent body and ride with them. "Sometimes buffalo hunters and Injuns have ta run the meat. Sometimes ya kin git close enuff without runnin' 'em, just whatever luck'll bring ya. And don't get close ta them bulls. The neck of a buffalo is strong enough ta toss a mule or a horse ten feet in the air."

Robert looked at Daniel not knowing which way to go. There were cows in all directions. "What about them red calves?" he asked.

"You nice Mormons otta pick a cow without a calf," Toothless said with a belly laugh. "And don't aim at the head. A ball cain't penetrate."

The hunt was less of a real adventure than Robert had envisioned. He left

Duke in camp. They rode the mules only a few hundred yards when a cow without a calf was spotted. Robert dismounted, aimed his gun, and fired. The crack of the musket startled the cow buffalo and instantly in the middle of a bare spot appeared a red dot. The cow shivered, jumped, and then staggered forward, not falling. For a few seconds the cow walked heavily, almost as if nothing had happened. But soon she stopped, tottered, her knees bent under her, and then her head sank to the ground. The buffalo then swayed her whole bulk to one side, rolled over in the grass, and died with barely a perceptible struggle.

Toothless and Robert's messmates brought one of Company E's wagons up and Robert began the task of butchering, with Duke licking at the blood. Toothless whacked off the tail and nailed it to the wagon, saying it was an emblem of the first Mormon to kill a buffalo on the Santa Fe Trail. Robert knew it really wasn't true—scouts had already killed one or two, but he went along with the little ceremony.

"Get the tongue out of her first," Toothless said.

"I've done this kind of work before, in England," Robert replied, feeling he didn't need the advice. He took of his hat to let his head cool. "I know what I'm doing." He slashed out the skin between the prongs of the jawbone, pulled the tongue through the opening, and cut it off. "Cook it up and give us all a taste," he said to Robert Pixton, the cook.

It took twice as long as it would have done a steer to gut the cow. "The wolves will have a meal, too, won't they?" Daniel remarked.

Coyotes and wolves had already made their appearance.

Toothless cast Daniel a reproachful glare. "Waugh! That's burro milk talk. Why, don't leave nothin' ta the wolves," he said. "Not only that, but it'll rile up the Injuns if ya waste the meat of a buffalo."

He explained that men trained in the Indian methods always opened the belly first to get out the warm, raw liver. Toothless pushed Robert aside and cut away the liver. "Indians take this liver and sprinkle a sauce on it from the gall bladder and refresh themselves. So do real mountain men. Try some?"

Robert pulled a face, looking aggrieved. "We always ate the liver in England and in Nauvoo, but we cooked it first. What if that stuff in raw form causes blindness?"

Toothless laughed. "If that's the case, every buck Injun around here would be blind, and so would the trappers. You otta try it. Buffalo gall can give a man quite a glow," Toothless said, grinning.

"It's all yours," Robert replied, sensing that the Indian delicacy must be something of a stimulant.

Toothless looked as though he were insulted, or puzzled over the Mormon's refusal to join him. "Well, the idea is ta not wait for the liver ta cool, but ta eat it while it's hot." And this he did, eating a healthy portion after he sprinkled gall juice over it, leaving the rest for Pixton to cook for the evening meal.

Robert grimaced. He had never thought of eating raw liver this way.

Toothless snatched a hatchet and cracked open the skull of the buffalo.

"Warm brains is the next best delicacy, long a favorite of the trapper." He scooped out a portion with his hands and thrust the brains into his mouth. He swallowed hardly without chewing. He offered a handful to Robert. "Better'n dog meat," Toothless said.

Robert cast a forlorn look at Duke. He couldn't imagine eating Duke, let alone warm buffalo brains.

"No thanks," Robert said. "I'm not that hungry." He had the sinking feeling, however, and he and the Battalion boys might be reduced to eating the brains of some animal before their journey was through.

"Now don't cha leave the heart, kidneys, and intestines for the wolves, either," he said, taking over from Robert, who reluctantly let him. "This part of butchering is likely to disgust the greenhorn." He pushed out the contents of the intestines and in time knitted the long tubes into a loopy chain.

Before getting to the main meat, Toothless showed Robert how to take the hump by skinning down each side of the shoulders, cutting away the meat, and chopping off the hump-ribs with a hatchet. "These're the choice parts," he said. "And so's the *depouille*, or the black fat." He cut out a strip of fatty matter lying along the backbone from the shoulder blade on.

"This piece," Toothless pointed out, "if scalded fer a few minutes in hot grease, will keep fer a long time, just a hangin' on a wagon. Out here we call it Injun Bread. Ya kin just saunter up and whack ya off a slice when ya want it."

A few minutes later the men had the huge cow propped up on her belly by stretching out her legs front and back. Toothless and Robert cut the hide in two along the backbone, and peeled down the hide from both sides. "We don't care if there's some meat left on the hide," Toothless explained in working fast. "We can take them pieces off with a dubber. Yer man Pixton can make an excellent soup outta that meat."

Toothless stretched the hide out on the ground, ready to receive the meat. By laying the meat on the skin, he said, the hunter kept the meat clean.

Next, the men cut away the outer blanket of flesh from the back and sides. "This we call the fleece," Toothless said. The front quarters were taken off next, the hindquarters removed at the hip joints, the hump removed, and the remaining meat stripped from the ribs.

Levi Roberts had been watching in almost stunned curiosity. "How many men will this feed tonight?"

"Dern near yer entire company," Toothless estimated.

"Good thing," Pixton said. "We're almost out of provisions already."

"Sometimes buffalo hunters leave the shoulders, hams, side ribs, and head to be cleaned up by the dern wolves and coyotes," Toothless said with a rueful smile. "But not in times of famine. As many men as you've got ta feed, bring everything. We'll even boil the hoofs."

"Even the hoofs?"

Toothless ignored the question. He cut away a gob of fat laced with just a little meat. "Watch this," he said as he threw the gob at the coyotes. A coyote snatched up the gob and took off running. It was quickly caught by a pack of wolves. The wolves not only stole the gob of meat but also killed the coyote. Toothless then aimed his musket and dropped one of the wolves. Within minutes the other wolves had eaten the wolf Toothless had shot.

"That's the way it is out here on the prairie, with wolves, Injuns, and even some of the whites," Toothless warned. "Even one of your own will eat you up."

"Dern, that's a fine tasting buffalo," Toothless said a little later.

The men were gathered around a campfire in the late afternoon heat. The bison meat had been cut up and shared with other messes. Private Pixton had boiled a portion of the tongue. Now he was baking it in a Dutch oven with portions of the kidneys, liver, and heart. Robert had a long stick onto which he had fastened a portion of a hump-rib, and he was roasting it over the fire. When it looked done on the outside he applied some more salt and ate it off the stick, and then cooked it some more over the red embers. The fat-covered depouille took the place of bread and butter, and loops of intestines were sizzling on the coals like hissing snakes. The fleece and muscles were already cut into thin sheets and drying in the hot sun and wind, "making meat," as Toothless described it. The men could eat the jerky later.

"You'll find that buffalo fat, unlike the fat of cattle, can be devoured by the pound without any unpleasant effects in yer gut," Toothless said. "I've never had a bellyache from buffalo meat."

Fires crackled under iron kettles in nearly every mess. Water boiled and bubbled as men cooked their meat. Laundresses were busy doing the washing; it was the last time water would be available for washing for a few days, Toothless predicted. Others went to work with needle and thread to mend clothes, sew on buttons, and darn socks. Others kneaded bread and baked it in the spider. Some soldiers were prowling through the brush with guns, trying to knock over a prairie hen or a rabbit.

By now, several Indians had made their way into the Mormon encampment. They wandered from mess to mess, looking for food and for trades. A Comanche eyed Daniel's musket.

"Watch yer rifles and the livestock," Toothless warned. "The Injuns never think they've got enuff guns."

"How well armed are they?" Daniel asked, almost gasping at the thought.

"More than ye know," replied Toothless. "Americans've furnished guns and ammunition to the Injuns fer twenty years or more. Guess it's part of the unofficial war with them Mexicans that's been goin' on fer a long time. Some of the traders hate the greasers worse than the Injuns. It's cause the Spaniards and Mexicans made slaves of the Injuns. The traders tell the Injuns to go into the interior of Mexico and kill Mexicans and bring their horses and mules back to'em. Pay 'em with whiskey."

"But doesn't that hurt the trade with Mexico?" Robert asked.

"Naw. Trade with the Injuns is just as good. They kin kill buffalo faster than the white hunter. Someday the buffalo'll be gone, but ye kin blame the Injun just as well as the white man."

As Toothless told his Indian stories, bad feelings about them erupted again within Daniel. Toothless told how the Indians slaughtered or ran off livestock of the Mexican settlers, destroyed or appropriated crops, captured women and children, killed men, and even rendered mining a risky operation. Lately, Apache and Comanche raiders had struck a climate of fear and pessimism that extended not only throughout New Mexico but northern Mexico as well. Comanches, Toothless said, only spared Mexico from complete destruction because it supplied them with horses. It was not in the Indians' best interest to destroy the Mexican economy entirely. The Indians would have long ago destroyed all the Mexican sheep if they didn't feel like they needed the sheep, too.

"Do you think the Indians will attack the Battalion?" Daniel asked.

Toothless laughed, half roostered by his consumption of whiskey. "No, that's not their style. They're smart. They attack the weak, the small ranchos, the small caravans."

Daniel's concerns were not resolved. "But couldn't the Indians band together? There must be thousands of them."

That was true, Toothless conceded. There were all kinds of Comanches, known by different names: Cherokee, Creeks, Pawnee, Cheyenne, Deleware, Shawnee, and Arapaho, just to name a few. The Apaches, too, had numerous tribes, although they wouldn't be seen until they got closer to Santa Fe, except for the Jicarilla and the Pueblos.

Now the whiskey had really wound Toothless up. "But the Injuns are broken up into so many small bands that don't get along with even each other. They've been fightin' and killin' each other fer so long that their scars go way back. Injuns have their temptations, too, but they're bad ones. They like to collect scalps and count coups. Horses the Injun can't resist, even the horses of friends and allies. Here in the West, there's always an endless series of raids and thefts, battles and stampedes. Horses're a measure of the Injuns' wealth. Of course, he might take wild ones and break 'em, and often does. But it's more thrillin' to steal well broken horses from his enemies. To the Injun, huntin' is drudgery, war is sport, but stealin' horses is the business of life. And the white man hates 'im fer it."

Indeed, they do, thought Daniel. He was thinking of the last wars among the Lamanites in the Book of Mormon. Since their utter destruction of the Nephites, they had truly become a backward, bloodthirsty people.

Toothless told hair-raising stories about dealing with Indians on the Santa Fe Trail. Once, he said, a large party of Indians came into a trading caravan, a party large enough to take the caravan and kill the traders. Toothless invited their chief to sit and smoke with him. The white men escaped with their hair intact only because the traders agreed to give up a good portion of their goods.

"The Mexicans have tried everything with the Injuns," Toothless concluded. "They had a velvet glove policy, fancy name of trade, gifts, and alliances that didn't work. But neither has their iron fist policy of tryin' to pound 'em into submission. A bad peace with Injuns is better than a good war, but neither is very good. This child don't have an answer fer the Injuns."

Daniel shuddered. Neither did he. And neither did the Book of Mormon prophets like Mormon and Moroni, both of whom died at the hands of the Lamanites. In many ways he felt sorry for the Indians he had seen wandering around the camp. But in another way he feared the huddle of insolent brown men with their sinewy, naked bodies, their long breechclouts, their bobbed black hair, their cloth headbands, and their strange yellow moccasins. But in other ways they were no different than the mobs of white men who had killed Joseph and Hyrum Smith, and had driven the Mormons out of Missouri and Illinois. Satan entered the hearts of men everywhere.

At the worst possible time, when Daniel was conjuring up visions of a big Indian aiming a hatchet at his head, a single Indian mounted on a gray horse rode into Daniel's camp. The Indian was gaudily ornamented with feathers and rode a handsome gray horse. He dismounted and began conversing with Toothless by sign language. As he did, another ten or twelve Indians appeared, but waited a few paces away without dismounting.

"What does he want?" Daniel asked Toothless after a while.

"He's Comanche. He's just returnin' from a gentleman-like horse-stealing expedition against the Kiowa. He wants ta know if he and his friends can smoke with us, share our food, drink the whiskey in my wagon, and even sleep with us overnight," Toothless said with a half fetched grin. The Comanche made a motion that he wanted to smoke in a gesture of peace. He carried a pipe decorated with glass beads, wool bands, silk ribbons, and horsehair.

Daniel shuddered. "You didn't tell him 'yes,' did you?"

Toothless laughed. "Ya turn 'em down, sometimes it angers 'em and they attack in the night. But if ya let 'em sleep in yer camp, they'll invite their hidden red gentlemen friends and slit yer throat. Ya cain't tell which'er friendly and which'er not."

Daniel shuddered again.

"What d'ya want me to tell 'im?" Toothless asked.

"Tell him to go away," Daniel said.

"I suppose I can say that," Toothless replied. "I don't think they'll make any trouble given the size of yer Battalion."

Using sign language that he had mastered, Toothless sent the Indians away.

As the men finished their meal of buffalo, express riders from Santa Fe bought the news that Santa Fe had surrendered to General Kearny's army.

"Yippee!" Robert squealed when he heard the news.

"And without even firing a shot!" Daniel exclaimed as the two men hugged each other and did a little dance. Daniel felt relieved to know that none of the New Mexicans would be shooting at him at least until he got to California. He still had his fears of Indians, though, and the pilots had said that the Pawnees were fierce and warlike in the area they were traveling.

Kearny now ordered the Battalion to skip the Bent's Fort route and travel directly to Santa Fe using the more direct trail, through the Cimarron.

"Well, that's not good news," Robert said. "I've only got one canteen."

"You should have kept those intestines—maybe they'd hold water," Levi Roberts said.

When Daniel heard of this he had mixed emotions. On one hand he wished the Battalion could be dismissed to return to the Iowa settlements and he could be free to spend the winter with Elizabeth, Moroni, and Harriet. But on the other hand, that would defeat the whole purpose of the Battalion. Funds from the Mormon soldiers' service were going to help get the main body of the Church to the Great Basin, and to help people survive the winter around Council Bluffs.

Later on, when the campfire had died to ashes and the moon appeared, and the gorged soldiers lay on their blankets telling stories and listening to the snarling of wolves in the distance, Robert and Daniel could hear the wail of orphaned buffalo calves that other soldiers had shot. Toothless had spread his buffalo robe on high ground, as was his habit in case of rain, and with his skinning knife he had ditched his bed all round against the rains. Hopeful thinking, Robert concluded. There were no clouds, and no rain expected during their desert travel.

Robert wondered how far Colonel Price and Henry were behind them. Price's regiment was supposed to have left Fort Leavenworth two or three days after the Battalion. Robert wondered when he would see Henry again, and under what circumstances.

34

Cimarron Cutoff, Kansas

September 1

WHEN PRIVATE HENRY EAGLES DROVE A WAGON into the Mormon Battalion camp loaded with provisions, Robert treated his arrival as good news and bad news. The good news was that Colonel Price once again had relented, sharing provisions with the Mormons. But just as before, the Mormon officers had to threaten him.

The bad news was that the Missourians were camped close to the Mormons, just a mile ahead on the banks of the Arkansas River where the Santa Fe Trail split into two directions.

One route led straight west toward Bent's Fort, and from there it struck south to Santa Fe; it was the long route, but safest because it had more water.

From Bent's Fort there was also a trail that led to Pueblo.

The route of the Santa Fe Trail led southwest and was called the Cimarron Cutoff because it cut the distance to Santa Fe by a hundred miles. It was also the deadliest; there was no water for sixty to eighty miles, depending on whether there had been any recent rainfall, leaving puddles in buffalo wallows. The trail was littered with the bones of man and beast that had failed. In Spanish it was called the *jornada del muerto*—journey of the dead man.

"What are Colonel Price's intentions?" Robert asked Henry.

One could see the bottom of the river and the water glistened in the afternoon sun. A morning mist had covered the country in the early morning hours, and clouds formed, but no rain had come, although it may have rained up country some. White tents were being erected along the banks of the river and hundreds of cattle were feeding over the meadows. Two big hawks were skimming the surface of the prairie, not far away.

For a while the trip had been pleasant, especially when the Battalion followed the Arkansas River because there was always water. The river had been seldom less than a quarter of a mile wide with low, barren banks, and the water flowed shallow and turbid over broad bars of sand. The sand sometimes rose here and there into small, shifting islands set thick with stunted, short-lived cottonwoods. The hills on either side of the river had been bare of trees, though, and the river had seldom been more than knee deep. Robert had wished he had twenty canteens to fill.

Alva Phelps was worse; Daniel was assisting him and so was Levi

Hancock.

"Why, aren't you glad to see me?" Henry said, answering a question with a question.

"I'm so happy I could kiss you, now tell me what's going on."

Henry smiled mischievously. "Your unit has been hauling some ammunition for us. Old Pap Price just took it back, that's all." He explained that Price's regiment had left Fort Leavenworth two days after the Mormon Battalion, as scheduled, but that a summer lightning and rainstorm had scattered their cattle in all directions. It took Henry and the other members of the regiment several days to round them up, so they had not caught the Battalion until today.

"You're not telling me everything," Robert said. He had seen that mischievous smile on Henry's face many times.

"Old Pap has sent your Lieutenant Smith some instructions, and I delivered the message," Henry explained. "Your Battalion is to take the Cimarron cutoff to Santa Fe. Smith is over yonder with your officers digesting the information now."

Robert's jaw dropped about two feet. "What? How did you get to be Price's messenger boy?"

"I'm Pap's favorite son now. He tells me everything."

"But I thought we were going straight west, to Bent's Fort, and then to Santa Fe," Robert said, still puzzled. "That's where our only provision wagon went and it's probably there already. We can't go out on that desert. We'd starve to death, if we didn't die of thirst first."

"I know," Henry said with a shrug. "Colonel Allen's plans were to use the Bent's Fort route, but things change. You waited around so long in Fort Leavenworth that you're behind schedule. Kearny has been promoted to general and he wants you in Santa Fe no later than the tenth of October."

Robert groaned. "It's not our fault Colonel Allen got sick and died. The army kept us in Fort Leavenworth those extra days. Now Colonel Price is making us pay for it by marching us through the desert without food or water? He must really hate Mormons."

Henry held up a hand. "The tenth of October is General Kearny's deadline, not Old Pap's. He's under orders, too, to get our regiment there at the same time."

"Whose idea was it to send us Lieutenant Smith? Kearny's or Price's?"

"What's wrong with Smith?"

Robert wrung his hands together and told Henry the problems the Battalion was having with the lieutenant, how he threatened the Battalion if they didn't accept him, how he treated sick soldiers, and how he supported the calomel doctor, George Sanderson.

"Then why did Lieutenant Smith send a messenger to Old Pap Price earlier, asking for some provisions for you out of our supply?"

Robert remembered the day in Missouri when Colonel Price showed up with Henry with a wagonload of flour, saying he wouldn't relinquish it to Mormons. "And what did Price say to the messenger? Stuff it up your nose? No provisions for the Mormons?"

Henry laughed. "Something like that. It'd make you turn green if I used the exact words."

"Are we getting the provisions?" Robert asked, eying the empty wagon. None of the Mormon soldiers had any flour or sugar left in their haversacks.

"Yep, you are. I brought a wagonload of flour and sugar. Your quartermaster had me unload at one of your camps up the river. Smith stuck up for you quite smartly. Said if he didn't get the provisions he would let loose the Mormons on us, and the artillery, too."

The statement caught Robert off guard. "He did?"

"Pap Price is a little perturbed, but he's getting' over it. Now he thinks Smith is a Mormon lover, just like Colonel Allen."

Robert thought of all the meetings the Battalion officers had been having with A. J. Smith. Apparently a little kindness was paying off.

Henry said, "Pap Price wants us to beat the Mormons to Santa Fe."

Robert groaned. He remembered when the members of the Daniel Browett Company from England were on a steamboat from New Orleans to St. Louis in 1841. The captain of the steamboat thought he was in a race with another steamboat, and it cost the life of his nephew—the nine-year-old son of Thomas and Dianah Bloxham. If Pap Price and Lieutenant Smith were in a race of some kind to get to Santa Fe just for the sake of pride, he was against it.

When Henry returned to the Missouri Volunteers, he found his camp visited by what a group the men called "eastern dandies." Their leader was a young man, only twenty-three, by the name of Francis Parkman, who had come from Santa Fe. He was from Boston, a graduate of Harvard. Henry took an immediate disliking to him, for he was the son of a minister in the Congregational Church. This even though Parkman claimed to be a writer and had crossed the prairies in Nebraska to the West, and was now returning—and he and his men still had their scalps.

"I'd stay away from the camp down yonder," Henry said to Parkman when he had the chance, just as everyone was about to find a camping spot.

"Why do you say that?" the young explorer queried.

"They're Mormons."

"Fanatics?"

"Yep, and armed, too."

"You got time to help me find a camping spot between here and them?"

Henry nodded, yes.

Henry was about to leave Parkman's camp when Lieutenant Smith pulled up in his wagon.

"Just curious, that's all. Who might you be?" Smith asked.

Parkman introduced himself and his friend, Quincy Shaw, and told him that he was planning to write a book about the American West. Thanks to a large family inheritance, he had been able to finance his own travels.

Henry hung around, fascinated by Parkman's stories, especially those about camping and hunting with the Sioux Indians, and experiencing tribal and frontier life.

When Parkman discovered Smith was commander of the Mormon Battalion, there ensued a conversation about Mormons that greatly pleased Henry. The men took turns bashing Joe Smith, Mormon doctrines, and their forced movement out of Missouri and Illinois. Smith called the appearance of the Mormon soldiers very striking in their half-military, half-patriarchal appearance.

Parkman took notes, shaking his head, and calling the Mormons armed fanatics again.

Robert returned to the main camp in time to find the sick ordered to line up in front of Dr. George Sanderson's wagon again. Robert and Daniel helped Alva Phelps to his feet and took him to the front of the line.

Robert's steely blue eyes bore into Sanderson. "This man will get worse if you give him more calomel."

There was a terrifying look on Alva's face. "Please, I beg of you. Let me be. I don't want the medicine."

"Nonsense," Sanderson said, cursing as was his Missouri habit. "You're getting worse because the fever is in you. Open wide."

"Please, doctor," Phelps pleaded. "No more medicine."

Robert shot Daniel a mean look. "Shall I?"

"What'd you say, private?" Sanderson asked Robert.

"Nothing," Robert said. Alva, who was pale and limp, leaned on Robert's shoulder.

Sanderson fouled the air with violent cursing. He pried Alva's mouth open with a rusty spoon, the same spoon that had been used to dispense pills and arsenic to other patients. "A double dose of calomel pills for you, and a spoonful of arsenic. Quit complaining and take it like a man."

The doctor forced Alva to wash down the pills and the arsenic with a few swallows of turpentine. The combination took the breath of the patient away for a few moments, and then he began to convulse. It took another two or three minutes until he righted himself.

With a reluctant sigh, Robert helped his fellow Company E soldier back to his tent. Several other company soldiers arrived with Levi Hancock and Levi gave Phelps a blessing.

There were so many things to worry about that Daniel couldn't sleep. Tomorrow the Battalion was to water the animals, fill barrels with water, fill their own stomachs with the precious liquid, fill their canteens, and strike out across the Cimarron Desert, the *jornada*. True, Colonel Price had sent one wagon with provisions, but the officers judged it would not be enough to feed nearly five hundred men from the Cimarron cutoff to Santa Fe. The Battalion had a deadline to meet—October tenth—or face the wrath of General Kearny. Lieutenant Smith claimed that there was a danger that the entire Battalion would be dismissed if they missed the deadline. That meant the entire plan as concocted by Brigham Young and the other leaders of the Church would fall on its face. The money needed to sustain Elizabeth, Harriet, and Moroni through the winter would fall short. Members of the Church in Council Bluffs would have no other way to raise money to buy extra flour and foodstuffs to sustain them until spring. Church representatives were scheduled to catch them any day so they would be available when the Battalion received their pay in Santa Fe.

Daniel began to picture in his mind running out of water in the *jornada*. One canteen of water would not last him for the eighty-mile trip. He could already feel his tongue swelling and turning black, his lips cracking, and his skin peeling from the burning sun. In the night he could hear the sounds of the cattle lowing, the mules braying, and the oxen stirring. He felt sorry for them, too. The few barrels of water the Battalion would be able to carry in the wagons would be gone within a half day, so great would be the demand from both beast and man. The first possibility of water would come after a hike of around thirty-five miles—if the hot weather hadn't dried up the creek bed at Cimarron Springs. Even if they found water there, it would taste like Epsom salts. Cimarron in Spanish was interpreted "lost river." If the river was truly lost—meaning that during the summer it disappeared into its sandy bottoms—then there was danger that the Battalion would be lost, too. Lost in delusions, in thirst, in mirages, and in death.

The Battalion was splitting up, not staying together. In the morning a detachment of sick men and women and children would leave on the western route leading to Bent's Fort and from there north to Fort Pueblo. At least there would be plenty of water and provisions along the way, and perhaps some foodstuffs they could purchase at Bent's Fort. The strain on soldiers who had wives and children with them was tremendous, and it was true the Battalion could move a little quicker without them. Captain Nelson Higgins, for example, had a wife and six children with the Battalion. Captain James Brown, who was also leaving, had a wife and four children. Captain Jefferson Hunt was staying, but sending his wife and seven children with the detachment. Private Montgomery Button was leaving with his wife and four children. In addition, seven other privates, all sick, were leaving.

There was a debate in Daniel's mind as to whether or not Private Alva Phelps, who was sick and trying to sleep in an adjoining tent, was even well enough to travel in the sick detachment. His messmates had helped give him a blessing and feed him, but Alva was terribly sick and had complained of feeling much worse after being forced to take his doses of medicine from Dr. Sanderson.

Daniel had barely fallen to sleep it seemed when he was awakened by a stirring in Alva's tent. The light of a lantern revealed the faces of Levi Hancock and Dr. William L. McIntire, a member of the Church whose opinions and practices had been brushed aside by Lieutenant Smith and Dr. Sanderson.

"Poor Brother Phelps is actually worse, not better," Hancock told Daniel when he got there.

Hancock went on to explain that Alva had been drooling uncontrollably for the past two or three hours. In Dr. McIntire's opinion, that was a classic sign of calomel or mercury poisoning. Mercury and arsenic were the two most active ingredients in calomel, and Dr. Sanderson had given Phelps an extra dose of arsenic. Dr. Sanderson earlier had told them that drooling was evidence that calomel was working. Alva also complained of a burning face, different than the burning from bilious fever attached to sicknesses like the ague. He also complained that it felt like his hair was falling out.

"What about his blessing?" Robert asked when he came out of the tent and stood by Daniel's side.

"Sometimes the will of the Lord is not life in this world, but entrance into the next life," Daniel confessed. "I remember the feeling I had on the ship when Nancy was failing."

Nancy was Hannah's younger sister, married to James Pulham, Daniel's cousin and employee in Daniel's cooper shop back in England. She had boarded the ship for the trip to America pregnant, not able to hold her food. The movement on the vessel during the storms that plagued the ship for the first part of the journey made her morning sickness worse and she quickly became dehydrated. Several blessings were given, but Nancy died anyway and was buried at sea. Daniel recalled the Savior's words as recorded in the Doctrine and Covenants, section 42: " *… and if they die they die unto me, and if they live they shall live unto me.*"

Robert shook his head in sad remembrance. It disturbed his mind. Nancy had seemed too young to have gotten herself in such a rough situation to die on the ocean. Alva Phelps had done nothing to deserve death, either. But it seemed likely, whether Robert thought that way or not.

Alva's drooling became worse, even more uncontrollable. Then came unconscious whimpering, followed by convulsions. There was nothing more the men could do. Within an hour, Alva passed away.

Robert was furious and it showed in the way he helped dig the grave by torch-light on the south bank of the Arkansas River. He had waken up soaked, though not from rain. He had rolled off his blanket in a sweat, dreaming about poor Alva. Now he took turns digging with Daniel and his other messmates, and the messmates of Alva. The soil was moist and they had to quit digging when the hole was only about four feet deep. Robert threw each spade full of dirt and extra yard or two. Sweat poured off from him, not from the work, but from his anger and from the heat of the night. He could still hear Alva's plead-ings with Dr. Sanderson: *Please—don't make me take more calomel.* Robert could still see the rusty spoon, the spoon that had been used to administer medicine to the other sick, too. He could still hear the terrible oaths Sanderson used to intimidate Alva and the others, and he could feel the quirt of Sanderson's contempt. Worse, he could feel the burn of his own regret. He should have exerted force over Dr. Sanderson, even if it meant a year in the stockade in Santa Fe. He could picture Sanderson lying on the ground with a broken nose, and worse. Unless Sanderson changed his ways, it could only be a sorry trip to California.

"I'll dig this grave a little wider at the top so it'll fit Dr. Sanderson's head,"

Robert said as he took his final turn. "That's who should be in this wet hole, not our good friend Alva Phelps. To die anywhere is hard, but to heave your last breath on this desolate prairie because of an incompetent doctor seems hard, indeed. "

Robert felt like crawling into the hole himself, so great was his regret. And then he thought of Hannah and his six children, and the one that wasn't born yet. He realized that's why he hadn't broken Sanderson's legs and his jaw and his nose. There would be a letter from her when the Church representatives caught the Battalion again. He had a desert to cross and a country called California to occupy for the army. And when it was all over he had to find the Church and his family. In the meantime, the Battalion had its hands full. There had been a lot of talk among the men about Smith and Sanderson. If it weren't for the fact that the Church needed the money, and that the reputation of the religion was at stake, most of the men would turn around and go home. Or they would lead a whole-scale mutinous revolt against them.

Levi Hancock ignored Robert's sarcasm. "That's good enough, boys. We'll have the services for Brother Phelps in the morning." Alva's body was wrapped in his blanket, lying in a tent, and watched over by Henry Standage.

Hancock waited until after all the men were up and had their breakfast of half-rations—a little bacon and a little bread—before he called them together for the brief funeral. Standage and Alva's other messmates had carved Alva's name in a tree next to the grave and they also used a long mesquite stick to mark the spot where they had lowered his body. Samuel Gully, quartermaster and third lieutenant of Company E, one of Alva's closest friends, spoke briefly of the resurrection.

After the grave was dedicated, Gully made a remark that rekindled Robert's anger as the men walked back to the camp. "Well, boys, it's not over yet. We have death with us, and hell, too, following in the way of our first surgeon. Let's get across that desert and into Santa Fe before he kills us all."

CHAPTER NOTES

It is a documented fact that Francis Parkman, eventual author of the famous book, *The Oregon Trail,* camped near the Mormon Battalion at the Arkansas River Crossing on the 16th day of September, 1846. He referenced the Mormons as "armed fanatics" in his book.

35

❦

THE DEATH OF ALVA PHELPS CAST a heavy gloom over the Battalion. Daniel could do nothing about it. For the next two hours it seemed that no one talked of anything but death. Most of the men had lived through rough times and had seen men die, but no one of their acquaintance had been force-fed poison and they could not keep the subject off their tongues. The worst by far was Robert, who was so unnerved by what he had seen that Daniel sensed he might be losing his mind. It seemed Robert had spent the last two hours uttering threats against the calomel doctor perhaps as a means of holding his own fears in balance. Messmates John Cox and Levi Roberts, in contrast, walked those two hours in silence, nervous and withdrawn, hoping that they would never have to submit to the doctor's whims. Levi Hancock was proving a treasure as the only Church general authority on the trip. He kept things in balance, as a rule, and kept reassuring the men. Private Davis, the young man who had been sent to the guardhouse in Fort Leavenworth for drinking, was still disappointing in his attitudes. He had taken homesick, missing his mother, and he begged the other men for money so he could buy whiskey from the supply Toothless still carried in his sutler's wagon.

"I hate Sanderson," Robert said as they marched along. "He's a murderer. I'll never forget what he's done."

"I suppose I hate him too," Daniel acknowledged. "But we've got more to worry about than just him and Smith. Like this desert, and Indians, too. It's curious how things get in your head. I've got an Indian in mine."

From the minute he'd left Nauvoo Daniel had begun to have his big Indian dreams, haunting his sleep. Sometimes just half dozing as he walked he would dream about Indians. He slept poorly as a result, and felt he would be tired and good for nothing by the time he reached Santa Fe.

"The next time I see Indians I'm gonna sic 'em on Sanderson," Robert said. "It'd do me good to seem them lift the doctor's scalp."

"I wish you'd quit talking about Sanderson and Alva's death," Daniel said. "We need to get over it."

"Wrong theory," Robert countered. "Talk's the way to defeat it. Anything gets boring if you talk enough about it, even death."

Daniel grew tired of this useless bantering and therefore was relieved when dust kicked up from behind the Battalion. A carriage drawn by two horses approached, followed by a yellow dog.

"It's not military men," said John Cox. "I don't see uniforms."

Daniel shaded his eyes. "It might be some of our people," he said.

"I'll bet its John D. Lee and Howard Egan," said Levi Hancock.

"Coming to get our pay?" Robert asked.

"Yep," Hancock answered. "We're due to get paid again when we get to Santa Fe."

Daniel blinked in the bright afternoon sun. "You're right, Brother Hancock," he said. "And I recognize Lieutenant Pace with them." Daniel's heart picked up more than just a few beats when the wagon drew nearer. There would be letters from Elizabeth and Harriet.

Pace had left the Battalion three weeks ago to ride back to Fort Leavenworth to check on the condition of Colonel Allen. Pace was a Tennessean by birth, thirty-five years old, and had been a member of the Church since 1840. While farming at Nauvoo, Pace had also served on the city police force.

Captain Davis told Daniel that all the officers should be the first to greet Lee and Egan, so Daniel left Robert and the others to do just that. By the time Daniel got to shake their hands the visitors already knew of Alva Phelps' death, and John D. Lee was worked up about it.

"Where is this Lieutenant Smith?" Lee asked. His chest was rising and falling in sharp, shallow little breaths so full was his anger.

Lee said he had heard in Council Bluffs that Colonel Allen had been sick and might have to relinquish command. Lee, along with Brigham Young and the entire Church leadership, favored the placement of Jefferson Hunt as the new commander. Lee was visibly shaken to find out that the men had installed A. J. Smith instead.

One of the officers pointed to Smith's wagon. "Over there," he said.

Smith stood out like a sore thumb in his blue uniform.

Most of the officers followed Lee, wanting to see the fireworks. Daniel was more interested in the mailbags. Daniel concluded that Lee had been working on his bad mood ever since Council Bluffs, and that the confrontation would be an ugly one. He'd had enough of such matters and found himself wondering what Elizabeth and Harriet had to say in their letters.

Only a short distance away Lee found Smith and the war of words began. Daniel could only catch part of it, but Smith was defending the use of calomel and the army doctor too, as well as his command authority. Lee was berating Smith on every count he could think of, including Alva's unfortunate death. Several of the Battalion boys had surrounded them, spellbound by the arguments.

But several other soldiers were just as curious as Daniel regarding the mailbags. Daniel rummaged through them, found his letters from Elizabeth, Harriet, Rebecca, and his mother, and sought for a private place to read. When he left, Robert was trying to find his letter or letters.

Daniel stared at Elizabeth's letter for a few moments before he opened it. When he was certain no one was looking, he drew it to his nose and sniffed it, hoping to catch the faint scent of his beloved wife. It was useless. The envelope only smelled like the musty leather pouch it had been carried in.

Daniel carried the letter to a rock protrusion, checked for lizards and tarantulas, sat down and began reading.

The first sentence of Elizabeth's letter stunned him. *No! No! No!* Tears welled up in his eyes. He wheeled to search for Robert, scanning dozens of men who, with their white belts looked strikingly similar, some reading letters as they walked, and others trying to find a place to sit before they opened their mail. Oxen were resting in the warm sun; wagons sunk a few inches in the dry, sandy riverbed. Dozens of prairie dogs scolded man and beast for the unwarranted intrusion into their domain. Less than a mile away, a small herd of buffalo grazed. Jackrabbits hid among the greasewood and sagebrush. The desert looked dry, felt dry, and smelled dry.

Robert!

Daniel dared not scream his name. He could see his other messmates, Levi Roberts, John Cox, Robert Pixton, and Richard Slater, but his eyes could not see Robert. He could see Lee and Egan having their heated discussion and Lee's round face was flushed with red. As Daniel passed by, Lee was saying, "I consider the oppression of your Mormon soldiers as great as it was in Missouri and Illinois."

"I'm not responsible for what Dr. Sanderson has done," Smith was explaining.

Daniel wanted to eavesdrop more, but he had to find Robert. He found his brother-in-law perched on the tongue of a wagon with a letter in his hands.

"Robert!"

Robert jerked his head up as though momentarily stunned. As he read Daniel's sad, shocked face, he began to look as though a premonition were building. "What's wrong?"

Daniel fought back his emotions. "Open your letter. I'd rather you read it for yourself."

Robert ripped open Hannah's letter and began reading. Tears streaked down his dusty face. "I can't believe it. I can't believe it."

The letter told of the death of his sister, Dianah. She had died in her sleep, in a makeshift tent, nearly three weeks ago, the night before John D. Lee and Howard Egan left Cutler's Park where most of the Saints had moved. She had suffered greatly, the victim not only of the ague and intermittent fever, but canker as well.

"I feel bad for poor Thomas, and worse for his five children," Robert said as he continued to weep.

Daniel placed a hand on Robert's shoulder. "At least Dianah's suffering is over. She's had quite a time of it these past few weeks."

There was a minute or two of silence between the two men as they contemplated the emptiness they felt.

The mustering bugle sounded and a stunned Robert Harris rose to his feet. "I suppose Hannah, Elizabeth, and Harriet can help Thomas with his children. They'll have to."

Aside from Robert's sorrow, the first thing Daniel noticed as the Battalion began moving again was that Lieutenant Smith, Captain Hunt, and Howard Egan were riding together in John D. Lee's carriage, and Lee was blistering Smith's ears. Daniel knew it was about Alva Phelps' death, about Dr. Sanderson, and about the Pueblo detachment. A pair of field glasses dangled from Lee's neck.

John D. Lee had seen the rough side of life. He was born in 1812 in Illinois, and raised by an alcoholic father after his mother's untimely death at age three. In Nauvoo, Lee had served as a member of the First Quorum of Seventy, helping direct the Church's missionary activities. He had spent much of his time during the past five or six years serving personal missions. He had also served as a bodyguard at the Prophet Joseph Smith's home.

Lee was fuming, speaking to Smith fast and furiously. "Your oppression of our men is just as terrible as the persecution heaped upon Mormons during the Missouri years." He had the field glasses in his hand, appearing ready to strike Smith with them.

"I've just been doing my job," Smith retorted with an acrimonious scowl.

"Inhumane treatment of fellow human beings is not your job," Lee countered. "To abuse the Mormon soldiers with threats to kill them if they didn't take their calomel medicine is not going to be tolerated for one more minute."

Smith denied threatening to kill Mormon soldiers.

Lee turned to Captain Hunt. "Didn't you and the other officers tell me that both Lieutenant Smith and Dr. Sanderson threatened to cut the throats of the men if they didn't take their medicine."

"Yes, there were dozens of witnesses," Hunt happily admitted.

Smith's voice was metallic and cold, laced with arrogance. "We had to do something to make the men follow orders."

"Well, you killed one of the soldiers," Lee charged.

"I'm not responsible for what Sanderson did," Smith said sheepishly.

Lee exploded. "You certainly are responsible. You're the commanding officer. You knew what Dr. Sanderson was doing, forcing calomel down the throats of our men—even administering double doses for the spite of it."

Smith slumped. To Daniel, it was like watching a mountain crumble.

"Correct me if I've misquoted the doctor, Captain Hunt," Lee said. "But didn't Dr. Sanderson say something like, 'I don't care a damn if the medicine kills or cures—the more Mormons it kills the better; the rascals ought to be sent to hell as fast as possible'."

"That's an accurate quote," Captain Hunt acknowledged.

Lee's mouth quivered in anger. "You'd better quickly realize, Lieutenant Smith, that your Mormon soldiers are on the verge of revolt. I wouldn't blame them if they did, and I wouldn't constrain them. They would be justified to rise up and burst off the yoke of oppression."

For a few moments Smith looked as though he were going to challenge Lee to a duel. He sat in the wagon rigid and still unyielding.

Finally when the Battalion stopped for a brief rest, Lieutenant Smith jumped out of the carriage and retreated to his own wagon. Levi Hancock emerged from a thick crowd of Mormon soldiers, many of whom had either heard the arguments direct or heard about them. "Thank you for supporting us, Brother Lee," he said. "I saw a bright falling star in the heavens last night. I took it as an omen that something good was going to happen to us. Your arrival has boosted our spirits. It's terrible enough to face the desert in front of us, but at least now perhaps the lieutenant and the doctor will treat us a little better."

Temporarily Lee had the air of some mystical hero, radiating charisma and authority. He smiled. "It's the least I can do."

From up ahead an order was given. Smith had called for the men to begin marching again.

Lee's authority had evaporated just that quickly. The Battalion moved out.

36

ROBERT HAD A BAD FEELING IN HIS HEART as he started walking across the desert again. A heavy burden had been placed there not only with the death of his sister, Dianah, but Alva Phelps, too, who had been in the same company and had slept in a tent right next to his the night he died. For a while he felt so sad that he almost embarrassed himself by crying in front of the other soldiers. He felt his eyes fill up. How could death come so quickly to people?

He felt the burn of hatred for the two men who had caused Alva's death—Lieutenant A. J. Smith and Dr. Sanderson. If Sanderson kept killing soldiers, the Battalion would be down to nobody before they got to California. He was happy John D. Lee had scolded the lieutenant and the doctor. Perhaps things might change for the better. Both Lee and Egan were committed to stay with the Battalion until it arrived at Santa Fe. Everyone was marching now with a sense of urgency. General Kearny's deadline of October tenth was a real one, and Lee agreed with Smith that it had to be obeyed.

As he marched along under a scorching sun, Robert tried to organize his thoughts. It had never struck him that his sister might die, or anyone else at Council Bluffs for that matter. Of course, he knew that anyone could die. Samuel Boley had died, Colonel Allen had died, and so had Alva Phelps. Back in England, his tiny baby sister twins had died when he was a young boy. His father had died at a fairly young age, and so had his mother. And his brother, William—a close friend—had died in England, too. Hannah's sister, Nancy, had died crossing the ocean, and her body had been committed to the deep somewhere southeast of Florida. Thomas and Dianah had lost a son to death off the back end of a steamboat. Yet death was a condition he had never associated with Dianah, or with any member of his immediate family—which included Hannah and his children. He had always refused to associate death with one of his own children. Now when he looked around at the Battalion boys, marching again in the heat, the thought came into his mind that any one of them might die. And death could come to a child of his. Robert knew at once that there was not much he could do to prevent death wherever death might strike, whether it might be in Council Bluffs or somewhere along the Santa Fe Trail, or in Santa Fe itself, or even in California.

When Robert looked ahead, to the west where the Battalion was headed, he felt very discouraged, for the country seemed endless. It seemed to him he could see almost a hundred miles across this flat country—just empty country and he had to walk it. He had never been an advocate of walking. In Nauvoo he'd seen to it that he always had a horse. Even in England his father had always provided him with a horse, even though most other folks walked their way around Gloucestershire. Before too many more miles his shoes were apt to wear out and he'd either have to walk barefoot or wrap rawhide around his feet. It was a blazing day, so hot it made him feel annoyed at the Cimarron weather. He stumbled on, feeling that the sun would burn the skin off his face and his hands. He felt so peculiar that he began to wonder what it would be like to die. His thirst began to work on him, and he wondered how long it would take to die from a lack of water. He had never known anyone who had died from thirst, but he knew it could happen. If the ague and black canker could take his sister, then thirst could take a man out here on the desert.

The *jornada* was turning out worse than he'd ever imagined. There was nothing in England to compare it to, and nothing he'd ever seen in the state of Illinois, not even in Galena where he'd seen the lead mines. Unfortunately, the first five miles through sand hills yesterday had been very heavy pulling and by the time the Battalion had reached the level plain beyond, the men and all the animals were tired, hot, and thirsty. Barrels of water had been used up by noon that first day.

It was a hypnotic experience to travel in this country, sort of like the silence of the ocean. The hot sun beat down on him and an even hotter wind whistled through the poor quality foxtail grass; the grass had turned brown here. He could hear mule's feet and soldier's boots rattling against dead alkali weeds. Mules and oxen staggered under their burdens. There were no trees, just clumps of mesquite, sagebrush, and the dry husks of soap weed yucca plants. Some of them looked uncannily like human beings and once or twice he thought he saw Indians. In his weariness he forgot that Indians were not likely to attack a Battalion of five hundred men, so he worried that Indians might appear over the horizon and shoot arrows at him, and throw spears, too. He raised his musket and took aim, only to realize it was only the yucca plants. How Indians could live anywhere near here was beyond his imagination. Several times he saw other soldiers—weary, thirsty, almost dozing as they walked—suddenly jerk awake at the mirage of Indians coming over the rise.

A few of the men could be seen resting on wagon tongues, something that Lieutenant Smith never allowed, but now that Lee and Egan were here, the officers said nothing. One man fell asleep due to the wagon's monotonous creaking, and he almost fell under the wagon. More and more the country became studded with prickly pear cactus. Spiny lizards resembling prehistoric monsters ran in and out of them. So did a few tarantula spiders. Several buffalo could be seen in the distance. Winding paths made by them cut innumerable lines across the desert. Rattlesnakes were so numerous that the progress of the Battalion had been accompanied by a continual popping of guns, as men shot them.

Robert found that he detested desert travel, especially now that it was hot and dusty and there was no water. His face and arms were tanned to a dark brown. It was clear that the other men didn't like desert travel either, nor did the animals. There wasn't enough grass and they were losing weight. The nights had been no better for Robert, sleeping on the hard ground rolled up in his wool blanket. He was so used to it, however, that he always fell to sleep quite quickly and the morning bugle was the noise that woke him up, so complete was his exhaustion. Walking all day beside a cowherd and five hundred men was proving monotonous, and death was threatening because of the lack of good water. This shortcut to Santa Fe, bypassing Bent's Fort, was proving to be perilous.

"Any water left?" Daniel asked later in the day.

"Not a drop," Robert answered, his tongue feeling thick. He had let the last drops in his canteen trickle down his throat last evening. "I'd even take alkaline water, the kind that rusts your boiler." A hot sun beat down on him, giving him a hard headache.

"I suppose the barrels are empty, too."

"Long ago."

The Battalion had filled every available vinegar barrel with water before they began crossing this part of the desert.

Toothless was still with the Battalion. He calculated that they would reach Sand Creek by nightfall, where water might be found by digging for it. "If we don't find water soon, we'll all be crow bait," Toothless predicted.

Right now Robert was feeling that death might come before nightfall for just about everyone in the Battalion. Probably due to the lack of water, John D. Lee had finally stopped trying to kick the frost out of Lieutenant Smith, so at least a quiet peace had settled over the men.

At camp last evening, Toothless had told Robert about the time fifteen years ago when an acquaintance of his, a trapper named Jedediah Smith, had died on the *jornada*. Back then there was no trail to follow and Smith and his party got lost after three blistering days. Taking courage, Smith struck out alone to find water for his men. Eventually he found the dry sandy bed of the Cimarron River. Smith spurred his horse forward, looking up and down the river for a pool, but found none. He did the only thing he could do, and that was to dig. After scooping out a basin two feet deep, water began to seep in. Smith watched it, smiling with cracked lips. He stooped to drink but when he raised his head, he found himself surrounded by Comanches. He jerked out his holster pistols but he had no chance. He dropped two of them, but they killed him. He had been a friend to the Indians all throughout the West, but to the Comanches, Toothless said, Smith was just a scalp.

"I've got to get some water soon, or I think I'll have to lie down and die," Daniel said.

Robert and Daniel talked about Indians again for a moment. Toothless had said that whenever a caravan was in difficulty, Indians were certain to appear. Even though caravans could circle and fight off the Indians for a while, holding off a long siege was not possible without water and the Indians knew it.

Robert felt like an insect inching along, trapped in a huge glass bowl that moved when he did. The inverted bowl of the sky met at the horizon. The

Cimarron River was nothing more than a dry, cracked bed of silt shimmering in the heat. In front of him, Robert could only see more desert, endless vistas punctuated by isolated volcanic uplifts. Barren slopes of yellow hills and mountains could be seen in the far distance. Here and there oxen bones littered the trail, a grim reminder that animals had been left to die many times.

"I wish one of them rainstorms would come up that soaked our camp and our bedding a month or so ago," Robert said. The rain and winds that night had blown nearly every tent over during their stay in Spring Creek. It was the first tornado the men had ever seen.

"Not in this desert," Levi Roberts mumbled through parched lips.

"Do you suppose Moses could come down and strike his finger against those rocks over there and send forth a gush of water?" he asked.

"Chew that a little finer," Toothless said, half squint-eyed.

"You'd have to read your Bible to understand," Daniel said.

Toothless pulled a face.

"You'd have to have more faith than I have," replied Richard Slater.

"Remember when we crossed Bluff Creek and Company C's wagon tipped over? How'd you like to jump in that creek right now?"

"Let's quit talking," John Cox said, his words hard to understand. "It's making my mouth worse. It's dry enough as it is."

In another hour the stark shadow of death seemed to hang over the Battalion. Occasionally an ox would stumble to its knees, its swollen tongue black and hanging out. Thirst-crazed teamsters got them to their feet and coaxed them to continue onward. Robert's tongue felt like the oxen's tongues, and he knew he had to have some water soon. The sun, though lower in the western sky, was beating down with a renewed fury, as if gloating over the failure of the Battalion to conquer the desert. Robert began to rehearse in his mind other horror stories Toothless had told about the *jornada*—men drinking the blood of horses to stay alive, or cutting the ears of mules and sucking on them for the blood.

The light bluish sky—almost white—was under the influence of a strong refraction of hot air at the surface of the desert. Black spots danced in Robert's eyes and he began to see mirages, one after another. He saw blue pools of cool water in the barren waste ground. He saw the image of Jedediah Smith, fighting the Indians as he died. He saw Hannah, rising from the desert floor, beckoning him to share a pail of fresh water drawn from a cool well. Robert ran toward her. She threw her arms apart in a caressing gesture and then slowly disappeared. And then he saw Dianah—she was dressed in pure white, ascending to heaven. She smiled at him as if to say all was well with her, and that all would be well with Thomas and her children.

The clatter of wagons all around him, and the braying of mules, awoke Robert out of his trance. The mules, and the oxen, too, were suddenly acting as if they were more alive than dead.

"Water!" someone yelled from the lead wagon. "Water!"

Robert staggered forward only to find a slough and a collection of filthy buffalo wallow puddles that had collected from a rainstorm that must have passed over four or five days earlier. Despite what Toothless had said about buffalo tea, the oxen, mules, and cattle were already drinking. The wallows were spread over a wide area and the soldiers were driving buffalo from them.

Robert collapsed to his knees next to Daniel. Some of the soldiers were sipping the water as they lay on their stomachs.

"How unique," Robert said, trying to salvage his sense of humor. "Pure water garnished with buffalo droppings and urine, swarms of insects, and mud, too."

It was either drink or face the possibility of dying. He, too, lay down and began to drink and tried not to think about how the water tasted. A few of the men began scooping up the water and placing it in buckets. Then they strained it through a handkerchief and drank it.

"Either way, it's going to make us sick," said Daniel morbidly.

In minutes, man and beast had sucked the puddles dry, and the Battalion pushed onward. Robert watched Daniel collapse, unable to go any farther. John D. Lee placed Daniel in a wagon along with three other sick men.

Robert felt terrible, too, certainly not very vigorous. The lack of proper food, water, and sleeping conditions was slowly breaking down his health, it seemed. He was appalled at the casual way Lieutenant Smith was taking over the situation they were in.

As the sweltering sun inched closer to the western horizon a cloud of dust startled Robert and the rest of the men. At first he thought it was a mirage, but it wasn't. It was a charging buffalo, or was it two? The two bulls seemed irritated at the sight of the mules, oxen, and the beef cattle.

"Load your muskets!" John D. Lee cried out.

Robert saw that the bulls were coming fast and that soldiers were already shooting at them. At close range, Toothless had said the size of the charge didn't count much. Robert poured in powder by guess, rammed a ball in place, and waited.

As the buffalo ran past, men were still shooting, several of the balls striking the two bulls. Robert took careful aim and pulled the trigger, sending a ball into one of the crazed bulls. Other soldiers in his mess blazed away, too, throwing lead into the huge bulk of the charging bull, and Robert was astonished that it did not fall. The bull ran by with a cloud of choking dust. Toothless had told him that a clean shot must be struck but a few inches above the brisket, behind the shoulder. A ball struck there would reach the vitals, but the maddened bull had not taken a ball there yet.

A hundred yards away or so one of the bulls staggered, slowed down, and then just stood there. Robert grabbed his knife and ran toward the huge bull, ready to do his duty as the Battalion butcher. The bull was still on its feet, resisting the drag of death with all his might, as if he knew that if he went down, he was finished. Blood poured from its mouth and a red tongue was protruding. The bull braced, looked at Robert with bloodshot eyes, and began to stamp the ground impatiently while he swayed from side to side. As Robert wondered if the bull had enough strength to charge, the bull lifted his shaggy head and bellowed out his agony.

Robert backed away as members of his mess arrived.

"Is he gonna die?" John Cox asked through his parched lips.

"Either that, or kill us both," Robert said, half joking.

The bull's head was swinging from side to side, as if looking for every soldier that had sent a ball to its body. Blood spurted from his mouth and nostrils, and from wounds on its body. Suddenly, the bull became rigid. A convulsive shudder shook him and the bull let go his last breath in a grunting gasp. He tumbled on his side with stiff, outstretched legs.

"Tell the others to bring a bucket and cups," Robert said to John as he cut the bull's throat.

"We're not drinking that blood, are we?" Levi Roberts asked, still feeling sick from the wallow water.

"No, but remember what Toothless said if we found buffalo?"

Levi's brain was in a fog, so desperate was he for water. After a few moments he remembered. "That buffalo only venture out into the desert after they've filled their bellies full of water?"

"Go get that bucket and some cups," Robert said as he slit the bull's hide open. By the time his messmates arrived with the bucket and cups, he had found the stomach. It was distended, with gallons of water in it. Using handkerchiefs as a strainer, the men strained partially digested grass from the mucous called water and began to drink.

"I hope this doesn't make us as sick as the water from the wallows did,"

Levi Roberts commented.

Daniel staggered out of the wagon, determined to try the new source.

"I don't know," Daniel answered. "But what a story for my journal. I can see myself telling about this around a fireplace someday. Little Moroni will never believe it. Neither will Elizabeth or Harriet."

"What do you say, Moroni, now that you're a year old?" Elizabeth asked her only child on his birthday.

The boy cast an innocent look at his mother.

"Ecclesiastes has nothing to say," Harriet responded. Robert had tagged the boy with the Biblical name a year ago during a debate over the boy's name.

Elizabeth laughed. She liked the Book of Mormon name better. She gathered Moroni in her arms and gave him a hug, fearing for his safety. Peter Sarpy had sent word that caused chills to course down Elizabeth's spine. A United States marshal from Missouri was reportedly on his way to Council Bluffs to arrest Brigham Young and all members of the Twelve. There was also a rumor that the Secretary of War had instructed the Indian agent, Robert Mitchell, to have all Mormons removed from Pottawatomi lands by next spring.

Elizabeth thought this move was beyond the realm of an Indian agent's duties. Agents were supposed to protect Indians from white encroachment, but the Mormons weren't encroaching. They were temporary settlers, not permanent. Agents were supposed to prevent liquor from being taken into Indian country, but Mitchell had totally ignored that rule. Mitchell quite liked his governmental duty to punish Indians who committed depredations on the whites. He still had a few troops at his command, ready to take punitive measures against the Indians when necessary. But he had lost some of his troops to the war against Mexico. Like most other Indian agents, Elizabeth suspected he was getting rich selling annuity goods that were meant for Indians.

"I wonder when they'll move us to Winter Quarters?" Harriet asked as she mixed a batch of bread. The Church had sent a contingent of men to St. Louis to buy supplies for the winter. A thousand dollars had been collected from among the Saints, who numbered around ten thousand.

"Soon, I hope," Elizabeth answered. She placed Moroni on the ground and watched him take a few awkward steps, finally collapsing on his rump. Brigham Young and the Twelve were in the new location called Winter Quarters at this very moment, laying out the new temporary city. It was located on the west side of the river, north of Cutler's Park. The original Grand Encampment was beginning to fall apart anyway; the livestock had eaten all the grass in the area.

A tear came to Elizabeth's eye. Moroni was taking his first steps and Daniel was not here to watch. She reveled in every little thing that Moroni did. She had waited for eleven years to be a mother, and now she was enjoying every minute of it. She had hoped and prayed that she would become pregnant again before Daniel left, but she didn't. And neither did Harriet.

"I wonder how close the Battalion is to California?" Harriet said.

"I don't know," Elizabeth answered. "It sounds so far away."

37

Los Angeles

September 23, 1846

VIOLENCE CAME WITHOUT WARNING during the early morning hours in Los Angeles. Gunfire was heard from both the front and the rear of the headquarters building, under guard by twenty-three marines commanded by Lieutenant Archibald H. Gillespie.

Gillespie tensed, all his senses tuned to his ears. Panic and fear swept through him as he shouted at his men. "Get on the roof and make it quick!"

From his perch on the roof, Gillespie had a hard time in the near darkness determining how many rebel Californios were swarming below, hiding behind houses. Finding a target, he raised his gun. His face was a mask of cold implacability as he calmly pulled the trigger and shot the rebel to the ground. Two hours later, morning light revealed more of the attackers.

"I see Serbulo Varela out there. That means they're just a bunch of street toughs," Gillespie said. "Kill a few of them and they'll go away."

Varela was a noted dissident who had opposed Pico the year before. But Gillespie had levied an arbitrary fine of fifteen pesos on Varela for breaking some rule, and now Gillespie couldn't remember what that rule had been. Varela had sworn revenge, saying he would rather die than live as he was doing under Gillespie's rule.

Gillespie had struck a bargain for trouble from day one by taking a haughty attitude toward the Californios during his occupation of Los Angeles. The port had fallen into American hands so easily that day in late July that Gillespie figured guarding it with the fifty men Fremont and Stockton had left him would be a piece of cake. But he had foolishly sent half of them to the garrison at San Diego and to Warner Ranch.

"I tried to warn you about the Californios," one of his men was saying as more gunfire was exchanged. "They don't like our strict martial law rules and the curfew hours." Gillespie had not only strictly enforced Stockton's curfew and the ban on Angelinos bearing arms, but also outlawed reunions in homes, closed shops at sundown, forbade the sale of liquor without his permission, and even forbade any two persons to walk in the street together. He had imprisoned a man named Don Francisco Rico on a suspicious whim, leaving him incommunicado in a dark dungeon.

Gillespie pulled a face, not about to admit being a petty tyrant. "You men should have held your liquor and behaved better. I should have smashed the wine and aguardiente bottles." Among his volunteers there were some very reliable men, but others were unaccustomed to discipline, and yet others were perfect drunkards.

Gillespie had never liked the Californios, calling them cowardly and inert. In his opinion, their governor, Castro, was devoid of principle, a usurper, and a despot. He had openly criticized the government as one of Mexican tyranny and military despotism. So he didn't mention the time that *Angelino* women gave him a basket of peaches in which they had embedded all-but-invisible cactus spines. It had taken him a week to get the sting out of his mouth.

A second marine responded. "You shouldn't have sent Zeke Merritt and his men to San Diego. We could sure use them now." The marine fired a shot. A second rebel fell dead.

Gillespie closed his eyes and cursed, regretting the way he had governed Los Angeles since being given temporary control of the pueblo by John C. Fremont. His diet had never been better, dining on a fare of fresh and dried beef, vegetables from a small kitchen garden, and lots of squash, corn, and beans. American ships, bartering for hides and tallow, had plenty of eastern goods to sell. Gillespie could still smell the fat that had been rendered into tallow in huge black kettles on the beach earlier in the day, and the meat that was being dried into jerky.

What could he do? The garrison he had taken over had no artillery. It was isolated inland from naval support, obviously offering a tempting invasion for attack for the Californios still in the area. His soldiers had taken advantage of too much wine in this free-living space. Besides that, he was hiding some twenty thousand dollars in gold for the military government, and the local gamblers coveted every penny. He had already uncovered several plots to steal it, and had made arrests that further aggravated the Californios.

"Oh, oh," said a third marine. "Look who's coming."

Gillespie wheeled his tall frame around to see more Californios grouping for an attack. "Jose Maria Flores."

"He's got us surrounded," said a fourth. "We can hole up here for a few days, but I don't see how we'll escape." It was common knowledge that Flores had access to around four hundred men.

Gillespie closed his eyes and cursed. He began thinking of a courier to relay the bad news to Commodore Stockton in San Francisco.

That night he sent a soldier named John Brown—known to the Californios as "Juan Flaco," or John "Skinny,"—to get help from Commodore Stockton at Monterey. Messages on cigarette paper were hidden in Brown's hair.

Six days later, however, with no relief in sight, Gillespie surrendered. Los Angeles was back in the hands of the Californios and Mexico, and he was a prisoner of Flores. There was no way he could escape, travel to San Francisco, and watch Fremont be appointed governor, and him accept the position of secretary under Fremont. He also wondered about Kit Carson—on his way to tell the president of the United States that California was American.

California was not on Daniel's mind, but mere survival was. The Battalion's march along the dry Cimarron River was taxing his will to live and the only thing that kept him going was thoughts of Elizabeth, Moroni, and Harriet, too. He felt this part of the Santa Fe Trail was cursed, so desolate was the landscape, and he hoped never to see it again. He had just passed a mournful sight—the bones of at least a hundred mules that had apparently died last winter during a snowstorm, and one human skull. A company of fur traders had owned the animals. At the last stop he and the other soldiers had dug holes in the sand and found a little water, and at times found tiny fish two or three inches long. Two days earlier the holes in the sand yielded only black water that tasted like poison, but there had been no choice for man or beast. They drank it. The day before that, the water from the sand holes had tasted like mineral salts.

The burden of controversy between John D. Lee and Lieutenant Smith weighed heavy on Daniel, too. Debate still raged among members of the Battalion as to who should be its leader, and the debate would be worse, Daniel admitted, if the men did not have to worry about the lack of water, the lack of full rations, and the heat of the desert.

Last evening Daniel had met with all the other officers to hear both sides of the issue again. Daniel could see both sides of the argument. Smith was better as a military leader. But in his view, Captain Jefferson Hunt ought to be leading the Battalion because he would have received more votes had Smith not intimidated and threatened the soldiers. It had finally boiled over to the point that Captain Hunt could see that Lee's constant criticism of Smith and Dr. Sanderson was ruining the morale of the Battalion, even stirring up the men towards revolt or even mutiny. Lee finally responded that he did not want to command the Battalion, but still felt that Hunt was the rightful leader. And he said he still felt angry that many of the officers had given their support to Smith. In the end, Jefferson Hunt had to tell Lee that for the good of the Battalion he needed to let the matter go, and if he didn't, he would support Lieutenant Smith's suggestion that Lee be put under guard.

Tensions were still high when Daniel left the meeting, found his messmates and motioned to Robert. "Get your fiddle out."

"Now?" Robert asked. "It doesn't look like the meeting is over. A. J. is playing the part of the devil."

"That's the problem—the meeting needs to be over. Start playing. The other men who play the fiddle will join you. Get the men to dance."

Lively violin music erupted from Robert's bow. Daniel took hold of Robert Pixton's arm. "Think of yourself as a girl, not the mess's cook. Dance with me."

In not too many minutes there were other violins playing, and other men dancing. And soon the meeting of the officers ended, and most of the officers joined the dance.

At the beginning of a new song, Daniel found John D. Lee.

"Could I have this dance?" Daniel asked. By now, dozens of men were dancing as couples, having a good time. In the distance loomed two mountain peaks known as the Rabbit Ears. A company of traders bound for Santa Fe had camped next to the Battalion, and a few of the traders had been attracted by the music and were highly amused at the sight of men dancing with men.

Lee's mood was still sour. "I don't feel like dancing."

"But I do," Daniel said as he took a grip on Lee's arm and gave a tug.

As the two men danced, Daniel said, "I've been saying my prayers that this controversy will end."

Lee sighed. "I don't see how. Smith shouldn't be leading the Battalion."

"Keep dancing," Daniel said.

The answer to Daniel's prayer came two weeks later as camp was made in the valley of Pecos, only a two-day journey from Santa Fe. While he and his messmates were strolling through the ruins of the Abbey of Pecos, built some two hundred fifty years earlier by Spaniards, a rumble broke through the camp. A messenger from Kearny's army had ridden into camp.

"What's going on?" Robert asked Daniel. He had just finished walking through the old cathedral, where the ruins had been divided into rooms that had been used for private apartments for the priests, confession chambers, and penance chambers.

"I don't know, but it must be something important," Daniel answered as he broke into a trot.

Camp had been made just north of a spring that gushed out of the north bank of Pecos Creek. Tents had already been set up, dotting the desert landscape. Mules and oxen grazed on a grassy landscape that ascended toward the mountains. The men had enjoyed a fine dinner of antelope, as the pilots had killed several earlier in the day.

Daniel found Jacob Kemp Butterfield near a huddle of men that included John D. Lee, Lieutenant Smith, Captain Jefferson Hunt, and Adjutant Dykes. Those men appeared to be in a state of shock.

"General Kearny's sent word that we're going to have a new commander," Butterfield told Daniel and Daniel's messmates.

Daniel's eyes scanned Lee, Smith, Hunt, and Dykes again. "Is it Captain Hunt?" he asked with a hopeful glint in his eye.

"Nope," Butterfield said. "It's someone waiting in Santa Fe."

"General Kearny himself?"

Butterfield laughed. "Impossible on two counts. Kearny has already left for California. Plus he's the general over the whole army, not a commander over any particular regiment or Battalion."

Daniel kicked himself on that count, knowing better. "Then who is it?"

"Take a guess."

Daniel shrugged. It couldn't be Colonel Price—his regiment of mounted volunteers was a day or two behind the Battalion, so that was a relief. He let his mind review the names of other officers under Kearny's command and settled on Colonel Doniphan as his choice.

"Colonel Doniphan?" Daniel asked.

"Nope, but a good guess," Butterfield replied.

"Who, then?" Daniel was tiring of the game.

"Captain Philip St. George Cooke."

The name struck Daniel like a blow. Names of all superior officers in Kearny's army had been discussed by the Battalion during the day marches, during nooning rests, and at night camps. Cooke was known to be quick tempered. If the Battalion commander had to be a non-Mormon, Doniphan would be best. At least Doniphan had the reputation of being a friend to the Mormons.

Daniel scanned the Battalion officers again. Lieutenant Smith, Dr. Sanderson, and Adjutant Dykes appeared to be taking the news even worse, anticipating something very different. Smith, he guessed, had been hopeful of commanding the Battalion clear to California and getting an advance in rank and pay as a result.

"Well," Daniel said, "at least this solves the controversy."

"But how do we know Cooke will be any better than old A. J.?" Robert asked.

"We don't," he answered. "But a least we know he can't be any worse."

At least it gave the soldiers a new subject to talk about. Conversation about the death of Alva Phelps had largely faded away. Daniel and Robert had found themselves talking about how they had spent their time in England before they joined the Church: how they met when the Browett family had moved to Deerhurst, how Daniel had felt when he first met Elizabeth, how Robert first met Hannah, how their parents objected to their courtship because of religious concerns, and their double marriage ceremony in the little Methodist chapel in Apperley. This kind of conversation made Daniel constantly see Elizabeth and Moroni in his dreams, even in daydreams. He was tired of seeing his family only in dreams. He was counting the days when his year's enlistment would be over and he could start home, wherever home would be next July.

Messengers from Kearny's army in Santa Fe had been carrying dispatches to the Battalion for the past ten or twelve days. Kearny sent word that he intended to start for California without the Mormon Battalion. Smith, in turn, sent back a message urging Kearny to wait until the Battalion arrived, even asking for permission for part of the Battalion—the sick ones—to winter at Bent's Fort. A few days later, with Smith getting more panic-stricken by the day, he called for a temporary halt at Ocate Creek and summoned the officers to his tent. He emphasized the importance of arriving at Santa Fe within a week—the tenth of October deadline—and made a proposal that threw Daniel into a spin. Smith wanted to divide the Battalion, sending fifty strong men from each company ahead to Santa Fe on a quick, forced march in order to meet the deadline. The others, he proposed, could travel behind at a slower pace. John D. Lee, Levi Hancock, and a few others strongly objected, not wanting to divide the Battalion for any reason.

"I don't feel too good about leaving the sick men behind," Daniel said when Smith asked for his opinion. "But I can see the military wisdom in the decision."

The ensuing debate brought the officers to erupt with old feelings again, some supporting Smith, others supporting Lee and Hancock. In the end, however, the vote favored Smith's proposal and the Battalion was divided into two parts. All of Daniel's messmates, being healthy, went in the vanguard group, breaking camp and traveling another eighteen miles that late afternoon and evening. Daniel voted for the division, but instantly regretted it. Dr. Sanderson, instead of staying behind with the sick, traveled with the advance group. After a while, however, Daniel began to think it was a blessing. At least Sanderson couldn't administer calomel and arsenic to sick men he couldn't see.

The next day the vanguard group passed through Las Vegas, a town of five hundred New Mexicans who lived among crudely built adobe huts, where Daniel saw only one window in the entire area. Men, women, and children stared at them as they passed, some climbed upon the roofs of the houses to see the spectacle of more American soldiers marching into New Mexico. Snow-covered mountains could be seen in the far distance. The vanguard group camped at Las Vegas for a few hours at night, and Daniel had walked through the village seeing what he thought was a most miserable set of poor, half-clothed people covered with vermin, who seemingly cared for nothing but a little food and a Fandango to kill time. There were no milk cows, only goats. Daniel saw a boy milking a goat from the rear, where the milk pail caught frequent droppings from the goat which landed right in the pail. The boy merely skimmed the droppings out of the pail and kept milking. The soldiers, however, were able to buy a little wheat, squaw corn, onions, red peppers, and squash to supplement their diet. While marching out of Las Vegas the next morning, another messenger arrived from Kearny. The Battalion was to report to Colonel Doniphan for orders as soon as it arrived in Santa Fe, and the October tenth deadline still stood. Doniphan had plans to install Cooke as their commander in Santa Fe.

38

Socorro, New Mexico

October 6, 1846

"THAT'S KIT CARSON?" Private Bernard Bogart asked Sergeant Waldo Peck. "I imagined him to be over six feet, and to talk like thunder. He's a dern sight smaller than I had 'im made out ta be."

Bogart scanned the famous western guide, another Missourian, from astride his black horse as General Kearny continued to question Carson. Carson, of medium height, was a plain, simple, unostentatious man. He had brown, curling hair, just a little beard, and a voice as soft as a woman's.

"Dern," Bogart said a few minutes later, after he heard Carson talk to General Kearny. "The Mexicans ran away in California, too, sounds like.

When am I gonna get ta shoot me some greasers?"

Carson told an incredible story. He had left Los Angeles twenty-six days earlier with dispatches for Washington, D. C., from Lieutenant Colonel John C. Fremont and Commodore Robert F. Stockton. California had been taken! Carson had promised Fremont and Stockton that he would deliver this news to Washington in less than sixty days. Already he had covered more than eight hundred miles in less than a month, accompanied by sixteen other men.

"You could ask General Kearny if you could transfer back to Santa Fe and go directly into Mexico with Colonel Doniphan," Peck answered.

Bogart thought this over for a few seconds. From Socorro, his present location in New Mexico—seventy-five miles south of Albuquerque, in the Rio Grande Valley—California was three months away, according to Carson. That's because Kearny was traveling with so many wagons and livestock that more rapid travel was impossible. If he could talk Kearny into a transfer, he could ride back to Santa Fe in about a week and hook up with Doniphan. Surely Doniphan would have an opportunity to kill greasers in Chihuahua.

"Dern, I don't dare talk ta the general now," Bogart said in a disgusted voice. "Kearny looks all bent out of shape, don't he?"

Peck agreed. Kearny was arguing with Carson over whether or not Carson should return to California with him.

Carson appeared stiff-necked. "But general," Carson was saying, "I pledged my word to Fremont and Stockton that I would deliver these dispatches to the President in person."

Kearny was equal to the task. "Don't worry about it. I'll assume all responsibility for the matter. I'll assign Fitzpatrick to carry your mail to Washington. I need you to show me the way to California. You've just passed over the country that my army needs to traverse."

Kearny had planned on striking due west from Socorro, but Carson had come from the south. Socorro was a way station on the *El Camino Real*—the Royal Road—that led from El Paso to Santa Fe. From the corner of his eye, Bogart could see the San Miguel Mission. Thousands of snow geese flew overhead. Hundreds of sand hill cranes stalked the marshes along the Rio Grande River. Roadrunners had been seen scurrying about all day in the desert landscape, where sheep and cattle of local Spanish settlers grazed. Only a few Indians had been seen, Apache and Pueblo. Baptiste Charbonneau, a guide Kearny had hired at Bent's Fort, had spotted the Apaches in the hills to the west. The other men had mistaken them for cedars and shrubs, but Charbonneau's practiced eye proved otherwise.

Thomas "Broken Hand" Fitzpatrick was another of Kearny's guides.

"Carson looks like he wish'd he'd taken another road," Bogart said. When he first saw Carson, he and Carson's men had charged down on Kearny's army, yelling like Indians. Now Carson looked like a coyote, wanting to slink away.

It must be true, Peck said to himself. Kearny's orders appeared to have shocked Carson profoundly. A mountain man like Carson, new to military life, couldn't understand a world in which one man could assume the responsibilities of another so lightly.

By nightfall, when Bogart lay rolled up in his wool blanket under his white tent, Bogart had the tussle between Kearny and Carson figured out. Easterners like Kearny did not like mountain men like John C. Fremont, who had virtually promoted himself from explorer to conqueror of California. Fremont had been commissioned a lieutenant in the Topographical Engineers. Kearny was plain jealous that Fremont and Stockton had already run off the Mexicans and secured not only San Diego, but Los Angeles, Monterey, Sonoma, and San Francisco as well. President Polk had sent Kearny to capture Santa Fe, and to march into California and take it as well. By now Bogart knew both sides of Kearny—cold, domineering, and harsh on one hand, and a diplomat, commander, and statesman on the other. Kearny, fifty-two, attended two years at Columbia University in New York City, served in the New York Militia, and had been a soldier for thirty-six years.

"Do you think the general will let me return to Santa Fe?" Bogart whispered to Peck as the moon began to hide behind dark clouds. He reached over and patted his musket. "Remember the Englishman, Henry Eagles? He's the lucky one, all right. He'll probably get to go straight into Mexico and kill greasers. I want to go with him."

"You have a two-thirds chance," Peck replied in a sleepy voice. "You'll find out in the morning."

Kearny had already disclosed the fact that he was going to reduce his forces from three hundred dragoons to a hundred and ten. Because California had already been secured, Carson recommended no more than that were necessary. That pleased Kearny, because the extra dragoons could be used for the invasion of Mexico, under Doniphan's command.

"Where do you suppose the Mormons are about now?" Bogart asked.

"Derned if I know. They're supposed to be in Santa Fe by the tenth."

"If all them Mormons make it to California, they'll outnumber us Missourians four or five to one."

Peck rolled over in his blanket. "You worry too much."

The next morning word sifted through the dragoons that Kit Carson had contemplated slipping away during the dead of night, knowing that none of Kearny's men could have caught him. The idea of obeying an arbitrary order against his better judgment seemed sheer nonsense, especially as he had no respect for the general. Plus, Carson had not seen his wife, Josefa, in almost two years, and she was waiting for him in Taos—less than a hundred miles away. But after talking it over with his men, he decided that he *ought* to obey. After all, Carson knew the way to California much better than Fitzpatrick.

As Bogart ate his breakfast, he could hear Carson laughing at Kearny's situation. "It'll take us four months to get to California with yer outfit," Carson was saying to the general. "Leave yer wagons and cannon behind, and yer foot soldiers, too. Men have two feet, mules have four. Men on mules—and horses—will be quicker than men afoot."

Bogart scratched his head, wondering why Kearny had not thought of that.

"But those wagons hold our supplies," Kearny argued. He had left Santa

Fe with a personal staff, three hundred dragoons, a party of topographical engineers under Lieutenant William H. Emory, experienced hunters and guides Antoine Robidoux and Jean Charbonneau. He also had a number of wagons.

"Load the supplies on mules," Carson countered. "We'll go south a few miles, then go west over the mountains. We'll follow Indian trails."

"Fine, but I'm taking just a few wagons, and the cannon, too. Just two of them."

Carson threw up his arms in despair. The howitzers were on wheels ten feet in circumference. "Those wheels ain't made fer goin' where we're goin'. The road's too irregular."

A while later Bogart was back to his own complaining. "Dern, why'd the general choose me to go ta California? I'll be surrounded by Mormons and won't get to shoot a single greaser."

It had been settled. Fitzpatrick was leaving for Washington. Carson was guiding Kearny to California. Charbonneau was to find the Mormon Battalion and lead it to California.

Peck, too, had been assigned to be one of the dragoons assigned to accompany Kearny. "Well, it won't be too bad. I can see us sittin' on the beach drinkin' whiskey and soakin' up the sun."

California, in fact, was in turmoil. Led by Jose Maria Flores, rebels had expelled Gillespie from Los Angeles. News of the attack had created a sensation and the Mexicans were rapidly organizing into rebel bands on horseback. More than three hundred of them signed a proclamation in Los Angeles, renouncing subjugation by the Americans. Electrified Californios began digging up arms, even a cannon, they had buried for safekeeping. A band of Mexicans drove a nine-man U.S. force from Santa Barbara. The nine men escaped into the chaparral, which the pursuing Californios set ablaze. San Diego, too, defended by only nineteen U.S. soldiers, under siege for a month, finally fell.

Thus Stockton and Fremont were right back where they had been when they drove Castro out of California and declared victory.

It was as if it hadn't happened at all.

39

❧

Santa Fe, New Mexico

October 9, 1846

ROBERT FELT A CHILL AS HE MARCHED into Santa Fe. Rain and hail pummeled his felt hat and water dripped into his face, but he didn't mind it at all. After walking eight hundred miles from Fort Leavenworth this was the first time in two months that he didn't feel hot and sticky. To get around the mountains that guarded Santa Fe the Battalion had marched southwest from Las Vegas and then turned northwest. A broad trail had been cut through the cedar trees and brush. Santa Fe looked to be around two miles long and a mile wide. Adobe farmhouses dotted the landscape, set in no particular order. Houses and buildings were more compact around the center of town. Oxen, horses, mules, and burros grazed on dried corn stalks and wheat stubble. There were lots of dogs, too, and Duke's hair was sticking straight out in a protective instinct.

"Not much here," Robert commented to Daniel as the Battalion boys marched down the hill toward the plaza with fixed bayonets and drawn swords, as ordered by Lieutenant Smith. American soldiers stood on top of the adobe roofs there; suddenly there was a military salute of a hundred guns.

The salute impressed Daniel. He could still see the gunsmoke from the muskets in the air above him. "You're right," he said, "but I'm anxious to look around." There wasn't much time; the sun was about ready to set.

Santa Fe was a huge disappointment to Robert. Given all the talk along the trail about it being a center of trade, he expected it to be another New Orleans, St. Louis, or Liverpool—at least until he heard Toothless Bayer's description of it. It was nothing of the kind. With a population of five to seven thousand, Santa Fe was more of a slum—a small town made up of an unlovely huddle of adobe buildings surrounding a bare, muddy plaza. The streets were muddy too, and narrow, unpaved, unkempt, and unlighted. The adobe houses looked dingy and forbidding from the outside, however cool, clean, and comfortable they might be on the inside. Everything in Santa Fe looked dirty, untidy, cheap, primitive, and even nasty. Medieval English farming hamlets such as Apperley consisted of rows of houses surrounding a central plaza. Here, the adobe houses had been built more hodge-podge and spread out in a confusing order. Homes had been built up and down both sides of the Santa

Fe River to keep marauding bears, raccoons, porcupines, and other wildlife from laying waste to crops.

As the rain quit and the sun came out, a few naked children appeared from adobe homes and splashed in the irrigation ditches that brought water from the mountains. A few women came out, too, to wash clothes. Dogs and burros ran at large in the ditches, extending the filth. No wonder the conquistadors were gone, Robert thought to himself. Their dream of an empire of wealth was gone. The people left behind had set their roots deep in a harsh, marginal land.

Colonel Doniphan, who ordered the hundred-gun salute to the Mormon Battalion, gave the Battalion a brief inspection. Lieutenant Smith explained to Doniphan that the other soldiers were two days behind, and why.

"I wonder how Henry feels," Robert said as the Battalion was dismissed to a camp located in a wheat field in back of the Santa Fe cathedral. "He wanted so bad to beat us to Santa Fe. And so did Pap Price."

The weather was mild with temperatures in the high sixties.

On a hill above the town, an American flag made of silk flapped in the breeze where construction on Fort Marcy had begun. Flocks of goats and cattle could be seen on all the other hills. Remnants of the corn harvest were evident in fields surrounding nearly every home. Long trains of Mexican men and women riding tiny gray burros, guided with a jab of a short stick behind, or a blow to the side of the head, were coming in from the mountains to catch a view of the newly arriving American soldiers. The common-class men were dressed in cheap-dyed goatskin pants, coarse shirts colored blue or red, palm-leaf hats, and serapes over their shoulders. Most were barefoot. Other men were better dressed in pants of cloth ornamented with stripes of colored goatskin, blue jackets with silver buttons, black oilskin over their wide-brimmed hats, and a hat-band ornamented with silver. The men here looked rough, like they might do worse than rob a man if the mood struck them. It wasn't long until Robert saw a fight between two Mexicans. He heard a yell and saw each man pull a knife. They went at one another like butchers. Their clothes were soon bloody, but evidently the cuts were not serious, for after a while they stopped fighting and went back to gambling together.

"Don't know and don't care," Daniel answered. "I want to meet Captain Cooke, and I'm certain the other officers do too. I just hope he's not in a big hurry to leave Santa Fe. We need a few days' rest."

Robert took a deep breath. "Like a month? But I suppose General Kearny is expecting us to catch him." Like Daniel, his shoes were nearly worn out and he was totally exhausted. Half the Battalion, two days behind them, was even worse off.

"What do you want for supper?" asked Robert Pixton, the cook. "Looks like we'll have a better choice tonight." Now that the dark storm had passed, women and girls were selling pine nuts, peaches, pears, apples, grapes, bread, boiled corn, and melons.

Daniel seemed to blush as the New Mexican women approached. Women here had never heard of petticoats, bustles, bodices, long sleeves, or high-necked blouses. They each wore a bright but skimpy *camisa* with loose, abbreviated sleeves, over which a gaily-colored shawl had been thrown because of the weather. Their red, yellow, or blue skirts were not long enough, leaving their ankles exposed. Slippers, instead of shoes, covered their feet.

After Robert's mess set up their tent, more women came around selling red pepper pies, tortillas, and penuche. Old men leading burros sold wood, or rather evenly cut sticks. Robert hated to buy any because the New Mexicans treated their burros so terribly. The small, thin animals were overloaded. One man, when the burro tried eating some green fodder, whacked the animal at the side of the head so hard it almost killed him.

Toothless closed his sutler wagon; there were too many competing goods. Robert found him half dejected, eating a melon.

"Say, that looks good," Robert said as he walked by.

"I've got this one all et up, I reckon," said Toothless. He signaled to a young brown-skinned girl. "The little muchacha will sell you one."

The girl came running and she bore one round watermelon. "Dos reals por una," she said.

"Un real media," countered Toothless.

The little girl surrendered the melon for a real and a half.

"Saved you a half real," said Toothless as he handed the melon to Robert. "Even these little muchachas know how to play the cheat. But it's the time of year for good melons in Santa Fe."

Robert nodded his approval and quickly cut the watermelon in pieces and shared it with members of his mess.

In another part of the camp, Colonel Doniphan was visiting with Levi Hancock and other Mormons he had known in the days the Church had been established in Missouri. Robert found out later that when Doniphan failed to extend Colonel Price's regiment a hundred-gun salute upon arrival, it was because Doniphan remembered the wrongs the Missourians committed against the Mormons.

When Private Henry Eagles arrived late in Santa Fe the next afternoon driving a wagon full of ammunition, he felt the wrath of Colonel Price immediately.

"As soon as I can find Colonel Doniphan I've a mind to shoot him," said Price, who was riding in the wagon with Henry.

Henry didn't say anything. Pap Price was angry that there was no hundred-gun salute for his Missouri Regiment as there had been for the Mormon Battalion.

"And how did the Mormons get here before us, anyway?" Price asked himself, clearly agitated. "I thought we were ahead of them."

Henry was afraid to give Price the answer. The Mormon Battalion had split in half, with the healthy troops moving ahead, and those who were sick or weak were not expected until tomorrow. Price's regiment beat the sick Mormons, but not the healthy ones. Henry was anxious to find out which group Robert and Daniel were in.

As soon as he could, Henry left his camp beneath Fort Marcy, lit a cornshuck cigarette, and found Robert at the Mormon camp south of the cathedral. Behind him, soldiers of Price's regiment were making their own salute, firing rifles and pistols into the blue sky. Their horses were rearing on their hind legs, and prancing around. Several of the Missouri soldiers had already found the La Fonda bar and were ordering drinks.

"All you Mormons sample the senoras and senoritas last night?" Henry asked when he found Robert. "Is that why you struck out ahead of us?"

Robert felt like sampling Henry's midsection with a right uppercut. "That may be the habit of many of the American soldiers, but not the Mormon soldiers, Henry. You ought to know that."

"Dern," Henry said, showing that he picked up on Missouri slang, "I lost the bet and you beat me to Santa Fe. What do you think of this place? Doesn't it remind you of the prairie dog town we saw on the trail a few weeks ago? Or a run-down brick kiln?"

Robert let his eyes scan the town again. He had to agree with Henry. Despite the dilapidated nature of the town, crowds of drunken Missouri volunteers already filled the streets, brawling and boasting. Mexicans, wrapped in their serapes, scowled at them as they passed. Donkey loads of *hojo*, corn shucks, were hawked for sale. Pueblo Indians and priests jostled the rude crowds of brawlers at every step. Under several portals were numerous monte tables, surrounded by Mexicans and Americans. Every other house was a grocery, not for food, but for gin or whiskey, and they continually disgorged reeling, drunken men.

"But I'll make you another bet," Henry said. "I'll bet there'll be more than one Mormon who'll imbibe in the Santa Fe whiskey and Mexican women. There's love for sale here. Take me on?"

"No, thanks," Robert answered. He knew one or two who might tarnish the reputation of the entire outfit before the Battalion left for California, but he didn't want to admit it to Henry. "But you can do me a favor."

"I just got here, and you're asking for a favor?"

"I am, Henry. Promise me that you'll stay faithful to Katherine while you're a solider. Promise me that you'll not act like a typical Missourian while you're here in Santa Fe, or if you end up in Mexico as part of the invasion army."

"It's none of your business what I do while I'm a soldier."

"You're my wife's brother. And I *am* my brother's keeper. Behave yourself."

Henry fell silent for just a moment.

Robert continued his lecture as another crowd of drunken soldiers staggered by, their cottonmouth Missouri drawl worsened by slurring caused by alcohol. There were blurred syllables, bad grammar, and the idioms and slang of uncouth dialects.

"I've been here only one night," Robert said, "but already the guardhouse is full of these ill-mannered soldiers. War is serious business, and soldiers usually leave a legacy that's a disgrace to their homeland's flag, whether they are British, French, Spanish, Mexican, or American."

"Bah! You worry too much," Henry replied.

"I mean it, Henry," Robert said. "Don't fall into the trap that the devil has set for you. These Missourians are bad characters. Don't do as they do."

"Dern, I ain't gonna go out on the town with you," Henry said a little sheepishly. "You're way too serious about all this."

Henry left the Mormon camp looking for a chance to defy Robert, and to return the New Mexican salute to another senorita. He already knew how to do it, because when he came into town this was demonstrated by a Mexican and another woman. When Henry saw a friendly woman he swept off his hat. Without hesitation the woman extended her right hand. Henry grasped it, shook it warmly, and gently drew her towards him. Then he threw his left arm about her waist, embraced her, and laid his bearded cheek against hers.

"Nauvoo was never like this," Henry called out to Robert, who was watching in disgust. "And neither was Carthage. Or jolly old England."

There was a clanging of church bells, creating a din that would wake the dead.

"I'm off to the fandango," Henry said to Robert. "You ought to at least come and watch. I've heard it's a festival not to be missed in Santa Fe."

New Mexican women could be seen coming out of their mud houses with their best dresses on, gold and silver bracelets on their wrists, large earrings, and massive crosses dangling around their necks. Cigarettes hung from their painted lips. Their Mexican tongue seemed outlandish.

Out of curiosity, Robert and dozens of other Mormon soldiers filed into the *sala*, along with other Mexican men, American traders, teamsters, and the Mexican women. The Mexican men were dressed in leather breeches, tight around the hips, and open from the knee down.

"You're coming to the fandango?" Henry asked.

"If it's just a festival," Robert answered, who didn't attend the previous night. He gathered that the women of Santa Fe went to a dance every night of their lives. "No alcohol for me. How about you?"

"Don't pass your morals on to me. I might end up with a warm-blooded Mexican woman for the night, if we can agree on the price."

Robert gasped and quickly changed the subject to the layout of the building.

At one end of the long room, under the eye of their leader, musicians were already seated, some with guitars, some with mandolins, and others with hand drums. Soon the sala was filed with men and women in native costumes, all smoking. The Mexican men wore knives and pistols on their hips, just below their gaudy calico shirts. In an eerie way, except for the musicians, it reminded Robert of the scene in the Carthage courtroom during the trial of the murderers of Joseph Smith. The music began and the Mexicans began to dance in the center of the dirt floor. Some were native dances, such as the cuna or cradle dance, and others were a form of the waltz. As the whiskey took hold of the dancers, they began to yell and whoop just like the Plains Indians. Between dances there was more drinking: the women became more coquettish, the Americans more truculent, and the Mexicans more jealous and envious of their entertainers.

"See you around, Henry," Robert said. "Looks like the makings of a fight."

To Robert, Santa Fe seemed to be a town where natives had no time for sleep. Tables for gambling surrounded the square and continually occupied the attention of crowds. Dice and faro banks were all the time in constant play. Even women had a passion for gaming.

"Stay here," Henry pleaded. "It's just like the old days, in the pubs back in England. I'll bet you and me could whip a dozen of them greasers at a time. The greasers here are a bunch of thieves and liars, mean and contemptible."

"Tomorrow's Sunday. We're having Church services in the morning. You're always invited. Goodnight."

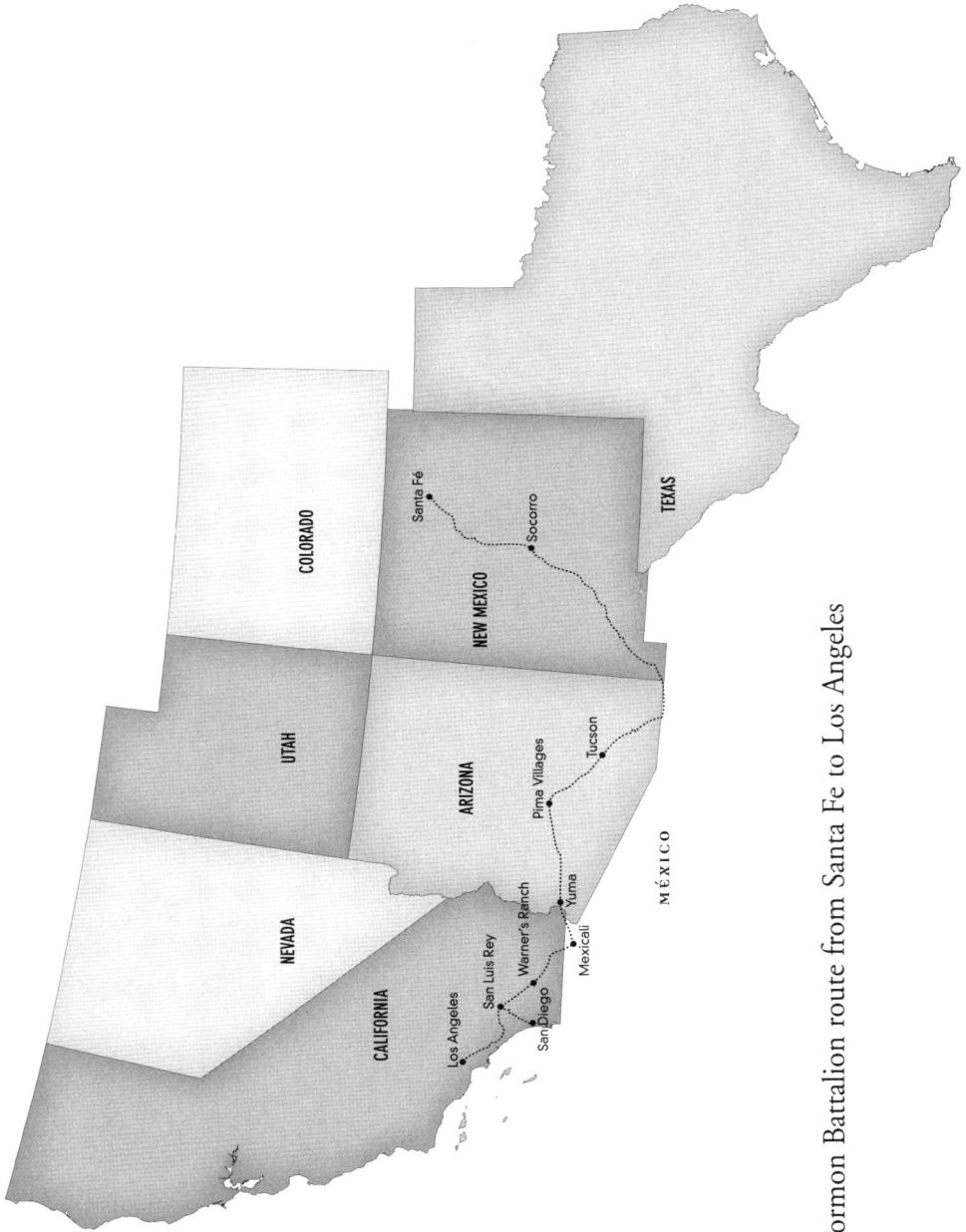

Mormon Battalion route from Santa Fe to Los Angeles

40

THE MOST INTERESTING PART OF THE Sabbath was not the Mormon services in which Levi Hancock spoke of repentance and baptism, but Robert's later attendance out of curiosity of a Catholic mass. Among the buildings on the west side of the plaza stood the parroquia, or parish church. It had a name; it was called the Chapel of the Holy Trinity. It reminded Robert of the Anglican Deerhurst Church—the Priory Church of St. Mary the Virgin—in England where he grew up. That old English church had been constructed by the Catholics in the 1500s, and taken over by the Church of England when King Henry VIII broke away.

Robert was standing near Daniel and another sergeant by the name of William Coray, and his wife, Melissa.

"I dare say there's enough holy water in here to swim an elephant," Coray whispered as they watched hundreds of New Mexicans go through the rituals of their religion. Robert concluded that Coray had never seen a Catholic or Anglican service. Instead of a church organ, a mixture of violins, triangles, drums, and other instruments supplied the music. The dingy mud walls were adorned with religious images, macabre *santos*, and pictures.

Robert was amazed at the fact that the New Mexicans the night before had been gambling, dancing, drinking whiskey and potent aguardiente, wearing revealing costumes, all in a drunken craze, and yet here they were the next day participating in their religious ceremonies as if no sin had been committed.

Afterward, Robert wandered a block or two west with Daniel and Toothless Bayer, past more mud houses, to the other side of the river, and came upon the San Miguel Chapel.

"What's the difference between the San Miguel and the Chapel of the Holy Trinity?" Daniel asked Toothless.

On top of the little chapel stood an uncharacteristic triple-story pagoda-like tower that housed a large bell. The bell had been cast in Spain and brought by oxcart to Santa Fe from Mexico City.

"I tolt you about the caste system here," Toothless replied. "This one's fer the Injuns and the color quebrado."

Robert concluded Toothless was right. Pouring out of the little church was a collection of mestizos and Pueblos. Robert felt lucky the Mormons didn't worship this way—the wealthy in one chapel and the unfortunate poor in another. He felt fortunate too, that in America people had freedom to choose their religion. Here, visitors had always been astonished at the blind zeal at which the people professed the Catholic religion. But given their propensity to lie, cheat, steal, gamble, and display the lowest morals of any people he had ever seen—including ignoring their marriage vows—he sensed that they ought to be taught better principles. There were open pastoral excesses too, with exorbitant fees charged for marriages, baptisms, and burials. The padres complained when American traders sold the locals liquors and ardent spirits, but the traders argued that the padres drank themselves and only complained because the process reduced the amount of money the locals had to pay for their church ordinances. When Robert mentioned this to Toothless, Toothless had a way of dealing with it.

"This is Santa Fe. Santa Fe has its own rules and its own morals."

"That's a poor way to look at it," Robert said. He suspected these kinds of rules and morals permeated throughout New Mexico, California, and even into Old Mexico.

"Whatever sins these ign'rnt people may have ta answer fer, ya haf'ta accord 'em at least two glowin' virtues," Toothless shot back. "And that would be gratitude and hospitality."

Robert readily agreed, but he still had concerns. "Did you attend mass today?" Robert asked Toothless.

"I'm Lutheran, not Catholic," Toothless replied. "If Martin Luther were here, he'd protest just like he did years ago."

"Protest what?" Daniel asked.

"If ye ain't noticed it yet, ye will," Toothless explained. "The priests here share all the vices and virtues of the people. You'll see the Santa Fe priests betting high at monte, loving good liquor, getting disgustingly tipsy, and even keeping a woman."

"For real?" Robert asked.

"It makes my blood boil," Toothless went on. "It's not unusual for 'em to have three or four wives. Unofficial, of course."

Daniel hung his head. He hadn't told Toothless that he had two wives. "I suppose you've heard of polygamy among the Mormons."

The old German sutler began to grin. "Yep, I have. I know my Bible. The ancients had more'n one wife. But ta preach celibacy, and then not practice it, why it smacks of hypocrisy."

"I suppose you're right," Daniel said timidly.

Daniel had a good feeling about Colonel Philip St. George Cooke when Cooke gave his first speech to the Battalion officers. It was a short one but covered a lot of territory. And it left no doubt as to who was in charge.

"Men," he began during a mid-morning meeting under bright sunlight at the Battalion camp, "my job is to get you to California so that you can be the occupation force there for the United States. But our travel will not be easy. For more than two centuries the lines of travel in the Southwest has run north and south in keeping with the course of Spanish expansion in the New

World. My job is to cut across the historic flow of colonization and open a new wagon route from here to California."

Daniel hadn't thought about that before, but he agreed it must be true. He wondered how far north the Spanish had explored, and how rough the country between Santa Fe and California would be.

At age thirty-seven, Cooke had already served nineteen years in the frontier army of the United States. He was one of West Point's youngest graduates. His six-foot-four-inch frame, dressed in blue, towered over every one of the Battalion boys. Cooke continued by saying, "To make this journey, we'll have to march eleven hundred miles through an unknown wilderness without any road or trail. We'll follow the old Spanish road for a while, the one that leads to Chihuahua and Mexico City, and then cut almost straight west to California."

Daniel grimaced. The trip along the Santa Fe Trail was rough enough, and it was an established road. He didn't know what to think of the prospect that the trip to California would be over territory that had never been traveled by a white man.

"Kearny has already depleted Santa Fe of its best mules," Cooke went on. "Not only that, but he had to take most of the provisions, too. Best I can determine, it'll take around ninety days to get to California. We'll probably have enough flour, sugar, and coffee for only sixty days. I estimate the salt pork will run out in thirty days, and soap in twenty days."

At this point Daniel wondered how the hunting would be in the desert that faced them between Santa Fe and California. There would be no buffalo, that was for certain.

"I have appointed Lieutenant Andrew Jackson Smith as our commissary of subsistence," Cooke said. "I've given him eight hundred dollars in treasury drafts to purchase cattle and sheep."

Levi Hancock whispered to Daniel, "Well, at least the lieutenant will be out of our hair for the most part."

"This will make the privates happy," Daniel said as he thought of Robert. Daniel had hoped that Smith would be reassigned to either Colonel Price or Colonel Doniphan. Daniel was about to ask about "Calomel" Sanderson but Colonel Cooke supplied the answer. "Dr. Sanderson will accompany us to California," he said.

Daniel felt the muscles in his stomach tighten. The Battalion boys were stuck with Sanderson.

"If California has been captured, and the fighting is over by the time we get there, you'll be taken by ship to the Bay of Monterey," Cooke said to the officers. He went on to propose that the sick, women, and children in the Battalion be sent to Pueblo for the winter. "In the spring, the sick detachment will be taken, at government expense, to join your people in the West, wherever Brigham Young has located."

Daniel agreed to this proposal, and so did the other officers—even John D. Lee.

"Come with me," John D. Lee said to Daniel with a concerned look. "I need some moral support."

"Where're you going?" Daniel asked as he finished his breakfast. Robert Pixton had made lumpy mush from local compounded flour, with goat's milk poured over it. Lee already had three or four other officers with him, and an enlisted man from Company D by the name of John Steele.

"We're going to find Colonel Cooke and give him a peace of my mind," Lee said, fuming. "Cooke wants to release twenty-five of the Battalion men, the ones who have been on the sick list. That means they'll not get paid. And you know what that means."

Daniel nodded. Twenty-five less paychecks—money that was needed by the Church to survive the winter in Council Bluffs. Daniel hoped Lee wouldn't push Colonel Cooke too hard. Cooke, he had learned, had been en route for San Antonio earlier in the year with hopes of being part of the invasion into Mexico. Kearny had countermanded the order.

"Cooke might not be too happy to have the Mormon Battalion thrust upon him," Daniel said.

"That's between him and Kearny," Lee said. "Not our problem."

Lee had hoped to find Colonel Cooke in the Palace of the Governors, a rundown adobe structure formed on the south side of the presidio. A walk under the portal disclosed a few soldiers and even a handful of Pueblo Indians, but no officers. Cooke was not in the town plaza either, located south of the palace. One-story adobe buildings surrounded the plaza. Missourians were trading with the Indians: a cotton shirt for a buckskin hunting shirt, a tin cup for a lasset, a buckskin for a small piece of tobacco, a knife for buckles and straps.

On the east side were government offices, private homes, and a squalid house where the ayuntamiento, or town council, met. Near here, in a long, low cellar, Lee finally found Cooke with about thirty other regular army officers. Over a meal of tortillas and cornstalk molasses, the officers were discussing provisions and military strategy. When Cooke arose to meet Lee, Cooke easily towered over him. To Daniel's surprise, Steele spoke before Lee could get out a word.

"I understand you have issued orders for the sick men and women to return to Bent's Fort," Steele said.

"Yes, that is so."

Steele's eyes bore into the colonel. "I think it is wrong to split up husbands and wives."

"This is an army, son."

"Well, my wife is on the list to return to Bent's Fort."

"That may be so."

"I would like the privilege of going back with her, although I'm not sick. Either that, or I want her to accompany me all the way to California."

Cooke took on a saucy tone. "Well, son. I suppose I'd like to have my wife along with me, too."

"Your wife is probably in Washington D. C., or in some seaport town, living very comfortably with her friends. Mine is here in Santa Fe among enemies. I will not stand for it to have her sent back to Bent's Fort with the sick of the Battalion."

Cooke looked at Lee as if he were pleading for help. He got none.

"I would consider it to be more honorable to command our sick men to be shot, and put an end to their suffering," Lee said, "than to leave them here to rot among these Missouri soldiers and the New Mexicans."

Daniel saw Cooke wilt. The colonel was clearly embarrassed in front of the other officers.

"Tell you what," Cooke said. "I'll meet with you in the morning about this matter. I promise to give it some serious thought."

"When are we leaving Santa Fe?" Daniel asked the colonel.

"As soon as our provisions arrive," he answered. "We're in competition with all the other armies, here. As you know, there was no specie, so I've had to pay your Battalion members with checks. Your mules are broken down after the trip from Fort Leavenworth to here, and I'm trying to find new mules. There is no salt pork here, but a shipment should be arriving any day. I'm also buying up as many beef cattle as I can find. Same with packsaddles and other rations. We need salt pork, flour, sugar, coffee, salt, and soap. I'm anxious to get going."

Daniel looked at the other officers in the low cellar. "Most of our Mormon men hate it here in Santa Fe. We'll be glad to get on the trail again, and get to California."

After a week in Santa Fe, Daniel was anxious to leave.

"The road to California's apt to be worse than the road from Fort Leavenworth to Santa Fe," he said to Robert as the men watched John D. Lee begin his journey back to Council Bluffs. Lee had collected around twelve hundred dollars in checks from the Battalion to be delivered to Brigham Young, and hundreds of letters. He traveled in a wagon, accompanied by Howard Egan, Samuel Gully, and Roswell Stevens.

Robert cringed at the remark. The Cimarron Desert had been no picnic. The deserts that lay before them promised to be just as bleak. "At least we're past the herds of buffalo. What little water we find won't be ruined, we hope."

Daniel was among the last to shake Lee's hand goodbye. "Give my love to my wives, Elizabeth and Harriet, and be certain they receive the money I've sent." In his letter, Daniel had explained to his wives that he had drawn his sergeant's pay for a month and a half, which consisted of seventeen dollars. He had also borrowed an additional eight dollars from another soldier, making a total of twenty-five dollars he was sending. He apologized to his wives for not sending cash, explaining that the commissioned officers in Doniphan and Price's regiments had first choice and took all the available cash. He also expressed his disappointment that he thought the Battalion might have received three months' pay instead of a month and a half.

He also wrote about traveling through the Cimarron Desert: "Sometimes we had to travel nearly sixty miles before we could reach water. The only thing we had to whet our dry lips with was the pint of water our canteens held, and that was used up quickly. The heat of the sun and the clouds of dust caused the death of many of our animals, and death and sickness of men. About a hundred miles out, a separation took place. The more hardy of the men continued on toward Santa Fe with the best teams in order to meet General Kearny's deadline, and we had to leave the sick and feeble amongst us to follow on in the rear."

Daniel went on to explain that the Battalion now had to face an additional eight-hundred-mile march to California, and that Colonel Cooke was hoping that the men could be taken by ship from San Diego to Monterey. He also commented on how grateful he was that his wives had not been sick as many others had been in Council Bluffs. He also commented on the death of Elizabeth's sister, Dianah: "It was a kind messenger to deliver Dianah from the hand of oppression that she has so long born patiently."

Daniel also sent a separate letter to his mother, Martha, and his sister, Rebecca.

41

ROBERT BEGAN HIS LETTER lamenting over his sister's death, and the fact that Hannah's letter had detailed the sickness of several of his children. He wrote: "Finding my children have been sick caused me to lament. But be of good courage my dear, and the God of heaven will bless you. My prayers are said continually that you and my children will be blessed."

Robert described his feelings about Henry, and that Henry was going to stay in Santa Fe with Colonel Price.

He also commented on Hannah's pregnancy: "Now respecting your being in a family way: if the child should be a girl I wish to have her named Maria. If it is a boy, name him what you'd like. Try to furnish yourself with everything necessary for your confinement and comfort. I am sending all my money, and I will send more for your trip out West in the spring. If you have to, sell my gun. I can buy it back later, when I am reunited with you and the children.

Try to keep my plough, for it will be very valuable, indeed, out West. Tell Joseph to be a good boy and do all that his mother tells him, and to read his book. Tell him, too, that I will try to get him a pony when I return. Give my love to all my dear children and tell them that their father will get them some nice playthings when I return."

Robert went on to describe Santa Fe: "It is a place of about seven thousand inhabitants. The Spaniards are a very dark-looking people. The women are small and their houses are like a lot of brick hills, built with mud and sticks. It predates America's Plymouth colony by ten years."

He described the hunting he'd done for his messmates: "I shot an antelope with my musket in early October. This animal is about the size of a deer, and was so large I could not carry it. I separated it with my knife and carried the hind quarters back to camp. My five messmates rejoiced. It was better than mutton." He also described hunting buffalo.

Robert concluded his letter talking about temple covenants and the money he was sending back with Brother Lee: "Now, my dear, be faithful. Do not forget the things that you and I heard and saw in the temple of the Lord. My faith is so strong in the things that Brother Brigham told us during the enlistment. If we will be faithful, we will not fail on this expedition, and we will see our families again. I believe all that Brother Brigham said, the same as if the Great God had told me himself.

"As a private, I received ten dollars in pay. I went about the camp and borrowed another sixteen dollars, agreeing to pay two dollars interest out of my next pay. Therefore, I am sending you a total of twenty-four dollars with Brothers Lee and Egan, and two dollars for the Twelve. I am enjoying good health, and I hope you and my dear children will enjoy the same. Please send word as soon as you can about how you are getting along. I pray for your brother, Elias, and for my sister, Dianah, who have departed this life. My prayer is that the great God of Heaven will preserve us in the hallow of his hand, forever and ever. I don't know how to tell you to direct your next letter, except to R. Harris, E Company, Mormon Battalion, Upper California."

John D. Lee and Howard Egan left Santa Fe as a caravan swarmed into the city. "Los carros! La entrada de la caravana!" the New Mexicans shouted as the collection of wagons, oxen, and mules descended into the village between endless adobe walls as high as the horses' heads. The air was filled with sharp pops, not unlike Fourth of July firecrackers. For the occasion, the wagoners had tied brand new poppers to the end of their whips, and they competed with each other to make the most noise.

From the southern end of Santa Fe, Robert could see wagons approaching Santa Fe from Chihuahua, and old ox carts, too. They were bringing Mexican gold and silver to trade for American goods. Mexican teamsters and carters acted as though there was no war going on between the two countries.

Robert was traipsing through town with Henry again, both men sucking on *panoche*, a Mexican candy made of raw brown sugar. Robert had learned to like the local diet, things like *frijoles*, pinto beans seasoned with hot peppers;

and *chili on carne*, lean pork cut into small pieces and boiled tender with sage, crushed garlic, salt, and chili powder. The streets were dusty today. Dogs and burros ran at large, mumbling the garbage in the narrow streets. A steady breeze brought the stench past Robert and Henry.

"What we ought to do is take over the customs house," Henry said.

The Missouri caravan merchants were there now, paying the required duties on their freight. Robert had heard it was an aggravating and wearisome process. The duties were high and the officials corrupt, especially during the time of Armijo. Robert wondered how many of the wagons had false bottoms, one of several devices used to escape paying duties. As the merchants paid, they scurried off to rent a store and commence selling. Others were selling at wholesale to local merchants. Their aim was to sell out as quickly as possible and return home with the profits before the first snowfall swept across the plains.

Robert laughed. "We're in the army, Henry. You can't be thinking of such crazy things."

"But Governor Armijo has been run out," Henry said. "He didn't even take his mistress with him. Who's in there collecting the money?" Armijo's mistress was the most famous lady in Santa Fe. Her name was Gertrudes Barcelo, but known locally as *La Tules*. She ran a bar and gambling casino that stretched the length of Burro Alley.

"That's simple," Robert answered. "The lieutenant governor stayed on. Hopefully, he's more honest and the money will go to improve everyone's lives, not just Armijo's."

Armijo had always had itchy palms as governor, but Americans provided the salve. Anything to keep on Armijo's good side.

Word had been received in Santa Fe in early July that an American army was on its way. Armijo and the priests quickly spread the word that the Americans would rape women and brand men on the cheek like cattle. Armijo had raised an army of four thousand New Mexicans and Indians, demanded funds from the city council and the Departmental Assembly, ordered the Catholic Church to give him all their silver and livestock to sustain the army, and then had fled without fighting.

"The Battalion is leaving tomorrow, Henry," Robert said. "I guess this is good-bye for us for a while."

"I won't miss you."

"I'm sure Katherine and Annie miss you. What are your plans?"

Henry looked perplexed. "I might go to Missouri after the war. The government is giving land grants to soldiers."

"Why didn't you tell me before Brother Lee and Brother Egan took our letters. I could have told Katherine. She could wait for you in St. Louis or Independence."

Henry took an evasive stance. "Maybe I'll end up in California—who knows?"

"Whatever you do, behave yourself here in Santa Fe." The Missourians had been fighting each other constantly. Two soldiers had been in a serious one, with one killing the other. The survivor had been court-martialed.

Henry was full of surprises. "I'd like to see Mexico. I might volunteer when soldiers are sent from here to invade. After the war, I might find me a cute little senorita."

"You already have a wife."

"Daniel has two wives. Maybe I'll end up with three or four. How about you? Gonna solicit another wife or two when you get out of the army?"

Robert ignored all this bantering. "If you do go to Mexico, try to behave yourself. Don't act like a Missourian."

"It's none of your business what I do here in Santa Fe, or down in Mexico—if I go there."

"I mean it, Henry," Robert said. "Soldiers commit atrocities that make Heaven weep, and we can only imagine what it would be like for someone to invade our country and murder, rob, and rape our wives and mothers. A year from now Mexican newspapers in Chihuahua and Mexico City are going to be filled with accounts of how the Missouri volunteers were bad smelling bandits, long-bearded drunkards, fornicators, adulterers, defied the laws of nature, drank whiskey out of holy vessels in the Catholic churches, and slept in the niches devoted to the sacred dead."

Henry fell silent for a moment. "Where'd you get all those ideas?"

"It just came to me," Robert admitted. "Shake my hand goodbye?"

"I guess so. See you around in a year or two, maybe."

When Philip St. George Cooke gave his pep talk to the Battalion boys before departing Santa Fe, Robert formed a quick opinion.

"I'm never going to learn to love a man like Colonel Cooke, but I'm willing to let him earn my respect," Robert whispered to Daniel. "And it won't be just because he's six feet four inches tall and about the same age as me."

"I guess I'm willing, too," Daniel whispered back. "Colonel Allen earned our respect. A. J. Smith failed miserably. The jury is now out on Philip St. George Cooke."

Robert had despised A. J. Smith, a runt of a man with small man's disease.

Cooke began his speech with a reference to the "Manifest Destiny" of the United States. "I suppose you've all heard the story about a group of prairie wayfarers who saw a vision of the republic's eagle spread across the sunset. They reportedly shouted in one voice that before the year was out the vision would exist in reality. Gentlemen, we are part of that vision. We are going to follow the sunset all the way to the Pacific."

Robert scoffed a little, feeling that visions belonged to Prophets like Joseph Smith, not to the cursing type of pioneers and teamsters he'd seen so far on the trail between Fort Leavenworth and Santa Fe.

"Gentlemen of the Mormon Battalion," Cooke went on, "now that New Mexico is in the hands of the United States, our job is to help General Kearny secure California and the West Coast. I have not the remotest idea of failing. You mustn't have any idea of failing, either."

Robert scoffed again. What all professional soldiers like Cooke really wanted were battle, glory, and promotion. Kearny had been promised a brigadier general's commission. Cooke had already been elevated from captain to colonel. It was well known that Cooke had been itching for a summons to battle from President Polk ever since the war broke out; it was no secret that Cooke had wanted to be part of the early thrust into Mexico. Cooke surely couldn't be real pleased with this assignment to baby-sit a Battalion of Mormons.

"I must make apology to you Mormons," Cooke suddenly said.

The statement perked Robert's attention.

"It is true that I initially referred to you as an ugly set of men," Cooke said apologetically. "You were ragged and seemed a bit angry. I have concluded that you had a right to look worn out and angry. Instead of buying proper uniforms, you sent money back to your families. You were worn out because of forced marches. You were angry because of a lack of specie here in Santa Fe, and the Mexicans refused to honor the government checks issued to you. I have criticized the fact you have had women and children with you. I apologize for all that."

Robert smiled, and so did all the other Battalion boys. Cooke had taken a giant step forward in the respect category.

"But lest you think I am a soft military officer, let me set the record straight," Cooke said. "We have a long ways to go and there has been a shortage of provisions here in Santa Fe. Your rations will be reduced to three fourths. Unauthorized raids on supply wagons will be halted by guards.

Straying from camp will be forbidden. There will be no gunfire from tent lines. You will carry your musket at all times. Teams will not be watered without my direct orders. Reveille must be attended by all men."

Robert gulped. Cooke was going to be tough. But already he sounded like more of a soldier than A. J. Smith.

CHAPTER NOTES

The author has in his possession copies of the actual letters written from Santa Fe by Daniel Browett and Robert Harris. Daniel wrote one letter, dated October 15, and a second one, dated October 17, both addressed to Elizabeth. He wrote a separate letter to his mother, Martha, and it contained a message to his sister as well. Robert began his letter to Hannah on September 19 and finished it a month later, on October 19, the day John D. Lee left Santa Fe. The letters were obtained from LDS Church Archives.

Knowledge of Philip St. George Cooke comes mostly from the book, *The West of Philip St. George Cooke,* by Otis E. Young (The Arthur H. Clark Company, Glendale California, 1955).

PART THREE

Destination: California

42

❧

Albuquerque, New Mexico

October 24, 1846

'I HOPE COLONEL COOKE DOESN'T BITE their heads off," Daniel said when he saw three riders approaching the Battalion from the west. The Battalion boys were entering country controlled by bands of Pueblo, Navajo, Apache, Piman, and Quechan Indians, much of it in the Mexican state of Sonora.

Cooke had been in a sour mood ever since the day the Battalion left Santa Fe five days earlier. Despite the colonel's orders, the Battalion boys had not realized the extent of discipline necessary to make their march a success. Pursuing their course to the south, averaging about ten miles a day through sleepy villages built of adobes and inhabited by curious Mexicans, there should have been no problems. But the Battalion boys drove their teams into creeks, holding up the entire column while the animals drank their fill. Sergeants failed in their duty. One sergeant was broken to the ranks for neglecting to hold reveille and attempting to excuse himself on the grounds that it was not light enough to call the roll. Sentries had to be constantly reminded that sleeping on duty was punishable by death. Not a single water bucket could be found in any of the thirty wagons that accompanied the Mormon army. The land was parched; buckets were a necessity.

"I'm glad it ain't more Indians coming," Daniel said. Yesterday Pueblo warriors had put on a show of their horsemanship. With their bodies painted all colors of the rainbow, they had amazed Daniel with their ability to ride at full speed and yet stoop to the ground to shield themselves and pretend to fire volleys from under their horses' bellies. The antics had scared Daniel; the Indians had been armed with muskets, lances, and bows and arrows. The Indians disappeared, but so did nineteen beef cattle and fourteen mules. That really seared Cooke, despite the fact that the animals were recovered later. The Indians had showed no interest in the three hundred long-legged Spanish sheep that were following the Battalion.

More recently Cooke had been angry over the fact that Indians at La Mesita would not accept American dollars for the melons, apples, and onions they had to sell. Twenty-four bushels of corn were acquired through trades, but not near enough to feed all the men. There was no wood where they were camped—wood had to be brought from a hill three miles away.

The three riders were approaching as Cooke and some of the teamsters were trading for more mules at the Ranches of Albuquerque. Three good mules had been acquired for sixty-five dollars plus three of the Battalion's most broken down mules. The leader of the three riders was a dark, swarthy, stocky man clad in buckskins. For the first time in a week, Colonel Cooke wore a smile. "This here's Pomp Charbonneau, one of Kearny's pilots," Cooke said. "He brings good news."

Daniel inched closer to Colonel Cooke and the pilot. Charbonneau was tall, with long hair down to his shoulders. Cooke told the Battalion boys that Charbonneau was the son of Toussaint Charbonneau and Sacajewea, born at a Hidatsa village in the winter of 1805. As an infant, Baptiste accompanied his parents on the famous Lewis and Clark discovery trip.

All eyes swept to Pomp Baptiste Charbonneau. Pomp took off his dusty hat, shuffled his feet a few times, let a broad smile grace his bearded face, and then spoke. "California has been captured," he said. "It is in American hands."

California captured? Daniel had a hard time digesting the news. It sounded too good to be true. His jaw dropped as a cheer went up from officers and enlisted men alike. Daniel cast a quick glance at Colonel Cooke. Cooke did not crack a smile. His hard face remained. Daniel couldn't tell if his commanding officer was elated, or angry that he would not get to see any military action in the California campaign.

Questions swirled. How did Pomp know these things? How did the capture of California come about? Were lives lost? Were the battles many or few? Was Kearny involved? How about the American Navy?

Pomp Charbonneau told the Mormon officers that General Kearny had hired him as Kearny passed through Bent's Fort. While on the road to California, Kit Carson and a party of sixteen other men had met Kearny's army in Socorro, bearing the news about the military victory in California. Pomp gave details about John C. Fremont's activities, the Bear Flag revolt, the support of Americans living in California, Commodore Stockton's presence, and Gillespie's involvement. Charbonneau's orders were to lead the Battalion to California. The Battalion boys were to help occupy California.

"Carson has led Kearny straight west," Pomp said. "But he wants the Battalion to take a more southern route, and build a road to California as you go. One that wagons can follow in months and years to come."

"Are we still required to catch Kearny before he gets to San Diego?" Levi Hancock asked.

"No," Charbonneau answered. "Captain Fremont has California under control. In fact, Kearny is sending two-thirds of his soldiers back to Santa Fe so they'll be available for the invasion into Chihuahua, and to occupy New Mexico. With this Mormon Battalion, he'll have more than enough soldiers to occupy California."

"How many dragoons did Kearny keep?" Captain Jefferson Hunt asked.

"Only a hundred."

"Are you certain California is contained?" Hunt asked. "What about the possibility of a counter attack?"

"The presidios are in shambles, according to Fremont," Charbonneau responded. "We know how Governor Armijo ran instead of defending Santa Fe. The Mexicans who were defending California have fled too. Fremont thought that a force led by Andres Pico might stand and fight, but he claims they have scattered to the four winds."

The men cheered again.

For a few moments, Daniel and the other officers listened as Colonel Cooke and Charbonneau discussed alternate routes to California. The most obvious appeared to be almost straight south, following the Rio Grande River, then southwest to San Bernardino Springs at the Mexican border, northwest to Tucson, follow the Gila River to the Colorado River and the California Border, and then west to either San Luis Rey Mission, San Diego, or Los Angeles.

"How long will it take for us to get to California?" Captain Hunt asked. The distance was eight hundred miles.

"Kearny wants you there as quickly as possible. We're nearly at the end of October now. You should see the Pacific Ocean before the first of February."

43

❧

San Pasqual, California
December 6, 1846

AT TWO O'CLOCK IN THE MORNING Private Bernard Bogart mounted his bony black horse and started down a long hogback ridge that sloped toward the valley. A cold wind was sweeping in from the snow-covered mountains. In the distance below, he could see the glitter of enemy bonfires.

"Yer finally gonna get yer wish," Sergeant Waldo Peck said to him in an excited breath. "Hold yer saber high. Yer gonna kill some greasers this morning."

Bogart summoned his courage and pride. "We'll litter the landscape with their bones." He patted his musket. "I can't wait to smell the gunsmoke."

"We'll make cemetery fodder out of 'em, all right," Peck replied. He wasn't making any notes. It was too dark, and besides, Bogart reasoned Peck's hands wouldn't work too well in the frostbitten air. His own hands were so frozen he could hardly hold onto the reins.

An icy breeze had almost frozen Bogart's face and a cold shiver wracked him from head to toe. His feet were cold and wet, too, owing to large holes in his worn-out boots. Despite that, he drew his face into a temporary fake smile. Peck the newspaperman had matched his witticisms. Bogart quickly thought of another. "Them greasers will soon be signing the guest register in hell."

"We'll each kill a hundred of 'em ourselves," Peck answered.

In truth, Bogart was more than a little frightened, and discouraged, too. It had rained hard the past two days since leaving a rancho in the Cajon Valley owned by a man named Warner. Bogart and his poor, worn-out black horse had been drenched in cold rain almost constantly since then. He had slept almost frozen and exhausted on the wet ground last night. The rain had quit, but he feared his powder wouldn't ignite when he tried to fire his carbine. If so, he couldn't kill even one Mexican. He had no real lust for battle, as did Kearny and the officers. Bogart hated to admit it, but he would rather be back at his parent's farm in Missouri, eating homemade pumpkin pie.

The enemy had been spotted during the night by a small detachment sent out by General Kearny under a native scout named Rafael Machado. Machado reported that the enemy commander, General Pico, had commandeered huts in a nearby Indian village. Pico's men had been seen lazily cooking over campfires. Machado told Kearny that he didn't know for certain if

Pico knew the Americans were closing in on them, but dogs had barked at them.

The knowledge that dogs had barked at Machado struck fear through Bogart. Not only was his powder wet but also there was a possibility that the Mexicans knew he was coming. Bogart hunkered down from atop of his horse. Suddenly, he had run out of clever quips to mask his fears.

Ahead of him, Bogart let his eyes train on a man named Lieutenant Gillespie. Machado had been brought to Kearny's camp by this Lieutenant Gillespie, along with a force of nearly forty men, none of them in uniform. It had given Bogart a temporary thrill, however, when Gillespie and those men rode into camp with the Stars and Strips fluttering from one of the riders. Gillespie had been part of John C. Fremont's force that had captured California. Gillespie had been left in charge of Los Angeles, but the greasers had driven Gillespie out—a fact that distressed Bogart even more than the wet powder. It proved that the Mexicans were still going to fight to maintain their precious toehold on their colonies. Gillespie seemed hell-bent for revenge and had told Kearny that a force of Californio insurgents under Andres Pico was hiding in the hills near this place called San Pasqual. During the battle plan meetings, Gillespie explained that Andres Pico was the brother of the former governor of California, and was hopping mad that the Americans were invading California. Pico commanded a whole company of Mexican lancers.

Bogart shuddered as he recalled Gillespie's description of Andres Pico. "Pico is a nasty customer. He means to kill us and throw our bodies to the vultures. I've been scouring the territory for good horses, but he's taken them all."

None of Gillespie's lengthy report had seemed to deter General Kearny. By now, Bogart had learned that adventure was Kearny's narcotic. Kearny's ambition to fight was real, not fake.

"Pico is out there in person?" Kearny had asked Gillespie.

"If you see him, you'll recognize him. He's a slimy-eyed, rat-faced man with a thick, black moustache."

"How many men does he command?"

"I've heard up to seven or eight hundred. But maybe in reality only a couple hundred."

"What do you advise?" Kearny asked.

"Simple," Gillespie hissed as he lowered his eyebrows. "Beat up their camp. Surprise them early in the morning. Pico is convinced that reports of American forces being in the vicinity are false. Now is the time to strike."

"What about the Indians?" Kearny asked.

"The Mexicans have not been good to the Indians," Gillespie answered. "They hope the Americans will chase them out of California. We won't have to fight any Indians. They've fled to the hills. They don't like the vaqueros. Mexicans around here hold the life of an Indian as worthless, less than an animal."

Gillespie seemed to have a talent for painting a picture of an eminent victory for Kearny. He told Kearny that the lancers would be easy to spot. They would be wearing the traditional rich and ornamental costumes of the Dons, with a leather cuirass to protect their body, and a red serape over one shoulder. Perhaps a few of them would carry old leather shields with their Castilian heraldry. When he had seen them earlier, bright pennants had fluttered from their medieval lances.

All of this seemed to embolden Kearny, but not Bogart. Bogart fretted about battling the Californios, that Kearny's forces might be outnumbered, that it might have been a mistake for Kearny to send most of his soldiers back to Santa Fe, that Gillespie might be leading Kearny into a fatal battle, and, most of all, Bogart worried that he might be wounded, or even killed.

44

THE TRAIL LEADING TO Pico's camp lay over a mountain that divided the valley of San Pasqual from the Santa Maria Valley, about six miles in length. Under a full moon, almost as bright as day, the valley was well defined. The trail had been used as a cart road by the Californios for more than a hundred years, and bore the prints of many burros. Bogart's eyes could barely make out fields of wild oats and large oak and sycamore trees.

As Bogart passed a ridge of white granite, Kearny ordered his dragoons to halt. Bogart shivered in the bright moonlight and tried to take stock. Every horse and every mule in Kearny's army of a hundred men was just as haggard as his own black horse. He felt fortunate that his horse was still alive. During the past week several horses and mules had given out, especially when Kearny's dragoons had crossed the dry, sandy bed of Carrizo Creek on a hot day. The men ate some; others were left behind for the wolves. There was such a shortage of horses now that some of the dragoons rode worn-out, skinny mules—the same mules that had pulled wagons from Fort Leavenworth. Other dragoons were on unbroken mules that had been purchased from local Californios. Bogart's horse was alive. But it was skinny, too, and worn out from the trip.

Kearny dismounted, and so did all the dragoons.

"Be steady, men," Kearny said as he began his pre-battle pep talk. His voice shattered an eerie silence that had settled over the men. "This is our chance. This is what we came for—to fight. Obey your officers implicitly as you go into battle. Your country expects you to do your duty. Lieutenant Gillespie has warned of their reatas, so watch for them. Don't let the enemy rope you. It'll be our sabers against their lances. One thrust of your saber point will be far more effective than any number of cuts the enemy may inflict upon you with their lances."

Lances? Bogart gasped, letting his emotions waver again. *The greasers have lances? Sharp lances? Do they cut off the heads of Americans? And they have reatas? They'll rope me off my horse?*

While Bogart tried to shake off his fears, Kearny paused for a moment to confer with Gillespie. Gillespie recommended a noisy approach, thinking that yelling combined with the clanking of the soldiers' arms and sound of the horses and mules' hooves marching down the valley would intimidate the Californios. Kearny, in turn, gave strict orders to Gillespie not the shoot the enemy unless absolutely necessary, but to capture them instead.

Bogart had the uneasy sense he was about to cross an imaginary threshold into another world. He longed for a larger army—another three or four hundred men. He leaned toward Peck and whispered, "Where are the Mormons when you need 'em?"

"They're still a few weeks behind us," Peck answered. "We've got to fight Pico without the Mormons."

"Dern," Bogart said. "I wonder how many greasers Pico has out there in the dark?"

Kearny's voice rose again. "Men, Captain Moore, Captain Johnston, and Kit Carson will direct the charge. Your orders are to surround the Indian village. Lieutenant Gillespie and his men are to follow behind and to capture or shoot any of Pico's men who try to escape, and to capture as many of Pico's horses as they can. Pico's men are mounted on strong horses, and it would be well for us to have them. Lieutenant Davidson is to follow in the rear with his howitzers. Good luck, men."

Kearny mounted his horse. "Let's get on with it."

Bogart began to tremble and the dreamlike quality of the morning began to settle over him. His general's plan was ridiculously simple. Ride head on into the enemy's camp. It didn't seem right. The clang of heavy dragoon sabers echoed against the frosty hills as Kearny's army descended into the valley.

"Dern," Bogart complained, "the greasers'll hear us comin'. We're nothin' more than a company of alarm bells."

"Trust Kearny," Peck replied. "He must know what he's doin'."

The trail ahead curved slightly and seemed to beckon Bogart, like the bony finger of death. With Kit Carson in the lead, Bogart and Peck trotted along with Captain Johnston—twelve men mounted on the best horses the army had. Next came the engineers, Emory and Warner. Following them were fifty dragoons under Captain Moore, upon tired mules, some ridden the thousand miles from Santa Fe. Then came about twenty volunteers under Captain Gillespie, with a four-pounder confiscated from Captain Sutter by Castro, abandoned in Los Angeles, and taken by Stockton to San Diego. The volunteers also had two mountain howitzers under Lieutenant Davidson, supported by more dragoons. The remaining force brought up the rear and protected the baggage.

"Maybe the greasers are heavy sleepers," Peck said. "They must not be good fighters. Kearny's not too worried, and neither is Gillespie."

The first gray light of morning appeared as Bogart descended into the valley, and a crisp December wind whipped by. Behind Bogart and Peck and the rest of the blue-coated mounted dragoons, Kearny's riflemen and Gillespie's men marched two-by-two.

Bogart's skin tingled with anticipation and fear. Ahead of him, Bogart could hear Kearny give a simple order. Bogart didn't understand it, and neither did any of the other men.

"Did he say 'trot' or 'charge' just now?" Bogart asked Peck.

"He must have said 'charge,' " Peck answered back, kicking his horse. "At least that's what the officers think they heard."

Bogart had no choice but do join a hasty charge down the hogback ridge. As fast as their tired, worn-out horses and mules could be urged, the dragoons sped toward the Indian village—still a half-mile away. Bogart hoped that a thick, foggy mist would somehow camouflage their approach. He had no answer for the clamor the charge was making. A gully came into view. Bogart could make out several campfires.

"I see the greasers!" Peck screamed out. As the other dragoons were going, Peck stood up in his saddle and flashed his saber.

"I see 'em, too, but they ain't runnin'!" Bogart answered. Reluctantly, he also stood in his saddle and slowly raised his saber. His black horse was slowing down and lathering hard under the strain of the early morning attack. Ahead of him, Captain Johnston and Kit Carson were whipping their horses, screaming threats and leading the frantic charge. Bogart sensed that he and the other dragoons had now far out-distanced the main force and new fears swept over him.

"*Why ain't them greasers runnin'?*" Bogart screamed out. Already, things weren't going as he had planned them out in his mind.

Indeed, the enemy was not running. The Mexican soldiers sat calmly on their horses, holding their long lances in their hands. Others held rifles. What Bogart didn't know is that Machado and his detachment had dropped a military jacket in their hurried retreat. The Californios had found it and delivered it to Pico. Pico had awakened his lancers, who had quickly saddled their horses and prepared for battle.

Bogart could see the trap, but it was too late. The Mexican lancers, wearing black hats and bright red serapes over their shoulders, spread as if herding cattle to encircle the oncoming line, and were countercharging, too. They not only had lances, but pistols, too. Their lances were much longer than the American sabers. They rode swiftly at Bogart and the soldiers in blue.

Shots began to ring out. Lead filled the air in both directions.

Bogart heard a dull thump from the damp, grassy ground. The first blue coat had fallen from his saddle.

"Dern! They've killed Captain Johnston!" Bogart exclaimed. Bogart jerked on the reins and his tired, foamy horse skidded to a stop, and then he gasped. There was a bullet hole in Johnston's forehead, and Johnston was dead.

"I thought them greasers were poor shots!" Bogart cried. The valley and hills seemed to be crawling with bloodthirsty Mexican soldiers hiding in ambush.

Bogart realized no one was listening. Ahead of him, Kit Carson's horse stumbled, throwing Carson to the ground and breaking his rifle. The lancers swept past, kicking up mud. Bogart whirled to see General Kearny coming into view, following his men into the swirling battle that was now taking place in the half-light of the morning. Peck was swinging his saber at the Mexicans who were trying to kill Kit Carson with their willow lances.

"Keep charging, men!" Kearny was saying.

All of a sudden, and to Bogart's amazement, the Mexicans began retreating on their strong, fresh horses.

Captain Moore repeated the order in excited spurts. "Charge! Get them while they're running!"

Bogart spurred his black horse again. "Come on, Peck! They ain't gonna kill any more of us! Let's get us a greaser or two!"

Bogart's fear left him, replaced by a confidence that the Mexicans were truly cowards. Surges of adrenaline made him feel warm, replacing the chill that had menaced him all morning. His black horse was tired, but managed to carry Bogart for more than a mile as Bogart happily pursued the fleeing Mexicans. More Americans followed the retreat in a long, disorganized line. Kit Carson was back in the fray; he had taken both the horse and a musket from a dead dragoon.

In the distance, Bogart could see the Mexican lancers regrouping. A menacing mass of horsemen loomed in the blackness ahead. "What's that they're going?" he screamed at Peck.

"Why, it looks like they're going to counterattack" Peck screamed back.

Carson galloped up on a foamy brown horse. "They're like mad dogs looking for revenge," he said, almost out of breath. "They'll attack again."

Bogart trembled all over. For a few seconds he neglected to spur his horse. He was awestruck by the sight of the lancers streaming toward him. They were among the best horsemen in the world and they knew the terrain.

Captain Moore and his dragoons surged past Bogart. Moore had spotted Andres Pico and quickly fired a pistol shot at him. Now Moore was slashing out at Pico with his saber. Pico swirled away. Bogart stayed put but became aware that Pico was riding almost directly at him with Moore in hot pursuit. Pico appeared to be a small man, and fairly young—perhaps in his late thirties. He also looked short and compact, beefy around the middle. He had a wide, square-jawed head and a massive thicket of black hair. His black eyes blazed with defiance, and his deathly smile had turned wolfish.

Moore came riding hard at Pico, swinging his saber. To protect Pico, right in front of Bogart, two Mexicans swarmed on Moore, piercing him with their lances. To Bogart's shock and dismay, Moore fell from his saddle and was finished off with a pistol shot from one of the Mexicans.

"Dern!" Bogart screamed. "I don't wanna die!" He spurred his black horse with all his strength and let the horse carry him away from the Mexicans.

Bogart could now see that the valley was a festering crisis of enemy soldiers everywhere. They looked like an approaching of swarming ants. The white teeth of the brown-skinned lancers gleamed in the morning light. They were small men, but rode their horses like they had been born on them. Another American soldier, Lieutenant Hammond, went down after a series of lance thrusts, aimed at his stomach, penetrated his ribs. Other dragoons were lassoed by the Mexicans, jerked off their horses and mules, and then stabbed to death. Like weeds before a scythe, the Americans fell in heaps.

A chill coursed through Bogart's blood as he watched his fellow soldiers die. He spurred his horse in the opposite direction. "Let's get out of here!" he yelled to Peck. Any remaining courage and rationality had totally dissolved.

"They're rubbing us out like flies!" Peck screamed.

The road was strewn with the dead and dying. Twenty or thirty dragoons were now fleeing, some of them against their will. Their new mules had panicked and were running away as fast as their bony legs would carry them. The rest of the dragoons and Gillespie's men were still approaching.

"Rally men, for God's sake rally!" Gillespie was screaming from his horse as Bogart passed. The muscles of his face were drawn taunt and he bared his teeth in an uncontrolled rage. "Show a front! Don't turn your backs! Face them! Face them! Follow me!"

Bogart ignored the mad American; he had already seen two captains and a lieutenant get killed by the Mexicans, and several dragoons. He felt cold again. His damp clothing gave him a chill, and so did the sight of all the blood. A weary numbness had long ago crept into his limbs.

"Ya, es Gillespie, adentro hombres, adentro!" the Mexicans screamed as they began to purse Gillespie.

Instantly, four lances were darted at Gillespie. He parried them but the fifth caught him on the back of his neck as he leaned over his horse. A sixth blow in the same area forced him out of the saddle, with his own saber under him. He attempted to rise but another Mexican thrust a lance, slicing Gillespie across his chest, making a severe gash open to the lungs. He turned to face his assailants but another Mexican, riding at full speed, lashed out with a lance and caught Gillespie in the face, cutting his upper lip and breaking a front tooth. Gillespie collapsed to the ground as the Mexican's horse jumped over him.

A man on a brown horse grabbed Bogart's black horse by the bridle. "Turn around and fight!" Bogart instantly recognized the man. It was Kit Carson.

Temporarily, Bogart felt an upsurge of courage. He followed Carson back into battle.

Bogart now could see that General Kearny had been singled out, too. As Bogart lashed out with his saber, fighting on sheer adrenaline, he saw that General Kearny had already taken the brunt of three lances—once in the arm, and two in the groin. Bogart gasped as Kearny toppled from his horse. Captain William H. Emory slashed his way to Kearny, killing one Mexican just before the lancer could finish off the general.

Two Mexicans attacked Bogart. Fear struck him with such shock, such stunning force, that he was for several seconds numbed with the realization of danger. A lance caught Bogart in his left shoulder, another in his thigh. Like a wounded beast, he lashed out with his sword while shouting the vilest of obscenities. Bogart caught another lance across his chest. There was a strangling, tortured gasp as the wind burst from his lungs. Blood began to seep through his shirt and his trousers. His body demanded air that wasn't there, and he barely stayed in the saddle.

Peck, too, was lanced in his side and he fell from his horse.

Incredibly, Gillespie was not dead. The lancers had been more interested in stealing his fine saddle, and had ignored him long enough for him to survive. The Mexicans captured one of the howitizers. But Gillespie motioned for another howitzer and managed to fire it using his cigar lighter. A few of the Californios temporarily scattered at the sound of the howitzer, which saved both Bogart and Peck. Gillespie collapsed on the field again.

In fifteen minutes, the Americans had been whittled down to half. But almost eerily, the Mexicans retreated once more. There was a disquieting moment as though the peeking of the sun had brought a sudden end to the battle. Bogart fell from his horse, still bleeding. Incredibly, the lancers left him alone and battled unwounded Americans.

"Dern Mexicans," he uttered as he lay on the damp ground. "Have they kilt me? I wished I hadn't taken God's name in vain so often. I wished I'd gone to Sunday School every week."

"I think I'm dying, too," Peck muttered as he sat on his haunches nearby watching blood ooze from his body.

"Does Joe Smith control the Pearly Gates, or does Saint Peter?" Bogart asked. He could taste the bitterness of defeat on his tongue. More regrets went through him.

The lancers began retreating, claiming total victory.

"Rest easy, son," a doctor told Bogart. "I'll get the bleeding stopped."

Not all the Mexicans had retreated just yet. Some were plundering the dead. One jerked Captain Johnston's gold chain from his neck.

With General Kearny and the other survivors, Bogart turned an uneasy eye to the battlefield. It was a sad, melancholy picture. Bogart stared petrified in disbelieving shock at the obscenely twisted corpses, curled in fetal attitudes, their gore spreading across the valley. Despite the bragging of the American soldiers, only one Mexican had been killed—and that had been by Captain Emory. To Bogart's horror, there were eighteen Americans counted already dead. Another thirteen were wounded, counting himself, Peck, and Gillespie.

The loss of the howitzer was an embarrassment for the whole outfit. Kearny gave the order to lash the dead men on mules so that they could be taken away and buried in a mass grave. After a march of two thousand miles, several fellow Missourians were going to stay permanently in California, planted a few feet under wet soil.

Three of Gillespie's volunteers began writing dispatches to Commodore Stockton and John C. Fremont. Ambulances were made for the wounded out of willows and buffalo robes, in frontier fashion, with one end suspended from a mule and the other dragging to the ground.

Bogart screamed in pain as he was lifted off the ground into the makeshift ambulance. The soldiers used Bogart's black horse to pull him. All the survivors eventually made it up a hill on the north side of the valley.

"Maybe we'd better stay the night here," Kearny said, wincing with pain from his own wounds and riding a horse despite it all.

"Dern, that Kearny's a tough man," Bogart said to Peck, who was being dragged along by a mule. Peck's horse had been killed.

After a while, Kearny gave orders to dig a large grave under some willows east of the camp. "Dig deep, men. But I suppose the Indians will plunder the graves no matter how deep."

The horrible consequences of his defeat had not sunk in, and Kearny talked of revenge. "The enemy will yet feel the full fury of the American army," he chafed. "I just hope the Mexicans don't know how to operate that howitzer they've captured."

Provisions had been exhausted, many of the horses were dead, the men reduced by one third, and San Diego was thirty-nine miles away.

Only one Mexican had been captured by one of Gillespie's volunteers. To Bogart's feverish brain, the Mexican looked like some ghastly apparition. He was covered with black powder, blood, and scorched flesh. The Mexican's musket had blown up in his face.

At the end of the day, when the wolves and coyotes began howling, eighteen men were laid to rest in the grave.

The next morning proved to be a painful day for Bogart on the ambulance. He was dragged several miles down the valley until Kearny's army reached Rancho San Bernardo, the ranch home of a man named Edward Snook. However, it was deserted except for a few Indians. Several chickens were killed and Bogart managed to eat some boiled chicken and parched corn.

Bogart heard gunshots.

"Dern," he moaned. "Are the Mexicans gonna finish us off?"

"Relax," a doctor said. "We still outnumber Pico and his horse soldiers. We've spotted them in a ravine. Captain Emory went out to dislodge them. I think he'll be successful."

In a couple of hours the doctor's prediction proved correct, but the army was still in dire straits. All the cattle had been stampeded and unless help arrived from somewhere, the army could either be starved out or wiped out in an attack, especially if Pico were able to enlarge his army with more California volunteers. Some of Kearny's men were killing a couple of mules for the soldiers to eat for the evening meal. Kearny sent four soldiers out of camp with the messages for Commodore Stockton.

"Where we going now?" Bogart asked as he was placed in his ambulance and the dragging started again. Gillespie, too, was in his ambulance, barely clinging to life.

"Up the hill where we can defend ourselves better," the soldier on Bogart's black horse responded. "Pico captured the four couriers. We're in a desperate situation."

"Where are Pico and his men?"

"Surrounding us."

"Dern," Bogart said, contemplating the murky scene. "I wish I was home. I hate army life."

"We're gonna send out more men."

"The Mexicans will kill 'em," Peck grumbled an adjoining ambulance.

"Not Kit Carson," came the reply. "He thinks he and two other men can get through as soon as it's dark enough." One of the others was a naval officer named Beale who had accompanied Gillespie, and the third was a mere Indian boy. Beale had suffered a head wound in the battle.

"Dern," Bogart said, thinking of the full moon the night before Kearny's army attacked Pico. "We'd better pray for clouds. Them Mexicans'll see old Kit if it don't cloud up." There were Mexican sentries posted all around the hill and three separate cordons of lancers had the Americans surrounded.

When night came, the clouds did come and Bogart could see no moon.

"Did Kit get through?" he asked, his voice groggy and on edge.

"I dunno," a soldier said. "I ain't heard no shot, nor any commotion. He'll have to worm on his belly for a long ways." Earlier in the evening some of the men had heard Pico warn his men to scour every inch of the hillside. Pico knew that Kit Carson might sneak through their lines.

Suddenly, there was a commotion. The thundering sound of a herd of wild horses echoed throughout the valley.

"The Mexicans have started a stampede!" the soldier yelled.

"Shoot one of them wild horses, then," Bogart muttered through the pain of his wounds. "Horse meat is better than nothing."

Other than the terrifying noise the horses made, the herd passed without inflicting damage on the Americans.

CHAPTER NOTES

Details of the battle between Kearny and the lancers at San Pasqual were taken from several sources: Pourade, Richard F., *The History of San Diego: The Silver Dons,* (Union-Tribune Publishing Company, Copley Press, San Diego, California, 1963); Norris, L. David, *William H. Emory, Soldier-Scientist* (University of Arizona Press, Tucson).

45

KIT CARSON KNEW THAT IF HE, BEALE, or the Indian boy were seen, it would not only be the end of them but the end of Kearny and his army, too. If an alarm sounded, the lancers would gather like hornets to the nest and kill them quickly. There would be no chance if they were discovered. They had to get through.

The way out was covered with rocks and brush. The three men's shoes made noise, so Kit ordered everyone to remove them and tuck them under their belts. Slowly he crept down the hill, through low bushes, among sharp stones, picking up cactus spines as he advanced. Kit's tin canteen rattled against the rocks, too, as he approached the first line of sentries, so he unbuckled his strap and made Beale and the Indian do the same. They made it through the first Mexicans they saw and drew near the second line of lancers. These were more active, as they had more ground to cover. The lancers kept riding up and down, often passing within a few yards of Kit and his compan-ions. Kit flattened himself against the rough ground.

A commander of the lancers rode past in the dark, warning his men to scour every square foot of the hillside. Kit understood the Spanish, especially about *el lobo*. "The wolf will get away if you're not careful," the commander said.

The lancers were everywhere, talking smugly.

Still Kit led on, worming forward on his belly with the other two follow-ing. In the darkness he could not avoid the cactus spines which penetrated his knees, elbows, bare feet, and even his hands. Stones cut his flesh and thorns scratched him. Inch by inch Kit passed the second cordon.

A third cordon lay just ahead. As Kit crawled through the lancers, one of them almost rode over him. Kit held his breath. He could hear his own heart beating, and Beale's and the Indian's, too. He figured it would take a miracle to prevent the lancer's horse from snorting at them, yet the horse did not. Kit waited. The lancer did not ride on. The lancer reined the horse, dismounted, and got out the metal-covered wick he carried. He was going to strike a light!

The lancer was a strapping fellow and seemed to be in no hurry. He struck steel on flint, ignited the wick, and prepared to light his cigarette. But first he held the flaming wick in his hand and appeared to glance around him. To Kit, the wick blazed like a searchlight. He held his breath. It seemed impos-sible that the lancer had not seen him.

Suddenly, the sentry quenched the wick, mounted, and galloped over to his nearest comrade. Through thinning clouds Kit could see the two lancers against the stars. *Had the sentry seen him?* Kit wondered. Was he quietly summoning the others?

"They've got us," Beale whispered. "Let's jump and fight."

Kit was cool. "No," he whispered back. "I've been in worse fixes. The boys back there in Kearny's camp are countin' on us. Hold tight."

The two lancers talked for a time, and then separated. Kit breathed again and crawled forward.

Within half a mile Kit saw trees along a creek. He let out a sigh of relief, thinking how refreshing the water would taste. When he reached the trees, he took cover, stood up, and began pulling the spines from his tortured flesh. He was startled to find that his shoes were missing. They had slipped from his belt, and so had the shoes of the other two men.

"I've been in a lot of scrapes, but I've never had to walk thirty miles without shoes before," Kit told Beale. "But let's get going. To make certain one of us gets through, we'll split up. I'll go left, you go straight, and the Indian can go to the right." He could picture the Mexicans slaughtering what was left of Kearny's army if they failed.

In the dark, the three men headed for San Diego.

The charming, dark-eyed senorita cast a sidelong glance at Henry from behind her colorful fan. Her tapping, red-heeled slippers kept perfect time with the music and the castanets as she danced with him. His head swimming with the dizzying affects of whiskey, Henry laughed and swung the senorita around. With two months under his belt, he had learned every New Mexican dance and knew the names of most of the senoritas.

"Show me a good time," Henry pleaded with the senorita as the dance ended. "I have to leave Santa Fe in a week or two." Leaning on the woman, he staggered to his table.

The senorita's English was excellent, although heavily accented. "You must leave with this colonel, the man who is known as Doniphan?"

Henry drank more whiskey at a table with a group of Missouri volunteers who were also leaving with Doniphan for the invasion of Mexico. Henry thumped his chest with a large fist. "We're gonna show them Mexicans that we're gonna keep Santa Fe."

"We're not givin' it back," said Sam Hughes, a private.

Henry gulped his whiskey like it might be his last. Pap Price had transferred Henry into Doniphan's unit because there was not much need any longer for a teamster in Price's unit. Doniphan, however, needed teamsters to get his men to El Paso and then into Chihuahua, five hundred miles away.

The gambling establishment owned by Senora Barcelo was full of Missourians. The senora was the best dealer in the house.

His speech slurred and slow, Henry pointed to the monte tables. "Let's gamble," he said to Hughes. "Maybe we'll get lucky tonight."

Hughes stood and began his slow, wavering walk to the monte tables. "Good idea."

Henry stood, took one step, and collapsed to the dirt floor, unconscious.

"Oh!" the senorita exclaimed. "My poor unfortunate *gringo!* Wake up! You promised to spend the night with me!"

46

❧

San Pedro River, Arizona

December 11, 1846

ROBERT WAS TERRIFIED THAT RUMORS might be true that a Mexican army of five thousand men was trying to overtake and capture the Battalion as it traveled toward Tucson. He recoiled at the thought. Last night a Spanish sheep driver had run away, fearing the rumor to be true. Now everyone was worried.

The Battalion boys were busy making camp along a canyon of the San Pedro River. The river flowed north from the Mexican state of Sonora, and was one of the Gila River's two main southern tributaries. Its water was clear and fit for drinking. It was welcome, too, because there had been very little water during the past week. All the livestock was grazing on the grass in the river bottoms, and some on the hills that lined the canyon. The grass on the bluffs was short and sparse, but along the river the grass was high—a kind of cane grass that in some places came up past the men's waists. There were hundreds of wild black cattle there, too, mostly bulls. The men had practically lived on bull meat the past few days. Deer and antelope had been seen, too, and a few bears. Bear scat littered the groves of black walnut along the river. Despite it being December, the weather was mild. A pleasant afternoon sun warmed the soldiers.

"It stands to reason that the Mexicans would send a big army out after us," Mathew Caldwell said as he set up a tent.

"There're millions of Mexicans living south of the border," Robert said as he let his fears build up. "Maybe there's an army of ten thousand coming our way, not five thousand."

Tonight there would be no story telling about their former life in Nauvoo.

"If there's a big Mexican army, I hope it heads toward Santa Fe, not toward us," Daniel added.

"I agree," said Ezra Allen. "They'll be wanting to recapture Santa Fe."

"Colonel Doniphan and Colonel Price would have a better chance against an army like that than we would," said Henderson Cox.

"That's true," said John Cox as he set his musket against a tree. "They've got dragoons. We're just foot soldiers."

"We wouldn't have a chance against Mexican lancers," said Levi Roberts.

"Have faith," Levi Hancock said, trying to force a smile. "Remember Brigham Young's promise. We might have to fight wild animals, but not Mexican soldiers."

Robert felt a rising uncertainty. "Well, I certainly don't like the looks of those wild bulls upon the bluff. Five thousand charging bulls would be worse than five thousand Mexican lancers."

Most of the wild bulls were black, but some were dark red.

"Pshaw," Daniel said. "I'm not worried about them bulls. Bulls can be scared off. Mexican lancers can't, especially if there're five thousand of them."

"Maybe the Mexican army is chasing General Kearny," Robert Pixton said in a hopeful tone.

"If it is, they'll leave us alone," agreed Henderson.

"Kearny's probably in California by now," Pixton said.

"And all his soldiers are sunning themselves on the beach," Ezra added.

"If they are, they deserve it," Hancock retorted, despite the fact that Kearny's army was made up of Missourians. "They're probably as worn out as we are."

The march since Albuquerque hadn't been quite as grueling as the trip across the Cimarron Desert for Robert, but it had been no picnic. Rumors of a Mexican cavalry had been consistent, sending a constant fear through the hearts of the men.

On November twentieth a near crisis had come to the Battalion. For a day or two Cooke had appeared dumbfounded over which route to take. Cooke had orders from Kearny to establish a wagon road between Santa Fe and the Gila River, but he was becoming convinced that it was an impossible task given the condition of the Battalion and the mules. After some deliberation with his guides, and traders who had arrived from the San Bernardino Ranch, he decided to head south for the copper mine country around Janos and Sonora, Mexico, and then turn west toward California. Cooke's decision was unpopular with all the Battalion. Despite the protest of the Mormon officers, Cooke forced a march toward Janos for more than a full day. Cooke felt there might be a chance to find provisions at some of the Mexican settlements.

Perhaps Mexicans had seen the Battalion during that day down south. Perhaps word had been sent to authorities in Chihuahua or Mexico City. For an instant, Robert relived the awkward situation.

"What if we run head-on into that big Mexican cavalry?" Levi Hancock had asked over and over during the Janos march. "An engagement with them will be certain."

Robert had felt the presence of Mexican spies hiding somewhere in the rocks. Not only that, but Dr. Sanderson had been trying to persuade Cooke to hurry toward Janos because of the possibility that liquor would be available there.

That night Hancock and David Pettigrew visited every man in the camp, requesting that they plead with the Lord to change Cooke's mind and the course of the Battalion. The next morning, after marching toward Mexico for more than an hour, Robert was relieved when Cooke suddenly rose from his saddle and ordered a halt.

Cooke consulted his pocket compass. Its quivering needle confirmed his suspicions. "This is not my course," he said, within hearing distance of Robert. His guides were leading him the wrong way. "I was ordered to California and I will go there or die in the attempt." Turning to his bugler he said, "Blow to the right!"

David Pettigrew immediately cried out, "God bless the colonel!" Cooke's guides looked perplexed, but simply shrugged their shoulders and began forging toward the west.

The incident was a testimony to Robert of the power of prayer. Cooke had been inspired somehow to climb a high peak and assess the route himself, and to consult with his guides. Cooke saw that the road he was following was gradually turning east, not west. That's when he began to go against his guides, and the feeling had been confirmed as the Battalion started out again. Then he gave the orders to turn west.

At one point, Robert tried to humor Cooke with a compliment. "Someday this will be known as Cooke's Wagon Road," he said to the colonel. All the other trails ran north and south but Cooke was leading the men on an east-west route, the first of it kind in this area of the Southwest.

The new western route had proven difficult too, despite the prayers. Robert and the other men had to walk in double file in front of the wagons, just far enough apart to make trails for the wheels for a day. Dirt and sand covered the men and their clothing. It had been worse than tromping snow, but it got the wagons through difficult sandy terrain. The next day Robert marched through country that reminded him of the Cimarron Desert. He saw a variety of deceptive mirages—a vast luminous lake, a grand city with churches and spires which was really the distant mountains, and the masts and sails of ships that reminded him of his trip across the Atlantic in 1841. At a huge dry lakebed, cattle fell through hollow spots and many had to be rescued by the men. Just as in the Cimarron, Robert suffered intense thirst and so did the animals. Once again, the mouths of the oxen and mules went black and their eyes became sunken, looking as if the monster death was close at hand. Robert remembered how he staggered on, dragging his feet.

Indians were a worry, too. More than a week earlier—shortly after Cooke sent out a company of twenty-one men at the request of the guides to improve the road through the Guadalupe Mountains—Cooke met with an Apache chief by the name of Manuelita. He tried to convince the chief that both the Americans and the Apaches were on the same side against the Mexicans. That night, Cooke castigated his guides for not knowing more about the difficult country the Battalion was crossing through.

Word came to Company E that a few men were going to climb the bluff and shoot a few of the black bulls. The meat was sure to be tough, but fresh meat was fresh meat, Robert reasoned. He began sharpening his butcher knife.

Corporal Daniel Frost had killed the first bull a few days ago, chased out of a stand of thick mesquite.

Daniel began cleaning his musket. "I think I'll join the hunting party."

"Not me," said John Cox as he retrieved his fishing pole from a wagon. "Think I'll catch a mess of fish."

"Be sure to clean them before you bring them back," Robert said. His duties as a butcher did not include cleaning fish. Last night, however, Cox had caught several. The fish had supplemented a supper of dried beef and beans.

Daniel stood to go. "Wish me luck. You want an old bull or a young bull?" he asked Robert.

"Just don't stir them up too much," Robert warned. He'd never had much luck with bulls, even back in the days he went to the cattle market with his father in England. One day a red bull tore out a fence and gored two cattle buyers from Ledbury.. The Battalion boys had seen several wild bulls during the day. Some merely ran off, startled. Others, to gratify their curiosity, came close as though bent on finding out who dared to intrude upon their quiet retreat. Just before Cooke had declared the camp sight, some of the boys had sighted a herd of bulls enjoying a "siesta" in the tall grass above the bluffs.

"How many do you want?" Daniel asked, joking. "Ten or twenty?"

"Just pick out a tender cow," Robert said as he thought how he had grown weary of all the butchering again, just as he had done in England. "Don't let a bull run over you."

A week ago, local Mexicans at Aqua Preita had told Robert that in 1832 the government had given a rancher by the name of Ignacio Eulalis Elias an extensive land grant and it had become the center of cattle ranching along the San Pedro. Apache depredations forced its abandonment, however, and the rancher had pulled out a few years ago, leaving the nearby San Pedro village in ruins. The cattle had multiplied voraciously over the years into a wild herd. Most of the herd were bulls; the Apaches regularly killed the cows because their meat was far more tender.

"I'll bring you twenty then," Daniel joked.

"Be careful," Robert warned. "The bulls I've seen look like they could tear one of our wagons apart if they got riled up."

Daniel picked up his musket. "It might have taken a dozen or so balls to bring down a running buffalo, but one ball ought to bring down a black bull." He walked toward the bluff to meet Charbonneau and the hunting party.

Out of the corner of his eye, Robert caught a glance of the teamsters as they led oxen and mules down to the river to be watered. As he began sharpening his knives, the first shots rang out. He felt his muscles tighten.

What happened next was almost beyond belief.

Several of the men began yelling, and there were more shots. Robert stood up to see twenty or thirty massive black bulls charging from the north, right up the river bottom toward camp. The smell of blood had turned the bulls into an angry herd, full of fight. The roar and bellows of the bulls were frightening. Men, mules, and oxen were scattering everywhere. A bull had a man trapped between its horns. Another man, nearly caught by a bull, threw himself flat on the ground. Still another bull charged a mule, running a horn into the mule's belly. Entrails and blood popped out. Soldiers scampered up trees; others ran away as fast as their legs would carry them.

"Load your guns! Protect yourselves!" Colonel Cooke screamed from his mount.

As Robert rammed a ball into his musket, another man was thrown high into the air by a maddened bull. Shots rang out from all along the camp as more bulls charged from downstream. Robert fired at a passing bull and then reloaded.

A coal-black bull closed in on Colonel Cooke and another soldier.

Cooke gave the soldier the order to load his gun and then scampered away. The soldier, however, stood fast and took dead aim.

"Run, run," Cooke yelled in disbelief. "Run, damn you, run!"

The soldier ignored the order and stood his ground, still aiming. The bull had been nearly a hundred yards away when Robert first saw it charging Cooke and the soldier, but now the bull looked as though it were going to smash head-on into the soldier. The bull was no more than ten or fifteen yards away when the soldier fired. The bull roared and then crashed to the ground at the soldier's feet. The bull shivered, rolled its eyes, and died.

"Damned if you ain't quite the soldier," Cooke gasped at the man with corporal stripes.

The rumble of musketry was now heard from one end of the camp to the other. In the distance, another mule was tossed in the air. A bull stove into the end gate of a wagon, shattering it to pieces. Men were now on the wheels of the wagons, pouring lead into the bulls. Others fired from positions behind mesquite bushes. Still others climbed trees and took aim on the bulls.

As Robert was loading his musket again, a large coal-black bull fell near him.

"Cut its throat, quick," yelled Robert Pixton, the cook. "We'll skin it right here."

Robert threw down his musket and drew out his knife. As he bent over the bull, a huge black eye stared back at him. The bull was far from dead, but a knife to the juggler would take care of that, he reasoned. Without warning, the bull leaped to its feet and tossed its massive head at Robert. With catlike reaction, Robert drew back, but one of the horns grazed his face with an upward blow.

Stunned, Robert realized the bull had hooked his black hat. Now the bull was running toward the bluff, the hat still stuck to its left horn.

"Stop you thief!" Robert screamed as he ran after the bull. "I'll have some beef!"

Robert lost ground, but pursued anyway, flashing his knife. "Don't shoot me!" he yelled at the other soldiers. "Shoot that bull!"

The bull had a seventy-five-yard lead now, but it began to falter from a loss of blood. Two more balls struck it. It collapsed to the ground, blood spurting from its nostrils. Robert pounced on it, plunged the knife into the bull's throat, and then retrieved his hat—which had a jagged hole in it now.

Later, as Robert skinned the bull and began cutting away the best parts of the meat, Daniel gave him an assessment of what had happened. Amos Cox of Company C was the most seriously injured. He had been gored on the inside of his thigh and suffered bruises all over his body after being thrown ten feet in the air. The gash on his leg was four inches long and three inches deep. Sergeant Albert Smith, Quartermaster Sergeant of Company B, was the soldier who had been trapped by the horns of a bull, but he had escaped with only bruised ribs. Levi Fifield of Company C had escaped serious injury too, by laying flat on the ground. Lieutenant George Stoneman had the upper joint of his thumb ripped off when he tried firing a fifteen-shooter rifle at one of the bulls. Dr. Sanderson promptly sewed up Cox with little ceremony. Stoneman and the others evaded Sanderson's attentions.

One of Paymaster Jeremiah Cloud's mules had been killed. And so had another, a mule belonging to Company D. A third mule had to be destroyed after a bull gored it in the stomach.

"How many bulls have been killed?" Robert asked, covered with blood and offal.

"I can count more than a dozen from here," answered Richard Slater, who was scraping the bull's hide.

Robert Pixton already had a fire going. Several men from Company E had gathered to broil fat ribs and tell stories. Pixton said, "I saw Doctor Spencer shoot six balls into one bull before it fell." Spencer was an assistant surgeon. "Two balls went through the bull's lights, and two square through the heart. He removed the heart—I saw it myself."

"I saw nine bulls killed at one place up the river," remarked Matthew Caldwell, who was cutting up the liver.

"Who was the soldier standing by Colonel Cooke, who killed the bull just before it ran over him?" Robert asked.

"Corporal Frost of Company A," answered Henderson Cox.

"We've got more bulls killed than we can use," Robert said mournfully. "If ever there were a true count, there might be seventy or eighty dead bulls. I need some help if we're going to save most of the meat."

Jacob Kemp Butterfield walked by. "I just came from Cooke's wagon. He's gonna have the bugle sounded soon. He wants us to move out of this place and get some more miles behind us. He's already sent Charbonneau on ahead to scout the country between here and Tucson. Once we leave the San Pedro, we've got to find the Gila River."

Robert threw down his knife and smiled. "I've never heard better news."

Butterfield's face twisted with concern. "Cooke originally wanted to avoid Tucson, but we need more supplies. Tucson is protected by a garrison of Mexican soldiers."

Pixton glanced up, astonished. "This war business will never end."

CHAPTER NOTES

The author visited the site of the "Battle of the Bulls" in early 2005. It is in southern Arizona, not far from Tombstone. A marker has been placed there, above the San Pedro River, by the Boy Scouts.

"Lights" is a term hunters used for lungs in those days.

47

Tucson, Arizona

December 16, 1846

BRIGHAM YOUNG'S PROPHESY THAT the Battalion would not fight any battles against wild beasts sounded to Daniel like it was doomed to failure here in the Mexican state of Sonora. The commandante of the garrison at Tucson had bulled his neck, warning Cooke not to pass through; he claimed that a large Mexican army stood ready to back him up.

The veins on Cooke's forehead were showing. "Load your muskets, boys," he ordered.

Daniel rammed a ball into his musket and set a charge.

Cooke had the air of some mystical hero in Daniel's view, radiating charisma and authority. "Our guides tell us the trail to California goes through

Tucson, and that's where we're going, Mexican soldiers or not. Any other course is a hundred miles out of the way, over a trackless wilderness of mountains, rivers, and hills. We will march, then, to Tucson. Boys of the Mormon Battalion, do I have your support?"

Daniel joined in a chorus of "yes!"

Cooked inhaled deeply and then smiled. "We came not to make war on Sonora, and less still to destroy an important outpost for defense against Indians. But we will take the straight road before us, and overcome all resistance. But I remind you that the American soldier ever shows justice and kindness to the unarmed and unresisting. The property of individuals you will hold sacred. The people of Sonora are not our enemies."

Daniel stared at his musket. He had never killed a man and hoped he wouldn't have to. But Cooke's words were dead serious. "It might be for real this time," Daniel said to Robert.

Robert shrugged his shoulders and framed Daniel with a resigned, fervent stare. "You might be right, but I hope not."

After leaving the battle site of the bulls on Saturday, the Battalion had passed around a canyon and the ruins of the Presidio Fortress of Santa Cruz de Terrenate. Nearby the guides had found a group of Apaches and Mexicans distilling whisky. From them the guides learned that the Mexican army garrisons of all little frontier posts in the area had collected at Tucson, numbering more than two hundred. Tucson also had cannons. Cooke sent the guides on ahead with instructions to gather more information and to inform the *commandante* that the American army, indeed, was on its way. They had orders to trick the *commandante* into believing that the Mormon Battalion was just an advance guard for a much larger army.

The next day, Cooke had marched the Battalion along the San Pedro River bottoms, which at that point were two miles wide. Mesquite trees there looked as though they had been arranged in orchards. At their new camp, Cooke acted as though he really expected a battle. He mustered the soldiers, ordered the men to clean their guns, inspected them, and had a long drill. He instructed them again on how to properly load and fire their muskets, and had them march in columns. Each man had been given twenty-eight cartridges.

On Monday, Cooke led the Battalion out the San Pedro River bottoms toward Tucson, but Daniel found the route covered so much with thorny bushes and prickly cactus that he almost wanted to turn back. Cooke sent a guide to the Mexican distillery to calm their fears and to prevent them running off. The guide returned saying the *commandante* still refused the American army's entrance into Tucson. Cooke sent back a message with Dr. Foster that his army was not their enemy. His men were interested only in purchasing flour and other provisions at Tucson.

When Daniel passed the distillery site the next day, he saw two dozen Mexican and Indian men, women, and children who lived in a collection of huts and wigwams. The distillery was in a small adobe house. He, along with some other men, peeked in. Whiskey was being made from mescal, and Daniel thought the place was the most muddy, filthy, wretched-looking place he'd ever seen. Rawhides were being used as vats and tubs.

Four Mexican soldiers appeared; Cooke took three of them prisoner and sent the other back to Tucson with a message: Release Dr. Foster if he was being detained. It was learned that one of the prisoners was the commandante's son, which Daniel felt was a stroke of good luck.

As the Battalion marched on, Daniel saw another extraordinary variety of cactus, the giant saguaro. Some were like pillars, thirty feet high, covered with thorns, and hooked. Still another variety of cactus proved particularly annoying. The cholla was jointed, and whenever the oxen and mules rubbed against it, it broke loose at the joints and sections would stick fast to the animals.

Daniel was asleep in his tent when the approach of horses and mules awakened him. He struggled to his feet and joined other officers at Cooke's tent to find out that Dr. Foster had returned with an escort of eighteen Mexican soldiers. He brought a proposal from Tucson, asking for a special armistice. This is when the Battalion learned that the *commandante* wanted the Battalion to march around Tucson, and then find the road to the Gila River just north.

For two hours Cooke talked to the Mexican soldiers, well into the night. "This Battalion is going to enter Tucson," he said in unyielding tones. Before he retired his bed, he demanded that the Mexicans surrender two cavalry carbines and three lances. "The people there are going to have a *Yanqui* invasion whether they want it or not."

Daniel had barely fallen asleep again when the bugle sounded. An alarm had been given by the picket guard who thought he saw a number of Mexicans approaching. There were none, but the false alarm served its purpose. The men were up, ready to go.

"Cooke wants an early start," Levi Hancock said with a stunned look. "We're on our way to Tucson."

Later in the morning, when the Battalion was only six miles from Tucson, a mounted Mexican soldier appeared.

"Now what?" Robert said to Daniel.

The soldier bore a letter from the *commandante*, a man named Antonio Comaduran. Colonel Cooke's terms could not be accepted.

"I can't believe this is happening," Hancock said, shaking his head in disbelief.

"Have faith," admonished David Pettigrew. "We're not there, yet. Say your prayers, men."

With his musket loaded, Robert marched double time with the Battalion. The saguaro seemed larger to him, the cholla stickier, and the prickly pears more irritable as he neared the garrison.

Two tiny dots appeared on the desert horizon. The dots increased in size. It was two Mexicans, approaching on burros.

Robert's eyes flew wide open. "What do you suppose this means?" he asked members of his mess.

"Good question," John Cox replied.

Ahead of the wagons and all the Battalion boys, Cooke summoned each of his officers. With his curiosity raging, Robert watched Daniel dance forward. After a brief huddle, the officers returned to their companies. Daniel had a calm look about him, and he was smiling.

"What was that all about?" Robert asked Daniel. He had come to expect an almost hourly change in the prospect of war.

"The soldiers are evacuating the garrison," Daniel said to everyone. "You can unload your gun."

"It's safe now?" Levi Roberts asked.

"According to those two Mexicans it is," Daniel answered. "Apparently we'll find Tucson nearly deserted, because the soldiers have already driven off most of the inhabitants."

"I hope we find some salt there," Robert Pixton said as he wiped the sweat off his brow. He pointed to the wild bull carcasses in one of the wagons. "All this meat, and no salt."

Robert found himself marching double-time again, wondering what he was going to find in the small town of Tucson. He wondered if the information was true, or if Cooke was leading them unawares into an ambush. The trail led over cobble rock, brush, cactus, and prickly pears. As a large stone church came into view, a dozen mounted men in plain clothes appeared, offering to accompany the Battalion toward the presidio. They said the Mexican soldiers had fled south, and would remain in a camp nine miles away.

At the gates of the presidio, Cooke brought the Battalion to a halt and began to address them. He informed the Battalion boys that the Mexican soldiers and most citizens had fled, leaving much of their property behind.

"Remember what I've told you about private property, men," he said. "Leave it be. The people who live here are not our enemy."

From the presidio, the Battalion marched into town.

Tucson apparently was the most important town in the region, but Daniel found it to be small and dirty. A small stream called the Santa Cruz River ran through the town, flowing northward from Mexico, the water alkaline and warm. Hogs wallowed there, and donkeys and cattle were drinking leisurely. Not everyone had abandoned the town. A few women could be seen, but they wore frightened looks. All told, there appeared to be around a hundred frightened men, women, and children in town, and a few elderly and sick people.

As the Battalion traveled from the Mexican border, Daniel had pieced together the story of Tucson. Its founder had been—of all people—a redheaded Irishman by the name of Don Hugo O'Conor, who in 1775 rode up from the presidio at Tubac to see about moving the post to a point farther north. He had been charged with inspecting and realigning the array of presidios between Sonora and Texas, which had been established to keep Indians on the north from raiding Spanish settlements on the south. The fort at Tubac—forty miles south—had been in existence since 1752, but even there, with soldiers for protection, survival for the Spanish and Mexican colonists was difficult and sometimes nearly impossible. As a result, the decision-makers far away in Spain and Mexico City decided on a reorganization of the presidial system. The Tucson presidio thus was established in an area where native Indian farmers built sand dams and diverted water into irrigation ditches. The Indian homeland was an enormous expanse of desert and mountains called *Pimeria Alta*. It was bounded, roughly, by the Colorado River on the west, the Gila on the north, and the San Pedro on the east. Even though the summers were hot, the Tucson location stood in sharp contrast to the enormous wasteland that surrounded it. There was game, wood, pasture, and people—Apache Indians the Spaniards called Papagos, or Bean People, who were experts in desert living. There were not only wheat fields surrounding Tucson, but beans, corn, watermelon, and squash.

The Spaniards held a low opinion of the Indians, who gave them occasional beatings just for the fun of it. As they had done in Mexico, the Spanish Empire had tried to convert, civilize, and exploit them. The Indians practiced plural marriage, easy divorce, indulged in ritualistic drunkenness when the cactus fruit ripened, and had a mystical religion difficult to understand. The Spaniards suppressed their ceremonials, derided their medicine men as witches, and forced them to work. In addition, Spaniards had been contemptuous of the Indians' belief in the great flood and their myth of a Savior.

On one hand, Daniel respected the Indians. He knew for a surety that they were Lamanites, descendants of the Book of Mormon people. How else would they know of Biblical stories like the flood, or the existence of a Savior? At times he would visualize himself as a missionary to the Indians, bringing them the truthfulness of the restored gospel of Jesus Christ. But on the other hand he feared them. He thought of passages in the Book of Mormon, how the Lamanites had fallen and had become a depraved people delighting in murders and whoredoms. He felt sorry for the Indians, too. From Florida to California, Spaniards had abused the Indians, tried to pacify them by converting them into their version of Christianity, and plundered their lands in search of gold, silver, and other riches. Diseases brought by the Europeans had decimated the Indians, too.

After the long morning march, Daniel was thirsty and his canteen was empty. "I guess that creek is the water supply," he said.

Sergeant Daniel Tyler agreed and made a gesture of thirst to a silver-haired Mexican. The man grabbed Tyler's canteen, ran to the creek, filled it in a spot above the wallowing hogs, and returned it. The old Mexican had never seen an American before.

Tyler's accepting smile was engaging. "I'm beginning to like Tucson already," he said.

Daniel judged the adobe houses in Tucson to be not nearly as good as those in Santa Fe, and the Santa Fe homes had been terrible. Compared to Nauvoo, Tucson was a primitive hovel. The effects of secularization were visible here, too. The mission and churches were in disrepair, and so was the presidio. An adobe wall with abutments and battlements was in shambles, but it surrounded the presidio barracks. The mission orchards no longer bore fruit and the Indians had stopped paying rent for the land they worked. It was a sad spectacle. But two small mills were in use, run by donkey power. Before the people fled, Tucson had been home to five hundred people, but they would be back soon.

"Looks like we'll be able to buy some flour," Robert Pixton happily concluded.

Beyond the dilapidated adobe walls Daniel could see young, green wheat fields, fruit trees, and other semblances of a farming community. It was music to his ears to hear the crowing of chickens and the snorting of the hogs.

In a short time, Cooke ordered the Battalion away from Tucson and found a place to camp about three-quarters of a mile northwest of the presidio. Daniel found an irrigation ditch there, containing water from the Santa Cruz River. He had barely time to bathe in the ditch and clothe again when the Mexicans from Tucson came into camp anxious to trade with the American soldiers. They brought wheat, corn, beans, and peas.

"We're gonna have a good meal tonight," Robert Pixton predicted. He gathered some of the food together and then walked into town looking for flour and salt.

Some of the men traded shirts for corn.

For the first time in history, the American flag was flying in Tucson. Daniel, along with David Pettigrew and Levi Hancock, drew a sigh of relief.

Brigham Young had been right again.

Henry's head felt like an overripe red pepper, ready to explode, as he drove his team of mules. Doniphan's army was following the Rio Grande River due south, toward El Paso. He had imbibed whiskey all night at Senora Barcelo's gambling house, and danced with several of the Santa Fe senoritas.

Evening camp came none too soon for Henry. He hardly felt like eating, and so he just nibbled on the beef.

"I'm glad to get out of Santa Fe," said one of the Missouri volunteers, a private named David Hastings. "As soldiers, we need to set a better example. The New Mexicans, I'm afraid, have a poor opinion of us."

"Bah!" said Henry. "You sound like my brother-in-law, one of the Mormons."

"I'm no Mormon," Hastings said. "But I take my Christianity serious. Our soldiers drank too much, incited too many riots, and abused the women."

Henry's friend, Private Sam Hughes, another of the Missouri volunteers, disagreed. "Drinking and rioting has been going on in Santa Fe for years. The New Mexicans are used to it. They can drink us under the table."

"Well," Hastings said. "It's no honor to conquer such a people then. In my view, we've strained our relations with the New Mexicans."

"I repeat. You worry too much, just like my brother-in-law," Henry said. "The senoritas like us Americans. The people in Santa Fe were glad to get rid of Armijo. It'll be the same all throughout old Mexico."

"You're right, Henry," said Hughes. "Doniphan ruled Santa Fe a lot better than Armijo did."

On that point, the three men agreed. Doniphan had spent the past two months administering affairs in New Mexico, as assigned by General Kearny. The invading American expeditionary force had supplanted Mexican civil authorities. Although Kearny and Doniphan had appointed trader Charles Bent as the figurehead governor, Doniphan had been the real governor. Doniphan had done an excellent job in drafting and adopting a territorial constitution along with a set of laws, successfully negotiated treaties with the province's bellicose Indians, patrolled public lands, took over the collection of custom duties, and imposed martial law. He did all this while training his regiment for the trek to El Paso and the planned invasion of Chihuahua, where he planned to join forces with an American general who was already in Mexico.

The only blip on Doniphan's record was the murder of Charles Bent. Not all New Mexicans had liked Kearny and Doniphan's military rule and the appointment of Charles Bent. The strong-willed Bent already had his enemies, including the powerful Martinez family of Taos and Indians who resented Bent's trading with their enemies. A revolt finally came, fueled mostly by resentment of the American conquerors and fears of land seizure. Bent's company had stores in Santa Fe, Taos, and at Bent's Fort. When Bent heard of unrest around Taos, he went there in hopes of restoring order. Early in the morning a mob broke down the door of Bent's home in Taos, shot him, and scalped him.

"I still think Doniphan is a Mormon-lover," Henry said. As an attorney, Doniphan had represented the Mormons in Missouri.

"I've forgiven him of that," Hughes said. "He's earned my respect."

Henry hung his head as a sign he agreed. Every man in Doniphan's army of 1,350 men respected the colonel, from the lowliest private to the vast array of officers. Dozens of wagons and hundreds of merchants were traveling with Doniphan for protection, too.

"Well, I'm looking forward to the women in El Paso and Chihuahua," Henry said.

48

❧

Near Maricopa Wells, Arizona
December 25, 1846

NEVER IN MY WILDEST DREAMS WOULD I have thought I would be in a desert like this at Christmas, Robert mused as he feasted on pieces of watermelon.

Maricopa and Pima Indians had also traded pumpkins, cornmeal, beans, and parched corn, which Robert Pixton had fashioned into a nice meal, along with beef saved over from the battle of the bulls. Colonel Cooke had been successful in trading six bushel of corn for wagon covers.

The Indians here lived in strange homes, a cross between a wigwam and a grass hut. They were nearly twenty feet across, dug slightly below the ground, and had a small door only about three feet high. Fires were burned in the center of the huts and the smoke escaped in a hole at the top. Robert judged them smoky and uncomfortable, ill suited for the warm climate here. But he quickly gained a huge respect for the Indians here. For the first time in his life he saw in these Indian tribes a people who had not been corrupted by Spaniards. Although nearly naked, they were handsome, intelligent, and charming. There was no degrading vulgarity, no pinching poverty, and no tippling loafers. These Indians had never shed the blood of white men, and they did not make war with other Indian tribes. With large farms they obtained their living by agriculture.

"It's Ecclesiastes' first Christmas," Robert said. "What do you suppose Elizabeth made for him? Or what Hannah and the children gave him?"

Daniel laughed. It had never bothered him that Robert called Moroni "Ecclesiastes." He bit into another large slice of watermelon. "I don't care what they got him for Christmas, as long as he's healthy. I can't wait to see him again."

Robert looked at his shoes. "I thought I'd wake up and find a new pair of shoes in the tent for Christmas. If there were someone here to carry back a letter, I'd complain about my blistered feet, my parched lips, scalded shoulders, weary legs, and ragged clothes. Other than that, I'd consider myself blessed. I only have another three hundred or so miles of bleak desert travel to survive until I get to the Pacific Ocean."

Daniel managed to laugh again.

Later in the day three guides who had been sent from California by

Kearny rode into the Battalion camp and brought news. The Californios were in a state of insurrection against the Bear Flag Republic. Cooke quickly decided to make a gamble with the elements. Rather than follow the great bend of the Gila River, he would make a forced march of forty miles across its waterless neck. This implied another inventory and repacking of the train, which resulted in the discarding of all packsaddles. Cooke was reasonably certain that he could get his wagons through to the Pacific.

Robert looked around him. They had started across the "Forty-Mile Desert" in the morning and the travel had been sandy and difficult. The animals had only sparse grass and mesquite to graze on. Kearny's army had passed through here weeks earlier, and the grass had not grown much since. There was nothing here to compare with Illinois or England. No green trees, no lush grasses, no verdant hills—and no family to celebrate Christmas with.

Yesterday, Colonel Cooke had issued two orders that had drawn Robert's ire. First, Cooke equalized the remaining rations between the five companies. Companies that had carefully managed their rations, like his, were forced to give up provisions to other companies who had been careless. Cooke also told the men that he wanted to lighten the over-burdened wagons, so he ordered all private luggage and provisions to be carried on the backs of the men—or leave them behind. This had followed a stern lecture on how to prepare to cross the barren deserts that lay between them and the Pacific Ocean.

"Without shoes, how can we carry our own provisions?" John Cox asked Robert.

"Same way we would if we had shoes," Robert answered. "On our backs."

Cooke had spent time with the guides to plan the route ahead. They decided to cut away from the Gila River for forty miles. This would save thirty or forty miles because the river made such a large bend to the north.

The Battalion had left Tucson a week ago. The ninety-five miles between Tucson and Maricopa Wells had been some of the most treacherous and waterless travel Robert had encountered yet. Within two days the Battalion had become stretched out in the dry, hot desert. Robert had searched for water all one night.

"Just think," Daniel said. "In two more months Hannah will have your seventh child. It'll take me a long time to catch up."

"But you have two wives," Robert countered, laughing a bit. "And I only have one."

"Ever think of what you'd do if the brethren asked you to take another wife?"

"If the purpose is to help Heavenly Father bring spirits to the world, Hannah and I are doing just fine, thank you."

"No argument from me on that point."

Henry Eagles pulled his team of mules to a halt. Doniphan had ordered his army to halt at a little arm, or old channel, of the Rio Grande called *Brazito*. The spot had good water and seemed like a likely place to consolidate the regiment.

"Deal the cards," Henry said to Sam Hughes as he spread a blanket on the ground.

To make a Christmas dinner, some of the men hunted for rabbits. Others gathered firewood. Even Colonel Doniphan was playing a few hands of three-card loo, and soon won a handsome stray horse that must have belonged to a Mexican officer.

Musket shots ripped through the air.

"Dern, what was that?" Private David Hastings asked.

"Nothing to worry about," said Hughes. "Just a few exuberant soldiers firing off their rifles in honor of Christmas day."

After a few hands of cards, a dust cloud appeared. "That ain't no Christmas gift," said Henry.

"Relax," admonished Hughes. "You've been worrying about greasers ever since we left Santa Fe."

Hughes no sooner got the words out of his mouth than scouts galloped into the camp yelling that they had seen Mexican soldiers in combat formations.

Doniphan jumped to his feet and began yelling orders. "To arms, to arms! Fall into line! Get your horses!"

The camp of four hundred men turned chaotic. Soldiers ran helter-skelter, dropping firewood, grabbing their rifles, and forming into some semblance of a line of battle. A captain assembled about twenty mounted men and held them in readiness.

Henry's rifle felt a hundred pounds heavy. "What if we get killed?" he asked no one in particular. Henry felt a nervous anxiety for good reason. Most of Doniphan's army was a few hours behind them. Henry was one of only four hundred men in an advance group.

"I'd hate to die clear down here in Mexico," Hughes admitted.

Henry knew he wasn't the only soldier trembling with more than just a little fear. By now the Mexican army could be seen plain as day. The Mexican cavalry had bright scarlet coats with snow-white belts, and high brazen helmets plumed with bearskin. They carried polished sabers, carbines, and long lances. Their uniforms stood in sharp contrast to the plain, worn-out clothes worn by the Missouri volunteers in Doniphan's army.

"Look at their horses," Hastings said in a trembling voice.

Muscular steeds pranced and tossed their heads to the sound of Mexican bugles. Their riders rode with backs erect and firm in their saddles.

"Well, look at that," said Hughes.

A Mexican officer approached on a horse flecked with foam. The officer carried a distinctive swallow-tailed black flag, decorated with two skulls and sets of crossbones on one side, and the words, *"Libertad o' Muerte,"* on the other side.

"What's that say?" Henry asked, wishing he had learned more Spanish while in Santa Fe.

"It says 'Liberty or Death' to me," Hastings said, shaking more. He had studied the Spanish language enough to read it and follow some of the conversation.

In minutes it was evident that the Mexican officer was demanding Doniphan's surrender, or the Americans would face battle with no quarter given. Through an interpreter, Doniphan rejected the terms. There was a hot exchange of words before the Mexican officer stormed away.

"The Mexican promised to break our ranks," Hastings reported to Henry and Sam Hughes. "He cursed the Americans and told Doniphan to prepare for a charge. He said no mercy would be shown."

Henry gulped. Suddenly he wished he were somewhere in Iowa with Katherine and Annie. Meanwhile, one of Doniphan's army was galloping back and forth explaining to the assembling American volunteers what was meant by the black flag and screaming, "Hurrah for the American stars and stripes!"

The gesture of waving a black flag emblazoned with skull and bones meant that it would be a fight to the death, Henry concluded. Within minutes, the Mexicans were firing at him from around four hundred yards away.

"Don't worry, men!" Doniphan screamed from his horse. "The Mexicans have nothing more than old British Brown Bess muskets. They'll have to get a lot closer, like within fifty or sixty yards, to do any damage. Hit the deck. Lie down. They'll think they killed a few of us. When they get closer, we'll fire back."

Henry's confidence surged. There were no lead balls flying in the air over his head. The Mexicans, however, looked well trained, and that concerned Henry. Doniphan hadn't drilled his men much at all during the trip. True to

Doniphan's prediction, the Mexicans came closer and fired again. Doniphan ordered more soldiers to lie on the ground. Soon, there was a third Mexican volley. More American soldiers lay down.

Hughes began to laugh. "I'll bet those Mexican officers really think we're dead."

"Don't shoot, men," Doniphan pleaded. He was walking among the soldiers, drawing upon his oratorical skills. "Reserve your fire until I give the order."

To Henry's amazement, the Mexicans were moving in remarkable concert in the center, and on each flank. *What targets*, Henry thought, aiming his American musket.

Doniphan gave the order. "Stand up, men! Fire!"

Henry fired, and so did at least two hundred other American soldiers. The heavy volley sent Mexican horses and riders tumbling in all directions. The Mexican line of infantry visibly faltered. Mexican lancers, however, were galloping around the American left flank.

"Fire at the horsemen!" Doniphan ordered.

A volley turned the horsemen and they began shearing off. Soon, the entire Mexican line of battle fragmented. Even Mexican officers were high tailing away, joining their frightened, now disorganized and retreating cavalrymen. Henry fired again, and then cheered as American dragoons began a pursuit.

Within an hour the dragoons returned. They had counted more than thirty dead Mexicans, with more dying as the Mexicans fled. They also estimated there were more than a hundred and fifty wounded lancers and infantrymen. The Americans had pursued them for four miles.

"Not one dead American," Hughes said to Henry, puffing out his chest.

"And only seven wounded," Hastings added.

Henry was drinking from a cask of captured wine. "Derned Mexicans sure ran away, didn't they?" At this point Henry was wondering if his old friend Bernard Bogart ever got to kill a greaser. The enemy had also left food, tobacco, cigarettes, British muskets, and pieces of uniform on the Brazito battlefield. The dragoons had even captured pieces of Mexican artillery.

"They're good runners," Hastings concluded.

"I like war," Henry said. "Merry Christmas."

When two men rode into the Mormon Battalion camp two days before the New Year, they brought news of an encounter between Kearny's forces and the Californios. Daniel and all the other officers were huddled with Colonel Cooke to hear the report.

"Did Kearny win?" Cooke asked one of the men, a youngster dressed more like a mountain man than a settler. Kearny had given the two men passports to Sonora.

"That's what we've heard," the man said. "But our accounts are second-hand."

Daniel let out a big sigh of relief. If Kearny had lost, it meant the Mormon Battalion would have to face the Californios next.

"But Kearny took a lot of losses," the other man said.

"How many men died, and who were they?" Cooke asked.

Daniel felt it was a natural question to ask. Cooke had friends in the men who were serving under Kearny, including Captains Abraham Johnston and Benjamin Moore.

"We don't know," the first man said.

"The Californios must have lost more men that Kearny, if Kearny won the battle," Levi Hancock concluded.

"Don't know that, either," the second man said. "But we do know that the leading Mexican generals are quarreling. Mexican settlers are restless and some of them are packing up to leave for Mexico."

For a while Cooke talked with his officers about these developments. There was nothing much he could do but send a dispatch to Kearny. The next morning Colonel Cook sent two of his guides, Leroux and Charbonneau, along with three other men, to inform Kearny of the Mormon Battalion approach and request that fresh mules and beef cattle be sent to Warner's Ranch, just outside San Diego.

49

~

San Gabriel River

January 8, 1847

THE BLAST FROM COMMODORE STOCKTON'S artillery on the American side was deadly accurate. One of Jose Maria Flores' cannons blew apart, and scattered the Californios.

"Dern, that Stockton knows what he's a doin'," remarked Private Bogart from the banks of the San Gabriel River, just outside Los Angeles. The river was only forty feet wide, knee-deep, but known for its quicksand bottoms. Bogart had crossed the river unguarded with the rest of Kearny's army, along with six hundred of Stockton's men—a collection of sailors, marines, and volunteers. Only the inferior quality of Flores' powder and the poor aim of his gunners had spared his life, and the lives of the other Americans. It had been a calculated risk, but it paid off. Kearny had wanted Stockton's artillery to protect the men as they crossed the river. Now, however, the artillery was on the same side of the river as the enemy and it was being used to cut the Californios to pieces.

"Flores must have poor quality powder," Sergeant Peck said as he made notes. Flores had made the water around him fly with grape and round shot, but none of the Americans had been killed. After the second shot flew over their heads, there had been laughter and jest from Kearny and Stockton's men.

"I don't think I'd quit ducking yet," said a soldier who arrived with Captain Archibald Gillespie. The soldier was assigned to one of the field pieces.

"How would you know?" Bogart asked; he liked the way he felt after Peck had said something about the poor quality powder. He hated the thoughts that he might have to duck a cannonball, or get his head blown off by grapeshot.

"I'm James Marshall," the soldier said. "I served with Colonel Fremont during the Bear Flag Revolt." He went on to say that he had helped secure northern California and that six months ago he had joined the Battalion of California Volunteers, now assigned to Gillespie. "Don't underestimate the Mexicans and the Californios. About the time you think they're done for, they surprise you."

The ground shook under Bogart' feet as a Californio cannonball hit. Dirt rained on him for a few seconds. When he looked up, James was splattered with the blood and brains of another soldier.

"Dern, does my face look like yours?" he asked Marshall, still in a state of shock.

Marshall was in shock too, but he straightened his long, lanky frame and locked his blue eyes onto Bogart. Marshall was from New Jersey, so he lacked a Missourian twang. "You're covered with blood and brains. I suspect we're lucky to be alive."

"Give 'em a stand of grape!" an officer screamed.

Marshall was quick to respond. Deftly avoiding the beheaded comrade whose body lay near the field piece, Marshall helped other soldiers take dead aim. Marshall's piece and other of Stockton's artillery fired incessantly. A second cannon of the Flores army exploded and Bogart could see more Mexican soldiers scattering, including lancers under command of Andres Pico. Pico had joined forces with Flores for the defense of Los Angeles. Kearny, wounded but full of fight, had been led safely into San Diego on January 12.

The Americans cheered.

The San Gabriel River was located just south of Los Angeles. If the combined armies of Flores, Castro, and Pico didn't hold, Los Angeles would be back in American hands within days. Gillespie said he wanted to be the one to raise the American flag there again. Flores had driven him out of Los Angeles.

"I'm surprised Fremont isn't here with men like Marshall," Bogart said.

"Me, too," answered Peck. "I wonder where he is?" He had questioned some of Stockton's men. The last Stockton knew, Fremont was in Monterey seizing arms, horses, saddles, bridles, and accoutrements for the war against the Mexicans.

"Attack, men, attack!" General Kearny yelled from his mule.

The Californios held a hill overlooking the river. Mexican lances and sabers glittered in the sun. Two squadrons of horsemen under Andres Pico were on the right, and a few hundred yards to the left another body under a man named Carrillo. Within minutes the hill was covered with Stockton's sailors and marines who were shouting, "New Orleans! New Orleans!"

Still recovering from battle wounds despite a seventeen-day rest at San Diego, Bogart sat on his black horse watching the action. "Why are they shoutin' *'New Orleans'?"* he asked.

"It's in memory of Andrew Jackson's great victory on this same day thirty-two years ago," answered Peck, the newspaperman.

All of Kearny's men, the healthy ones numbering fifty-seven, were charging the hill, too. Kearny showed remarkable courage, leading his men despite the wounds he had suffered at San Pasqual. There was a reason that Bogart and Peck were still alive after the tragedy at San Pasqual. Although Pico's force had been doubled shortly after the battle, and he appeared ready to charge the weakened Kearny force, reinforcements consisting of a hundred tars and eighty marines had arrived from San Diego, sent by Commodore Stockton. That's because Kit Carson, Beale, and the Indian had gotten through.

"Dern," said Bogart. "I wish I was in that charge. I still need ta kill some greasers."

Bogart soon changed his mind. Within full view, Flores' army made a furious charge on the left flank. Pico's lancers suddenly threatened the right flank. However, the Americans quickly formed hollow squares as Stockton had trained them to do in the hasty weeks before the battle. Hundreds of rounds of lead were simultaneously fired at the Californios, and the air was filled with gunsmoke.

As the main body of Kearny's troops advanced, Kearny led the way on his brown mule. "Steady, my lads, steady. Keep perfectly cool." Midstream of the river, Kearny's mule stopped. Kearny gathered his pistol in one hand, leisurely dismounted, and led his mule to the other side.

"Dern," Bogart said. "I should have given the general my black horse."

At this point, the Californios began a charge. Their red blankets, black hats, and bright lances seemed terribly threatening to Bogart.

"Steady my Jacks; reserve your fire," Kearny said above the uproar. "Front rank—kneel to receive cavalry."

The columns halted. Quickly each man dropped upon one knee and placed his spear-tipped bayonet at an angle of forty-five degrees. Simultaneously the files of the rear cocked their muskets in preparation.

"Fire!"

A sheet of flame flew along the line. The volley was deadly, with a few Californios tumbling from their horses. Another charge, however, was made on the right but veered off, and then came a third.

"Fire!"

Again the Californios met a wall of fire and steel.

"Charge, and up the hill!" Kearny commanded. Both he and Commodore Stockton stormed up the hill, pistols in hand.

They found the hill abandoned. That's because Flores and Castro had already given the command to withdraw. Flores' foot soldiers fled first, followed by Pico and his lancers. Bogart counted only two dead men on each side, and several wounded. He didn't know how many dead the Californios carried with them, or how many wounded.

"Do you think Kearny will pursue?" Bogart asked Peck.

"It doesn't look like it," Peck answered. "None of Stockton's men have horses, and Kearny doesn't have enough dragoons to fight Flores and Pico alone if he happened to catch them."

Bogart was full of questions. "But what if they don't scurry back toward Mexico, and stand to fight another day?"

After what he'd just witnessed, Peck was full of confidence. "Then we'll fight them again."

That proved to be the case the next day. The two forces met again on the plain of La Mesa, about six miles from the river. It was remarkable to see that there were far fewer Californios fighting this time.

"Flores and Pico have suffered some desertions," Peck said, taking more notes.

"Dern, I wish Kearny'd let me fight today," Bogart said, not meaning it.

After two or three hours of fighting, during which Flores' army used up nearly all its powder but accomplished little, the Californios retired from the field, apparently for good. No one was killed in the exchange.

"This is going to make a great story," Peck said. "We whipped the greasers at San Pasqual and at San Gabriel, too."

"We whipped them at San Pasqual?" Bogart said, raising an eyebrow. His memory had not faded. "Seems to me Pico gave us a beatin'." Eighteen American dead had been forever etched in his memory. Only one of Pico's lancers had been killed.

"You're lookin' at it wrong," Peck said. "Quit thinkin' of statistics. Who controls California now—the greasers or us?"

"You've got a point."

"That's the way I'm writin' it up."

"Do you think them greasers are headin' to Mexico?"

Peck had a gift. "Think about it, Bogart. If you were a greaser, would you go to Mexico? Especially if you knew that five hundred soldiers of the Mormon Battalion were bearing down on you?"

Five men, sent by Colonel Cooke, had arrived with news that the Mormon Battalion was about to reach California.

"I dunno. I surely ain't one, so I can't think like they do."

"If they go down to Mexico, they'll be put into the Mexican arm to fight the United States. I think they'll just lay low, wait on the course of events here, and end up citizens of our country."

"Really?"

"I'd bet on it."

50

THE STARS AND STRIPES flew over the Government House in Los Angeles once again. Captain Gillespie raised the flag himself, the same flag he had lowered when he had retreated from the pueblo back in September.

"Dern, that flag looks good up there," said Bogart. "Captain Gillespie knows how to fly 'em, don't he?"

Early that morning a delegation from El Pueblo de Los Angeles appeared in the town square to surrender the town. Commodore Stockton and his forces marched in with the military band playing.

"I wish Colonel Fremont wuz here," James Marshall said half dejectedly. "He'd like to see the Stars and Stripes flying again."

"Well, where is he?" Bogart asked. "They ain't nothin' keepin' him away."

Marshall pursed his lips deep in thought. "If I know him, he's up to somethin'."

Four days later, in a driving rainstorm, Bogart emerged from a Los Angeles grog shop with James Marshall just in time to see Colonel Fremont ride into town with his four hundred men.

"I'll bet there's good news," said Marshall as he ran toward his former commander.

Bogart stared at the rain, which was coming in sheets. "Dern, the good news can wait until this storm quits, can't it?" He went back into the grog shop.

It wasn't ten minutes later when Marshall burst back into the grog shop. He wiped the rain off his face but not his smile, which was broad, showing all his teeth beneath his heavy brown mustache. "I told you Fremont was up to somethin'," he said.

Bogart felt like kidding around a little. He had been drinking aguariente all morning. He knew Fremont was Marshall's hero "Fremont's been promoted to general, and he's gonna run fer president of these United States."

"The war's over," Marshall said.

"Over? Mexico surrendered?"

"It's over in California. The Californios surrendered."

Bogart tried to focus. He knew he wasn't seeing too well, but before Marshall burst though the door he thought his hearing was just fine. "What'd ya say?"

"You remember Andres Pico."

Bogart let his tongue hang out. Pico's men had severely wounded him at San Pasqual. "I remember the scoundrel, dern it."

"Pico surrendered to Fremont."

"Yer kiddin'."

As Bogart collapsed on a stool and all the other men in the grog shop gathered around, Marshall dried his hair and explained what Fremont had just told him. Fremont had learned of the recapture of Los Angeles while camped at Mission San Fernando Rey de Espana, north of the pueblo. Andres Pico had been fleeing north because he, too, knew about the fall of Los Angeles. Pico had done the intelligent thing and simply surrendered to Fremont. At Fremont's headquarters in the old Cahuenga ranch house Fremont arranged Pico's capitulation. The document both men signed was called the Treaty of Cahuenga. It gave very favorable terms to the defeated Californios.

Bogart slowly returned to his senses and began analyzing the details. "Dern, boys, Fremont's gonna be in big trouble over this."

Marshall reeled a couple of steps backward. "Trouble? What do you mean?"

"He shoulda let General Kearny and Commodore Stockton sign that treaty," Bogart said, showing remarkable astuteness for the number of drinks he had consumed.

Marshall snorted derisively. "You just say that 'cause you were in Kearny's army."

"Kearny won't like the terms, I can tell you that," Sergeant Peck added as he took a step toward the door with his notepad. "But this is a great story for my newspaper."

"Dern, I can't wait to go home," Bogart said.

"Thinkin' of your land grant in Missouri again?" Peck asked.

"Yes, sir," Bogart answered. "When the Mormons get here, they can hold Los Angeles."

"Sergeant Peck, the general wishes you to be in attendance at the meeting between him and Colonel Fremont."

Sergeant Waldo Peck quickly responded to the lieutenant's words and strutted toward the adobe building in Los Angeles where Brigadier General Stephen Watts Kearny sat ramrod straight in a chair. He looked ticked, and Peck and Bogart had already made a bet with Marshall that Kearny would go after Fremont's hide.

"You're a newspaperman, so I want you to witness what is about to transpire," the general said abruptly.

"Yes, sir," Peck said meekly as he saluted. He took a chair around an oak table in the low-ceilinged room. Kearny had been in Los Angeles only one week. There had been leaks among his officers that he was not only mad about the treaty Fremont had negotiated, and the terms, but also mad over the fact that Fremont thought Kearny ought to answer to him.

This is going to be good, Peck said to himself. It had been the shock of Kearny's life when Fremont refused to obey his orders.

"Show Colonel Fremont in," Kearny said to an aide.

Within a minute the Missouri explorer stood in front of the general. Kearny looked at Fremont and asked if he had received the communication of the previous day, referring to the organization and command of Fremont's California Battalion.

With more than a touch of defiance Fremont said that he had, and that he had drafted a reply that was being copied and would arrive shortly. As the two officers spoke of other trivial matters, Kit Carson appeared with the letter and handed it to Fremont. Fremont read it over, making certain there were no errors. Using a pen that was on the general's table, he signed the letter and handed it to Kearny.

"Please have a chair while I read your letter," Kearny said sternly.

Peck was situated so that he could read Fremont's letter as Kearny read it. Kearny slowly turned beet red. Fremont had put something in writing that no subordinate officer should have done. If Fremont had talked the matter over with Commodore Stockton, perhaps Stockton would have cautioned against such an obvious disregard for military rank. No matter how correct his case might have been, Peck concluded that Fremont was committing a cardinal sin by telling a senior officer that he was not going to obey him until he was given a proper reason for doing so. Only one reason was needed, and Kearny possessed it—the difference in rank.

Fremont believed Commodore Stockton to be the governor and commander-in-chief in California, that he had received a commission from

Stockton, and that Stockton was still exercising the functions of civil and military governor. Stockton had promised to transfer the functions of governor to Fremont, and Fremont aimed to accept it.

Peck could see that Kearny was collecting his thoughts while trying to bring his temper under control. There was a keen edge of anger in his voice as Kearny spoke. Kearny wished to put a stop to the actions of this upstart Missourian, who fancied himself to be become both a military commander and a governor. Peck concluded that Stockton should have counseled Fremont to obey the general or at least try to reach an agreement with him. Peck suspected Fremont was not politic enough to make terms and therefore was about to be forced to quit drinking from his cup of temporary prosperity. From Fremont's success in negotiating the treaty at Cahuenga, and his exultant entry into Los Angeles, Fremont, if he were not careful, was one step away from isolation and degradation. Peck, by virtue of being under Kearny's command for many months, knew his boss to be a man of hot temper and iron will.

"Colonel," Kearny began as he gritted his teeth, "I hold both your wife and your father-in-law, Senator Benton, in high esteem. I have received many acts of kindness from the senator. But I need to give you some advice. Take back your letter. Destroy it. If you'll do that, I'll forget I ever read it. Commodore Stockton will not support you in disobeying the orders of a senior officer. If you persist in this attitude, you will ruin yourself."

Peck admired, for the moment, Kearny's patience in his irritation.

It was Fremont's turn to boil over. He refused to give in and make a tactical retreat. Instead, he rose to his feet, stood at attention, and spoke stiffly. "I will not do that. Stockton will support me."

"Stockton will never support anyone in disobeying the orders of a superior officer," Fremont shot back.

"Goodbye, sir," Fremont replied. He turned and walked briskly out of the room. To Peck's view, it was a matter of pride and vanity, and an outright act of disobedience. From now on, it would be war to the knife for the two men.

Kearny turned to Peck and his aides. "That man gives me no choice. The day will come when that young officer will discover the meaning of military discipline."

"Do you mean to take him prisoner?" an aide asked.

"No, he is too popular here," Kearny answered. "But I may have to take him back to the United States and arrest him there."

Peck left the adobe building with a sad look. The situation between Kearny and Fremont was unfortunate, and a collision had been inevitable. Peck now realized that had Kearny not appeared on the scene, it would have been possible for the nation to assume that one man, Fremont, had conquered California. On the basis of that prestige, Fremont would well be president of the United States within ten years.

Peck, Bogart, and the other dragoons who had traveled with Kearny to Ciudad de Los Angeles the week previous were exhausted and in poor shape. The combination of their long overland trip, the dreadful days and nights at

San Pasqual and Mule Hill, and the battles to retake San Luis Rey and Pueblo de Los Angeles—including the battle at San Gabriel River—had left the small detachment in terrible shape. Low in spirit, their clothing worn out and torn, some of the men even without shoes, they looked like the last survivors of the losing side in a war. Peck recalled the day when General Kearny saw that one of his foot soldiers was sick and had bleeding blisters on his feet, Kearny dismounted and gave the soldier his own horse to ride. Ahead of them they had a march of nearly a hundred and fifty miles over rough terrain.

As Kearny walked along, within earshot of Peck, he was joined by Lieutenant William Emory, who thoroughly disliked Fremont. He spoke freely and asked Kearny what was to be done about this officer who had taken over the governorship of California, even though the President of the United States had vested that authority to Kearny.

Kearny was still suffering from his wounds at San Pasqual. "As soon as I heal up, I'll take affairs into my own hands."

"Does that mean force will be used?" Emory asked.

"If necessary," Kearny said bluntly.

The next day, as Kearny's mangled army marched toward San Diego, he was overtaken by Commodore Stockton and his mounted escort of thirty sailors and marines. Both commands stopped for the night at San Juan Capistrano, but Peck recalled how both groups maintained different messes and had very little to do with each other. The next day, Stockton's unit rode past Kearny and his men, gave a polite salute, and struck out.

Not long after Stockton and his men had vanished from view, another rider overtook the remnant of the Army of the West. This was newly elected Congressman Willard P. Hall of Missouri. He reported to the general that Colonel Cooke and around three hundred and fifty men of the Mormon Battalion had arrived at Warner's Ranch.

"Good," Kearny had said. "Good. This will tip the balance of power in my favor."

Kearny immediately sent a messenger with orders for Cooke to march his force to San Diego. The arrival of the Battalion would tip the balance of power to Kearny, Peck deduced. Cooke was faithful to Kearny, and the Mormons, to Cooke. The Mormons apparently feared neither Californians nor trappers, obeying only God, Brigham Young, and Philip St. George Cooke.

At San Diego, five days later, Kearny learned that Stockton was ready to sail south along the coast of Baja California.

"Another good development," Kearny said to his men. "Stockton won't be around, and the Mormons are on their way."

The next day, Kearny sailed for Monterey. He left orders for Peck, Bogart, and the other dragoons to return to San Diego and join the Mormons to protect the southern part of California.

51

A COLD JANUARY WIND, forming hard drifts of snow, whistled through the collection of crude log homes, sod hovels, lean-tos, and tents known as Winter Quarters. The town was situated on the south bank of the Missouri River about eighteen miles above Bellevue in the Omaha country. Hannah's sod home was located on Woodruff Street, on the north end of the settlement.

"Mommy, when will Daddy be home?"

Eight-year-old Lizzy's question had been asked almost daily and Hannah had no definite answer. She didn't know exactly when, and she didn't know where home would be either. "Maybe sometime late next summer, or certainly before winter," she answered as she added another log to the sod fireplace.

"I hope we're still not in this place," Hannah's oldest son, ten-year-old Joseph said.

"Me too," said his younger brother, William, seven.

"We're lucky to have this little house, even if it is made of sod," Hannah said. "Don't complain."

Hannah and her six children had lived out of a tent and her wagon box until mid-October. Thanks to George Bundy, Job Smith, Thomas Bloxham, and a few other men, she now had this twelve by eighteen small, crude one-room home. Some of the homes were made of cottonwood logs rafted down the Missouri before winter, but most had large cracks that allowed the wind to whistle through. Hannah's shanty was fairly air tight and had a dirt floor, frozen solid around the edges but warm near the hearth. Her sod chimney had just been installed a month earlier during a warm spell.

"But Brother Bundy says it'll leak come spring," Joseph said. The roof of their cabin was sod too.

"We'll stretch our wagon cover over the roof if we have to," Hannah retorted. "Maybe by then the men will make us some shake shingles."

Joseph wrinkled his face as he wondered how shakes could be nailed to pieces of sod.

A knock came to the door. It was Elizabeth and Harriet, and sixteen-month-old Moroni. The women stooped as they entered the cabin, avoiding the low door frame. The ceiling was only seven feet high.

"We brought you a treat," Elizabeth said.

"What is it?" five-year-old Thomas asked.

"Applesauce cake," Elizabeth said as she sat on a barrel and opened her basket. Enoch and Sarah Ann, three and two years old, scurried to their aunt's side and took a peek, eyes wide open.

"We used the last of our apples," Harriet commented.

Little Moroni Browett, bundled in homemade woolen clothing and a coat, took awkward steps from one barrel to another, and to Hannah's chest.

Hannah's heart did a tumble as she watched her six children begin devouring the cake. "I used the last of ours two weeks ago. I don't know how to thank you." Not only had her apples disappeared, but gone too were the wild chokecherries, melons, strawberries, grapes, and other fruits and vegetables she had obtained from Missouri farmers. Her and her children's diet had long been reduced to cornmeal, bacon, and a little beef. The dregs of ague and canker had already struck other families; Hannah prayed daily that sickness would not strike hers.

"Better get some," Elizabeth told Hannah.

"Let the children have it," Hannah answered.

Elizabeth pointed to Hannah's bulging tummy. "Then feed number seven, silly."

Hannah blushed and took a small piece of the cake.

"Still going to name it Robert, if it's a boy?" Elizabeth asked.

"Yes, I am," Hannah said with a wide smile.

"Well, in another month you'll know," said Harriet.

Besides feeling worn out, Hannah also felt lucky to be heavy with child again. Harriet had expressed disappointment many times about the fact that she was not pregnant with Daniel's child.

"I wonder where Robert and Daniel will be by then?" Elizabeth asked as she watched the last of the cake disappear into the children's hands.

"California, I'd guess," Hannah answered.

"Let's see—your baby will be born toward the end of February," Elizabeth said. "By then, our husbands will have only four months until they're discharged."

Hannah did a quick calculation. "It'll be fall when we see them again. I hope I can keep the new baby healthy after it's born."

"I don't know how Brother Brigham is going to get us all to the Great Basin by next summer, or by fall," Harriet said with a puzzled look.

Hannah nodded her understanding. A ward-by-ward census had just been conducted; there were more than four thousand people in Winter Quarters, with an estimated three thousand Latter-day Saints in other locations near Council Bluffs. And that didn't count the members of the Church wintering out in locations such as St. Louis, Garden Grove, Mt. Pisgah, Burlington, Galena, and Iowa City.

"Well, at least I think he'll get us Mormon Battalion wives out West next summer," Elizabeth said. "That's the promise."

"Mommy, how far is the Great Basin?" Thomas asked.

Hannah shook her head. "I don't know. A long ways from here; if we leave by May, we'll get there in July or August I suppose." Hannah grimaced: there was already talk that perhaps all the Mormon Battalion families might not be included in the first wagon companies.

Lizzy knelt to talk to Moroni. "Do you miss your Daddy?"

The little boy just smiled. His mouth was full of cake.

"He was only nine months old when Daniel left," Elizabeth said. "I don't know if he even remembers his Daddy. I can just picture Daniel swooping Moroni up in his arms when he sees him again."

EPILOGUE

As stated in the introduction, the author's original intention had been to complete the Light & Truth series with this fourth volume. There will be a fifth volume, to be entitled *The Journey Home*. That's because this volume swelled to be nearly a thousand pages, so it became necessary to divide the work into two volumes. Therefore the fourth volume will begin with the Mormon Battalion's arrival into California and conclude with the story of how Robert and Daniel struggle to become reunited with their families again.

BIBLIOGRAPHY

While it is not normal to publish a bibliography for a novel, I do it here to demonstrate the depth of the research it has taken to write the fourth book in this series.

Bennett, Richard E. *We'll Find the Place, The Mormon Exodus, 1846-1848,* Deseret Book Company, Salt Lake City, Utah, 1997.

Bigler, David L., and Bagley, Will. *Army of Israel, Mormon Battalion Narratives,* Utah State University Press, Logan, Utah, 2000.

Bishop, M. Guy. *Henry William Bigler, Soldier, Gold Miner, Missionary, Chronicler,* Utah State University Press, Logan, Utah, 1998.

Bryant, Edwin, *What I Saw in California,* University of Nebraska Press, Lincoln, Nebraska, 1985 (original printing in 1848).

Chalfant, William Y. *Dangerous Passage, The Santa Fe Trail and the Mexican War,* University of Oklahoma Press, Norman, Oklahoma, 1994.

Crockett, David R. *Saints Find the Place, Winter Quarters to the Salt Lake Valley,* LDS-Gems Press, Lehi, Utah, 1997.

Dary, David. *The Santa Fe Trail, Its History, Legends, and Lore,* Alfred A. Knopf, a division of Random House, Inc., New York, N.Y. 2000.

Dawson, Joseph C. *Doniphan's Epic March, The 1st Missouri Volunteers in the Mexican War,* University Press of Kansas, 1999.

DeVoto, Bernard. *The Year of Decision, 1846,* Truman Valley Books, St. Martin's Griffin, New York, N.Y. 2000.

Egan, Ferol. *Fremont, Explorer for a Restless Nation,* University of Nevada

Press, Reno, Nevada, 1985.

Gardner, Mark L. *Wagons for the Santa Fe Trade,* University of New Mexico Press, Albuquerque, New Mexico, 2000.

Gay, Theressa. *James W. Marshall, The Discoverer of California Gold; A Biography,* The Talisman Press, Georgetown, California. 1967.

Hancock, Levi Ward. *The Levi Ward Hancock Journal,* 1803-1846 (unpublished), LDS Church Archives.

Harlow, Neal. *California Conquered, War and Peace on the Pacific 1846-1850,* University of California Press, Berkeley and Los Angeles, California, 1982.

Holmes, Gail George. *Old Council Bluffs; Mormon Developments, 1846-1853, in the Missouri and Platte River Valleys of SW Iowa and E Nebraska,* Omaha LDS Institute of Religion, Omaha, Nebraska, 2000.

Hyslop, Stephen G. *Bound for Santa Fe, The Road to New Mexico and the American Conquest,* University of Oklahoma Press, 2002.

Larsen, Karen M. and Paul D. *Remembering Winter Quarters/Council Bluffs, Action Group,* Omaha, Nebraska, 1998.

Maynes, Shirley N. *Five Hundred Wagons Stood Still, Mormon Battalion Wives,* Corporate Edge Printing, 1999.

McLynn, Frank. *Wagons West, The Epic Story of America's Overland Trails,* Grove Press, New York, N. Y., 2002.

Nevins, Allan. *Fremont, Pathmarker of the West,* University of Nebraska Press, Lincoln, Nebraska, 1939.

Noble, David Grant. *Santa Fe; History of an Ancient City,* School of American Research Press, Santa Fe, New Mexico, 1989.

Norris, David L., *William H. Emory, Soldier-Scientist,* The University of Arizona Press, Tucson, Arizona, 1998.

Owens, Kenneth N. *Gold Rush Saints, California Mormons and the Great Rush for Riches,* The Arthur H. Clark Co., Spokane, Washington, 2004.

Peterson, Charles S. *Mormon Battalion Trail Guide,* Utah State Historical Society, Logan, Utah, 1972.

Ricketts, Norma Baldwin. *The Mormon Battalion, U.S. Army of the West,* Utah State University Press, Logan, Utah, 1996.

Roberts, David. *A Newer World; Kit Carson, John C. Fremont, and the Claiming of the American West,* Simon & Schuster, New York, New York, 2000.

Scott, Richard. *Eyewitness to the Old West,* Roberts Rinehart Publishers, New York, N. Y., 2004.

Standage Family, *Henry Standage's Journal; An Account of His Experiences in the Mormon Battalion* (unpublished), 1972.

Talbot, Dan. *A Historical Guide to the Mormon Battalion and Butterfield Trail,* Westernlore Press, Tucson, Arizona, 1992.

Bowen, Ezra. *The Old West, The Forty-Niners,* Time-Life Books, New York, N. Y., 1974.

Bowen, Ezra. *The Old West, The Mexican War,* Time-Life Books, New York, N. Y., 1974.

Bowen, Ezra. *The Old West, The Pioneers,* Time-Life Books, New York, N.

Y., 1974.

Tyler, Daniel, *A Concise History of the Mormon Battalion in the Mexican War,* Publishers Press, Salt Lake City, Utah, 7th printing, 2000.

Vestal, Stanley. *Kit Carson, The Happy Warrior of the Old West,* Houghton Mifflin Co., New York, N.Y., 1928.

Vestal, Stanley. *The Old Santa Fe Trail,* University of Nebraska Press, Lincoln, Nebraska, 1996.

Weber, David J. *The Mexican Frontier, 1821-1846, The American Southwest Under Mexico,* University of New Mexico Press, Albuquerque, New Mexico, 1982.

Weems, John Edward. *To Conquer A Peace, The War Between the United States and Mexico,* Doubleday and Company, Inc., Garden City, New York, 1974.

Woolsey, Ronald C. *Migrants West, Toward the Southern California Frontier,* Grizzly Bear Publishing, Claremont, California, 1966.

Mormon Battalion Roster

The following is a documented, researched roster of the Mormon Battalion, as listed on the official Mormon Battalion web site. The compiler, Major Carl V. Larson, U.S. Mormon Battalion, Inc., has spent the past 20 years researching and documenting the names that comprise this roster. The sources searched include the following primary documents:

Mexican War Service Records 1845-1848. United States National Archives. Muster-in and payroll. U.S. Archives microfilm numbers 351-1, 351-2 and 351-3.

Return lists. The Returns Lists were compiled on the members of Companies A and B at Council Bluffs, Iowa, July 21 and 22, 1846. Available at the LDS Church Family History Library, Salt Lake City, Utah. Microfilm number 001922.

Final Muster Roll of Companies B and C and of the re-enlistment company which was called Company A. Compiled in July 1846. Available at the LDS Church Family History Library, Salt Lake City, Utah. Microfilm number 937032.

U.S. Government Pension Records. Pension records of many of the Battalion members. Available at the LDS Church Family History Library, Salt Lake City, Utah. Microfilm numbers 480129 to 480149. These microfilms contain only pension data of the Mormon Battalion and were compiled by Dr. Ben Bloxham.

Veterans with Federal Service. Utah State Archives. Salt Lake City, Utah. Records of war veterans who are buried in the State of Utah, containing burial records of veterans of the War of 1812 through the year 1966.

Personnel of the Mormon Battalion

Kearny, Stephen Watts, Brigadier General; Commander, Army of the West, to May 1847

Stevenson, Jonathan D., Colonel; Commander of the Army in California, appointed by General Kearny, 10 May 1847

Battalion Commanders

Colonel James D. Allen, Battalion Commander to 23 August 1846

Lieutenant Andrew Jackson Smith, Acting Commander to 13 October 1846

Colonel Phillip St. George Cooke, Battalion Commander to 16 July 1847

Battalion Staff:

Cloud, Jeremiah H., MAJ, paymaster

Stoneman, George, 2LT, Assistant Quartermaster

Dykes, George Parker, 1LT, Adjutant, to 1 Nov 1846

Merrill, Philemon Christopher, 2LT, Adjutant, from 1 Nov 1846

Glines, James Haravey, SGT-MAJ, to 16 Oct 1846

Ferguson, James, SGT-MAJ, from 16 Oct 1846

Allred, Reddick Newton, QM Sgt, from 11 Feb 1847

McKissock, M.D., Assistant Quartermaster

Sanderson, George, MD, Surgeon

McIntyre, William L., Assistant Surgeon (Dr. McIntyre served with the rank of Assistant Surgeon; he was not a private)

Battalion Guides

Appolonius

Chacon

Charbonneau, Jean Baptiste

Foster, Stephen G.

Francisco

Hall, Willard P.

Tasson

Thompson, Phillip

Weaver, Pauline W.

Roster of Company A

Hunt, Jefferson, Captain

Oman, George W., LT

Willis, William Wesley, 2LT

Clark, Lorenzo, 2LT

Muir, William Smith, 1SGT

Brown, Ebenezer, 2SGT

McCord, Alexander, 3SGT

Chase, Hiram Berry, 4SGT

Wright, Phineas R., SGT

Hunt, Gilbert, 1CPL
Frost, Lafayette N., 2CPL
Weir, Thomas, CPL
Packard, Henry, CPL
Shepherd, Marcus D.L., CPL
Averett, Elisha, Musician
Joseph W. Richards, Musician

Privates
Allen, Albern
Allen, Rufus Chester
Allred, James Riley
Allred, James Tillmon
Sanford
Allred, Reuben Warren
Bailey, James
Beckstead, Gordon Silas
Beckstead, Orin Mortimer
Bevan, James
Bickmore, Gilbert
Blanchard, Mervin S.
Brass, Benjamin
Brown, John
Brown, William Walton
Bronson, Clinton Doneral
Bryant, John Strange
Butterfield, Jacob Kemp
Calkins, Alvah Chauncey
Calkins, Edwin R.
Calkins, James Wood
Calkins, Sylvanus
Casper, William Wallace
Clark, Joseph L.
Clark, Riley Garner
Clifford Isaac Newton
Clifford John Price
Coleman, George
Cox, Henderson
Curtis, Josiah
Decker, Zachariah Bruyn
Dobson, Joseph
Dodson, Eli
Earl, James Calvin
Egbert, Robert Cowden
Fairbanks, Henry

Ferguson, James to 16 Oct 1846
Fredrick, David Ira
Garner, David
Glines, James H. 16 Oct 1846
Goodwin, Andrew
Gordon, Gilman
Hampton, James
Hawkins, Benjamin
Hewit, Eli Buckner
Hickenlooper, William F.
Holden, Elijah Edward
Hoyt, Henry Pike
Hoyt, Timothy Sabin
Hudson, Wilford Heath
Hulett, Schuyler
Hunt, Martial
Ivie, Richard Anderson
Jackson, Charles A.
Johnson, Henry
Kelley, Nickolas
Kelly, William
Kibby, James
Lake, Barnabas
Lemmon, James William
Maxwell, Maxie
Mayfield, Benjamin F.
Moss, David
Mowrey, James
Naegle, John Conrad
Oyler, Melcher
Pierson, Ebenezer
Ritter, John
Rowe, Caratat Conderset
Sessions, John
Sessions, Richard
Sessions, William Bradford
Sexton, George S.
Sharp, Norman
Steele, George E.
Steele, Isaiah Clark
Swarthout, Hamilton
Taylor, Joseph
Thompson, John Crow
Vrandenburg, Adna
Weaver, Franklin

Weaver, Miles
Webb, Charles Young
Weir, Thomas
Wheeler, Merrill W.
White, Joseph
White, Samuel Stephen
Willey, Jeremiah
Wilson, Alfred Gideon
Winn, Dennis Wilson
Woodworth, Lysander

Women and children of Company A

Allred, Elizabeth Briget Manwaring, wife of James T. S. Allred; son, Fent. Allred, Elzadie Emeline Ford, wife of Reuben Warren Allred. Brown, Phoebe Draper, wife of Ebenezer Brown.

Hunt, Celia Mounts, wife of Jefferson Hunt. Harriet, Hyrum, Jane, Joseph, John, Mary, Parley.

Hunt, children of Jefferson Hut; Matilda Nease, another wife of Jefferson Hunt; and their children, Ellen, Peter, sister and brother of Matilda Nease. Kelley, Malinda Allison, wife of Milton Kelley. Malinda Catherine Kelley, Sarah, wife of Nickolas Kelley. Parley. Sessions, Emmeline, wife of John Sessions.

Roster of Company B

Hunter, Jesse Devine, Captain
Luddington, Elam, 1LT
Barrus, Ruel, 2LT
Merrill, Philemon C., 2LT
to 1 Nov 1846
Coray, William, SGT
Hyde, William, SGT
Smith, Albert, SGT
Rainey, David P., SGT
Dunn, Thomas John, CPL
Chase, John Darwin, CPL
Wilcox, Edward, CPL
Alexander, Horace M. CPL
Hunter, William, Musician
Taggart, George W., Musician

Privates

Allen, Elijah
Allen, Franklin
Allen, George
Bigler, Henry William
Bingham, Erastus
Bingham, Thomas
Bird, William
Bliss, Robert Stanton
Boley, Samuel
Borrowman, John
Brackenberry, Benjamin B.
Brown, Francis
Bush, Richard
Bybee, John McCann
Callahan, Thomas William
Camp, James G.
Carter, Isaac Philo
Carter, Richard
Cheney, Zacheus
Church, Haden Wells
Clark, George Sheffer
Clawson, George
Colton, Philander
Curtis, Dorr Purdy
Dalton, Henry Simon
Dayton, Willard J.
Dunham, Albert
Dutcher, Thomas P.
Eastman, Marcus N.
Evans, Israel Evans
Evans, William
Follett, William Alexander
Freeman, Elijah Norman
Garner, William A.
Green, Ephraim
Hanks, Ephraim Knowlton
Harris, Silas
Haskell, George Nile
Hawk, Nathan
Hawk, William
Hinkley, Arza Erastus
Hofheinz, Jacob
Hunter, Edward
Huntsman, Isaiah

Jones, David H.
Keysor, Guy Messiah
King, John M.
Kirk, Thomas
Lawson, John
McCarty, Nelson
Martin, Jesse Bigler
Miles, Samuel
Morris, Thomas
Mount, Hiram B.
Murdock, John Riggs
Murdock, Orrice Clapp
Myers, Samuel
Noler, Christian
Owens, Robert
Park, James (I)
Park, James (II)
Pierson, Ephraim
Pierson, Harmon Dudley
Prows, William Carroll
Richards, Peter F.
Rogers, Samuel Hollister
Simmons, William Alpheus
Sly, James Calvin
Smith, Azariah
Steers, Andrew J.
Stevens, Lyman
Stillman, Dexter
Stoddard, Rufus
Study, David
Walker, William Holmes
Watts, John
Wheeler, John L.
Whitney, Francis Tufts
Wilcox, Henry
Willes, Ira Jones
Willes, William S.
Winters, Jacob
Workman, Andrew Jackson
Workman, Oliver Gaultry
Wright, Charles
Young, Nathan
Zabriskie, Jerome

Women and children of Company B

Coray, Melissa Burton, wife of William Coray. William Hunter, Lydia Edmonds, wife of Jesse D. Hunter. Diego. Ludington, Mary Eliza Clark, wife of Elam Ludington. At least two children were in the Ludington family. Luddington, Lena Monger, mother of Elam Ludington

Roster of Company C

Brown, James, Captain to 16 Oct 1846
Rosecrans, George, 1LT (Company Commander from 1 Nov 1846)
Thompson, Samuel, 2LT
Clift, Robert, 2LT
Elmer, Elijah, 1SGT
Adams, Orson Bennett, SGT
Terrell, Joel Judkin, SGT
Tyler, Daniel, SGT
Martin, Edward, SGT
Brownell, Russell G., 1CPL
Wilkin, David, CPL
Brown, Alexander, CPL
Peck, Thorit, CPL
Squires, William, CPL
Sprague, Richard D., Musician
Allen, Ezra Hela, Musician

Privates

Adair, Wesley
Babcock, Lorenzo
Bailey, Addison
Bailey, Jefferson
Barney, Walter
Beckstead, William Ezra
Blackburn, Abner
Boyle, Henry Green
Brimhall, John
Brown, Jesse Sowel
Burt, William
Calvert, John Hamaker
Carpenter, Isaac
Carpenter, William Hiram
Catlin, George Washington
Clift, James

Condit, Jeptha
Covil, John Q.A.
Dalton, Edward
Dalton, Harry
Dodge, Augustus Erastus
Donald, Neal
Dunn, James
Durphee, Francillo
Fellows, Hiram W.
Fife, John
Fifield, Levi
Forbush, Loren
Gibson, Thomas
Gould, John Calvin
Gould, Samuel J.
Green, John
Hancock, Charles Brent
Hancock, GeorgeWashington
Harmon, Ebenezer
Harmon, Lorenzo Frazer
Hatch, Meltiar
Hatch, Orin
Hendrichson, Abraham
Hendrichson, James
Holdaway, Shedrick
Holt, William
Hulse, Lewis
Ivie, Thomas C.
Johnson, Jarvis
Johnstun, Jesse Walker
Johnstun, William James
Landers, Ebenezer
Larson, Thurston
Layton, Christopher
Lewis, Samuel
McMullough, Levi Hamilton
Maggard, Benjamin
Mead, Orlando Fish
Moore, Calvin White
Mowrey, Harley
Mowrey, John T.
Myler, James
Nowlin, Jabez Townsend
Olmstead, Hiram
Owen, J.

Parke, George
Peck, Isaac
Perkins, David Martin
Perkins, John
Pickup, George
Pierson, Judson A.
Pulsipher, David
Reynolds, William
Richie, Benjamin
Richmond, Benjamin
Riser, John J.
Rust, William Walker
Shipley, Joseph
Shumway, Aurora
Shupe, Andrew Jackson
Shupe, James Wright
Smith, Milton
Smith, Richard D.
Steele, William
Taylor, Norman
Thomas Elijah
Thomas, Nathan T.
Thompson, James Lewis
Tindell, Soloman
Truman, Jacob Mica
Tuttle, Elanson
Wade, Edward Davis
Wade, Moses
Welsh, Madison
Wheeler, Henry
White, John Stout
Wilcox, Matthew
Wood, William

Women and children of Company C

Adams, Susanna, wife of Orson Bennett Adams. Brown, Mary McCree Black, wife of Captain James Brown. George David Black, son of Mary McCree and George Black. Shupe, Sarah, wife of James Wright Shupe. Elizabeth Margaret Wilkin, Isabella, wife of David Wilkin.

Roster of Company D

Higgins, Nelson, Captain to 1 Nov 1846

Dykes, George Parker, 1LT, Company Commander from 1 Nov 1846

Hulett, Sylvester, 2LT

Canfield, Cyrus C., 2LT

Tuttle, Luther T., 1st SGT

Williams, Thomas S., SGT

Jones, Nathaniel V., SGT

Haws, Alpheus, SGT

Hunsaker, Abraham, SGT

Stephens, Arnold, CPL

Barger, William W. CPL

Buchanan, John, CPL

Jacobs, Sanford, CPL

Hovey, Silas, Musician

Jackson, Henry Wells, Musician

Smith, Willard Gilbert, Musician

Privates

Abbott, Joshua

Averett, Jeduthan

Badham, Samuel

Boyd, George W.

Boyd, William W.

Brizzee, Henry Willard

Brown, James "P"

Brown, James Stephens

Button, Montgomery

Casto, James

Casto, William W.

Chase, Abner

Clawson, John Reese

Cole, James Barnett

Collins, Robert H.

Compton, Allen

Coons, William

Cox, Amos

Curtis, Foster

Davis, Eleazer

Davis, James

Davis, Sterling

Douglas, James

Douglas, Ralph

Fatoute, Ezra

Finlay, Thomas

Fletcher, Philander

Fosgreen, John Erick

Frazier, Thomas Leonard

Gifford, William

Gilbert, John R.

Gilbert, Thomas

Gribble, William

Hendricks, William Dorius

Henrie, Daniel

Higgins, Alfred

Hirons, James P.

Hoaglund, Lucas

Holmes, Jonathan Herriman

Huntington, Dimick Baker

Kenney, Loren E.

Lamb, Lisbon

Lane, Lewis

Laughlin, David Sanders

McArthur, Henry Morrow

Maxwell, William Bailey

Mecham, Erastus Darwin

Merrill, Ferdinand

Mesick, Peter

Oakley, James DeGroat

Owen, James

Peck, Edwin Martin

Perrin, Charles

Pettegrew, James P.

Rawson, Daniel Berry

Raymond, Alonzo Pearis

Richmond, William

Roberts, Benjamin Morgan

Robinson, William J.

Rowe, William

Roylance, John

Runyan, Levi

Sanderson, Henry Weeks

Sargent, Abel Morgan

Savage, Levi

Sharp, Albert

Sharp, Norman

Shelton, Sebert C.

Smith, John Grover

Spencer, William W.
Steele, John
Stephens, Alexander
Stewart, Benjamin
Stewart, James
Stewart, Robert Boyd
Stillman, Clark
Swarthout, Nathan
Tanner, Myron
Thomas, Hayward
Thompson, Jonathan Miles
Tippets, John Harvey
Treat, Thomas W.
Tubbs, William
Twitchell, Anciel
Walker Edwin
Whiting, Almon
Whiting, Edmond
Woodward, Francis Snow

Women and children of Company D

Abbott, Ruth Markham, wife of Joshua Abbott. Brown, Eunice Reasor, wife of James "P" Brown. Robert, Newman, John, Mary Ann, Sarah. Button, Mary Bittles, wife of Montgomery Button. Charles, James, Jutson, Louisa. Higgins, Sarah Blackman, wife of Nelson Higgins, Capt.

Druzilla, Almira, Wealthy, Carlos Smith, Heber Kimball, Hirons, Mary Ann, wife of James P. Hirons. Huntington, Fanny Maria Allen, wife of Dimick B. Huntington. Martha Zina, Betsy Prescinda, Clark Allen, Lot. Sharp, Martha Jane Sargent, wife of Norman Sharp. Sarah Ellen.

Caroline Sargent, daughter of Abel Sargent and sister to Martha Jane Sargent Sharp Mowrey.

Shelton, Elisabeth Trains Mayfield, wife of Sebert C. Shelton. John Mayfield, Jackson Mayfield, Sarah Mayfield, Caroline Shelton, Mariah Shelton. Steele, Catherine Campbell, wife of John Steele. Mary. Tubbs, Sophia, wife of William Tubbs. Williams,

Albina Marie Merrill, wife of Thomas Stephen Williams. Caroline Marie, Ephraim Merrill, Phoebe Lodema, sister of Albina Marie Williams.

Roster of Company E

Davis, Daniel C., Captain
Pace, James, 1LT
Lytle, Andrew, 2LT
Gully, Samuel, 2LT
Brown, Edmond Lee, 1SGT
Brazier, Richard, SGT
Hanks, Ebenezer, SGT
Browett, Daniel, SGT
St. Johns, Stephen M. CPL
Burns, Thomas R. CPL
Scott, James Allen, CPL
Ewell, John Martin, CPL
Hancock, Levi Ward, Musician
Earl, Justice C., Musician

Privates

Allen, John
Bates, Joseph William
Beers, William
Beddome, William
Binley, John Wesley
Brown, Daniel
Bulkley, Newman
Bunker, Edward
Caldwell, Mathew
Campbell, Jonathan
Campbell, Samuel
Cazier, James
Cazier, John
Chappin, Samuel
Clark, Albert
Clark, Joseph
Clark, Samuel Gilman
Cox, John
Cummings, George Washington
Davis, Walter L.
Day, Abraham Eli
Dennett, Daniel "Q"

Dyke, Simon
Earl, Jacob Sylpher
Ewell, William Fletcher
Follett, William Tillman
Fornay, Fredrick
Glazier, Luther William
Harmon, Oliver Norton
Harris, Robert
Harrison, Isaac
Hart, James S.
Hess, John Wells
Hickmott, John
Hopkins, Charles A.
Hoskins, Henry
Howell, Thomas CharlesDavis
Jacobs, Bailey
Jameson, Charles
Judd, Hiram
Judd, Zadock Knapp
Karren, Thomas
Kelley, George
Kelley, Milton
Knapp, Albert
Lance, William
McBride, Harlem
McClellan, William Carroll
Miller, Daniel
Miller, Miles
Park, William Ashberry
Pettegrew, David
Phelps, Alva
Pixton, Robert
Porter, Sanford
Pugmire, Jonathan
Richardson, J.
Richardson, Thomas
Roberts, Levi
Sanders, Richard T.
Scott, Leonard M.
Skeen, Joseph
Slater, Richard
Smith, David
Smith, Lot
Spidle, John
Standage, Henry

Stephens, Roswell
Strong, William
Tanner, Albert
West, Benjamin
Whitworth, Robert Walton
Williams, James V.
Wilson, George Deliverance
Woolsey, Thomas

Women and children of Company E

Brown, Agnes, wife of Edmond Lee Brown. Davis, Susannah Davis, wife of Daniel C. Davis, CPT. Daniel C. Jr. Hanks, Jane Wells Cooper, wife of Ebenezer Hanks. Hess, Emeline Bigler, wife of John W. Hess. Smith, Rebecca, wife of Elisha Smith and Thomas R. Burns. St John, Harriet, wife of Daniel Brown.

Servants to officers

Colton, Charles Edwin
Higgins, Nelson Daniel
Mowrey, James
Pace, William Byram°
Palmer, Zemira
Smith, Elisha, teamster